THE CAMBRIDGE RITUALISTS RECONSIDERED

PROCEEDINGS OF THE FIRST OLDFATHER
CONFERENCE, HELD ON THE CAMPUS OF THE
UNIVERSITY OF ILLINOIS AT URBANA–CHAMPAIGN
APRIL 27–30, 1989

edited by

William M. Calder III

Scholars Press
Atlanta, Georgia

The Cambridge Ritualists Reconsidered

edited by

William M. Calder III

©1991
The Board of Trustees
University of Illinois

Copies of the supplement may be ordered from:
Scholars Press
1650 Bluegrass Lakes Parkway
Alpharetta, GA 30201

Library of Congress Cataloging in Publication Data

Oldfather Conference (1st : 1989 : University of Illinois at Urbana
-Champaign)
    The Cambridge ritualists reconsidered : proceedings of the First
Oldfather Conference, held on the campus of the University of Illinois
at Urbana-Champaign, April 27-30, 1989 / edited by William
M. Calder III.
    p. cm. — (Illinois classical studies. Supplement ; 2)
(Illinois studies in the history of classical scholarship ; v. 1)
    Includes bibliographical references.
    ISBN 1-55540-605-X (alk. paper)
    1. Religion—History—Congresses. 2. Cambridge (England)—
Intellectual life—Congresses. I. Calder, William M. (William
Musgrave), 1932-   . II. Title. III. Series. IV. Series: Illinois
studies in the history of classical scholarship ; v. 1.
BL21.048 1989
480'.9041—dc20   91-640
                                      CIP

Printed in the United States of America
on acid-free paper

The Cambridge
Ritualists
Reconsidered

Illinois Classical Studies
Supplement 2

Editors

WILLIAM M. CALDER, III (Reception)
HOWARD JACOBSON (Latin)
MIROSLAV MARCOVICH (Greek)

Editor-in-Chief

MIROSLAV MARCOVICH

Camera-Ready Copy Produced by
Michael J. Spires

Illinois Studies in the
History of Classical Scholarship
Volume 1

Editor

William M. Calder III

Preface

Great scholars are admired and feared during their lives, disparaged and libelled after their deaths and, when passions have cooled and their victims and friends are gone, they are reconsidered. That means they are seen in context, their work explained and an attempt, perhaps illusory, made to separate the ephemeral from what abides. In recent years this has been done with the great Germans, Otto Jahn, Eduard Meyer, Friedrich Gottlieb Welcker, and Ulrich von Wilamowitz-Moellendorff. It has also been done, to the dismay of many, with Heinrich Schliemann. I thought it time to assemble a group of experts for three days to discuss a group of innovative and brilliant English scholars, long neglected and ridiculed by those lesser men who came after them.

When J. G. Frazer died, blind and forgotten, on 7 May 1941, few mourned or even noticed his passing. Arthur Darby Nock, a Cambridge man, in the fifties presented Jane Harrison's views to his Harvard students (of whom I was one) as irresponsible and bizarre. Sterling Dow dismissed Cornford's book on Thucydides as wrong-headed and pernicious. Only Cook's *Zeus* was lauded for its collection of details. Nock reported that the Cambridge printers who set the massive tomes observed on finishing: "We've got a few epithets for Zeus what old Cook don't 'ave." Cook survived because of his sheer accumulation of data and his reluctance to draw conclusions from it. As late as 1985, an historian of Cambridge classics, himself a Cambridge professor, had not a word for the Ritualists' achievement.

The change began in the United States, not in England, and in an English, not a Classics, Department. Twenty years ago, Robert Allen Ackerman wrote *The Cambridge Group and the Origins of Myth Criticism* (Diss. Columbia, 1969).[1] This was the first attempt to see them as part of the intellectual life of their time rather than to list "mistakes" made by them. Ackerman's work culminated with his great book *J. G. Frazer: His Life and Work* (Cambridge, 1987). Meanwhile, book-length lives of Murray and Harrison have appeared, and a life of Cornford is on the way. Books on the tyranny of Greece over England by Jenkyns and Turner have made work much easier. In 1990, authoritative brief lives of Cornford, Frazer, Harrison, and Murray that provide invaluable background material and informed hints for further reading became available.[2] These American

---

[1] See now Robert Ackerman, *The Myth and Ritual School: J. G. Frazer and the Cambridge Ritualists* (New York/London 1991).

[2] By Woods, Ackerman, Schlesier and Fowler, respectively: see *Classical Scholarship:*

efforts coincided with a renewal of interest on the Continent (German and Italian) in *Religionsgeschichte* and, therefore, in the *Geschichte der Religionsgeschichte*. I mean the attention paid to Meyer, Rohde, Usener, Welcker and Wilamowitz as historians of ancient religion. I therefore thought the time ripe to reconsider the achievement of the Cambridge Ritualists.

I had learned from conferences I had earlier organized in Germany that to succeed three sorts of specialists would be necessary.[3] One needs modern authorities in the fields of the scholars being considered. They can rule on what for the moment is "right" and "wrong." They can show which investigations proved fruitful for subsequent research and which were dead-ends. However, it must be stressed that specialists are usually the worst historians of their own disciplines because they are too close to them. One need only recall the reaction of Bronze-Age archaeologists to the new Schliemann-Forschung. Next, specialists in the intellectual history of the time in which the Ritualists lived are needed. These scholars have little interest in whether Jane Harrison was "right" or "wrong" in her interpretation of some detail of Greek religion. They want to explain what in her time caused her to reach the conclusions she reached. Certainly it was not the ancient evidence. Finally, *Wissenschaftshistoriker*, historians of scholarship, are required. They are trained, for example, to see Frazer within the history of his discipline and within the history of the English university system. Because no one scholar can be equally competent in three such diverse and demanding disciplines, only by a collective effort can progress be attained.

This was the first Oldfather Conference on some aspect of the modern history of classical scholarship (held the last weekend of each April at the University of Illinois at Urbana/Champaign and financed by the Annual Research Fund of the William Abbott Oldfather Professorship of the Classics). The intent is to bring these diverse specialists together for productive discussion. Papers are submitted one month before the conference, then circulated to and read by all participants. Each participant gives only a ten-minute summary of his paper, followed by a searching fifty-minute discussion, all the more searching because the papers have been critically read beforehand. The conference is a working seminar and not a lecture series. The product is better published papers.

For ease of consultation by occasional users, I have arranged the contributions alphabetically by the author's last name. There will be more readers of selected articles than those who will read the book through from beginning to end. The papers at the conference were presented in historical

---

A Biographical Encyclopedia, edited by Ward W. Briggs and William M. Calder III (New York, 1990).

[3] For just this see William M. Calder III and Justus Cobet (editors), *Heinrich Schliemann nach 100 Jahren* (Frankfurt/Main 1990).

order: 1) antecedents of the Ritualists (Vaio, Naiditch, Smith, Ackerman);
2) the individual Ritualists, Harrison (Peacock, Calder, Africa, Schlesier),
Murray (Fowler), Cornford (Chambers), Cook (Schwabl); 3) two papers on
reception (Newman, Jones). Those with the time and interest to approach
the Ritualists historically should read the papers in that order. I regret that
two invited scholars were unable to participate because of prior
commitments: George W. Stocking, Jr. (University of Chicago) and Frank
M. Turner (Yale University).

Apart from the participants who worked devotedly and whose revised
papers appear within, I should like to thank the following Urbana colleagues
who chaired sessions: Professors J. J. Bateman, Gerald M. Browne, Howard
Jacobson, Miroslav Marcovich and David Sansone. I thank as well five
scholars who, although they did not present papers, contributed vigorously
to the discussion: Shelley Arlen (University of Oklahoma at Norman),
Susen Guettel Cole (University of Illinois at Chicago), David P. Kubiak
(Wabash College), Annabel Robinson (University of Regina) and Robert A.
Segal (Louisiana State University). Special thanks are due Shelley Arlen,
who generously allowed participants to consult her invaluable, then
forthcoming bibliography of the Cambridge Ritualists.[4] Michael
Armstrong elegantly translated Renate Schlesier's German. Dr. Robert
Ackerman beneficially read proof for the whole volume. Michael Spires,
whose name deservedly appears on the title page, expertly prepared camera-
ready copy. Our gratitude to the founder and editor-in-chief of *Illinois
Classical Studies* is expressed by all of us.

William M. Calder III
The Villa Mowitz
The 140th Birthday of Jane Harrison

---

[4] See now Shelley Arlen, *The Cambridge Ritualists: An Annotated Bibliography of the
Works by and about Jane Ellen Harrison, Gilbert Murray, Francis M. Cornford, and Arthur
Bernard Cook* (Metuchen/London 1990).

List of Contributors

Robert Ackerman is Director of Humanities at the University of the Arts, Philadelphia, Pennsylvania. His biography of J. G. Frazer was published by Cambridge University Press in 1987.

Thomas W. Africa is Professor of Ancient History at the State University of New York in Binghamton, New York. He has published widely in the modern reception of classical antiquity.

William M. Calder III is William Abbott Oldfather Professor of the Classics at the University of Illinois in Urbana/Champaign, Illinois. He has published and edited numerous books and articles on the history of classical philology in Prussia in the nineteenth and twentieth centuries.

Mortimer H. Chambers is Professor of Ancient History at the University of California, Los Angeles, California. He has published widely in the history of classical scholarship. His life and letters of Georg Busolt was published by Brill in 1990. He is working on a life of Felix Jacoby.

Robert L. Fowler is Associate Professor and Chairman of Classics at the University of Waterloo, Waterloo, Ontario, Canada. He has edited, with W. M. Calder III, the letters of Wilamowitz to Eduard Schwartz and to Gilbert Murray, and he has published lives of Murray and Wilamowitz.

Robert Alun Jones is Professor of Sociology at the University of Illinois in Urbana/Champaign, Illinois. He is author of a study on Robertson Smith and James Frazer (1984).

P. G. Naiditch is Publications Editor for the Department of Special Collections, University Research Library, University of California, Los Angeles, California. He has written numerous articles on A. E. Housman and is author of *A. E. Housman at University College, London: The Election of 1892* (1988). He is working on a history of classics in Victorian England.

J. K. Newman is Professor of the Classics at the University of Illinois in Urbana/Champaign, Illinois. He is author of many articles and books on Greek and Latin Poetry.

Sandra J. Peacock is Assistant Dean in the Graduate School of Emory University, Atlanta, Georgia. Her biography of Jane Harrison was published by Yale in 1988.

Renate Schlesier is Research Associate in the Institute for the History of Religion at the Free University in Berlin. She has published widely in the history of classical scholarship in Germany, especially on Otto Jahn, Eduard Meyer and Ulrich von Wilamowitz-Moellendorff.

Hans Schwabl is Professor of Classical Philology at the University of Vienna. He is the author of the article "Zeus" in Pauly-Wissowa.

Morton Smith is Professor (emeritus) of Ancient History at Columbia University, New York, New York. He is author of numerous articles and books on Greco-Roman paganism, Hellenistic Judaism, and early Christianity.

John Vaio is Associate Professor of Classics at the University of Illinois at Chicago, Illinois. He is author of articles on George Grote, Gladstone, and Heinrich Schliemann.

Contents

Preface   v
List of Contributors   viii

1. The Cambridge Group: Origins and Composition   1
   ROBERT ACKERMAN, University of the Arts, Philadelphia

2. Aunt Glegg Among the Dons
   or Taking Jane Harrison at Her Word   21
   THOMAS W. AFRICA, State University of New York
   at Binghamton

3. Jane Harrison's Failed Candidacies for the Yates Professorship
   (1888, 1896): What Did Her Colleagues Think of Her?   37
   WILLIAM M. CALDER III, University of Illinois at
   Urbana/Champaign

4. Cornford's *Thucydides Mythistoricus*   61
   MORTIMER CHAMBERS, University of California, Los Angeles

5. Gilbert Murray: Four (Five) Stages of Greek Religion   79
   ROBERT L. FOWLER, University of Waterloo

6. La Genèse du Système? The Origins of Durkheim's
   Sociology of Religion   97
   ROBERT ALUN JONES, University of Illinois at Urbana/Champaign

7. Classical Studies in Nineteenth-Century Great Britain as
   Background to the "Cambridge Ritualists"   123
   P. G. NAIDITCH, University of California, Los Angeles

8. A Ritualist Odyssey: Victorian England to Soviet Russia   153
   J. K. NEWMAN, University of Illinois at Urbana/Champaign

9. An Awful Warmth About Her Heart: The Personal in
   Jane Harrison's Ideas on Religion   167
   SANDRA J. PEACOCK, Emory University

10. Prolegomena to Jane Harrison's Interpretation of
    Ancient Greek Religion   185
    RENATE SCHLESIER, Freie-Universität, Berlin

11. A. B. Cook, *Zeus: A Study in Ancient Religion*
    (1914 / 1925 / 1940): Nachdenkliches über Plan und
    Aussage des Werkes   227
    HANS SCHWABL, Universität Wien

12. William Robertson Smith   251
    MORTON SMITH, Columbia University

13. Seventy Years Before *The Golden Bough*: George Grote's
    Unpublished Essay on "Magick"   263
    JOHN VAIO, University of Illinois at Chicago

14. An Unpublished Essay on Magick by George Grote   275
    Edited by JOHN VAIO, University of Illinois at Chicago

1

The Cambridge Group: Origins and Composition

ROBERT ACKERMAN

Some of the facts about "origins and composition" are quickly and straightforwardly stated. In the biographical sense, the Cambridge Ritualists began on 24 August 1900, the date Jane Ellen Harrison, recently appointed as Newnham College's first research fellow, wrote a fan letter to Gilbert Murray, sometime professor of Greek in the University of Glasgow, after reading his *A History of Ancient Greek Literature* (1897).[1] He responded, they met at the home of their mutual friends, the Verralls, and soon became fast friends. Around that time too, Francis Cornford, then a fourth-year student in ancient philosophy at Trinity College, heard Harrison lecture at Newnham and wrote a letter that once again led to a meeting and friendship.

Clarity departs when one considers whether to regard A. B. Cook as a full fourth "member" of the group. I count him as such, but I recognize that reasonable people can differ on this.[2] There is no doubt that at the high noon of ritualism (1908–14) he worked closely with Jane Harrison on *Themis* and that he was in some ways more sympathetic, both intellectually and personally, to the three of them, than was any other classical scholar in Cambridge. There is also no doubt that his major work, *Zeus*, had its origins in the controversy over the sacral kingship to which ritualism was one response, and that ritual is one of the motifs that give that vast work what unity it may be said to possess.[3] At the same time, it must be said that his strong reservations about the general direction their work was taking in regard to the origins of religion (to be discussed later) constituted a strict limit beyond which he would not go. Indeed, Murray himself was of two

---

[1] The letter is published in Jessie Stewart, *Jane Ellen Harrison: A Portrait in Letters* (London 1959) 30.

[2] Sandra Peacock (*Jane Ellen Harrison* [New Haven 1988] 130) does not grant Cook full membership of the group, on the considerable authority of Murray, who in retrospect said as much ("ABC was a great help to us, but not one of us," although only eighteen months earlier Murray *had* included Cook in the group). The arguments on both sides notwithstanding, the fact remains, however, that at least for classicists, the most important product of the entire Ritualist episode is *Zeus*.

[3] For the collaboration between Cook and Frazer that led ultimately to *Zeus*, see Robert Ackerman, *J. G. Frazer: His Life and Work* (Cambridge 1987) 197–200.

minds about Cook's status *vis-à-vis* the others. In any case, when Harrison met him is not known, but it probably was around the turn of the century, for she had returned to Cambridge only in 1898.

Jane Harrison probably introduced each of the others to one another, but again the specific dates or occasions are not known. It is always possible that Cornford, then the equivalent of a graduate student, met Murray and Cook at a scholarly or social gathering, but the difference in their ages and status, and the improbable speed with which they became friendly, argues strongly for the encouraging presence of Jane Harrison, her enthusiasm, and her affection for all concerned.

Two others, A. W. Verrall and J. G. Frazer, were never members but in different ways were significant intellectual presences. Verrall was perhaps Harrison's closest male friend in Cambridge in the years immediately after her return, but as a quintessentially literary scholar, he could never be induced to interest himself even in archaeology (which he called "stuffage"), much less anthropology and folklore.[4] Jane Harrison dedicated *Prolegomena* to him out of deep and abiding affection and because she tried out and sharpened many of her ideas on the whetstone of his skepticism. Frazer knew and was on cordial terms with all the Ritualists, but the combination of his workaholic tendencies, paralyzing shyness, and the jealous presence of his difficult wife effectively prevented him from being a member of any group, much less one with irrationalist tendencies with which he would have been out of intellectual sympathy. In the event, the only Ritualist with whom he worked at all closely was Cook, and that only between 1902 and 1905, essentially before the group's heyday.[5]

The Ritualists having been professional scholars, a full discussion of their origins must of course draw upon social and intellectual history as well as biography. Because Jane Harrison stood at the heart of the group (in more than one sense), and because all the important connections in her adult life were indissolubly emotional and intellectual, the biographical

---

[4] Stewart 56. Although Verrall was a "splendid emendax," and never could be convinced that anthropology had anything to offer, he had, besides boldness and brilliance in his way with a text, "a lively idea of the conditions of dramatic poetry. No English scholar before Verrall, and no earlier scholar save Otfried Müller...was possessed of a similar capacity of visualizing a Greek tragedy as a play to be performed upon a stage. Consequently, one vital aspect of this poetry was more adequately brought out in Verrall's commentaries than in those of his forerunners." Eduard Fraenkel, *Aeschylus Agamemnon* I (Oxford 1950) 57.

[5] For Frazer and Cook, see above, note 3. For Harrison on Frazer, in an unpublished letter to Murray (Newnham College Library) she refers, half-mockingly, to Frazer as "old Adonis." Her genuine affection for Frazer is demonstrated in a witty letter to Lady Mary Murray (Stewart 37): "Mrs. Frazer (your double!) has been sitting on my bed for two hours, telling me 'who not to know', i.e. who has not paid Mr. Frazer 'proper attention'! This is the price I pay for a few shy radiant moments under the Golden Bough—Good Conservative tho' I am I am ready for any reform in the Game Laws for the Preserving of Eminent Husbands."

component must trace the course of those complex relationships with the other members, especially during the most important years of the group's activity. Further, in view of the fact that she was the first female British classical scholar to achieve international recognition, something must also be said about women's education at Cambridge and classical scholarship as a profession. Finally, university and national politics occasionally intrude (should Cambridge grant degrees to women? should women be granted the vote?) because the Ritualists' conservative opponents did not confine themselves to academic matters only. Instead, they viewed ritualism as a symptom of the intellectual and moral decline of all that was great and worthwhile in British life and attacked it root and branch as the subversive rot they believed it to be. Sorting all this out has become appreciably easier now that we have useful modern lives of Jane Harrison and Gilbert Murray.[6]

Inasmuch as the Ritualists were more or less a unified group with a coherent program (itself an unusual event within the individualistic tradition of British scholarship), the intellectual-historical element must include something of the larger classical context—assumptions, traditions, and expectations—along with a discussion of the Ritualists' education and early work, the questions they addressed and the way they made them their own, their methods of collaboration, and finally the reception their ideas met. Many of these matters—especially in the detail that anyone interested in the fine structure of the group would like to have—are unknowable because most of their work was conducted face-to-face in Cambridge, and because Murray's letters to Harrison no longer exist.

Because for years the Ritualists and their work have been dismissed by classicists and ancient historians, relatively little has been written about them; the proceedings of this conference will doubtless go far to make up for that neglect.[7] In my limited space here I have elected to shuttle between biography and the history of ideas, using each to illuminate the other. I hope to shed some more light on what may have been "in the air" that made possible the complex network of passionate intellectual friendships that we call the Cambridge Ritualists. Finally, in evaluating the achievement of the Ritualists as a group, I also wish to remind us of some of the uncertainties inherent in the historical record and therefore to suggest a certain caution in moving very far beyond what the documentary record will support.

---

[6] Peacock, *op. cit.*; Desmond Wilson, *Gilbert Murray OM* (Oxford 1987); Francis West's *Gilbert Murray: A Life* (London 1984) is useless. For Cornford, see D. K. Wood in W. W. Briggs and W. M. Calder III (editors), *Classical Scholarship: A Biographical Encyclopedia* (New York, 1990) 23–36. A life of Cook is wanted.

[7] The prevalent attitude was summed up in M. I. Finley's irritable aside, tossed off while discussing the possibility of opening up the classics to other disciplines: "We all know the standard retort: look at the mess Jane Harrison and even Cornford got into, playing about with Frazer. Let's have no more of that. Indeed not, but Frazer was neither the alpha nor the omega of sociology" ("Unfreezing the Classics," *Times Literary Supplement* [7 April 1966] 289–90).

I

To begin with long-term tendencies, ritualism may usefully be seen as part of the gathering wave of vitalism and irrationalism that crested throughout the West in the quarter-century before 1914. Specifically, it represents the confluence of five analytically distinct movements and tendencies: (1) the 150-year-long romantic investigation of the unconscious mind and the concomitant gradual undermining of the older associationist psychology; (2) the end-of-century scramble for colonies among the imperial powers, which threw off as a by-product unexampled quantities of ethnographic data about so-called primitive peoples which in turn permitted generalizations of a scope quite unimaginable at any earlier time; (3) the 200-year-old process of demythologization of the classics which made it even thinkable for the Ritualists to compare the Greeks to the barbarians in the first place and at the same time produced the scandalized reaction of the Ritualists' conservative opponents; (4) the nineteenth-century passion for seeking out origins, which often were confused with essences[8]; and (5) the triumph of evolution (usually understood as progress), both as intellectual method and cultural metaphor, with its implication that the human mind and social institutions were just as much products of development as the physical world. All this made it possible for the Ritualists not merely to talk about the Greeks and the primitives in the same breath, but also to advance a general theory of the origins and evolution of religion in terms of a social psychology based on collective emotion.

Although I believe that this sort of bird's-eye view is helpful, especially for those who are not in the habit of taking long views, I also admit that there is not much oxygen to be breathed at such *zeitgeistlich* altitudes. Choosing where to land rather nearer the subject is not so easy, however. On the one hand intellectual history, like other kinds of history, is uneasy with the notion of origins; on the other, one recognizes the need to begin somewhere. To my mind, a reasonable (that is, intellectually appropriate and chronologically proximate) place to start is the publication of William Robertson Smith's *The Religion of the Semites* in 1889. A book we badly need now is an intellectual biography of Smith, who was both conduit and advocate, in the 1870s and 1880s, for German Higher Criticism in Britain.[9] If this book existed, I should be especially interested

---

[8] A splendid example of the manic pursuit of origins for their own sake is afforded by William Ridgeway, redoubtable antagonist of Jane Harrison. Along with being the self-appointed scourge of all things ritualistic, he also published the following articles: "The Origins of the Homeric 'Talent'" (1887), "The Origin of the Stadion" (1897), "The Origin of Jewellery" (1903), "The Origin of the Turkish Crescent" (1908), and "The Origin of the Indian Drama" (1917). To these must be added, among books, *The Origin of Metallic Currency and Weight Standards* (1892), and *The Origin and Influence of the Thoroughbred Horse* (1905).

[9] The outdated and otherwise inadequate biography is J. S. Black and G. Chrystal, *The Life of William Robertson Smith* (London 1912). See also Frazer's obituary essay,

in its comments on the question of how and why Smith came to reject the dominant rationalist assumptions of British historiography of religion.

Aside from the evident influence of the speculations of his fellow Scot, the trail-blazing social theorist J. F. McLennan, and in the absence of better information, I suggest that the answer may be related to his own religious position. It cannot be a coincidence that most of the major writers on mythology, ancient religion, and folklore in late Victorian Britain came from non-Church of England families.[10] For intellectuals, the experience of growing up outside the Established Church may in itself have predisposed some of them to adopt a critical viewpoint about religion at a moment when they felt compelled to take sides in the great battle between science and faith.[11] For this first generation to come to intellectual maturity after Darwin, the decision to study (in David Hume's phrase) "the natural history of religion" often represented a way to resolve personal conflicts concerning the claims of faith and reason. In many cases, however, the assumption of an attitude of neutrality was little more than a moral and intellectual ruse, permitting the would-be objective student to occupy the moral high ground, i.e., to attack religion while seeming to study it scientifically, thus obviating the need for any vulgar polemic. Of all these writers, Smith was among the few who remained a believing Christian, although obviously of a sophisticated kind.[12] Unlike Tylor or Frazer, he was not engaged in an undeclared war on Christianity. Perhaps for this reason he had a far better sense than either of them of the communal basis of religion and the many social and emotional needs that it fulfills, and this awareness may have made him doubly unwilling to follow them in their hostile rationalist reductionism.

Whatever Smith's motives, *The Religion of the Semites* undoubtedly put forward a collectivist and sociological interpretation of ancient religion, as opposed to the individualist and psychological explanations advanced by Spencer and Tylor that were current in Britain at the time. This meant that

---

"William Robertson Smith," in *The Gorgon's Head and Other Literary Pieces* (London 1927), pp. 275–92; orig. pub. *Fortnightly Review* (May 1894). *The Religion of the Semites* (2 ed., 1894) is all that remains of the three series of Burnett Lectures that Smith gave from October 1888 to October 1891 on "The primitive religions of the Semitic peoples, viewed in relation to other ancient religions, and to the spiritual religion of the Old Testament and of Christianity."

[10] Examples: Herbert Spencer (Methodist); E. B. Tylor (Quaker); J. G. Frazer (Free Church of Scotland); A. C. Haddon (Congregationalist); Jane Harrison and Edward Clodd (Baptist); Gilbert Murray (Roman Catholic); Joseph Jacobs and Moses Gaster (Jewish). Counterexamples: both Cook and Cornford were Church of England.

[11] Thus B.M.G. Reardon: "The issue of science *versus* religion was most prominent from about 1862 to 1877, when both sides were in the mood for conflict" (*From Coleridge to Gore* [London 1971] 13).

[12] S. A. Cook, a disciple and friend, states flatly that Smith was always a Christian, and that "he had no sympathy with...any thorough-going humanism or rationalism" (*Centenary of the Birth on 8th November 1846 of the Reverend Professor W. Robertson Smith* [Aberdeen 1951] 16).

in studying ancient Semitic religion Smith was unwilling naively to make late Victorian assumptions—e.g., private property as the economic norm; religion understood as synonymous with theology, to be judged entirely on rational grounds. Most importantly, because of his social perspective he focused on the group and its emotional behavior rather than the solitary thinker and his intellectual belief, and on ritual (i.e., action) rather than myth (i.e., text). What the ancient community really worshiped (Smith believed) was the social order—society itself—idealized and divinized. That is, ancient religion provided what we should call supernatural sanctions that legitimize the existing order of things, an order that seemed to the primitive worshiper to be natural and inevitable and therefore divinely ordained.

Basically, Smith claimed, myths have grown up as elaborations on rituals, and only when the original sense of these rituals has been misunderstood or forgotten. It follows, then, that the only way to understand a myth is to examine the ritual it attempts to explain, or if the ritual is no longer extant, then to read backward through the myth and thus to reconstruct the ritual.

> So far as myths consist of explanations of ritual, their value is almost secondary, and it may be affirmed with confidence that in almost every case the myth was derived from the ritual, and not the ritual from the myth; for the ritual was fixed and the myth was variable, the ritual was obligatory and faith in the myth was at the discretion of the worshipper.[13]

This polemic generalization enunciates the basic tenet of ritualism, which the Cambridge group would adopt as their method.

We know that Jane Harrison was having her students read Smith in 1900; she herself, always *au courant*, doubtless read him a decade earlier.[14] I suspect that Smith was useful to her at two different moments and in two different ways. The first occurred around 1890, when she had come to reject the prevalent idealization of the Greeks which she had earlier shared.[15] That Smith had had the temerity to demythologize the ancient Hebrews, who were after all God's Chosen People, by comparing them to contemporary Arabs, must have encouraged her mightily as she moved toward a more primitivistic view of the Greeks.

[13] The above paragraph is drawn from my "Frazer on Myth and Ritual," *Journal of the History of Ideas* 36 (January–March 1975) 119; the quotation comes from Smith, *The Religion of the Semites*, 2 ed. (1894; repr. New York 1956) 18.

[14] Stewart 14; Jane Harrison, *Reminiscences of a Student's Life* (London 1925) 82–83. Although we do not know exactly when she read Smith, we know that by 1892 she had read the first edition of *The Golden Bough* (1890), which was explicitly indebted to Smith. See her preface to Katherine Raleigh's translation of A. H. Petiscus, *The Gods of Olympos* (London 1892) vi, where she declares herself a follower of "the Folk-lore method, of which Mr. Andrew Lang and Mr. J. G. Frazer are, in England, the best known exponents."

[15] See Robert Ackerman, "Jane Ellen Harrison: The Early Work," *GRBS* 13 (1972) 209–30.

The point to bear in mind, however, is that when she read Smith she was ready to understand him. There can be no doubt that she was already, on her own, moving toward a Smithian position regarding myth and ritual. The decisive break came as a result of her first visit to Greece in 1888, when she was doing the research for a guidebook for modern travelers based on Pausanias' "Attica" called *Mythology and Monuments of Ancient Athens* (1890). In Athens, Dörpfeld himself had personally guided her through his excavations, showing her how closely and strongly cultic reality stood behind mythic narrative, whether told in a story or painted on a vase. In the preface to *Mythology and Monuments*, written nearly certainly *before* she read Smith or Frazer, she writes:

> ...I have tried everywhere to get at, where possible, the cult as the explanation of the legend. My belief is that in many, even in the large majority of cases, *ritual practice misunderstood* explains the elaboration of myth....Some of the loveliest stories the Greeks have left us will be seen to have taken their rise, not in poetic imagination, but in primitive, often savage, and I think, always practical ritual.[16]

That is, if myth arises from ritual misunderstood, to study myth we must focus on what the primitives—Greek or otherwise—did, not on what they (might have) thought. This is not to argue that the publication of *Myths and Monuments* marks the start of ritualism, which was the result of a lengthy and complex scholarly interaction, but rather that, for the rare person who is ready, willing, and able actually to see what is in front of her, as she was in Athens in 1888, personal experience is a more powerful solvent to old ideas than is any book.

Twenty years later, when she began writing *Themis*, Smith would have been important in quite a different way. As we who are gathered here today know only too well, whenever scholars have need to move outside their own specialty, they are often made uncomfortable by the new assumptions, codes, and ways of thinking which they encounter. For this reason, even when disciplinary boundaries within the social sciences were less well demarcated than they are now, and even for a person as dedicated to ignoring those boundaries as Jane Harrison, Smith would have provided her with a most welcome entrée to the work of Émile Durkheim and his colleagues in *L'Année Sociologique*, for Durkheim drew freely and heavily on Smith. She seems to have discovered the *Année* group around 1907, when she was struggling to revise *Prolegomena*, after the anthropologist A. R. Radcliffe-Brown had made them known in Britain. Thus, although she probably found Durkheim's thoroughgoing rationalism chilly and even repugnant, she surely recognized his central concept of "collective representations," or ideas held in common by the entire society, as derivative from Smith's notion of the faith of primitive people in the power that orders the world.

---

[16] *Myths and Monuments of Ancient Athens* (London 1890) iii. Italics in the original.

Smith's friend and protégé was J. G. Frazer (1854–1941), a classical Fellow of Trinity College, Cambridge. In the mid-1880s he had begun working on Pausanias when he met Smith, who as editor of the ninth edition of the *Encyclopædia Brittanica* introduced him to anthropology by assigning him the articles on "Taboo" and "Totemism." Frazer, deeply interested in philosophy and psychology, already had wider horizons than could comfortably be accommodated within the usual Cambridge classical career consisting of textual scholarship. Fascinated by the vistas of "primitive" life and thought which were revealed by this first foray into ethnography, and doubtless liberated by the feeling of wide-open intellectual space in that relatively young discipline, he never looked back.

Salomon Reinach remarked in 1912 that a sufficient epitaph for Smith would have been "*genuit Frazerum*," but Frazer and Smith, close friends though they were, from the start must have agreed to disagree about virtually everything concerning religion.[17] Pure types are rare enough in life, but Frazer was as undiluted an individualist, cognitionist, and reductionist regarding myth, ritual, and religion as one might ever expect to find. He appears here not because he was especially sympathetic to ritualism, for that sympathy, sporadic at best, was in any case later explicitly disavowed.[18]

Instead, his importance was essentially literary, expressing itself in several ways. His generally limpid and elevated style became a model for those who would write about ancient myth and ritual to a non specialist audience. From the start, he was able to guide his genteel readers with agreeable assurance through what in other hands might have been deserts of repugnant or dreary facts. British reviewers, whether lay or scholarly, whether friendly or hostile, universally agreed that Frazer, though as industrious as any German, was never dull.

Nor was pedantry the only reef on which he might have foundered. Given the deep and abiding interest at the time among educated Britons in anything that might help in deciding whether religion retained its authority, Frazer struck exactly the right note of respectful gravity about religion, relieved by frequent acid asides about the perseverance and ubiquity of superstition which served to flatter the up-to-date modern reader. He tactfully presented himself as a self-effacing follower of Science, pursuing the Facts wherever they might lead. This etiquette of disinterestedness permitted him neatly to suppress his rationalist agenda, thereby eschewing confrontation, for which he had no taste. He went so far as to avoid even mentioning Christianity, although his discussions of Attis, Adonis, Osiris, Dionysus, and the rest of the pantheon of the ancient Near East made it clear to any but the slowest reader that those cults, founded in mental confusion

---

[17] Ackerman (1987) 70.
[18] Ackerman (1975) 131–32.

as they were, bore unmistakable resemblances to that of Jesus.[19] In *The Golden Bough* and his many subsequent works, he thus created, virtually single-handedly, a non specialist audience for books on primitive psychology, myth, and ancient religion. This was an audience that Gilbert Murray especially tapped. Whereas Harrison's, Cornford's, and Cook's "big" books were too complex and technical for lay people, Murray was a gifted popularizer whose most important work would have appealed precisely to Frazer's earnest and high-minded readers.

Finally, Frazer's main ideas and especially his memorable metaphors (the figure of the priest-king in the grove at Nemi, "the slayer who would himself be slain"; the recurring pattern of death and resurrection in the cults of the ancient Near East) constituted a fund of attractive and accessible dramatic imagery that soon became available by reference to all who came after him, including the Ritualists and their followers, who treated him respectfully even when they disagreed with him.[20]

The Golden Bough (1890, 2 vols.; 1900, 3 vols.; 1911–15, 12 vols.; 1922, 1-vol. abridgement) focused on sacrificial cult ritual, primarily of the vegetation-magical kind, in the ancient and classical world, along with its alleged analogues and survivals among modern savages and peasants. The work was based on the bold assertion that the peoples of classical antiquity, far from being the shining cultural heroes familiar since the Renaissance, had climbed no higher on the ladder of mental evolution than the (low) level attained by contemporary savages and peasants. If the Greeks were no further advanced than savages, then ethnography—which silently was made equivalent to the study of primitive epistemology—afforded us nothing less than a mental time machine. If we succeeded in extracting and articulating the assumptions underlying the world-view of the benighted peoples then being observed and documented by missionaries, explorers, traders, and folklorists, then we also and at the same time gained entry to the otherwise inaccessible mental and moral universe of the ancients.

---

[19] His ambivalent attitude toward Christianity is expressed in a remarkable metaphor in which he pictures himself as a reluctant artilleryman, compelled by his research to bombard the walled citadel of religion and eventually to destroy it: see the preface to the second edition of *The Golden Bough* (London 1900) I xxi–xxii.

[20] In view of the fact that Frazer was an obscure Cambridge don writing on what would seem to be a recondite subject, it is worth remarking just how soon the priest at Nemi, the "corn king," and the rest of the Frazerian *dramatis personae* entered the public domain and became part of what a literate person was expected to recognize and know. An excellent indication of just how quickly this entry into subacademic consciousness took place is provided by E. C. Bentley's *Trent's Last Case*, a runaway best-selling mystery novel of 1912 (i.e., a year after the appearance of the last volume of the third edition of *The Golden Bough* but fully a decade before Frazer's real "best-seller," the abridged *Golden Bough*). In it the Frazerian figure of the slayer who would himself be slain appears as a metaphor in the climactic revelations of the last chapter. Among the many early followers, the most important were Jessie Weston (*From Ritual to Romance*) and Margaret Murray (*The Witch-Cult in Western Europe*).

II

Having sketched some of the more important early influences—and I could go on for many more pages—I must now enter a crucial biographical *caveat*. The history of ideas is rather like a glacier, scouring and smoothing everything in its path and covering over important individual differences in the intellectual terrain. It cannot be overemphasized that the Ritualists, their close personal and intellectual relationships notwithstanding, were quite different one from the other in terms of background, interests, and personality; that by no means did they always agree; and that each of them found congenial and chose to emphasize different elements from within the complex intellectual context in which they worked. It is therefore both useful and important to expose some of the differences as well as similarities in the work of the members of the group.

The single most important fact about the Ritualists was that Jane Harrison stood at their center. It was she who, in the process of resolving questions that mattered deeply to her, brought them together in the first place, talked and wrote to them continually, and throughout set the group's agenda.[21] She was the spark; it is perfectly plain that without her, there would have been no group. Further, it was she who led the others to (at least) Durkheim, Nietzsche, Bergson, and Freud. I don't mean by this that the others had not heard of these writers, but that it was she who read them first, saw their potential importance for their work, and pressed them on her friends. Thus, returning to the specific case of Robertson Smith, my remarks were made from *her* point of view and tried to estimate the impact on and value of Smith to *her*.

From Cornford's perspective, however, one might note that whereas he undoubtedly read Smith, he probably did so at the urging of Harrison, which is to say that he encountered *The Religion of the Semites* at least ten years after she had. But the 1890s were an extremely productive decade in the study of comparative religion (I am thinking especially of the work of Tylor, Frazer, and Lang), which is to say that reading Smith in 1900 was not at all the same as reading him in 1890, when Harrison did. (Not to mention the fact that he read Smith while he was in his mid-twenties, whereas she read him at forty.) Moreover, he read Smith not in the context of a "deconversion" from idealization as she had, but while already moving toward primitivism under her powerful influence. There can be no doubt that as part of her passionate intellectual friendship with him, she opened a

---

[21] For a good example of such agenda-setting, see the conclusion to her brief, non scholarly introduction to *The Religion of Ancient Greece* (London 1905) 63, where, in speaking of the work still to be done, she writes: "...the history of Greek religion is yet to be written...how in its early stages did religion act on philosophy? Philosophy react on religion?...finally, a difficult and delicate task, what is the outlook of each literary author, his personal outlook and bias, how did each modify the material ready to his hand?" The philosophical task was to be undertaken by Cornford and the literary by Murray.

new way for him to see the pre-Socratics, and within that re-ordered framework, Smith was only one of the writers to whom she introduced him (none, of course, was as important as Durkheim later would be).

The other Ritualists were hardly blank slates, and the abiding temperamental differences among them must always be borne in mind when one tries to understand the group and its achievement. To take another important example, I have little doubt that Harrison was always more favorably disposed toward irrationalism than was Murray.[22] Although he later became a tireless propagandist for the *eniautos-daimon*, I suspect that if we had his letters to her, we would find many a polite attempt on his part to beg off reading whatever Continental scholar was her newest enthusiasm.[23]

Because Duncan Wilson was not especially interested in or knowledgeable about Murray's classical work, he paid ritualism relatively little attention; his biography nonetheless does make it possible to see that Murray's path to ritualism was quite different from Harrison's. To demonstrate, here is the very passage from *A History of Ancient Greek Literature* that so moved Harrison in 1900 that she wrote her fateful letter to him:

> Reason is great but it is not everything. There are in the world things not of reason, but both above and below it; causes of emotion which we cannot express, which we tend to worship, which we feel, perhaps, to be the precious elements in life. These things are Gods, or forms of God: not fabulous immortal men, but "Things which Are," things utterly non-human and non-moral, which bring man bliss or tear his life to shreds without a break in their own serenity.[24]

Considering where she then was on her own intellectual odyssey, having jettisoned Attic serenity a decade earlier in favor of chthonic turmoil, it is easy to see why Harrison should have greeted those lines as the announcement of the welcome existence of a fellow seeker on the same path. But I suggest that an equally relevant biographical subtext here may well have been Murray's own deeply unsettling experiences with paranormal

---

[22] In other words, I am unwilling to accept (at face value, at any rate) her protestation to the contrary, in the preface (p. viii) to *Prolegomena*: "I have tried to understand primitive rites, not from love of their archaism...but with the definite hope that I might come to a better understanding of some forms of Greek poetry." (This is repeated in the preface to *Themis*, where she claims that she has "little natural love of what an Elizabethan calls 'ye Beastly Devices of ye Heathen.'") Certainly Harrison's post war, post classical writings (e.g., *Epilegomena*) lean heavily toward mysticism.

[23] Thus, the following are suggestive: in an unpublished letter than can be dated by Jessie Stewart no more closely than 1908, Harrison writes to Murray: "Have you read Bergson's *L'Évolution Créatrice*? If not, it is likely that I may be a nuisance when I come [to see you]." And again, in a letter of December 1909: "I have been re-reading *Die Geburt der Tragödie*. Have you read the book at all lately, it is real genius, and if you hate the German there is a French translation" (MSS: Newnham College Library). She is "re-reading" because she had read it at least once by 1903, for it is cited in *Prolegomena*.

[24] (London 1897) 272.

phenomena. For many years a well-known "sensitive," he had often participated in experiments carried out by the Society for Psychical Research, of which he served twice as president. Indeed, the Verralls were his great friends in Cambridge twice over: Arthur as a fellow Euripidean and Margaret (Jane Harrison's classmate at Newnham, collaborator on *Myths and Monuments*, and good friend) as a well-known psychic investigator. Wilson makes it clear that Murray was always uncomfortable with this side of his own nature and experience, with which he never fully came to terms. Whatever its final role in his psychic economy, it must have acted to undermine fatally any tendencies toward, or hopes for, rationalist certainty that he may have had.[25]

Murray and Harrison were both complex personalities, and neither "rationalist" nor "mystic" suffices to describe either of them. Because her own childhood was made miserable by a hateful Calvinist stepmother, and because she possessed a naturally caustic wit, Harrison was always ready to laugh at religious cant and hypocrisy, so prevalent in late Victorian Britain. She combined this streak of mockery at humbug in the present with a taste for the wild and even barbaric side of the Greek experience in the past, neither of which the gentler and more abstemious Murray shared. (To which must be added as well a capacity for transcendent experience. I am thinking of the "vision" that was vouchsafed her in 1912 at the end of her long depression after Cornford's marriage.[26]) His extrasensory gifts notwithstanding, Murray seems generally to have been content to remain within the envelope of more "normal" experience. That is, Harrison and Murray had much but by no means everything in common, and these differences never disappeared. Indeed, I suspect that they acted as a piquant ingredient in the recipe of their friendship.

Thus, for all his great and growing importance to Harrison in the latter stages of the writing of *Prolegomena* and his active collaboration with her in the years that followed, it should come as no great surprise that as late as 1907 Murray had no difficulties in accepting William Ridgeway's (Harrison's arch-enemy) euhemerist position on the origins of tragedy.[27] By 1907, that is, the notion that tragedy might have been the product of an unconscious collective sentiment or process, much less a specific Dionysian ritual, had not even glimmered in his mind. Harrison seems always to have

---

[25] Wilson, chap. 20.

[26] See her letter to Murray of September 1912, in Stewart 113.

[27] See the preface to the third (1907) edition of his *History of Ancient Greek Literature*, where he says "that one most important element in the origin of tragedy was the ritual performed in so many parts of Greece at the grave of an ancestor or dead hero." These performances were later transferred to Dionysus. Thus Murray: "Almost every tragedy, as a matter of fact, can be resolved into a lament over the grave of some canonised hero or heroine mixed with a re-enacting of his death." Having said that, he admits that he still does not see how a complete historical case can be made, and awaits Ridgeway's book (viz., *The Origin of Tragedy*).

been the intellectual leader of the group, and always she led the others toward the irrational roots of religion. Murray's acceptance of the *eniautos-daimon* hypothesis may well have occurred virtually on the spot when Harrison sent him the manuscript of the first chapters of the new book for comment. That would have happened in 1908 when she gave up trying to revise *Prolegomena* and instead began a new book that would be called *Themis*. She had finally found a way forward as a result of having read Henri Bergson's *L'Évolution Créatrice* (1907) and specifically in grasping the importance of his notion of *durée* to Greek experience.

But in this context perhaps the most astonishing item in Murray's *oeuvre* is *Euripides and His Age*, which appeared in 1913 as part of the burst of Ritualist publications in the two years immediately preceding the war. By then the group had been together for a decade, and Murray had been working on Euripides for twice that length of time. A book with this title may therefore reasonably lead one to expect a definitive Ritualist statement on the dramatist whose work, Murray had argued only a year earlier in his "Excursus" in *Themis*, illustrated the prehistoric ritual pattern most clearly of all. Yet, although written to a Greekless audience and therefore requiring a different rhetorical strategy than the "Excursus," which was intended for scholars, it is disappointing in its own terms. Take, for example, his discussion of the *Suppliants*, where he notes that the play opens with a scene of supplicants before an altar. But that is all he says—he does not even mention, as he had in the "Excursus," that the scene has or might have a ritual basis. And indeed the analysis of this play, as with many others, contains nothing about ritual at all.

But odder still is the frequent and intrusive presence of a tone that would sound natural in hard-core rationalists like Verrall or Frazer, but which is not at all what one comes to expect in a full-blooded Ritualist, with all the irrationalist connotations of that label. One gets nowhere in this book, as one does everywhere in Jane Harrison's mature work, any sense of the terror or darkness of the chthonic *cultus*; instead, Murray prefers to focus on what he is pleased to call the Athenians' "superstitions." An example: Murray has been (over-)emphasizing the importance of philosophy in the fifth century, and he says that despite the intellectual and moral advances made by the great thinkers of the time, most Greeks never stopped practicing "the silliest and cruelest old agricultural magic."[28] If one is psychobiographically inclined, it is possible to read the gratuitous irrelevance of such a remark as a manifestation of resistance to Harrison's relentless promotion of the chthonic. Psychobiography aside, the remark is at least a genuine expression of a temperament altogether less attracted by primitive "excess" than hers.

[28] (London 1913) 115.

Finally, consider this passage, in which Murray, in an analogy meant to be helpful to non classical readers, tries to sum up the spirit of the *locus classicus* of ritualism, the *Bacchae*:

> Let us imagine a great free-minded modern poet—say Swinburne or Morris or Victor Hugo, all of whom did great things—making from some local anniversary a rhymed play in the style of the Mysteries on some legend of a mediaeval saint. The saint, let us suppose, is very meek and is cruelly persecuted by a wicked emperor, whom he threatens with hell fire; and at the end let us have the emperor in the midst of that fire and the saint in glory saying, "What did I tell you?" And let us suppose that the play in its course gives splendid opportunities for solemn Latin hymns, such as Swinburne and Hugo delighted in. We should probably have a result something like the *Bacchae*.[29]

It seems to me that, *mutatis mutandis*, in such a case nothing at all like the *Bacchae* would result, for one important reason that Murray should have been aware of: namely, in his use of myth Euripides was unselfconscious in a way that modern writers are not and can never be. This is true without getting into the difficult question of Euripides' personal religious views—in exactly what sense he may be said to have believed in the gods at all. For whatever his position was—atheism or rationalism or severely qualified belief—Dionysian myth and ritual were in his bones in the way, say, that a belief in progress was in those of someone born at the end of the nineteenth century, regardless of whether he ever thought about it, much less consciously espoused it. The analogy isn't exact, but Euripides' relationship to myth is perhaps comparable to that of Cervantes to knighthood and chivalry in *Don Quixote*. Dionysus was probably closer and more "available" to Euripides than was chivalry to Cervantes, but in both cases the relation between author and subject was complex; in neither case was there any of the antiquarianism implied in Murray's example. Indeed, as we know from the numerous attempts over the last hundred years to employ ancient myths as a basis for works of literature, the aesthetic distance implicit in historicism makes possible pathos, but tragedy seems to be beyond reach. The necessity for "research" on the part of the modern writer (wholly absent in Euripides' case) vitiates whatever numinous power the myth may hold. Only in irony or fantasy (such as science fiction) is myth usable in literature now.

Finally, Cook ought not to be left out. Conclusive evidence exists that he was distinctly unwilling to go the whole primitivistic way with Harrison, Murray, and Cornford in their analysis of the irrational origins of religion. I believe that the chief reason for his reluctance lay in the fact that he remained a committed evangelical Christian throughout his life. Like Smith, he could accept the notion of a sacral king in earliest society, and perhaps he understood Jesus as the omega point of that tradition; he was

---

[29] *Ibid.*, 183–4.

unwilling, however, to go further. Specifically, he found totally
unpersuasive Jane Harrison's recasting of the evolution of Greek religion
based upon Durkheim's analysis of Australian aboriginal religion. He must
have seen that this model, when turned on Christianity, dissolved Jesus into
a froth of collective primitive emotion. (Recall that Jane Harrison says in
the preface that *Themis* is really offering a general theory of the origins of
religion, with the examples drawn from classical antiquity because that is
what she knows best.)

Here are relevant extracts from two unpublished letters. Writing to
Murray as late as 23 August 1913, Cook expresses at considerable length
his distaste for "*eniautos-daimon*" as a phrase. His throwaway conclusion—
"but I daresay it is all a question of words. I hate 'daemons' of all sorts, and
'year-daemons' worse than any"—underlines the seriousness of his
objections.[30] We all know that when good friends differ deeply on an
important intellectual question, a seeming retraction such as Cook's is a
formula that permits the writer to show how important the matter is while
at the same time indicating subtextually that he nonetheless remains a
friend.

The other letter, written by Jane Harrison to Cook about two years
earlier (on 8 September 1911), is intended to counter his substantial
objections to the *eniautos-daimon* hypothesis, which he must have
expressed to her (in a lost letter) upon reading the manuscript of *Themis*.
(An interesting small point: Cook clearly at this time has not read
Murray's "Excursus," which implies either that he saw only parts of the
manuscript, or that the decision to include it was made relatively late.) She
writes:

> The point at which we are really at issue lies deeper. I do not believe
> that the drama took its form from the cult of Dionysus except in so far
> as he was one of the thousand-year daimons. The Mummers and May
> Day plays are not survivals of the cult of Dionysus but of a thing far
> more widespread...I am greatly pleased that the analysis of drama in
> general commends itself to you—it will I think be immensely
> strengthened by Prof. Murray's excursus which is to follow chapter VIII
> and which will I think interest you. It teems with facts. To conclude,

[30] When in the 1970s I spoke with Cook's daughter Phyllis Cook, she told me of her
father's abiding religious faith. She also said that he had a special interest in "uncanny"
occurrences and phenomena such as extrasensory perception, telepathy, "prophetic
dreams," and the like, whether they happened to him or to anyone else. He collected
reports and notices of such things in a series of large ledgers that he entitled "Explicanda,"
one of which she showed me. I suggested that she donate these volumes to a library, either
that of her father's college (Queens') or some other place.

and it is time: I am intensely conscious that my theories (and my book will be a tissue of theories) need a much broader basis both of psychology and probably ethnography, and it is probably rash to publish it as it stands, and I stand to lose such reputation as I have. I write really not to instruct but because I cannot begin to think until I have discharged all the theories that welter inside me and put everything out of focus, but the bits you accept I have confidence in.[31]

From the first three sentences one may infer that Cook, essentially a historical scholar, had balked at Harrison's willingness to move speculatively from the historical deity Dionysus to the generalized class of year-spirits of which he was putatively a member. Cook appears to have wished to try to derive the mummers' plays historically from the cult of Dionysus rather than make what must have seemed a leap into the philosophical and psychological void. (This also suggests why he would have felt intellectually comfortable collaborating with Frazer, who, though equally speculative, at least employed a simple associationist psychology. It may also explain why he was not asked to contribute to *Themis*.)

The possibility of making such a direct historical connection was not as fanciful then as it may seem now. Only five years earlier, in 1906, R. M. Dawkins, in Thrace to examine inscriptions, by chance happened upon a performance of a springtime "mummers' play" that reproduced with remarkable fidelity many features of Dionysian worship as reported by ancient writers.[32] His description created a sensation because, unlike the many similar ancient and modern rituals from various locales collected and recounted by Mannhardt and Frazer, this one came from Dionysus' own "home," Thrace. The temptation for historically inclined philologists like Cook must have been irresistible to believe that they had against all odds uncovered the genuine article, a demotic "survival" that had somehow been preserved more or less intact through two and a half millennia.

In the absence of the relevant correspondence, and so far as one can tell, this gap between Cook and the others persisted, which I believe goes far toward explaining why (as noted) Murray retrospectively denied Cook full membership in the group. Because of the extent of these intellectual differences with the others, I suspect that Cook would soon have veered off or even broken with them publicly. In the event, that was not necessary, for the winds of war snuffed out the Ritualists along with the rest of scholarship. By the time Jane Harrison left Cambridge for Paris in 1922, she had abandoned Greek for Russian, Murray was committed to the cause of international intellectual cooperation within the League of Nations, and Cornford had moved from the study of the mythical foundations of philosophy to the study of philosophy itself. It was all over.

---

[31] Jessie Stewart papers, Newnham College Library.
[32] "A Modern Carnival in Thrace and the Cult of Dionysus," *JHS* 26 (1906) 191–206.

III

Patricia Hampl, discussing the genesis of fiction in view of the uncontrollability of the imagination and the sense in which writers are more its servants than its masters, remarks, "Every story has a story."[33] Every idea has a story, too. Sometimes an idea seems to spring full-blown in the mind, and one is unaware of the combination of conscious effort and unconscious process that produced it. Other times, and especially when one is working closely with others—trying out thoughts on colleagues, who having knocked them down sometimes pick them up, transformed, and play them back—when ideas come in such settings they may be experienced more as the products of the mitigation or resolution of tension between people than as intellectual constructions within one's individual consciousness. The result may be the same, but the process is quite different. Because of the individualistic tradition in which modern scholarship has developed in the West, intellectual biographers have had relatively little practice in exploring and documenting the ways in which groups of scholars work closely together, and specifically in analyzing the ways in which groups become more than the sum of their parts. Beyond the sometimes feverish comic *brío* of Jane Harrison's letters to Gilbert Murray—and Jessie Stewart emphasized that side of their relationship in the letters she chose to print—we do not know much about the Ritualists *as a group*. Specifically, although the new biographies certainly help, there is a great deal more that I should like to know about Harrison's changing relationships with Murray and Cornford.

Obviously, mastering the dense intellectual context, delineating the complex interaction of the main personalities, conveying the excitement that they felt as they applied Frazerian anthropology and Durkheimian social psychology to classical religion, at the same time throwing open a window in the airless museum of classical studies—all these constitute real and considerable analytical and narrative problems in themselves. Because Jane Harrison burned her papers when she left Cambridge, we shall never have a clear idea of Murray's side of their correspondence (and therefore how he viewed their relationship), and we shall never know much about other important parts of her life, especially the difficult early years she spent in London. To be sure, the Cornford archive is now accessible, but because he and Harrison saw one another so often, sometimes daily, in Cambridge, there is much we shall never know about "the *Themis* years." No one, however, seems to have remarked the importance of the loss of Cook's papers, which are nowhere to be found. Their absence is especially unfortunate precisely because his growing differences with the others, to the

---

[33] Patricia Hampl, "The Lax Habits of the Free Imagination," *New York Times Book Review* (5 March 1989) 37.

extent that they were committed to paper, would provide an admirable index of the evolution of the Ritualists' ideas and the way they worked together.

The lives of intellectuals on the close-up, day-to-day level often contain an element of seeming randomness that historians of ideas tend not to notice, or at least not to take much interest in. By its nature, biography concerns itself with psychological processes (including the possibilities for confused or aimless action that neurotic behavior implies), whereas the history of ideas emphasizes social consequences—the diffusion and dissemination of information and its effects in intellectual terms. That is, to some extent the disparities between intellectual history and biography highlighted in this essay should be understood as the products of inherently different perspectives and in that sense unavoidable.

The existence of complex and shifting fields of emotional and intellectual tension is precisely what one might expect in a small group of scholars like the Ritualists, working under various kinds of pressures. In this case the turbidity was heightened by the cloud of unresolved sexual emotion between Harrison and Cornford. Much of *Themis* was written while its author's feelings were in a knot, the nature of which was only intermittently acknowledged. This tension must have contributed to the opacity of some of the text, if only in that it may have made her more impatient than she might otherwise have been. Indeed, were we to encounter only sweetness and light among them, that fact alone should cause us to suspect that wishful retrospective smoothing or even doctoring of the sources may have taken place.

Such smoothing is precisely what I believe may have taken place in the case of Murray's ambivalence about Cook's contribution, already noted. Murray may have decided to exclude Cook largely because the latter's differences with the others, which must have been known to all concerned, had by the 1920s come to take on a somewhat different aspect. Before the war, when the group was in full swing, the best response to the skepticism and hostility that their work engendered was the strength and energy of the work itself. After the war, with the group dispersed and in the face of continuing opposition from mainstream scholarship, Murray, who had become the group's public defender and advocate, may have wished to present more of a semblance of a united front to the world. Such an impression of unity (which was real enough for himself, Cornford, and Harrison, but not for Cook) may have become more important after the fact than it had been during the group's heyday, when Cook's demurrings were in any case expressed only in private.

My conclusion, then, is that although ritualism's brief moment occurred only seventy-five years ago, we are far from having taken its measure, either intellectually or biographically. The main problems are easily listed: the gaping documentary lacunae; the lack of modern lives of Cook, Cornford, and Robertson Smith; the lack of intellectually adequate histories of anthropology, the history of religion, and classical scholarship.

In view of the magnitude of these needs, it is indeed a great pleasure to contribute in some small way to this first (and in my view overdue) examination of an absorbing and problematic episode in modern intellectual history.

University of the Arts, Philadelphia

2

Aunt Glegg Among the Dons
or Taking Jane Harrison at Her Word

THOMAS W. AFRICA

"Sometimes a matter of less moment, an expression or a jest,
informs us better of their characters and inclinations."—Plutarch,
Alexander 1.

Salvaging an individual from the obscurity of the past is the most
demanding task of a historian. While any historical topic can be clouded by
lack of data, even well-documented cases are not necessarily clear. The long
view that posterity is afforded may only seem a clearer perspective, for
contemporaries knew warts and much else that Clio omits. The human
personality hides behind many masks, some deliberately assumed, others
unconscious. How should we evaluate a self-assessment that seems playful?
Presumably, an appropriate epithet is consistent with a pattern of reliable
data in the life and work of the individual. Another problem lies in the
weight given to evidence that lies in the realm of the irrational—visions,
dreams, and fancies; superstitious acts and slips of the pen; whatever shows
the unguarded self. Such data make the subconscious audible, as Jane
Harrison said of Joyce, "dredging the great deeps of personality."[1] Here, the
only criterion should be authenticity, for if it can be validated, a dream or
hallucination is historically significant as evidence. What such data tell us
about an individual again depends upon the plausibility of the pattern that
emerges through its addition. Both of these biographic problems—the
colorful epithet and irrational data—are illustrated in the case of Aunt Glegg
among the dons at Cambridge, which is how Jane Harrison says she saw
herself.

Though always controversial, Jane Ellen Harrison (1850–1928) was
once a name to reckon with in Classical Studies, for she was an ardent
advocate of applying anthropological insights to the prehistory of Greek
religion and adamant in insisting on the priority of ritual as a group
experience from which emerged various myths and philosophic notions.

---

[1] Jane Ellen Harrison, *Reminiscences of a Student's Life* (London, 1925), 26.

Changing tastes in Classics and Anthropology eclipsed her fame, but her star has risen again with the revival of ritualist theory and feminist focus on neglected women scholars. Flanked like a Minoan goddess by two younger males, she was the presiding spirit of the Cambridge Ritualists, a scholarly trinity (Jane Harrison, Gilbert Murray, and Francis Cornford)[2] who stirred up the Edwardian intellectual world with a series of heretical books that were brilliant, eloquent, and intuitive to a fault. "Behind their bright splendours," Ms. Harrison wrote of the high culture of Hellas, "I see moving darker and older shapes."[3] Not only did she see savage survivals and primitive practices in Classical Greece, but also remnants of an earlier social order, "matriarchal" in spirit and mediated by intensely emotional ritual group experiences. Much of this imagined idyllic past was later swept aside by the Olympian cults and patriarchal social structures. Although Murray and Cornford viewed Olympian "rationality" in a more positive light, the Cambridge Ritualists agreed on the emotional basis of society, then and now, and their sense of life as a drama fitted *fin-de-siècle* sensibilities. Like Frazer's *Golden Bough*, Harrison's *Prolegomena to the Study of Greek Religion* (1903) and *Themis* (1912) used a wealth of anthropological data and classical material to demonstrate that there are more things in heaven and earth than positivist science dreamed of. Not surprising, D. H. Lawrence and T. S. Eliot read her with enthusiasm,[4] and Virginia Woolf ranked Jane Harrison with Jane Austen, the Brontes, and George Eliot in the feminist literary pantheon.[5] Edmund Leach recognizes Harrison as "a classical scholar who profited from the writings of anthropologists; the succeeding generation of anthropologists in turn profited from hers. Malinowski and Radcliffe-Brown...were both indebted to Harrison."[6] Murray recalled that Malinowski "remarked on the soundness of her anthropological understanding."[7] Conservative classicists were less appreciative of the heresies of the Cambridge Ritualists, and some were candid about the roots of their discontent. Though he balked at her

---

[2] A. B. Cook was a loyal friend of Jane Harrison and an important ritualist scholar who battled her foes and helped "do proofs" on her books, but he did not share the intimate bond between Harrison, Murray, and Cornford. "ABC was a great help to us," recalled Murray, "but not one of us"—see Sandra J. Peacock, *Jane Ellen Harrison: The Mask and the Self* (New Haven & London: Yale University Press, 1988), 130.

[3] Harrison, *Reminiscences*, 86–87.

[4] T. S. Eliot, *The Sacred Wood* (New York: Knopf, 1930), 75. D. H. Lawrence, *Collected Letters* (New York: Viking, 1962), I: 234, 249.

[5] *The Diary of Virginia Woolf* (New York: Harcourt Brace, 1978), II: 339. Jane Harrison also appears in Ms. Woolf's *A Room of One's Own* (New York: Harcourt Brace, 1957), 17—the most sacred feminist text.

[6] Edmund R. Leach, "Ritual," *International Encyclopedia of the Social Sciences* (1968), XIV, 522.

[7] Gilbert Murray, "Francis M. Cornford," *Proceedings of the British Academy* 29 (1943): 424. See Bronislaw Malinowski, *Magic, Science, and Religion and Other Essays* (New York: Doubleday Anchor, 1954), 22–23.

imaginative reconstructions of a social order before history, Lewis Farnell of Oxford was not averse to anthropology *per se*. Rather, he objected to Harrison's "two dominant prejudices—the prejudice against the personal individual God, and the matriarchal prejudice."[8] In Farnell's eyes, "the writings of the gifted Jane Harrison, the leading woman scholar of the time, were marred by the spirit of feminist propaganda."[9] As Vice-Chancellor of Oxford, he was a leading opponent of admitting women to the universities, and the chain-smoking Ms. Harrison seemed to embody his worst fears. Her implacable enemy, William Ridgeway, was another outspoken antifeminist.[10] Ironically, Ms. Harrison was not a suffragist, though she was a highly visible champion of women in higher education.

To her allies and admirers, Jane Harrison was an inspired scholar whose intuitive forays into the unmapped terrain of prehistory often outran the factual logistical support demanded by conventional pedants. If she was over-assertive about guesses and fancies, the price was a small one to pay for her exciting presentations and the glimpses of lost realities that broke through when she was at her best. To her critics, she was the archetypical Crazy Jane, a creature of uncontrollable emotions, eccentric in dress, theatrical in mien, and deluded by her own ravings[11]—in short, the epitome of feminine emotion, and an old maid to boot. Wrongly assuming that she was a disciple of Frazer (who was not a ritualist), Edmund Leach claims that she was titillated by Frazer's subtext, "a Dionysian, sex-inspired, primitive undercurrent sapping at the roots of conventional Victorian society...It seems clear that part of Jane Harrison's interest in *The Golden Bough* lay in the fact that she was fascinated by the brute sadism of primitive sacrifice."[12] Unfortunately for Leach's surmise, Harrison had declared her adherence to ritual theory and "savage survivals" in *Mythology and Monuments of Ancient Athens* in 1890,[13] the same year that Frazer published *The Golden Bough*. More importantly, her books deal less with the "brute sadism of primitive sacrifice" than with orgiastic dances and possession of worshipers by a god who is the collective feeling of the group. Because these rituals were at their purest during the matriarchal social order that she presumes

[8] Lewis R. Farnell, rev. "Themis," *Hibbert Journal* 11 (1912): 455.

[9] Lewis R. Farnell, *An Oxonian Looks Back* (London: Hopkinson, 1934), 281.

[10] Jessie Stewart, *Jane Ellen Harrison, A Portrait from Letters* (London: Merlin, 1959), 184–186. Peacock, 120–122—"Alas," laments Ms. Harrison, A. B. Cook "is on the wrong side...with the old dragon Ridgeway."

[11] Elaine Showalter, *The Female Malady: Women, Madness, and English Culture 1830-1980* (New York: Pantheon, 1985), 10–16. When George Meredith's *Jump-for-Glory Jane* appeared in 1892, some of her critics may have been mindful of Harrison.

[12] Edmund R. Leach, "Golden Bough or Gilded Twig?" *Daedalus* 90 (1961), 383.

[13] Jane E. Harrison, *Mythology and Monuments of Ancient Athens* (London: Macmillan, 1890), iii; "In the large majority of cases, *ritual practice misunderstood* explains the elaboration of myth." The source of myth is "not in poetic imagination, but in primitive, often savage, and...always practical ritual." D. S. MacColl had already alerted her to the work of Wilhelm Mannhardt and J. Theodore Bent—Peacock, 75.

preceded the Olympians, Harrison downplays the violence of Dionysian religion and emphasizes the loving attitudes of young males to the female personification of the group, Themis. Such is the theme of *Themis* (1912), which was "written in a white heat"[14] to exorcise her despair when Francis Cornford married Frances Darwin.[15] Even the format of the book (Murray and Cornford each contributed a chapter) recapitulates Harrison's model of a small group of males in attendance on a beloved female "spirit of the group." In correspondence with Murray, she sometimes signed herself as "Themis,"[16] and she did not choose pet names for her friends lightly. Once, Harrison and Cornford were "Sheba" and "Solomon"; at other times, he was "Zeus" and "Comus," but when he married Ms. Darwin, Cornford was demoted to "Francis."[17] It should come as no surprise that scholars act out their fantasies in books that purport to be scientific.[18] Mommsen's Caesar is as romantic a creation as Harrison's pre-Olympian matriarch, Themis, and her open attacks on the Victorian family are as uncompromising as his on German politicians.

Like the heroine of a Victorian novel, Jane Harrison was the darling daughter of a doting widower who, when she was five years old, married her beautiful governess and bred a large family with the new wife that rivaled Jane and her sisters. The personal tragedy of her life forms a major component in her critique of Victorian patriarchy;[19] another was the hostile

[14] Farnell, *Hibbert Journal*, 454. Francis Cornford, *Newnham College Letter* (1929), 75, recalls: "When she was writing *Themis*, she astonished me by producing, week by week, a new chapter almost in its final shape."

[15] Stewart, 101–113, first revealed the Harrison-Cornford-Darwin triangle; Cornford, who was twenty-five years her junior, did not realize that Jane Harrison was in love with him. Peacock, 151–178, 194–211, 217–218, provides a detailed account of this contretemps and relates the writing of *Themis* to Ms. Harrison's efforts to cope with the crisis.

[16] Stewart, 35, 78. Usually, Harrison signed herself as "Ker," a Greek death *daimon*, an appropriate name for one who blamed herself for her mother's death from puerperal fever— Peacock 8, 141. (I owe this insight to Professor Renate Schlesier.)

[17] Peacock, 163–164.

[18] Gibbon, Mommsen, Prescott, and Kantorowicz are sufficient examples of great scholars who lived vicarious lives in their books; the list could be extended indefinitely. Leon Edel, *Writing Lives* (New York: Norton, 1984), offers sage remarks on transference and other habits of biographers. William M. Calder III, "Ulrich von Wilamowitz-Moellendorff: *Sospitator Euripidis*," *Greek, Roman, and Byzantine Studies* 27 (1986) 409–430, shows convincingly how Wilamowitz identified with Euripides and how Rohde used the poet as a mask for Nietzsche.

[19] Jane Harrison's eloquent essay, "Homo Sum," *Alpha and Omega* (London: Sidgwick & Jackson, 1915), 80–115, must be read on both a personal and a gender level—the same dictum applies to her many offhand remarks on religion, such as "the god or force of the family, a god violently dominant up to quite recent days, demanding and receiving holocausts of human and especially feminine lives, a god sometimes a tower of strength and joy, but often also a terror and a paralysis." (52) See also representative samples in *Prolegomena to the Study of Greek Religion* (Cambridge: Cambridge University Press, Ed. 3, 1922), 274, and *Themis: A Study of the Social Origins of Greek Religion* (Cambridge: Cambridge University Press, Ed. 2, 1927), 491.

social structure that impeded the fulfillment of talented women in her times. A pioneer in many ways, Jane Harrison was one of the first generation of British women to attend a university, Newnham College at Cambridge, and she opted for a career in Classics when knowledge of Greek was a symbol of gender and class privilege.[20] Later, she lived alone in London and supported herself as a public lecturer. She did not receive an academic post (Research Fellow at Newnham) until she was forty-eight years old, and her major books were written when she was in her fifties and sixties. Like many Victorian intellectuals, Jane Harrison rejected Christianity as an Evangelical nightmare of gloom and injustice—it was also the fanatical creed of her hated stepmother, and the patriarchal Olympians paid heavily for the sins of her parents in her eyes. Patterns of personal agony and gender issues are clearly discernible in her books and resonate in her celebrations of chthonic rituals, orgiastic enthusiasm, and the irrational in general. Happily, her sense of intense emotion underlying much Greek religion was closer to historical realities than were the intellectual constructs of conventional scholars, to whom orgiastic abandon was both improper and alien.

Controversial people never lack attention, and both critics and friends have provided versions of Jane Harrison, provocative in public, moody in private, stimulating and exasperating, academic crank and near-genius. "When she was speaking about Ritual," Cornford recalled, "she became for the space of an hour a hierophant herself. I have never witnessed anything quite like it."[21] How did she see herself? Revealingly, as a character in a novel by George Eliot, whom she admired as a writer and a woman. When she was a student at Newnham, Harrison fainted when the novelist visited her room and praised her William Morris wallpaper—"It was in the days when her cult was at its height—thank heaven, I never left her shrine!"[22] In her final years, Harrison recounted this incident in a sprightly memoir that is no more selective and evasive than most autobiographies.[23] Perhaps, recalling the episode with George Eliot prompted Harrison to declare:

> Until I met Aunt Glegg in the *Mill on the Floss*, I never knew myself. I
> *am* Aunt Glegg; with all reverence I say it. I wear before the world a
> mask of bland cosmopolitan courtesy and culture; I am advanced in my
> views, eager to be in touch with all modern movements, but beneath all

[20] Harrison, *Alpha and Omega*, 117. R. Fowler, "'On Not Knowing Greek': The Classics and the Woman of Letters," *Classical Journal* 78 (1983–4) 337–349.

[21] Stewart, 174.

[22] Harrison, *Reminiscences*, 45.

[23] Harry C. Payne, "Modernizing the Ancients: The Reconstruction of Ritual Drama 1870–1920," *Proceedings of the American Philosophical Society*, 112.3 (1978), 189 n. 45, says of *Reminiscences*: "Like many post-Stracheyan accounts of nineteenth-century lives, it is almost a set-piece, providing stock characters in a Victorian melodrama." While Harrison is not always candid in her memoir, her life was not unlike a Victorian novel, as Jessie Stewart's book had shown.

that lies Aunt Glegg, rigidly, irrationally conservative, fibrous with prejudice, deep-rooted in her native soil.[24]

Her close friend, Gilbert Murray, admitted that "there is a fragment of truth" in her identification with Aunt Glegg, but he rejected the notion itself:

> No, it is not true. It was not Aunt Glegg nor anything like Aunt Glegg that lay beneath; but there was something rather traditional, a habit of manners rather better than our manners, a standard somewhat stricter than our standards, a grace and dignity that most of us have somehow lost, and also...unbounded generosity toward her fellow-workers.[25]

In his old age, Murray was recalling a lost friend with fondness, but not necessarily with accuracy. It is not wise to disregard Flaubert when he said, "Madame Bovary, c'est moi!"[26] and we should not take Jane Harrison lightly when she says that she *is* Aunt Glegg.

Like Proust,[27] Jane Harrison admired *The Mill on the Floss*, and she was drawn to both its portrayals of strong women and its depiction of life in the premodern countryside. Among the denizens of St. Ogg, George Eliot tells us, "one sees little trace of religion, still less of a distinctively Christian creed. Their belief in the unseen...seems to be rather of a pagan kind; their moral notions...hereditary customs" (362).[28] The child Maggie "kept a Fetish which she punished for all her misfortunes," a large wooden doll with nails driven in its head (78–79). Her Aunt Glegg carried a mutton bone in the pocket of her dress to guard against cramp (185). "Big checks and live things, like stags and foxes, all her table-linen is" (574). Jane Harrison approved of fetishes and amulets and scorned Christian creeds; she adored animals, especially bears, and bestowed totemic names on her closest friends.[29] Eliot's description of Jane Glegg also fits Jane Harrison: "For a woman of fifty, she had a very comely face and figure" (108). Mrs. Glegg, however, was more renowned for prudence and thrift. Both women were outspoken and did not suffer fools gladly (125, 185–186). For Jane Glegg, kinship ties had priority, and she offered support and shelter for Maggie

---

[24] Harrison, *Reminiscences*, 11–12.

[25] Gilbert Murray, "A Great Scholar," *The Listener* 45 (March 8, 1951), 374.

[26] Francis Steegmuller, *Flaubert and Madame Bovary* (Boston: Houghton Mifflin, 1970), 339, 342.

[27] Mario Praz, *The Hero in Eclipse in Victorian Fiction* (New York: Oxford University Press, 1956), 376–383. Two pages of *The Mill on the Floss* could reduce Proust to tears; he was also intrigued by Eliot's technique of recollection.

[28] All quotations from George Eliot, *The Mill on the Floss* (1860), are from the Penguin edition, 1979, edited by A. S. Byatt.

[29] Stewart, 34–35. Peacock, 84, 109–114, 164. "The shedding of plant and animal form marks the complete close of anything like totemistic thinking and feeling. It is in many ways pure loss....There are few things uglier than a lack of reverence for animals."—*Themis*, 449–450. For Virginia Woolf's private animal language, see Jean O. Love, *Virginia Woolf, Sources of Madness and Art* (Berkeley and Los Angeles: University of California Press, 1977), 243–245, 294.

Tulliver in her distress (197, 631). There is a matriarchal aura about Aunt Glegg who describes herself as "head o' the family on his mother's side! and laid by guineas" (422). She expects Maggie to feel "respect and duty to her aunts and the rest of her kin," (575) and she bids Maggie's brother Tom to "bear in mind that it is his mother's family as he owes it to" (577). Of that family headed by Jane Glegg, Eliot comments, "no individual Dodson was satisfied with any other individual Dodson,...but with the Dodsons collectively" (97). The imperious figure of Aunt Glegg evokes themes that were precious to Jane Harrison in her mature years—folk magic, pagan survivals, kinship ties, and group solidarity under strong female leadership. Happily, both ladies were named Jane, and both were provincials to the core.

"I am intensely proud of being a Yorkshire woman,"[30] proclaimed Jane Harrison, whose *Reminiscences of a Student's Life* (1925) begins with a fanfare on the merits of Yorkshire folk. Elsewhere, she boasts of "the true Yorkshire spirit" and describes herself as "a Yorkshire tyke," who was outraged by the Scarborough raid in 1914.[31] Ms. Harrison also shared a Yorkshire familiarity with the unseen world. "I am by nature," she admits, "rotten with superstition and mysticism."[32] In *Alpha and Omega*, she declares: "The unseen is always haunting me, surging up behind the visible."[33] Francis Cornford recalls "coming in one summer afternoon at Southwold, when she had been lying exhausted in a long chair, looking out at the sea. She told me she had become totally blind for perhaps an hour, and she was wrought up by a visionary experience, which she described in terms I cannot recall. There were other neurotic symptoms, such as a terror of journeys."[34] In April 1915, she wrote to Gilbert Murray: "I was kept from Paris by a very *daimonion* experience, I should like to think that it was my Guardian Angel, but it...is too long to write." Her friend and biographer, Jessie Stewart, adds: "Jane sometimes had these experiences; she told F. M. Cornford that once in Greece, when about to get into a railway carriage, she looked in and saw her own figure sitting in the far corner. She drew back and did not travel. The train had a smash."[35] In literature, the specter of a double is an effective device; Hoffman, Dostoevsky, and Henry James employed it successfully. Apparently, poets are apt to see their own doubles—Goethe saw himself only "in his mind's eye" in 1771,[36] but Shelley saw himself literally walking on a terrace and

---

[30] Harrison, *Reminiscences*, 11.

[31] Stewart, 157–159.

[32] *Ibid.*, 38.

[33] Harrison, *Alpha and Omega*, 206.

[34] Cornford, *Newnham Letter*, 76. Harrison's state of euphoria after "electric treatment" in 1912 was not mystical but produced by the catharsis of "black despair" and "hate against Frances"—Stewart 113.

[35] Stewart, 160.

[36] K. R. Eissler, *Goethe, A Psychoanalytic Study* (Detroit: Wayne State University Press, 1963), II: 1219–1220, is skeptical even of the account in *Dichtung und Wahrheit*.

also strangling his wife,[37] and Robert Frost based a celebrated poem, "The Road Not Taken," on an encounter with "himself" in 1912.[38] However, Jane Harrison's glimpse of herself in a Greek railway carriage was not a hallucination such as Shelley's, or a pure fancy such as Goethe's; rather, like Frost, she saw someone who resembled herself, but she reacted like a Yorkshire peasant and fled. Among the country folk in Yorkshire, the folklorists assure us, "it is unlucky in the highest degree to meet one's own double; in fact, it is commonly regarded as a sign of early death. There's but one path of safety; you must address it boldly."[39] In Whitby, sometime in the nineteenth century, we are told, a man encountered his double (*waff*) in a store and chased it away, but Jane Harrison balked at the death omen. That she took a person who may have looked like her for a *waff* suggests a preoccupation with death at the time. In any case, she reacted like Jane Glegg, saw the presumed *waff* as a warning, and thus evaded a train wreck.

Both Janes were proud, confident women who faced down opponents with unshakable stubbornness. They also stuck loyally by those close to them, as provincial folk are wont to do. Jessie Stewart describes an encounter between Jane Harrison and the redoubtable Hilaire Belloc late in 1902. Belloc was ranting that Trinity College, Cambridge, had offered a fellowship without examination: "Jane demurred and said that A. W. Verrall was examining, she was sure he would not admit of such proceedings. H. B. let fly, Jane bit her lip until it bled and made an excuse to go out and fetch her handkerchief. H. B., when asked why he had stuck to his point, said, 'When she said "there wasn't one jot or one tittle of truth in it," he could see the woman was a Jewess and resolved not to spare her.'"[40] As usual, the back end of the Chesterbelloc was wrong—he had been addressing "Aunt Glegg," and Yorkshire women do not submit to bullying. Similarly, Jane Harrison saw herself as Aunt Glegg when attacked by academic foes as fierce as William Ridgeway and as catty as Lewis Farnell. Secure within the charmed circle of the Cambridge Ritualists, she defied her critics and stood her ground, defending with equal aplomb real insights and dubious fancies. Her opponents dismissed her theories as wild and subversive, her scholarship as slipshod and vague, and her manner as most unladylike. When she defended Bertrand Russell's opposition to the First World War, Ridgeway roared that she was a pacifist traitor and Newnham a "notorious

[37] Richard Holmes, *Shelley, the Pursuit* (New York: E. P. Dutton, 1975), 727. Newman Ivey White, *Shelley* (New York: Knopf, 1947), II: 368.

[38] Lawrence Thompson, *Selected Letters of Robert Frost* (New York: Holt, Rinehart, & Winston, 1964), 45–46. Elizabeth S. Sergeant, *Robert Frost, The Trial by Existence* (New York: Holt, Rinehart, & Winston, 1960), 87–89.

[39] Arthur H. Norway, *Highways and Byways of Yorkshire* (London: Macmillan, 1899), 139. William Henderson, *Notes on the Folklore of the Northern Counties of England* (London: Longmans, Green, 1866), 30–31, 46. Richard Blakeborough, *Wit, Character, Folklore, & Customs of the Northern Riding of Yorkshire* (London: Wakefield, 1898), 122.

[40] Stewart, 52.

centre of pro-German agitation."[41]   Aunt Glegg was not swayed by the raging of the dons.

Despite its appeal for the idealistic and the indolent, academic life has considerable drawbacks—fierce struggles for insignificant aims, insular attitudes and myopic perspectives, a craze for fads combined with a horror of heresy and an awe of authority. Some of these characteristics reflect the habits of the clergy (which once most academics were), others are inherent in institutions and professions, and all are exacerbated by personality and neurosis. When the renowned anthropologist, Ruth Benedict, died, her bitter rival, Ralph Linton, boasted "that he had killed her, and produced,...in a small pouch, the Tanala material he said he had used to kill Ruth Benedict."[42] Jane Harrison's enemies entertained similar thoughts but lacked such potent magic. When Arnold Toynbee was a student at Oxford, his tutor warned him "not to read Professor Gilbert Murray's books and not to go to his lectures, because he is a very dangerous man."[43] When Murray retired as Regius Professor of Greek in 1936, he picked as his successor another "dangerous man," Eric Dodds, although other academics had their eyes on the position. So rudely did Maurice Bowra, Denys Page, and other worthies treat their unwelcome colleague that Dodds dreamed that he had cerebro-spinal meningitis and awoke after a twenty-five year coma to find himself an old man in 1961. "The span of my twenty-five-years' 'illness,'" he explains, "is the span of my tenure of the Oxford Chair from 1936 to my retirement....The year 1961 was to be the first in which, too late, I was to be 'disinfected' of Oxford."[44] Earlier, Jane Harrison had braved the wrath of Ridgeway, Farnell, and lesser lights with the intransigence of Aunt Glegg and the support of her paladins, Murray and Cornford, and her friend, A. B. Cook. In 1916, she argued in *The Classical Review* that Salome with the head of John the Baptist was performing "the ritual dance of Agave with the head of Pentheus"; her "proofs" included a Russian puppet play, and the article provoked the Provost of King's College, M. R. James, to a savage critique. Although Murray came to her defense in print, Ridgeway gloated over her discomfort: "Never was such an audacious, shameless avowal of charlatanism, debauching young minds wholesale, and that too in a generation whose loose thinking has been doing immense harm to national life and international politics." Unswayed by the polemics, Ms. Harrison

[41] *Ibid.*, 151.

[42] Sidney W. Mintz, "Ruth Benedict," in *Totems and Teachers, Perspectives on the History of Anthropology*, ed. Sydel Silverman (New York: Columbia University Press, 1981), 161. See also Adelin Linton and Charles Wagley, *Ralph Linton* (New York: Columbia University Press, 1971), 48–49. Linton was an authority on the Tanala magicians of Madagascar.

[43] Arnold J. Toynbee and G. R. Urban, *Toynbee on Toynbee* (New York: Oxford University Press, 1974), 32. The warning was not heeded; young Toynbee rushed to read the books and attend the lectures of "a very dangerous man," and in time he married the ogre's daughter.

[44] Eric R. Dodds, *Missing Persons* (Oxford: Clarendon Press, 1977), 128.

acknowledged a few errors but stuck by her thesis: "I abide by it unmoved."[45] Aunt Glegg could do no other.

In the first Jane Harrison Memorial Lecture in 1928, Gilbert Murray claimed that *Prolegomena to the Study of Greek Religion* (1903) "transformed the whole approach to the study of Greek Religion" with its emphasis on chthonic cults and visual evidence for what the Greeks actually did in religious matters; but he concedes that, with regard to Dionysus and Orpheus, "the skeptic will say that she was, for psychological reasons, determined to bring out a certain result."[46] A sampling of reviews in 1904 ranges from polite chiding to sarcastic dismissal of "a too facile fancy, which is attracted by explanations more specious than true."[47] The response at Newnham was more positive; Jessie Stewart recalls that "the College jubilated" over the publication, which "met with instant success and quickly took its place as a standard text-book," at least at Newnham. She adds that, "Jane writes: 'I blush for the Examiners. Five questions are out of [*Prolegomena*]'...In the Classical Tripos Part II, the paper on Mythology and Religion included questions on the Cult of Dionysus, the *Anodos* of Gaia, Orphic hymns, and Attic festivals."[48] Mrs. Stewart does not tell us what were the "correct" answers on topics that in fact were not the exclusive property of Ms. Harrison. Sadly, Gilbert Murray reports that "*Themis* had a less favorable reception than the *Prolegomena*...It was too full of new ideas," and the argument was not always clear. "There was also, in conservative or orthodox circles, rather more dislike of *Themis* as a 'dangerous book.'"[49] In classical circles, *Themis* (1912) was roundly rejected as "a stimulating companion but a dangerous guide";[50] "magnificent—but how much of it is science?";[51] "full of bold conjectures and perilous inferences";[52] "extraordinary dogmatism...and perverse archaeology; her matriarchal prejudice...is past praying for or reasoning with";[53] "the primitives are upon us."[54] In the *Oxford Magazine*, an

---

[45] Jane E. Harrison, "The Head of John the Baptist," *Classical Review* 30 (1916) 216–219. M. R. James, "Some Remarks on 'The Head of John the Baptist,'" *Classical Review* 31 (1917) 2–4; letters by Harrison (63) and Gilbert Murray (63–64). Ridgeway's comment: Stewart, 88.

[46] Gilbert Murray, "Jane Ellen Harrison Memorial Lecture," 1928, in Jane Harrison, *Epilegomena to the Study of Greek Religion and Themis* (New Hyde Park: University Books, 1968), 567–568.

[47] W.H.D. Rouse, *Classical Review* 18 (1904) 465–470. Unsigned review, *Journal of Hellenic Studies* 24 (1904) 174. Unsigned review, *Cambridge Review* (March 10, 1904) 245. Lewis Farnell, *Hibbert Journal* 2.8 (1903–04) 821–827.

[48] Stewart, 54. Mrs. Stewart is always protective of Ms. Harrison and very much a Newnham booster.

[49] Murray, *Harrison Memorial Lecture*, 569–570.

[50] Joseph W. Hewitt, *Classical Weekly* 7 (1913–1914) 86–88.

[51] W.M.L. Hutchinson, *Classical Review* 27 (1913) 132–134.

[52] Unsigned review, *Journal of Hellenic Studies* 32 (1912) 397–398.

[53] Lewis Farnell, *Hibbert Journal* 11 (1912) 453–458.

[54] Clifford Moore, *Classical Philology* 7 (1912) 359–363.

ungallant reviewer (probably Lewis Farnell) quipped: "Miss Harrison's work has always a freshness that is at first attractive, but the freshness is often found to be that of the dew on cobwebs."[55] Some Gallophobic reviewers noted her enthusiasm for French emotionalism (Bergson) and French social science (Durkheim), although *Themis* received only a cool review by Maxime David in *L'Année Sociologique*.[56] While some of the resistance of traditional classicists to Harrison's heresies was due to mental inertia or prudence in the face of unrestrained imagination, the shrillness of the response to a "dangerous book" arose from the gender of its author. A woman who disdained Olympian "restraint" and patriarchy, sang the praises of Dionysian abandon and matriarchy, and celebrated the orgies of Bacchic women roused a variety of disquieting emotions in male scholars. Farnell identified Jane Harrison with the insurgent New Women who were trying to seize both the ballot and the university. Paul Shorey saw her, not as a rebel, but as a temptress drawing men into sexual excess and madness. In an oft-quoted tirade, he denounced "the corybantic Hellenism of Miss Harrison" as part of "the irrational, semi-sentimental, Polynesian, free-verse, and sex-freedom Hellenism of all the gushful geysers of 'rapturous rubbish' about the Greek spirit."[57] It did not matter that Ms. Harrison was not a promiscuous maenad, much less a devotee of *vers libre*; in Shorey's mind, she is connected with female abandon and unrestrained sexuality in Edenic climes. The frenzied corybant, the lustful maenad, the Bacchic dancer were women out of control and unabashed in their emotionalism, the terrifying and irresistible "idols of perversity" who haunted the minds of late Victorian and Edwardian males.[58] In various stages of undress, their bodies were displayed in the lurid art of the era; Gilbert Murray's versions of Euripides' *Bacchae* and *Hippolytus* (1902) offered Greekless readers horrific examples of feminine excess; and academic critics of Jane Harrison had long pondered Euripidean women in their conscious and unconscious minds. The critics dismissed Crazy Jane and sniped at Gilbert Murray, who at least was "sound" on the Olympians.[59] Soon, changing fads in academe allowed the

[55] Peacock, 212.

[56] Maxime David, *L'Année Sociologique* (ser. 1) 12 (1909–1912) 254–260.

[57] Paul Shorey, review of Murray's *Classical Tradition in Poetry*, *Saturday Review of Literature* 4 (1928) 608. Whether Shorey knew it or not, Miss Harrison had encouraged the young Isadora Duncan—Peacock 261, n. 58.   Paul Delany, *The Neo-Pagans: Rupert Brooke and the Ordeal of Youth* (New York: Free Press, 1987), 93, claims that Jane Harrison encouraged "bathing naked by moonlight." While Brooke invoked her authority, his circle did not need it, for Brooke, Frances Darwin, and their friends bathed naked in sunlight.

[58] Bram Dijkstra, *Idols of Perversity: Fantasies of Feminine Evil in Fin-de-Siècle Culture* (New York: Oxford University Press, 1986), explores both art and literature.

[59] The late Duncan Wilson, *Gilbert Murray O. M.* (Oxford: Clarendon Press, 1987), 119, describes Jane Harrison as "a student of Nietzsche and a precursor of D. H. Lawrence,...something of a Bohemian." He deplores her "pernicious influence" (155) on Murray, and his allusion to the "wilder shores of conjecture" (156) surely invokes Lesley

defenders of scholarly propriety to replace the veils that Jane Harrison had rent so dramatically.

A half-century after her days of renown and controversy, Jane Harrison had faded into a figure of legend. The Biblical scholar, S. H. Hooke, of Myth and Ritual fame, cited "a story which Jane Harrison tells of her experience at an Easter Sunday celebration in Greece. She said to an old peasant woman..., 'You seem very happy.' 'Of course I am,' replied the old woman. 'If Christ were not risen, we should have no harvest this year.'"[60] Of course, Jane Harrison said no such thing; in *Themis*, she quoted the story quite accurately from John Lawson's *Modern Greek Folklore and Ancient Greek Religion*.[61] As Francis Cornford said of legends, "the facts work loose."[62] In a study of Cornford's son who died in the Spanish Civil War, Peter Stansky and William Abrahams refer to "a revolution in classical studies inspired largely by the work of...Jane Harrison."[63] While she did trumpet the irrational and emphasize chthonic elements in Hellas, Ms. Harrison was not alone in using anthropology and comparative religion in her work; many of her fiercest critics used a similar methodology, though for different aims. Be this as it may, Jane Harrison is still cited and still chided. The former Regius Professor of Greek at Oxford, Hugh Lloyd-Jones, notes her enthusiasm and stimulating effect on Gilbert Murray, but finds her wanting: "She did not know Greek well, her judgment was erratic; and like other pioneers, she made many errors."[64] W.K.C. Guthrie marks her reaction to a "narrow evangelical upbringing" and doubts that she was really disgusted by the "beastly devices of the heathen."[65] In his obituary of Gilbert Murray, J.A.K. Thomson considered Jane Harrison a bad influence who "had not a classical elegance and restraint...She was not always logical in argument, [and]...she overflowed with suggestions highly stimulating but of the kind that drive 'conservative' readers to distraction."[66] G. S. Kirk observes that "Miss Harrison had an almost physical passion for the past. Her books are lively, learned, yet unpedantic—and utterly uncontrolled by

Blanch's *Wilder Shores of Love*. In 1931, Murray guided a party of wealthy Americans to Delphi; one of them was Walter Lippman, who complained to Learned Hand of Murray's prudishness and whitewashing of the Greeks—Ronald Steele, *Walter Lippmann and the American Century* (Boston: Little Brown, 1980), 278–279.

[60] S. H. Hooke, *The Siege Perilous* (London: S. C. M. Press, 1956), 40.

[61] Harrison, *Themis*, 202 n. 2, cites John C. Lawson, *Modern Greek Folklore and Ancient Greek Religion* (Cambridge: Cambridge University Press, 1910), 573. Lawson adds: "I regret that my notes contain no mention of my informant's name."

[62] Francis M. Cornford, *Thucydides Mythistoricus* (London: Arnold, 1907), 131.

[63] Peter Stansky and William Abrahams, *Journey to the Frontier* (Boston: Little Brown, 1966), 140.

[64] Hugh Lloyd-Jones, *Blood for the Ghosts* (Baltimore: Johns Hopkins University Press, 1983), 202–203. Like Harrison, Lloyd-Jones "made many errors" in his sketch of Murray's life—William M. Calder III, *Gnomon* 57 (1985) 314, n. 3.

[65] W.K.C. Guthrie, *The Greeks and Their Gods* (Boston: Beacon Press, 1954), xi, 20.

[66] J.A.K. Thomson, "Gilbert Murray," *Proceedings of the British Academy* 43 (1957) 264–265.

anything resembling careful logic." Yet, he admits of the Cambridge Ritualists, "even now there is a widespread feeling that these people, although they used a new method to excess, were in most important respects correct."[67] Professor Kirk, of course, does not share this feeling. In the Jane Harrison Memorial Lecture for 1972, the late Moses Finley opined: "When Jane Harrison was wrong,...that was because she mishandled the Greek evidence, not because she had spent long hours reading of the tedious doings of savages." He deplored the "bad reasoning and strong emotion" that fueled hostility against "the legendary Cambridge School" and led to an "almost total cessation in the dialogue between anthropology and the classics."[68]

Like the arid Sahara, the Academy is a region of constantly shifting sands, blown by the winds of chance, while the bedrock beneath slowly reacts to geological forces. The shifting dunes can bury the tallest steeples or uncover unsuspected terrains—often the winds reveal forgotten idols or show them in another perspective as vistas change. So, too, the image of Jane Harrison has altered in recent years as the Academy has changed its interests and composition. Like her old protagonist Ridgeway, Ms. Harrison "has gone where the noise of battle is for ever hushed,"[69] but the woman and her work have taken on new stature. With greater sophistication and wider learning than Jane Harrison could muster, Walter Burkert has illuminated the Greek past with a deeper understanding of human behavior and the role of ritual, and he gives due credit to Jane Harrison with Murray and Cornford "in her wake."[70] Both ritual and its champions seem respectable again. In *The Greek Heritage in Victorian Britain*, Frank Turner places Jane Harrison in the company of those British scholars whose interest in things Hellenic was more than purely academic. His account of her contribution to classical studies is informed and impartial, and he appreciates her use of vases and other visual data. Turner realizes that "she yearned for a fuller appreciation of the unity of life and of the connectedness of things than either traditional rationalism or traditional Hellenistic humanism could afford. In that respect, she struck a responsive chord with the major

[67] G. S. Kirk, *Myth, Its Meanings and Functions in Ancient and Other Cultures* (Berkeley and Los Angeles: University of California Press, 1970), 3, 4–5.

[68] Moses I. Finley, *The Use and Abuse of History* (New York: Viking Press, 1975), 104. This thoughtful essay, "Anthropology and the Classics," (102–119) should be read in conjunction with Clifford Geertz, *Works and Lives: The Anthropologist as Author* (Stanford: Stanford University Press, 1988).

[69] Harrison, *Themis*, viii.

[70] Walter Burkert, *Greek Religion* (Cambridge: Harvard University Press, 1985), 2–3; *Structure and History in Greek Mythology and Ritual* (Berkeley and Los Angeles: University of California Press, 1979), 35–36, 158. On p. 160, n. 30 of the latter, Burkert dryly remarks of Evans-Pritchard's sneer at "if I were a horse" arguments: "Still the method has undeniable heuristic value."

impulses of early twentieth-century intellectual life."[71] In *Jane Ellen Harrison: The Mask and the Self*, Sandra Peacock draws a psychological portrait of an aspiring Victorian professional woman, whose personal emotional crises are reflected in her academic works.[72] This view of Ms. Harrison reflects the impact of women's history and feminist concerns on academic subjects. In a 1984 article in the *American Historical Review* on "The Contribution of Women to Modern Historiography," Bonnie Smith singled out Jane Harrison as a "woman worthy" but identified her primarily as a "polymath" and a matriarchist, rather than as a classical scholar of religion: "A separate feminine culture, in particular, is the thesis of Harrison's *Themis*."[73] Ms. Smith's version of her is a matter of selective emphasis that might have provoked a retort from Ms. Harrison. Popular books about "the Goddess" and attempts to "revive" female cults in the modern world sometimes invoke the name of Jane Harrison as a venerable (if unread) Wise Woman. Given her feel for the authentic and love of antiquity, she would not feel honored by such attention. Jane Harrison was not a dabbler in patchwork religion, but a lover of Wordsworth and Keats and a celebrant of Bergson's *durée*. Like Faust, she went to the Mothers in search of some universal truth, something "real." Murray recalls that "she was so eager to penetrate beneath the surface that she almost grew to dislike the surface itself and to love what lay below—and the deeper below the better."[74] Her quarrel with patriarchy was both a personal and a gender issue; her dream of ancient matriarchy was both a search for her lost mother and a Utopian hope for a life untroubled by male oppression. The world of *Themis* was also a very private fantasy that projected into Greek prehistory relationships that had come unstrung in her own life.

Since she was often pilloried for subjectivity, Jane Harrison would welcome current critiques of the illusion of objectivity, but she would lose patience with most ventures into theory because she had a sense of humor and no tolerance for jargon. With its gnostic aridity and text-fixation, Deconstructionism would repel her, for Jane Harrison believed that reality

[71] Frank M. Turner, *The Greek Heritage in Victorian Britain* (New Haven and London: Yale University Press, 1981), 28, 53–54, 120–128, 153.

[72] The pioneer work on Jane Harrison's life was Jessie Stewart's charming "portrait in letters" to Murray, augmented by valuable personal memories of Ms. Harrison and the Cambridge scene. Two significant additions were made by Robert Ackerman, "Some Letters of the Cambridge Ritualists," *Greek, Roman, and Byzantine Studies* 12 (1971) 113–136, and "Jane Ellen Harrison: The Early Work," *Greek, Roman, and Byzantine Studies* 13 (1972) 209–230. Peacock's book is the first full-length portrait of the person, whom even Lewis Farnell called "the leading woman scholar of the time." See also Renate Schlesier, "Jane Ellen Harrison," in *Classical Scholarship: A Biographical Encyclopedia*, eds. Ward W. Briggs and William M. Calder III (New York/London, 1990), 127–41.

[73] Bonnie G. Smith, "The Contribution of Women to Modern Historiography in Great Britain, France, and the United States, 1750–1940," *American Historical Review* 89 (1984) 722–723.

[74] Murray, "Cornford," *PBA* 29 (1943) 424–425.

was a matter of feeling and tactile verification, not word-play or academic arts. Francis Cornford saw Ms. Harrison as one who had strayed in time:

> To live ahead of one's generation must needs be to live dangerously....A spirit that belonged of right to the twentieth century had strayed back to the middle of the nineteenth. This meant that she had to live down the really uncongenial influence of the late Victorian rationalists (the Old Rats, as she came to call them) and of the disillusioned littérateurs of the nineties.[75]

At the age of fifty, this woman ahead of her time began to battle with the Old Rats. Deep within her was a lonely Yorkshire girl, who would not survive if she showed that vulnerable side to her critics. She would have been swept into the flood like Maggie Tulliver. Instead, Jane Harrison stiffened her back and faced the Old Rats as Aunt Glegg. The strategy worked until the Maggie Tulliver in her fell in love with Francis Cornford.

State University of New York at Binghamton

[75]Cornford, *Newnham Letter*, 76.

3

Jane Harrison's Failed Candidacies for the Yates Professorship (1888, 1896): What Did Her Colleagues Think of Her?

WILLIAM M. CALDER III

I. Introduction

There are two sorts of evidence for what Jane Harrison's professional colleagues thought of her during her lifetime: published and unpublished. Of the published, most obvious are reviews of her books. She tells us in her letter of application for the Yates Chair what she had done by April 12th 1896[1]:

> In 1882 I published "The Myths of the Odyssey in Art and Literature"; in 1885, "Introductory Studies in Greek Art." I have from time to time published in the "Journal of Hellenic Studies," original monographs on special subjects connected with Mythology and Ceramography, *e.g.* an article on "Monuments relating to the Odyssey": on "The Judgment of Paris," &c. The work of drawing up the Report for the year 1887, on "The Progress of Archaeology in Greece," was entrusted to my care. In 1890 I published in conjunction with Mrs Verrall, "Mythology and Monuments of Ancient Athens," and in 1895[2] in conjunction with Mr. D. S. MacColl, "Greek Vase Painting."

Of the four books mentioned the bibliographer of the Cambridge Ritualists, Shelley Arlen, lists for *Myths of the Odyssey* only an anonymous notice;[3] for *Introductory Studies* six reviews, not one in a scholarly journal, four of

---

[1] I cite here and throughout the unpublished documents concerned with Jane Harrison's candidacy for the Yates Chair in 1888 and 1896 preserved in the Archive of the Library of University College, London (AM/C/216; AM/D/52). I am grateful to the archivist, G. M. Furlong, for copies and the permission (*per litt.* June 29 1990) to cite them here.

[2] In fact the book was published in 1894 and hence reviewed in that year.

[3] *Notes and Queries* (5 November 1881) 379. I wish to express my gratitude here to Shelley Arlen of the University of Oklahoma Libraries for generously allowing me to use an early MS of her book *The Cambridge Ritualists: An Annotated Bibliography* (Metuchen/London 1990).

the English first edition and two American notices of the 1892 reprint;[4] for *Mythology and Monuments* 11 reviews, four in scholarly journals, one on the continent, and a review article by a leading English authority;[5] of *Vase Painting* only three anonymous notices in the semi-popular press and a signed review in *Art Journal*.[6] That is, she was never reviewed in Germany, the center of study in her subject. Her name was barely known in France. She had a reputation in America which, if anything, would have been used against her. Her reputation was in fact insular. Later there would be criticisms of her work in *Forschungsberichte*[7] and published replies to her writings[8] or citations of it by scholars working in her field. Only after her

---

[4] Anonymous, *Athenaeum* (19 December 1885) 812–13; *New York Times* (18 January 1886) 116; *Notes and Queries* (21 November 1885) 420; *Saturday Review* (27 February 1886) 311; A. S. Murray, *Academy* (13 February 1886) 116; (of the 1892 edition): Anonymous, *Nation* (31 March 1892) 248 and Martin L. D'Ooge, *Dial* 12 (1892) 392.

[5] Apart from notices in *Athenaeum, Atlantic Monthly, Critic, Nation, Speaker*, and *Spectator*, I notice Anonymous, *American Journal of Archaeology* 7 (1892) 72–73; G. C. R<ichards>, *Journal of Hellenic Studies* 11 (1890) 218–20; F. B. Tarbell, *Classical Review* 4 (1890) 430–32; and a reviewer in *Revue des Études Grecques* 4 (1891) 410–11. The book was not reviewed in Germany. The most important published document concerning Harrison's work available to the Yates Committee in 1896 was Anonymous, *Quarterly Review* 171 (1890) 122–49. Arlen (33) identifies the reviewer as Percy Gardner, then Lincoln and Merton Professor of Archaeology at Oxford, earlier (1880–1887) Disney Professor of Archaeology at Cambridge. Gardner was elder brother of Harrison's victorious adversary, Ernest Arthur Gardner (1862–1939), and did not encourage the higher education of women. See Percy Gardner, *Autobiographica* (Blackwell, Oxford 1933) 67–68: "...the Great War, which has shaken so many things, has led to the wider activity of women, and to their admission to the Parliamentary franchise. After that, Oxford and Cambridge were compelled to admit them on almost equal terms. But since, there has come a certain reaction. To the advocates of the admission of women, the question seemed extremely simple. There was only an unreasonable prejudice to set aside, and the question would solve itself. But simple as is such a view it is not in accord with many important facts of human nature, which all have their roots in the supremely important truth that the function of women is childbearing, and so in the whole future of humanity is not the same as that of men. In any stable condition of society this truth, with all its never-ending corollaries, must be fully recognized. So matters did not go quite as they were expected by the women's advocates to go. The phenomenon, well known in America, that the mass of the women took up less educational—though in their own way good—subjects, such as modern languages and modern history, has shewn the danger of letting women control the Oxford curriculum. Both Oxford and Cambridge have taken measures to limit the number of women admitted, and to secure male predominance." He certainly took Harrison's work seriously: see e.g., Percy Gardner, "A New Pandora Vase," *JHS* 21 (1901) 1–9.

[6] See Anonymous, *Athenaeum* (20 October 1894) 533–35; *Nation* (24 May 1894) 394–95; *Spectator* (7 April 1894) 468–70 and R.A.M. Stevenson, *Art Journal* NS 57 (1894) 208–09.

[7] Especially important because from so erudite a source is O. Gruppe, *Bursian* 137 (Leipzig 1908) 276ff. (*Prolegomena*), *s.n.* 648; (1921) *s.n.* 443 and his dismissal of her, Durkheim and F. M. Cornford at *Geschichte der klassischen Mythologie und Religionsgeschichte während des Mittelalters im Abendland und während der Neuzeit* (Leipzig 1921) 243.

[8] Often extraordinarily damaging: see, e.g., M. R. James (1862–1936), "Some Remarks on 'The Head of John Baptist,'" *Classical Review* 31 (1917) 1–4, the lead article of the

death would there be remarks about her in the memoirs of contemporaries. But for one review article and the books and articles themselves, the Yates Committee owed its decision to a second sort of evidence.

Then there is that which was not published in her lifetime: letters to her[9] and from her, diaries, and, perhaps most valuable, letters about her. Classical scholars often make the mistake of thinking that all that is important must be published. This is true for Plato but not for figures of the nineteenth century, where normally official versions are published and truth languishes in archives.[10] In the case of Jane Harrison, 24 letters[11] of recommendation, most written in 1888 and seven in 1896, survive and provide the most important sources extant for her contemporary evaluation by peers or indeed superiors. Who wrote these letters and for what purpose?

II. The Yates Chair

The Yates Chair of Classical Archaeology was created at University College, London in 1880. It bore the name of its founder, James Yates (1789–1871), the antiquarian, contributor to Smith's *Dictionary of Greek and Roman Antiquities*, and author of numerous articles on archaeological subjects. Its first holder was Sir Charles Newton (1811–1894), concurrently (and since 1861) the first Keeper of Greek and Roman Antiquities at the British Museum. In 1888 he was "compelled by increasing infirmity to

---

volume. Letters of congratulation poured in to James, then Provost of Kings and earlier Headmaster of Eton: see Richard William Pfaff, *Montague Rhodes James* (London 1980) 254–56. W. Ridgeway, a member of the board of management of *Classical Review*, wrote him (Pfaff, 256): "Never was such an audacious, shameless avowal of charlatanism, debauching young minds wholesale, and that too in a generation whose loose thinking has been doing immense harm to national life and international politics." Harrison briefly replied at *CR* 31 (1917) 63 ("To me the keenest joys of science...are always perilous"). Murray loyally sought to make the best of a weak case: see *CR* 31 (1917) 63–64, where he raps James' fingers for his severity. See further *YWCS* 13 (1918/19) 191. This may have been one of the discouragements that caused Harrison to leave Cambridge and the field in 1922. Peacock never alludes to the *Auseinandersetzung*.

[9] Upon leaving Cambridge for reasons that are not clear Harrison burned a treasure of letters to her, including some 800 from Gilbert Murray: see Stewart, 12: "Unfortunately Jane made a holocaust of letters and papers when she left Cambridge in 1922."

[10] See my remarks at *Mnemosyne* 43 (1989) 256–62 (review of C. O. Brink, *English Classical Scholarship*: a book inadequate just because confined to published and censored sources).

[11] I do not include a hastily-written note, dated only Red House Hornton St. W. 5 May, to Petrie from W. Martin Conway (1856–1937), Baron Conway of Allington, Roscoe Professor of Art at University College, Liverpool (1885–1888) and a famous mountaineer: "I write to urge the claims of *Miss Harrison* to the Archaeological Chair of U.Coll. Of course you know what they amount to. I heard her lecture at Liverpool & her matter & manner were alike admirable. I am just off to explore the interior of Spitzbergen. Don't trouble to answer this." A guess would be that Harrison met him through MacColl. There are two letters by Verrall, who in 1896 updated his earlier letter of 1888.

give up the Yates professorship."[12] Percy Gardner, a friend and colleague at the British Museum, describes his tenure of the chair:

> Newton did not attempt to teach, but to lecture, and his careful but somewhat frigid style did not long attract the general public. Hence the lectures were soon delivered in the presence of only three or four auditors: but Newton never ceased to prepare them with care, and to illustrate them with drawings of great size and costliness. He thought of his own ideal rather than the class before him. Thus as a Professor he could scarcely be called successful.[13]

A scholar was needed: but, if the new discipline were to survive, he must be a teacher as well. Jane Harrison, resident in London since 1880, living on unearned income and occasional lectures, applied. For 100 years her application has been unnoticed. In her *Reminiscences* Harrison avoids the matter.[14] Jessie Stewart in her *Portrait* says not a word about her heroine's failures.[15] Much to her credit, Sandra J. Peacock first in 1988 noted the two candidacies, although allotting them less than one page in a chapter of 35 pages covering the London years (1880–1897), some fifteen of which concern her friendship with D. S. MacColl. Peacock attributes Harrison's failed candidacies to misogyny and the hostility of classical scholars toward innovative thinking. We shall see whether the archival evidence supports these charges. She writes:

[12] See Cecil Harcourt Smith, *DNB* II. 2450. The standard life is Percy Gardner, "Sir Charles Newton," *BiogJahr* 19 (1896) 132–42. He was the friend of Ruskin since student days: see E. T. Cook and Alexander Wedderburn, *The Works of John Ruskin* vol. 35 *Praeterita et Dilecta* (London 1908) 198, 384–85 (their disagreement on the statue of Mausolus).

[13] Gardner, *Newton*, 138–39.

[14] Jane Ellen Harrison, *Reminiscences of a Student's Life*[2] (London 1925). Readers of Peacock should be warned that she never cites the standard edition but a pirated reprint in a Texan journal, *Arion*: see Sandra J. Peacock, *Jane Ellen Harrison: The Mask and the Self* (New Haven/London 1988). Her book is reviewed by Mary Beard (Fellow of Newnham) at *TLS* (January 27–February 2 1989) 82; R. L. Fowler, *Classical Views*, forthcoming; Carolyn G. Heilbrun, *The Women's Review of Books* 6 No. 8 (May 1989) 8–10; Robert A. Segal, *Journal of American Folklore* 103 (1990) 370–72; C. A. Stray, *LCM* forthcoming and by me in *Gnomon* forthcoming. The book is henceforth cited "Peacock, *Harrison*." Although I must often criticize this book I wish to emphasize that I have learned from it and indeed found the subject for this paper in its pages. The best biography of Harrison in print is Renate Schlesier, "Jane Ellen Harrison, 9 September 1850–15 April 1928," in *Classical Scholarship: A Biographical Encyclopedia*, edited by Ward W. Briggs and William M. Calder III (New York/London 1990) 127–41 (henceforth cited: "Briggs–Calder"). Schlesier alludes only briefly to the Yates Professorship (130).

[15] Jessie Stewart, *Jane Ellen Harrison: A Portrait from Letters* (London 1959). The octogenarian Stewart, a former student of Harrison's and a friend of Hope Mirrlees, is as much a source as a biographer and her book remains indispensable. No critical review of the book ever appeared. There are notices: Anonymous, *TLS* (24 July 1959) 432; Jacquetta Hawkes, *New Statesman and Nation* (20 June 1959) 870–71; Edmund Leach,

...her [Harrison's] expertise could not conquer the fears of those who questioned the wisdom of granting the distinguished professorship to a woman. In addition, the hidebound world of classical scholarship had no room for innovative thinking. Classicists considered Jane's work far too unconventional to merit such a prestigious position.[16]

A word is necessary on procedure. A candidate wrote himself to scholars who, in his opinion, were competent to evaluate his work and sympathetic to his cause. The sponsors sent their letters to the candidate, not to University officials. Certainly this affected their matter and style. The candidate gathered the letters, introduced them with a letter of application and—in those pre-Xerox days—had them printed up for use by the University, distribution to the sponsors and (in Housman's case) to friends and relatives. We know most of the election of A. E. Housman in 1892.[17] He had a bit over 50 copies printed.[18] Who were Harrison's sponsors? Are we able to evaluate their competence?

III. The Twenty-Three Sponsors

The number of sponsors seems not to have been limited by statute. Housman had 17, Harrison had 23. Their names, in the elusive order in which she arranged them (neither alphabetical nor by seniority nor by prestige of position), follow:

1. S. H. Butcher, Litt.D., LL.D., Professor of Greek in the University of Edinburgh; formerly Fellow of Trinity College, Cambridge and University College, Oxford.[19]

Spectator (31 July 1959) 145; Harold Nicolson, *Observer* (21 June 1959) 18. It was never noticed outside England. Until Schlesier, I have never seen it cited by a German.

[16] Peacock, *Harrison* 90. She earlier writes (*loc. cit.*): "Her references included R. C. Jebb, Henry Sidgwick, Henry Jackson, A. W. Verrall, and Walter Leaf of Cambridge; Henry Butcher and Arthur Sidgwick of Oxford; F. H. Middleton, director of South Kensington Museum; and Sir Edward Maunde Thomson, librarian of the British Museum; and Continental archaeologists Wilhelm Dorpfeld, Ernst Curtius, Wilhelm Klein, Otto Bindorf and Cavalier Luigi Melina, among others." Correct as follows: (1) *Henry Butcher* is the Hellenist S. H. Butcher; (2) Butcher was not *of Oxford* but professor at Edinburgh; (3) for *Sir Edward Maunde Thomson* read *Sir Edward Maunde Thompson*; (4) Thompson was not *librarian of the British Museum.* He was *Principal Librarian, British Museum*; (5) For *Dorpfeld* read *Dörpfeld*; (6) for *Otto Bindorf* read *Otto Benndorf.* Correct p. 279. The name was apparently conflated with Dindorf; (7) for *Cavalier Luigi Melina* read *Cavaliere Luigi Milani.*

[17] See P. G. Naiditch, *A. E. Housman at University College, London: The Election of 1892* (Leiden 1988). This thoroughly admirable book is henceforth cited "Naiditch, *Housman*." Housman's election falls precisely between Harrison's two candidacies and sheds much light on procedure in her cases.

[18] Naiditch, *Housman*, 235: "The edition of the *Testimonials* therefore consisted of at least fifty-one copies and, since that is an improbable number, probably more." Housman sent twenty copies to UCL (*Ibid.*, 234). We may assume that Harrison did the same.

[19] For S. H. Butcher (1850–1910), see his brother-in-law, G. W. Prothero, *DNB* II. 2545. For a delightful glimpse of the Butchers at Paris in 1886, see E. M. Sellar,

2. R. C. Jebb, Regius Professor of Greek in the University of Cambridge.[20]
3. Professor W. M. Ramsay, D.C.L., University of Aberdeen.[21]
4. F. H. Middleton, D.C.L. Oxon.; Litt.D. Camb.; V.P.S.A.; Director of the South Kensington Museum.[22]
5. Dr. Wilhelm Dörpfeld, Prof., I. Sekretar des Kais. Deutschen Archäolog. Instituts in Athen.[23]

Recollections and Impressions (Edinburgh/London 1907) 325–26. He is remembered by scholars today for his *OCT* Demosthenes and his edition with translation of Aristotle, *Poetics*. Peacock, *Harrison*, 52, documents "a mysterious unhappy love affair" between Harrison and Butcher, which Mirrlees unsuccessfully sought to cover up. The wretched Butcher married the daughter of Archbishop Trench and deserted Harrison. I see little more than an undergraduate crush and should be surprised if this were the reason why Butcher is placed first among the 23.

[20] For R. C. Jebb (1841–1905), see Caroline Jebb, *Life and Letters of Sir Richard Claverhouse Jebb O.M., Litt.D.* (Cambridge 1907) with the review of Ulrich von Wilamowitz-Moellendorff, *LittZentralblatt* (1907) 1469–71 and Mary Reed Bobbitt, *With Dearest Love to All: The Life and Letters of Lady Jebb* (London 1960). Full references are at Naiditch, *Housman*, 172ff. esp. n. 60–1, to whom add Roger D. Dawe, "R. C. Jebb," Briggs-Calder 239–47.

[21] For Sir William Mitchell Ramsay (1851–1939), see P. G. Naiditch, "Classical Studies in Nineteenth Century Great Britain as Background to the Cambridge Ritualists," [henceforth cited "*Studies*"] n. 74. He was Regius Professor of Humanity (1886–1911) at Aberdeen. His great work was his exploration of Anatolia. With Leaf, he was one of the two English-speaking sponsors competent to evaluate Harrison. He writes: "I would point to her stimulating influence as a lecturer as her pre-eminent claim to recognition in the world of scholars."

[22] For John Henry Middleton (1846–1896), archaeologist, architect, art historian and museum director, see Lionel Henry Cust, *DNB* II. 2445. He was a close friend of J. G. Frazer: see J. G. Frazer, *Pausanias's Description of Greece* I (London 1913) viii. A wrong first initial is given him on the printed testimonials.

[23] For Wilhelm Dörpfeld (1853–1940), see Peter Goessler, *Wilhelm Dörpfeld: Ein Leben im Dienst der Antike* (Stuttgart 1951). The life is uncritical and must be read with caution: see A. von Gerkan, *Gnomon* 24 (1952) 166–68. For a recent *laudatio* with bio-bibliography see Klaus Herrmann, "Wilhelm Dörpfeld 1853–1940," *Archäologenbildnisse: Porträts und Kurzbiographien von Klassischen Archäologen deutscher Sprache*, edited by Reinhard Lullies and Wolfgang Schiering (Mainz 1988) 112–13 [henceforth cited "*Archäologenbildnisse*"]. A critical life is desiderated. Dörpfeld certainly at first glance would have been the most impressive sponsor. Three points must be made: (1) Dörpfeld never earned a doctorate in archaeology. He was educated to be an architect. Schliemann went to Olympia in 1881 to hire him (they may have known each other since December 1876). He learned field archaeology working at Troy with Schliemann. In short, he was never one of the guild. Ludwig Curtius, *Deutsche und Antike Welt: Lebenserinnerungen* (Stuttgart 1958) 155, records Dörpfeld's appalling insensibility to poetry and beauty. His controversial excavations of the Theater of Dionysos at Athens exerted lasting influence on theories of fifth-century production. For Harrison's interest see her "Dr. Dörpfeld on the Greek Theatre," *Classical Review* 4 (1890) 274–77. (2) Wilamowitz saw to it that Dörpfeld never became a member of the Prussian Academy. On 24 June 1900 he wrote of "the infantilities" of Dörpfeld and declared his work "rubbish [Blödsinn]," adding "In comparison spiritualism is harmless." See William M. Calder III and David A. Traill (editors), *Myth, Scandal, and History: The Heinrich Schliemann Controversy and a First Edition of the Mycenaean Diary* (Detroit 1986) 31.

6. Dr. Paul Wolters, Kaiserlich Deutsches Archäologisches Institut.[24]

7. Dr. Ernst Curtius, Professor of Archaeology in the University, Berlin.[25]

8. Dr. Wilhelm Klein, Professor of Archaeology in the University, Prague.[26]

That is, the highest authorities in the field queried his competence. Robert Ackerman reminds me that Harrison's *Primitive Athens as Described by Thucydides* (Cambridge 1906; reprinted Chicago 1976) is dedicated to Dörpfeld and defends him throughout against his detractors. E. A. Gardner reviews the book at *CR* 21 (1907) 114–16 and W. Judeich at *Wochenschrift für Klassische Philologie* 13 (February 1907) 173–74. (3) *Ca.* 1890 Harrison gave Dörpfeld £100 to be used for his excavations (Goessler, 98). Dörpfeld's letter is dated Athens 28 March 1896. Harrison's gift substantiates Beard's contention (*supra*, n. 14) of Harrison's wealth against Peacock. She called Dörpfeld "my most honoured master" (*Reminiscences*, 65).

[24] For Paul Wolters (1858–1936), see Reinhard Lullies, *Archäologenbildnisse*, 124–25 (with portrait and bio-bibliography). Wolters (1887–1900) was Second Secretary (=Vice-Director) of the German Institute in Athens. He worked closely with Dörpfeld and presumably Harrison met him in Athens through Dörpfeld. His letter is dated Athens, 24 October 1888. In 1908 he succeeded Furtwängler in Munich.

[25] For Ernst Curtius (1814–1896), see his son's, Friedrich Curtius', *Ernst Curtius: Ein Lebensbild in Briefen* (Berlin 1903). There is a recent bio-bibliography at Richard Lullies, *Archäologenbildnisse*, 40 and see M. H. Chambers at Briggs-Calder 37–42. For the archaeological importance of Curtius, see Adolf Heinrich Borbein, "Ernst Curtius, Alexander Conze, Reinhard Kekulé: Probleme und Perspektiven der Klassischen Archäologie zwischen Romantik und Positivismus," in "Die Antike im 19. Jahrhundert in Italien und Deutschland," *Jahrbuch des italienisch-deutschen historischen Instituts in Trent* Beiträge 2 (Bologna/Berlin 1988) 275–302. For Wilamowitz' famous dismissal of the man see *Aristoteles und Athen* I (Berlin 1893) 377–78, repeated at *Geschichte der Philologie*[4] (Leipzig 1959) 69. His only book of permanent value was his description of the Peloponnesus. Wilamowitz underestimates Curtius' direction of the Olympia dig, possibly because of his distaste for the site. Harrison had met Curtius in Berlin and he "took me round the museums of Berlin" (*Reminiscences*, 64). She does not date the meeting. Curtius writes: "Miss Jane Harrison hat mit einem für Damen wöhnlichen Ernst und Erfolg sich in das Studium der Antike eingelebt. Sie hat durch Unterricht und durch Schriften gezeigt, daß sie die Gegenstände der Klassischen Archäologie beherrscht, und die Geschichte der Malerei und der Sculptur richtig aufzufassen versteht."

[26] For Wilhelm Klein (1850–1924), see Wolfgang Schiering, "Wilhelm Klein 1850–1924," *Archäologenbildnisse*, 98–99 (with portrait and bio-bibliography). He was an ancient art historian rather than an archaeologist. He habilitated under Benndorf in 1879 and succeeded Eugen Petersen on the Prague chair in 1876. He was one of several great Jewish scholars in the field. One thinks of Freud's friend, Emanuel Loewy. He retired in 1923. Harrison presumably met him in London. Klein draws attention to her museum work which led to the assignment of new fragments to named painters. "Ausser Ihrer literarische Arbeiten sind noch Ihrer Forschungen in den Museen zu gedenken, die der Wissenschaft hervorragende Dienste geleistet haben. Die Wiederentdeckung der Troilos Schale des Euphronios ist nur das Bekannteste aber nicht das Einzige dieser Art." Klein refers to Harrison, "Some Fragments of a Vase Presumably by Euphronios," *JHS* 9 (1888) 143–46, which he had recently read. Harrison early stated her indebtedness to Klein at *Myths of the Odyssey in Art and Literature* (London 1882) xiv, 215–19. See further *infra*, n. 44.

9. Dr. Otto Benndorf, Professor of Archaeology in the University of Vienna.[27]

10. Ernest Babelon, Director of the Bibliothèque Nationale, Paris.[28]

11. Cavaliere Luigi Milani, Director of the Archaeological Museum, Florence.[29]

12. Henry Craik, C.B., LL.D., Secretary to the Scotch Education Department.[30]

13. Sir Edward Maunde Thompson, D.C.L., Principal Librarian, British Museum.[31]

14. Richard Garnett, C.B., LL.D., Keeper of the Printed Books, British Museum.[32]

[27] For Otto Benndorf (1838–1907), see Hedwig Kenner, *Archäologenbildnisse*, 67–68 (with portrait and bio-bibliography). He was excavator, art historian, and organiser. He was the only sponsor who provably wrote without being asked. He writes from Vienna two days after Klein. He heard of her candidacy from Klein and hastened to wish her luck. He continues: "Ich habe leider noch nicht das Vergnügen Sie persönlich zu Kennen [*sic*], habe aber ihre [*sic*] archäologischen Arbeiten stets mit grossem Vergnügen und persönlichem Gewinn verfolgt. Wir danken Ihrem Scharfblick schon manchen glücklichen Fund und ich vergegenwärtige mir gern wie das klare, scharf getreffende [*sic*! =getroffene?], Urtheil das sich in Ihren Recenzionen <zeigt?>, und der resolute Sinn für das Thatsächliche und Wesentliche welcher überall in Ihren Untersuchungen hervortritt, Ihnen besondere Lehrerfolge sichern werde." This is one of the most authoritative as well as perceptive and intelligent of the letters. Benndorf's judgment was not clouded by Harrison's charm. Nor had she paid him one hundred pounds. He says that he had never met her. From her writings he deduces her intelligence and divines her pedagogical gifts. Are the textual errors a clue to her knowledge of German in 1888?

[28] For Ernest Babelon (1854–1923), see J. Nostos, *DBF* 4 (Paris 1948) 997–99; Peter and Hilde Zazoff, *Gemmensammler und Gemmenforscher: Von einer Noblen Passion zur Wissenschaft* (Munich 1983) 224–25, where he is considered the peer of Adolf Furtwängler; and David Le Suffleur, *Ernest Babelon* (no date) which contains a full bibliography (*non vidi*). Harrison twice calls him "Director of the Bibliothèque Nationale, Paris." In fact he was after 7 December 1897 "conservateur du Cabinet des médailles," a prominent numismatist. His letter is dated merely "Paris, le 24 Octobre." Whether written in 1888 or 1896, Babelon, although widely published, was merely something like an assistant keeper in the numismatic department of the Bibliothèque Nationale, a far cry from Director, a title which in fact was never his. I assume that Harrison carelessly or naively misrepresented his post.

[29] For Cavaliere Luigi Milani (dates unknown), see Harrison, "The Judgment of Paris: Two Unpublished Vases in the Graeco-Etruscan Museum at Florence," *JHS* 7 (1886) 196–219. The vases were published with his permission.

[30] For Sir (after 1897) Henry Craik (1846–1927), see G. MacDonald, *DNB* II. 2584. He studied classics as a schoolboy and undergraduate with distinction (double first at Oxford) but never held a professional post in classics or archaeology nor published on them. His courteous letter is worthless. He ought not to have been included.

[31] For Sir Edward Maunde Thompson (1840–1929), see F. G. Kenyon, *DNB* II. 2925. He was knighted in 1895 but not yet on "Oct. 19th, 1888" when he wrote for Harrison. He was a self-taught palaeographer (he never completed his Oxford B.A.). He had no professional interest in archaeology. His letter compliments Harrison's lecturing style.

[32] For Richard Garnett (1835–1906), see Sidney Lee, *DNB* II. 2646. Harrison again inflates his title. Garnett on "Oct. 20th, 1888," the date of his letter, was not "Keeper of the Printed Books, British Museum." He was appointed to that post in 1890. He was a

15. Henry Sidgwick, M.A., Litt.D., Praelector in Moral Philosophy, Trinity College, Cambridge.[33]

16. Henry Jackson, Litt.D., Fellow and Praelector in Ancient Philosophy, Trinity College, Cambridge.[34]

17. A. W. Verrall, M.A., Litt.D., Fellow of Trinity College, Cambridge.[35]

---

self-educated bibliographer and belle-lettrist with no competence in Harrison's subjects. He describes her as he might a conscientious schoolgirl and enthusiastic amateur: "As Superintendent of the British Museum Reading Room while you were engaged in preparing the Lectures you delivered in this Institution, I had the opportunity of appreciating your extraordinary diligence and research. As a reader of many of your Archaeological Essays [= the *JHS* articles], I can speak with no less emphasis of your power of rendering your favourite themes luminous and attractive, and of inspiring the student with the interest you feel in them yourself."

[33] For Henry Sidgwick (1838–1900), see A. S<idgwick> and E. M. S<idgwick>, *Henry Sidgwick: A Memoir* (London 1906). He was a founder of Newnham, an ardent supporter of women's education, and so inclined to support his former pupil. His university career was hindered by his stammer: see G. P. Gooch, *Under Six Reigns*[3], (London 1960) 24: "He was better to read than to hear, for his stammer was incurable." He attests her excellence as an undergraduate, disclaims competence in her subject and writes in a future most vivid that "If she is appointed...she will prove an interesting and impressive teacher..." Harrison again muddles a title. Sidgwick had resigned the Praelectorship in 1883 to become Knightsbridge Professor of Philosophy. His letter is dated "Oct. 22nd, 1888."

[34] For Henry Jackson (1839–1921), see R. St. John Parry, *Henry Jackson O.M., Vice-Master of Trinity College & Regius Professor of Greek in the University of Cambridge: A Memoir* (Cambridge 1926) and P. G. Naiditch, *Housman*, 165–72 with the extensive collection of testimonia at n. 58-1. He praises her undergraduate work, adding, "Of Miss Harrison's Archaeological attainments I am not competent to speak."

[35] For Arthur Woollgar Verrall (1851–1912), see Naiditch, *Housman*, 211–14 with the vast bio-bibliography at n. 64-1. The standard biography is M. A. Bayfield, "Memoir," in A. W. Verrall, *Collected Essays Classical and Modern* (Cambridge 1913) ix–cii; and for his criticism of Greek tragedy see James E. Ford, *Rationalist Criticism of Greek Tragedy: A Case Study in Critical History* (Diss. Chicago 1981). Both Verralls were close friends of Harrison, who would later (1903) dedicate *Prolegomena* to them. Mrs. Verrall was also a collaborator and Newnham colleague: see Jane Harrison, "In Memoriam—Mrs. A. W. Verrall," *Proceedings of the Society for Psychical Research* 29 (1918) 376–85. Verrall's letter is among the longer; and he is the only sponsor to update a letter of 1888 with a second brief one of March 31st 1896. He is scrupulously honest, for he considered "the paraphernalia of archaeology" to be "stuffage" (Stewart, 56–57). He admits "my own acquaintance with Archaeological subjects" is "superficial," and he reveals to the Committee that Harrison missed a First in the Classical Tripos: a miss he attributes to inadequate schooling. His generous assessment deserves citation. It is the most precise and revealing from a non-specialist and must have strengthened her case: "She has...a prudence in dealing with evidence and a clearness of perception which would secure her from avoidable error, even if her linguistic knowledge were far less than it is...Of the admiration which I feel for her industry, acuteness, and power of exposition, I could say much; but keeping to my province, I will say only that if her work had been liable to injury from inaccuracy or insufficient knowledge of the language concerned, I could not have failed to discover the fact; and I can warrant that, in this respect, she is well-equipped for her work. In her own field, it is Miss Harrison who instructs me, and she is far above any commendation of mine. Both writing and speaking she always commands my interest, and her enthusiasm has illuminated many regions into which for myself I should scarcely have

18. Arthur Sidgwick, M.A., Fellow and Tutor of Corpus Christi College, Oxford.[36]

19. R. G. Tatton, Formerly Fellow and Tutor of Balliol College, Oxford; Member of the Council of the London Society for the Extension of University Teaching.[37]

20. Walter Leaf, M.A., Trinity College, Cambridge.[38]

21. Edmond Warre, D.D., Head Master, Eton College.[39]

22. Rev. W. F. Fearon, D.D., Head Master, Winchester College.[40]

---

looked. I can hardly conceive any one more likely to make successful the work which she proposes to undertake." I have not seen Jane Harrison, "In Memoriam—Dr. Arthur Woolgar Verrall," *Newnham College Letter* (1912) 53–55. Two of her recollections of Verrall are preserved at Verrall, *Literary Essays*, xix–xx; xciv.

[36] Arthur Sidgwick (1840–1920), a minor classicist, the lesser brother of Henry, friend of Gilbert Murray, writes about "my friend" and is not competent to speak of "Miss Harrison's technical knowledge." He repeatedly turns "never without profit" to her *Archaeology of Athens* and then praises at length her lecturing ability.

[37] R. G. Tatton (dates unknown) is called by Peacock (68) "a suitor of Jane's." He will "speak only of her teaching powers" and he seeks to anticipate "a certain prejudice amongst some of the students against being taught by a woman." "...her command of the subject, her natural distinction, her sincerity and good sense" would dispell that. Tatton was involved in the administration of adult education and had no expertise in archaeology or classics.

[38] For Walter Leaf (1852–1927), see Charlotte M. Leaf, *Walter Leaf 1852–1927: Some Chapters of Autobiography with a Memoir* (London 1932) and Gilbert Murray, *DNB* II. 2745–46. With Jebb and Verrall, he was the greatest English classical scholar to write for Harrison. A banker, not an academician, he was interested in *Realien*. Persuaded by Harrison in 1890, he delivered a series of extension lectures for London University on ancient houses, dress, art and "Homeric Geography": see Leaf, *Leaf*, 154. There was a sympathy of interest. In his exegesis of Homer he used archaeological evidence and topography in a way that neither Jebb nor Verrall could and so his competence to judge Harrison's work was greater than theirs. Like Babelon, he refuses to judge her work on vases. He then writes: "In the best sense of the word, however, she has, during the last few years, popularised Archaeology in a quite extraordinary degree. The secret of Miss Harrison's success lies in the union of thorough and systematic knowledge of her subject matter with great natural endowments of clearness, fluency, and voice, all cultivated by long practice to a high pitch of perfection, and inspired by deep enthusiasm for Greek art." In June 1889, Leaf wrote a similar letter supporting William Ridgeway's candidacy for the chair of Greek at Glasgow. But for the phrase "an inspiring teacher," the whole letter concerns Ridgeway's research with citation of three specific articles: see Walter Leaf, in *The Testimonials of William Ridgeway, M.A.* (Cambridge 1889) 26 No. XVIII. I am grateful to the Librarian of the University Library for a copy. For Leaf's evaluation of E. A. Gardner, see *infra*.

[39] With Edmond Warre (1837–1920) we have the first of three schoolmasters, each of whom attests Harrison's ability to impress youthful hearers, not accustomed to being lectured at by women. None of them can evaluate her archaeological competence. For Warre, see Henry Elford Luxmore, *DNB* II. 2949. I have not seen C.R.L. Fletcher, *Edmond Warre* (1922). A classicist devoted to *Realien*, his famous models of Odysseus' raft, Caesar's bridge, and a trireme would have enticed Harrison.

[40] As at Eton, so at Winchester: Harrison delivered a successful lecture, "admirably clear, attractive and stimulating." So writes William Andrewes Fearon (1841–1924). The middle initial is wrong.

23. Rev. J. M. Wilson, M.A., Head Master, Clifton College.[41]

IV. Analysis of the Letters

The chair was one of archaeology. It had been the chair of Newton, arguably the most distinguished archaeologist in the English-speaking world. It was not a chair of classics. The matter was not the appointment of a University Extension Lecturer. Because Newton had been so dismal a teacher, one may safely surmise that attested teaching ability would be welcome, though not decisive. The sponsors fall easily into three groups: (A) People not entitled to a professional opinion on Harrison's archaeological work; (B) Witnesses to her lecturing ability; and (C) the Hard Core. Some straddle more than one group. I arrange sponsors alphabetically, rather than as Harrison has:

A. Persons not entitled to a professional opinion[42]

Butcher	Arthur Sidgwick*
Craik*	Henry Sidgwick*
Fearon	Tatton*
Garnett	Thompson
Jackson*	Verrall*

Wilson

B. Witnesses to Harrison's lecturing ability

Butcher	Middleton
Craik	Ramsay
Dörpfeld (!)	Arthur Sidgwick
Fearon	Tatton
Jebb	Thompson
Leaf	Warre

Wilson

C. The hard core

Babelon	Klein
Benndorf	Leaf

[41] For J. M. Wilson (1836–1931), Head Master of Clifton 1879–1890 (sc., no longer at the time of the second election) see H. B. Mayor, *DNB* II. 2968. I have not seen James M. Wilson, *An Autobiography 1836–1931*, edited by A. J. and J. S. Wilson (1932). Peacock (61–62) calls Wilson "Archbishop." That he never was. After retirement from Clifton, he served as Archdeacon of Manchester (1890–1905). Harrison lectured twice at Clifton to 200–250 masters and senior boys. Wilson writes: "I may say at once that (with the single exception of Faraday's) I have never heard such delightful lectures." For Wilson at Clifton see O. F. Christie, *Clifton School Days (1879–1885)* (London 1930) 144 *s.n.*. The frontispiece of the volume is a portrait of Wilson.

[42] An asterisk indicates those honest enough in their letters to confess their incompetence.

Curtius   Milani
Dörpfeld   Ramsay
                              Wolters

Who is missing? Newton may have declined to write because he was the previous holder of the chair. Percy Gardner may have pleaded conflict of interest, as his brother was a candidate. Adolf Furtwängler, arguably the greatest living archaeologist, is not represented.[43] Harrison may not have asked them. No woman writes for Harrison. Neither of her two collaborators, MacColl or Mrs. Verrall, writes for her. One would think they were best informed on her capacity for research.

Of the nine letters that count, only one is from an Englishman, and he is a banker. One is from a Scot, one from a Frenchman, and one from an Italian. Five are from German-speaking archaeologists. Two, Babelon and Leaf, declare themselves incompetent to judge her work on Greek vases. Leaf and Ramsay, the only two English-speaking sponsors competent to judge her work, call her a popularizer, a *damnatio* for a scholar. Babelon and Milani write polite phrases, but nothing specific. Of the five Germans, Curtius says little more than that she is a good student: "She has shown by her teaching and writings that she controls classical archaeological material and she knows how to interpret correctly the history of painting and sculpture." Wolters, just thirty years old, praises an older "valued colleague in the field of archaeology" for her "surety of scholarly method" and her "lucky zeal." His letter is well-intentioned and superficial.

Klein attests a European reputation and praises specifically three articles in *JHS*.[44] He wisely draws attention to the value of Harrison's museum work, because of which she has discovered a new masterpiece of Greek vase-painting. Benndorf's letter, the only unsolicited one and owed Klein, is probably the greatest. He has read her work with great pleasure and personal profit. "We already owe to your keen eye many a fortunate find and I foresee with pleasure how the clear, trenchant criticism, that is found in your reviews, and the resolute sense for the factual and essential, which comes to the fore constantly in your scholarly work, will insure for you extraordinary success as a teacher."[45] Dörpfeld, because of his spectacular finds and earlier

---

[43] Harrison had disagreed with his views: see *JHS* 14 (1894) xli–xlii and her "Some Points in Dr. Furtwängler's Theories on the Parthenon and its Marbles," *CR* 9 (1895) 85–92 and "The Central Group of the East Frieze of the Parthenon: Peplos or στρωμνή?" *CR* 9 (1895) 427–28. This may have made her unsure of his support. For his response, see "The Lemnia of Pheidias and the Parthenon Sculptures," *CR* 9 (1895) 269–76. See now Andreas Furtwängler's life of his grandfather at Briggs-Calder, 84–92.

[44] See *supra*, n. 26. The articles are: (1) "Monuments Relating to the Odyssey," *JHS* 4 (1883) 248–65; (2) "The Judgment of Paris: Two Unpublished Vases in the Graeco-Etruscan Museum at Florence," *JHS* 7 (1886) 196–219; (3) "Some Fragments of a Vase Presumably by Euphronios," *JHS* 9 (1888) 143–46. I think most scholars today would agree that these articles were Harrison's permanent contributions before October 1888.

[45] For the German text, see *supra*, n. 27.

association with Schliemann, the darling of Gladstone, was for Englishmen the most famous of the five. He writes twelve lines:

> I attest gladly here that Miss Jane E. Harrison has through long and serious studies acquired an outstanding knowledge of archaeology and has proven herself a virtuous scholar through her valuable publications of various sorts in many scholarly journals. Her book, *Mythology and Monuments of Ancient Athens*, belongs without question to the best books which have been written about Athens. Her public lectures too are known to be excellent. I can, therefore, without any hesitation, highly recommend Miss Harrison for the Yates Professorship of Archaeology.[46]

None of the German letters is cited in the recorded deliberations either of 1888 or of 1896.

In 1888, Harrison was 38; in 1896, she was 46. Certainly in 1896 she ought to have made up a better dossier. Undergraduate teachers and personal friends, not to speak of the "suitor," ought to have been omitted. More care should have been given to providing accurate titles and to proofreading the German. Three, rather than thirteen, sponsors would have been sufficient to attest her lecturing ability. We have scrutinized the testimonials she provided. An equally important source must now be examined: the minutes of both elections have been preserved.

V. The Election of 1888

Two documents (AM/C/216) survive attesting the election of 1888. The first is entitled: "Yates Professorship of Archaeology. Report of Committee." It is a seven-page handwritten document, dated "Dec. 14, 1888" and signed "Alfred Church, Chairman."[47] It is a summary of the deliberations of the Committee, and served as a recommendation to the Senate, which body emended and adopted the report on December 17, 1888. It was adopted by the Council on January 12, 1889. The text falls into two

---

[46] The German text, with corrected errors (e.g., *Ich* for *Tch*; *Ihr* for *Thr passim*) follows: "Ich bescheinige hierdurch sehr gerne, daß Miss Jane E. Harrison sich durch lange und ernste Studien hervorragende archäologische Kenntnisse erworben und sich auch durch ihre wertvollen Veröffentlichungen verschiedener Art in mehreren wissenschaftlichen Zeitschriften als tüchtige Gelehrte erwiesen hat. Ihr Buch *"Mythology and Monuments of Ancient Athens"* gehört unstreitig zu den besten Büchern, die über Athen geschrieben worden sind. Auch ihre öffentlichen Vorträge sind als ausgezeichnete bekannt. Ich kann daher Miss Harrison aus voller Überzeugung bestens empfehlen für das Yates Professorship of Archaeology."

[47] For Rev. Arthur John Church (1829–1912), since 1880 Professor of Latin at University College, see Naiditch, *Housman*, 53–54 with the material gathered at n. 14-1. Naiditch writes (*Housman*, 1–2): "But by the late 1880's, Church had lost the respect of many of his students. They circulated tales of his falling asleep whilst pupils were construing texts and of leaving the classroom to consult the dictionary for the meaning of Latin words." In 1887, 29 students had submitted a letter of protest. An ad hoc committee

parts. The first part establishes the duties of the Yates Professor. Of interest are the subjects for which he will be responsible:

> The Committee resolved to recommend...that provision must be made by the Professor for the teaching by himself, or by the aid, if necessary, of assistant lecturers of the three following branches at least, viz.
>
> (1) Classical and Oriental archaeology
> (2) Medieval archaeology
> (3) Prehistoric archaeology and the history of arts of savage races
>
> That the Professor should himself give an elementary course on General Archaeology.

There is no distinction between what we would call archaeology and art history. The professor is responsible for far more than Greece and Rome. He must give what we should call an undergraduate survey course from pre-historic times (Schliemann was still alive) through the medieval period and by no means limited to the Mediterranean basin. He is further to provide "two lectures and two demonstrations in every week of the Session." These may be held in the College or in a museum. The Committee further recommended "that with the consent of the Senate and Council, the Professor may in every year be granted leave of absence during one term for the purpose of archaeological research." On return the following term, he would be required to present three public lectures "(open to the Public without payment)" stating the results of his research. Finally, the professor will be "required to defray out of his salary the cost of adequately illustrating his lectures." One wonders if Newton had.

Next, "The Committee had to consider the qualifications of nine Candidates." Nine candidates had put in. The first two are quickly disposed of: "Mr. J. F. Hodgetts, late Professor of English in the University of Moscow"[48] and "Mr. Penrose, who has long occupied an honourable place in the Profession of Architecture."[49] They lacked credentials. An amiable youth, Mr. Talfourd Ely ("favourably known...both for social and intellectual qualities") is too young. Not discouraged, he would try again in 1896. They next turn down a candidate arguably superior to Harrison:

---

was appointed. On February 9th 1889, Church resigned. The chairmanship of the Yates Committee was one of his last college functions shortly before an ignominious retirement.

[48] For the adventurer and writer J. F. Hodgetts (1828–1906), see Alexander Gordon, *DNB* II. 2698. He was author of "Harold the Boy Earl" and "Edwin the Boy Outlaw," neither of which I have read.

[49] For the neo-classical architect, Francis Cranmer Penrose (1817–1903), see Paul Waterhouse, *DNB* II. 2832. He designed the British School at Athens in 1882 without fee and was its first Director (1886-1887).

Mr. Waldstein, University Reader in Classical Archaeology, and Director of the Fitzwilliam Museum at Cambridge, has achieved a high reputation in his subject, and has unquestionably done much to make the study of it popular in the University of Cambridge. Mr. Waldstein sent in no testimonials: but submitted a scheme for the work of the Professorship. The Committee was not satisfied that the solidity of his attainments was equal to the reputation which he enjoys.

Charles Waldstein (1856–1927), later Sir Charles Walston, educated at Columbia College, New York and at Heidelberg, was denied a career in the United States because of American anti-Semitism. Henry Bradshaw and Henry Sidgwick arranged that he be made lecturer in archaeology at Cambridge in 1880. After being unsuccessful for the Yates chair, he accepted the Directorship of the American School in Athens 1889–1893. His tactlessness offended the English. *The Times* obituary says "He was neither shy nor reserved." At a famous public occasion in Cambridge, Sir Charles Stanford had cried out in the presence of Waldstein: "I wish that German-American-Jew would go back to his respective countries."[50] In short, anti-Semitism may have been a factor.

The next three candidates are dismissed *en bloc* in spite of their virtues. "But, in view of the superior claim of two candidates now about to be mentioned, the Committee had no hesitation in passing them by." They were L. R. Farnell, Fellow of Exeter;[51] A. H. Smith, assistant in the Department of Greek and Roman Antiquities in the British Museum;[52] and E. A. Gardner, British Archaeological School [*sic*] at Athens,[53] the latter to

[50] For Waldstein (Walston), see *The Times* 23 March 1927. For the Stanford incident and the most revealing description of Waldstein, see E. F. Benson, *As We Were: A Victorian Peep-Show* (London 1930) 139–42, 146. Farnell (*op. cit., infra*, n. 51) remarks: "It is hardly to our credit that his [Brunn's] pupil Waldstein found in England a lucrative career which Germany denied him." Harrison alludes briefly to him (*Reminiscences*, 60). It is revealing that he was never included in *DNB*.

[51] For Lewis R. Farnell (1856–1934), see his *An Oxonian Looks Back* (London 1934), where (281) he writes: "the writings of the gifted Jane Harrison, the leading woman scholar of the time, were marred by the spirit of feminist propaganda." See further Naiditch, *Classical Studies*, n. 80.

[52] For the distinguished career of Arthur Hamilton Smith (1860–1941), see F. G. Kenyon, *DNB* II. 2890.

[53] For Ernest Arthur Gardner (1862–1939), see Naiditch, *Classical Studies*, n. 84, to which for his activities at the British School add Helen Waterhouse, *The British School at Athens: The First Hundred Years* (London 1986) 167 *s.n.*

be successful in 1896. The Committee then turned to the two finalists:

> Miss Jane Harrison comes recommended by testimonials of the very weightiest kind. Her large attainments (though the Committee did not[grant?] that she is eminent in scholarship properly so called), her enthusiasm in the study to which she has given herself, her unselfish devotion to the pursuit of knowledge, and her singular success in imparting that knowledge to her hearers, were described in terms of the heartiest praise by persons who had every right to speak with authority. The Committee were agreed in thinking that her claims were of the very first order, and would indeed have been irresistible (the question of sex being supposed to be set aside), but for the competition of a candidate of European reputation in the person of Mr. R. S. Poole. [So strongly, however, did the Committee feel the strength of Miss Harrison's claims that they resolved that it would be advantageous if her acknowledged ability as a teacher could be utilized by her acting as an occasional lecturer for the Professor.][54]

Finally, the winner:

> Mr. R. S. Poole,[55] Keeper of Coins in the British Museum, has scarcely a rival in the breadth & profundity of his archaeological knowledge. He is an Egyptologist of high repute, an expert in Oriental archaeology, not less proficient in the archaeology of Greece and Rome, and, in his special occupation of Numismatology, an authority second to none. The Committee had also evidence of his efficiency as a lecturer, and they were satisfied that he had wise and liberal views of the work which the Professor should do. They have therefore no hesitation in recommending him to the Choice of the Council. They also recommend the acceptance of Mr. Poole's offer to spend £200 per annum out of the endowment of the Chair in providing instruction in those branches of the study in which he is not himself expert.

The evidence substantiates the Committee's preference for Poole. His biographer writes: "...he converted what had been a special chair of Greek archaeology into a centre of instruction in a wide range of archaeological studies. His own stimulating teaching of Egyptian, Assyrian, and Arab art and antiquities, and numismatics, was supplemented by the co-operation of specialists in other branches."[56] Poole resigned the chair in 1894 because of declining health.

A second document, a minority report, is attached to the Report of the Committee. It is the following:

---

[54] A later hand has bracketed the paragraph and adds "See Senate Minutes Dec. 17.88 for the paragraph substituted for this." *Non vidi.*

[55] For Reginald Stuart Poole (1832–1895), see Naiditch, *Housman*, 93–94 with the rich material at n. 32-1. He was a numismatist and Egyptologist of prominence, and 18 years senior to Harrison.

[56] Anonymous, *DNB* II. 1687.

The undersigned disagree with that part of the report which recommends that the Professor of Archaeology should be assisted by Miss Harrison. They think it undesirable that any teaching in University College should be conducted by a woman.

E. S. Beesly[57]
G. D. Thane[58]

Dec. 15, 1888.

Beesly, although opposing women on the teaching staff, was no conservative. M. L. Clarke reports[59] that he was "a strong supporter of the cause of Labour, and aroused much criticism by a speech he made in defence of Trades Unions after some acts of violence in Sheffield. A move was made in Council to have him dismissed from his professorship, but Grote, though he was by no means pleased with Beesly's conduct, used his influence to ensure that no action was taken." That is, a leftist, indeed, a friend of Karl Marx, opposed Harrison's appointment on the grounds of her sex, as did an anatomist.

VI. The Election of 1896

Harrison added seven letters to her testimonials of 1888 (Butcher, Dörpfeld, Jebb, Middleton, Ramsay, Tatton and Verrall 2). The document for what follows (AM/D/52) is in the hand of W. M. Flinders Petrie,[60] and dated June 1, 1896. The second covering page contains the following:

Report of Committee of Senate
on Candidates for the Yates Professorship
of Archaeology

Candidates
J. Romilly Allen
Prof. W.C.F. Anderson
Talfourd Ely
E. A. Gardner
Miss Jane Harrison
J. Stanley Rogers

---

[57] For Edward Spencer Beesly (1831–1915), then Professor of Ancient and Modern History at University College and concurrently Professor of Latin, Bedford College, London, see Naiditch, *Housman*, 73–74 with the material at n. 29-1. The minority report is written in the hand of Beesly.

[58] Sir George D. Thane (1850–1930) was Professor of Anatomy at University College (P. G. Naiditch). Beesly, Church and Thane are the only Committee members identified. There may have been six others.

[59]M. L. Clarke, *George Grote: A Biography* (London 1962) 158–59.

[60] For the great field archaeologist and Egyptologist W. Flinders Petrie (1853–1942), see Flinders Petrie, *Seventy Years in Archaeology* (New York 1932; repr. New York 1969) and Margaret S. Drower, *Flinders Petrie: A Life in Archaeology* (London 1985).

Committee (10)
Professors
Barker
Bendall
Brown
Rhys Davids
Ker[61]
Housman (Chair)[62]
Petrie
Platt[63]
Roger Smith
Strong

Attendance at first meeting 7
at interview of candidates 9

Two candidates did not submit printed testimonials and their fields were considered remote from the advertisement of "a chair where Classical Studies are a first requirement." There has been a change since 1888. These candidates were T. Stanley Rogers (legal institutions) and J. Romilly Allen (British Archaeology). Talfourd Ely was not up to the other candidates.[64] The first candidate seriously considered was W.C.F. Anderson.[65] His testimonials impressed the Committee. It was twice debated whether to invite him for an interview, but his lack of experience in archaeology decided them against it. "Accordingly, Miss Jane Harrison & Ernest A. Gardner were invited to see the Committee." The comparison of Harrison and Gardner is preceded by the following:

> Before considering the respective position of these candidates an allusion was made in the Committee to the question involved of the

[61] For William Paton Ker (1855–1923), then Quain Professor of the English Language and Literature, University College, London, see Naiditch, *Housman*, 57–64 with the material collected at 57–58 n. 22–1.

[62] The bibliography on A. E. Housman (1859–1936) is *fast unübersehbar*: see Naiditch, *Housman*, 100 ff. and Briggs-Calder, 192–204, which is certainly the safest guide. Mr. Naiditch informs me that because he was Dean, Housman was Chair.

[63] Arthur Platt (1860–1924), Professor of Greek at University College, has been immortalized by A. E. Housman in one of the finest necrologies in the English language: see Arthur Platt, *Nine Essays*, with a Preface by A. E. Housman (Cambridge 1927) v–xi.

[64] P. G. Naiditch informs me that Ely was Professor of Greek at Bedford College (1891–1893), later Secretary of University College School, London. A trip to Greece in 1889 is attested. He lectured occasionally at the South Kensington Museum. He seems to have been an amiable amateur.

[65] Elusive, Anderson published reviews in *CR*, and an occasional article and schoolbook. From the two testimonials cited by Petrie, he seems to have been Professor of Classics at Firth College, Sheffield. J. Arthur Munro, Tutor of Lincoln College, Oxford, writes of him: "...we studied together at Oxford ten years ago under Professor W. M. Ramsay...We have done practical work together at excavations in Montenegro and exploration in Asia Minor." The Committee overestimated him.

position of women on the teaching staff. It was unanimously agreed that such a question did not enter in any way into the reference to this Committee; that the sole business before this Committee was to decide which candidate appeared to be the most able, irrespective of sex; and that it rested rather with the Senate and the Council to consider if such a matter should have any weight. No prejudice was hinted at by any member against a woman holding such a post, and several members were in favour of it. It should be remembered that in the following deliberation the general question of a mixed professoriate is not touched on in any way; and any views for or against that order of things are external to the present report.[66]

What Petrie did—after the interviews—was to arrange the credentials of the two finalists under six headings. He cut up sets of their testimonials and pasted relevant bits onto his pages, interspersing them with handwritten comments. The headings are: (1) Scholarship; (2) Lecturing; (3) Work with Students; (4) Breadth & Originality; (5) Work Abroad; (6) Official Business [= Administrative Experience]. Verrall (twice), Jebb and Butcher are cited for Harrison's scholarship: none of the foreigners! Her four books are noted, and her papers in *JHS*. For Gardner, Sandys, Jebb and Henry Pelham, Camden Professor of Ancient History, are cited. Then Gardner's letter of application is quoted:

> I was placed in the First Division of the First Class in the First Part of the Classical Tripos in 1882, and in the Second Part of the same Tripos I obtained in 1884 a First Class with Distinction in Section D (Greek and Roman Archaeology).

His principal publications are listed:

> "Naukratis II" (and chapter on inscriptions in Naukratis I) 1886–8
> "Excavations at Megalopolis" 1892
> "Handbook of Greek Sculpture" 1896 (part 1)
> and many papers in Journ. Hellen. Studies.

Petrie then writes:

> Questions were asked of both candidates as to the study of Roman archaeology & Latin authors. Miss Harrison had a general acquaintance with this time, but had not made it a detailed study. Mr. Gardner had necessarily grounded himself on this branch in order to pass (First Class with Distinction) in Greek and Roman Archaeology; but his

---

[66] Whether this reflects the minority report of 1888, I do not know. The passage is briefly summarized at Naiditch, *Housman*, 63 n. 22-10, where he cites a letter of Harrison to her undergraduate teacher, Henry Jackson (TCC Add. Ms. c 32.10), dated 1 May 1896. In the letter, Harrison alleges that one member of the Committee was averse to appointing a woman and she names W. P. Ker as the misogynist. (1) There is no other evidence that Ker was a misogynist. (2) Petrie writes that the Committee was unanimous in not making sex an issue. (3) I doubt that the Committee had even met by 1 May. The final report is dated 1 June 1896; only two meetings are recorded. Things were done with dispatch.

subsequent work had thrown him on the Greek examples of Roman age, more than on Italian work. Another scholastic branch—that of epigraphy—was Mr. Gardner's principal subject before he went to Athens.

It was generally felt that although Miss Harrison's abilities might be equal to Mr. Gardner's, she had not enjoyed the same opportunities for a thorough scholarly grounding in the details of the various branches. And the testimonials bear witness mainly to her natural ability, insight, & artistic impulse. While Mr. Gardner's testimonials notice especially his accuracy & distinction in scholarship & close practical acquaintance with the facts of his science. The balance of intuition may be on Miss Harrison's side, while the balance of knowledge may be on Mr. Gardner's side.

Under lecturing, Petrie records: "This subject was felt by the Committee to be that in which Miss Harrison undoubtedly had most advantage." Gardner was helped by a valuable testimonial from Nathaniel Wood,[67] Fellow of Kings College, Cambridge, who heard Gardner lecture successfully in the open air to a mixed crowd in Greece. Petrie noted that "Mr. Gardner's position at Athens has been more connected with individual than collective teaching." That is, Harrison never had "students." Petrie then reports (8–9):

Some of the Committee were mainly influenced by the importance of securing the most popular lecturer, who would draw large classes and make the subject as widely followed as possible in the interests of the College; while others attached more weight to the founding of a school of studies, & the encouragement of a wide grasp of the whole subject. Varying weight was therefore given to the claims of Miss Harrison on the ground of proved success in popular lecturing.

Under the rubric "Working with Students," Harrison suffered. "Miss Harrison does not appear to have had so much opportunity of close work with students, as she has of lecturing. Hence there are not many allusions to this branch of work." The anti-Harrison, Ridgeway, lauded "Mr. Gardner's unselfish devotion to the interests of his students" and adduced "the testimony of brilliant young men trained by him to his zeal and ability as a teacher." Gardner was astute enough to submit a "Joint testimonial of former students of the School at Athens." The students write:

As Director of the School, Mr. Gardner has always placed his knowledge and his services ungrudgingly at the disposal of the students; and the generous interests which he has taken in their several

---

[67] For Nathaniel Wood (1864–1940), editor of Euripides, *Orestes*, tutor and friend of E. M. Forster, see *Selected Letters of E. M. Forster*, Volume 1 (1879–1920), edited by Mary Lago and P. N. Furbank (Cambridge 1983) 26 n. 1 and P. N. Furbank, *E. M. Forster: A Life* II *Polycrates' Ring 1914–1970* (New York/London 1978) 347 *s.n.* His unpublished memoirs survive.

studies, however remote from those in which he has been himself engaged, is very remarkable.

Petrie summarizes the discussion (11):

> This ability to discuss questions with students, & help them personally in their original work has been a specialty of Mr. Gardner's at Athens, & constitutes one of his strongest claims.

Comparison under this heading may have been decisive. Petrie summarizes the discussion (10–11):

> The Committee feel that in this branch of work across the study-table there is an advantage with Mr. Gardner; and how essential such work is, was shown by the lack of any school of archaeology being formed from the lectures of Prof. Newton & Prof. Poole. It appears that in this line of the formation of future scholars Mr. Gardner has much the same superiority that Miss Harrison has in popular lecturing & interest. In neither case is the proficiency of one candidate any reflection on the abilities of the other.

The next rubric is Breadth & Originality. Here Harrison has only Ramsay:

> Her successive books show that steady growth in width of knowledge and in the power of applying knowledge, which proves freedom of mind, and gives hope of a continuance of similar work and still further development.

David Hogarth[68] wrote for Gardner:

> I was intimately connected with Mr. Ernest Gardner in archaeological work four years ago, and had full opportunity of learning how genuine is his sympathy for archaeological study and how extraordinarily wide and comprehensive his knowledge. We, who worked with him in Cyprus, though no younger than he, always regarded him as possessed of an archaeological experience which placed a gap of years between us: and in the publication of our results we relied greatly on his acute and critical judgement. He has as much acquaintance with many subjects in Archaeology, as most specialists on each subject severally possess: and I do not believe that anyone in the United Kingdom is better qualified to fill a chair of Archaeology.

---

[68] For the distinguished field archaeologist David George Hogarth (1862–1927), see David G. Hogarth, *The Wandering Scholar* (Oxford 1925); Janet E. Courtney (Hogarth's sister), "David George Hogarth 1862–1927," in *An Oxford Portrait Gallery* (London 1931) 3–48; and F. G. Kenyon, *DNB* II. 2699." In the tradition of Colonel Leake, he combined archaeological surveying with intelligence work, and thus assured the financing of his digs: see Richard Symonds, *Oxford and Empire: The Last Lost Cause?* (London 1986) 141; Jeremy Wilson, *Lawrence of Arabia: The Authorized Biography of T. E. Lawrence* (New York 1990) 1173 *s.n.*; and H.V.F. Winstone, *Woolley of Ur: The Life of Sir Leonard Woolley* (London 1990) 27–28, 61, 286–87. In 1897 he succeeded Gardner as Director of the British School at Athens.

Under the last two rubrics, Work Abroad and Official Business, Harrison does not even appear. Of the first qualification, Leaf, identified here as "Treasurer, British School at Athens," writes of Gardner:

> There is perhaps no English archaeologist with the single exception of Sir C. Newton, certainly there is not one of the younger generation, who can approach his experience in practical study of the subject in its home in Greece.

Finally, George A. Macmillan,[69] "Hon. Sec. British Sch. at Athens," writes: "I have much pleasure in bearing my testimony to his business capacity, and his conscientious discharge of the duties of his position." It may have been that at this point in the deliberations Gardner's triumph was not yet assured. For, thirty-six years later, Petrie recalls:

> On the death of Reginald Stuart Poole, the Yates Chair of Archaeology was vacant at the College. A Committee was appointed to see candidates, and the two considered were Jane Harrison and Ernest Gardner. It was my duty to draw up the report, which I did as impartially as I could. The committee were on the point of naming Jane Harrison, but I remarked that, though an authority on religion,[70] she had not as wide a view and knowledge as Gardner, and that carried the day.[71]

The final summation (14) deserves citation:

> The issue between the two candidates appeared to the Committee to rest much on the kind of work that was to be expected in the Chair. If the main object were to be the spread of a general interest in Greek Art and Mythology, undoubtedly Miss Harrison is a specialist in this branch, whose abilities appear to be pre-eminent. But on looking to the other questions,—of well grounded scholarship & high accuracy,—work with students in their own special researches, & the founding of a school of general archaeology,—breadth of interests outside of the very specialised branch of Greek Art,—power of independent work,—the interpretation of evidence from actual discovery,—& general business capacity,—the evidence was all in favour of Mr. Gardner, as being the fittest person to forward the interests of archaeology in a position in which too great specialisation would be a misfortune. The general scope of the position has been already much limited by the requirement of particular capacity in one branch: and the main object after satisfying the first requirement of a high position in Greek work, should be to preserve as much breadth, & sympathy with all branches of Archaeology, as possible. In view of these considerations the Committee by a final vote recommend that Ernest A. Gardner be appointed to the Yates Professorship of Archaeology.

---

[69] For George Macmillan's work for the British School, see Waterhouse, *British School*, 168 *s.n.*

[70] She was in fact not an authority on religion until 1903.

[71] Petrie, *Seventy Years*, 174.

Notice is found on the first covering page that the recommendation was adopted by the Senate on 1 June 1896 and by Council on 7 June 1896. "E. A. Gardner appointed for 5 years."

VII. What have we learned?

Peacock attributed Harrison's failures to "fear...of granting the distinguished professorship to a woman" and alleged that "the hidebound world of classical scholarship had no room for innovative thinking." Only two members of the Committee of 1888, one a friend of Karl Marx, objected to Harrison's sex. The Committee of 1896 explicitly stated that sex played no role in their deliberations. The Committee of 1888 placed her before seven men; the Committee of 1896, before four men. Harrison's "innovative" books did not begin to appear before 1903. As late as 1896, her work was conventional. None of her 24 testimonials even raise the question of "innovative thinking." Harrison failed because in both cases there was a stronger candidate.[72]

University of Illinois at Urbana-Champaign

[72] I am grateful for valuable help to Robert Ackerman (Philadelphia), Alexander Košenina (West Berlin) and P. G. Naiditch (Los Angeles).

4

Cornford's *Thucydides Mythistoricus*

MORTIMER CHAMBERS

I. The Stance of a Ritualist

Our leading Greco-Roman historian, E. Badian, has said, "That general books on Thucydides appear at the rate of about one a year does not require demonstration."[1] Yet it may be surprising to learn that, at the beginning of this century, even after the commentaries of Bloomfield, Arnold, and Jowett, there had not been a single such general book in English. Only as classical scholarship began to awake and rub its eyes, as it were, did anyone dare to write an analytic treatment in English of the greatest historian of antiquity.

F. M. Cornford's *Thucydides Mythistoricus* was not the fruit of decades of thought, written by a scholar at the height of his maturity. The author was but 33 and had published only a few short papers, none of them on the historian. Moreover, the first English book on Thucydides was not a respectful demonstration of the historian's greatness or an encomium from an ancient university that might further justify the unchallenged place of the classics as the queen of academic disciplines. It was, rather, an attempt to show that Thucydides was deficient in the analysis of historical causes, that he did not understand the real issue behind the Peloponnesian War, and that he was in the grip of certain intellectual, even psychological, influences that made it impossible for him to control the structure of his own narrative. The young Fellow of Trinity College, Cambridge, must have known that he was inviting rebuke from traditional academics, but he was to show comparable originality in all his other writings and he was, besides, a member of a group that was attempting little less than a revolution in classical scholarship.

Cornford dedicated his first book to Jane Harrison, with whom he had already held long conversations; and by this declaration of allegiance clearly took his stand with the Cambridge Ritualists. The dedication itself is significant—"To Jane Ellen Harrison: ὄναρ ἀντ' ὀνειράτων πολλῶν τε καὶ καλῶν." The first three Greek words vary slightly those of Socrates

[1] *Échos du Monde Classique/Classical Views* n.s. 7 (1988) 297 n. 14.

to Theaetetus: "Listen, then, to a dream in exchange for your dream": Ἄκουε δὴ ὄναρ ἀντὶ ὀνείρατος.[2] But Cornford was doing more than thanking Harrison or giving her a fantasy in return for the many beautiful speculations she had shared with him. In the passage from Plato, Socrates goes on to say that he has heard some people say that the elements (στοιχεῖα) of which we and all other things exist can only be named: we cannot make any statement about them, or even define them. Socrates does not go on to accept this theory, but Cornford may have alluded to it as a way of hinting that we can only name, but never scientifically analyze, the pre-theological forces that (in the opinion of the Ritualists) controlled mythology and religious lore.

As all know, this group did not think that classical studies could fulfill their task through the expert syntactical decoding of polished texts or through ever more erudite commentaries on the acknowledged models of style. They knew their Greek authors as worthy members of Richard Porson's university should, but they did not necessarily find, as many Victorians did, a pattern for modern life within the gentle precepts of Horace and the balanced ethics of Aristotle.

They sought rather to penetrate to the origins of thought and behavior, and they found these origins in dimly felt, scarcely known impulses that humanity has long concealed through controlled social forms. Complex civilizations like Greece and Rome, if we may so refer to the many communities and peoples included under these convenient names, cannot survive without moving away from primitive rituals and replacing them with laws and magistrates. Yet, if we are to understand what they were really doing, or what we ourselves are doing and saying, we do well to read the clues that disclose to us the origins, the hidden yet still flowing springs of our thoughts and, even more, of our emotions. Anthropology was no longer merely a species of travel on the Herodotean model but had taken on a deliberately scientific manner.[3] Sociology had recently been born. Above all, there was "her more speculative but far more effective younger sister" (as Sir Isaiah Berlin[4] has called her), psychology, powered by Freud.

The Ritualists could expect to find fertile ground in such literary forms as drama and poetry: in these intellectual products mythology is everywhere and the comparative method of Sir James George Frazer was removing the thin veil of civilization and disclosing the reality beneath. As for religion, students of the Cambridge-trained Arthur Darby Nock will remember his

---

[2] Plato, *Theaet.* 201d. Cornford discusses the passage in his *Plato's Theory of Knowledge: The Theaetetus and the Sophist of Plato translated with a running commentary* (New York and London, 1935) 143 ff.

[3] Robert Ackerman reminds me that the first anthropological voyage to be sponsored by a British institution had gone as recently as 1898 to the Torres Straits; see A. C. Haddon, *Reports of the Cambridge Anthropological Expedition to Torres Straits* (Cambridge, 1901–1935).

[4] *Historical Inevitability* (London, 1954) 75.

definition of it: "man's feeling of helplessness in the face of what he cannot control, and what he does, says, and thinks—*in that order*—to overcome this feeling."[5]   Ritual, symbolic action, rather than Nock's "the demon, thought," often designs religious behavior. But what of historical writing? Is it not a calm, reflective ordering of the past through the patient collection of facts, the subordination of the insignificant to the more important, the cool evaluation of men and motives?   The two pillars of fifth-century historiography are the candid, witty Herodotus and the austere, detached Thucydides: could there be better examples of that logical analytic method that leads through the Sophists to Plato and Aristotle?

Exactly here did Cornford show his intellectual courage, as he discovered a Thucydides who could not understand or even recognize the causes of his Peloponnesian War, because he was still not freed from modes of thought, really patterns of feeling, that arrived with the Greek psyche and emerged most clearly in the other magnificent literary form of the fifth century, tragic drama.   Nor could he give realistic portraits of his main actors, because for him they were merely types of characters, as mechanical as those in Aeschylus.   Cornford's work is especially valuable to the historian of scholarship because it shows a Ritualist applying his methods to a single large classical text.   Justice to his challenging analysis demands that we restate it, severely compressing an argument of some 250 pages.

II. A View of Thucydides

Cornford's arresting title resolves itself into the two parts of his book, "Thucydides Historicus" and "Thucydides Mythicus."   He begins by confessing his inability to obtain, from Thucydides' narrative, a clear idea of why the great war started at all. "This very question seems to have puzzled contemporaries; for various accounts were already current when Thucydides wrote, and it was partly his object to correct vulgar opinion and readjust the perspective to his own view."[6] He briefly dismisses the calumnies against Pericles: that he started the war in order not to have to reveal his misuse of public money,[7] or because his friend Phidias had been prosecuted for alleged malversation of materials given him for the famous statue of Athena[8] and he "set the city on fire," that is, started the war, before any such thing could happen to him.[9] Even easier to dismiss are the suggestions that the war was a "racial conflict of Ionian against Dorian" or an ideological clash between

[5] In a Harvard seminar, 1953.

[6] Cornford, 4.

[7] Diodorus 13.38.

[8] Discussion: G.E.M. de Ste. Croix, *The Origins of the Peloponnesian War* (London, 1972) 236. Phidias did go into exile at Elis, where he made the statue of Zeus for Olympia, one of the Seven Wonders of the ancient world.

[9] Aristophanes, *Peace* 605–18, obvious satire that nevertheless found its way into Plutarch, *Pericles* 31–32, cf. Diodorus 12.39.1–2.

democracy and oligarchy. The Spartans did not want to fight and had to be goaded into the war by their allies and the fiery ephor Sthenelaidas. As for Pericles, Thucydides says indeed that he kept urging the Athenians to war; they must not yield to the Spartans,[10] yet in neither place where Thucydides refers to Pericles' wish to fight a war "is any motive assigned for this course of action." Thus "[w]e can only conclude that Thucydides was at a loss to understand what the motive could be."[11]

Cornford constructs a model of Athenian society based partly on the Old Oligarch, who gives us an Athens in which the well-off are opposed to, and offended by, the people.[12] And yet the writer admits that the Athenians, having chosen the system they have, do manage it well. In particular, Athens imports everything it needs through the Piraeus; by this means the commercial-industrial class prospers. Meanwhile, the country people had little interest in commerce or in empire; "and they had everything to lose by war, which meant the destruction of their olive trees."[13] This much is clear at once in Cornford's favor, that many Athenians moved into the city only reluctantly at the beginning of the war,[14] and that those whose farms were ravaged during the invasions by the Peloponnesians were vindictive toward Pericles because of their losses.[15] As we know from Thucydides, Pericles was the undisputed leader of the democracy, but "time does not stand still; a new generation is growing up under Pericles' feet, with new aims and new demands."[16] When the new generation became mature and woke up to its own power, "Pericles must go under or take the lead whither they will."

What was it that this army of tradesmen and workers wanted? Cornford took a hint from the ancient sources who make the "Megarian Decrees" the major immediate cause of the war. The "main" Megarian Decree, moved by Pericles in the late 430s, excluded the Megarians from the Athenian Agora and from all harbors in the Athenian Empire. As is well known, the decrees have been subjected to a lengthy and highly original analysis by G.E.M. de Ste. Croix.[17] He finds that the exclusion from the Agora means only that, in the narrowest sense: the Megarians could not enter the Agora under the Acropolis, but they were not barred from the Piraeus, from its Agora, or indeed from anywhere else in Attica. The exclusion from harbors in the empire was, in de Ste. Croix's interpretation, mainly an attack on the dignity and status of Megarians, who could however continue to trade, if they wished, on little boats or nearby beaches. Thus the Megarian Decrees

[10] οὐκ εἴα ὑπείκειν, 1.127.3; cf. Pericles' advice to the Athenians, μὴ εἴκειν Πελοποννησίοις, 1.140.1.

[11] Cornford, 13.

[12] [Xenophon], *Constitution of the Athenians*.

[13] Id. 17.

[14] χαλεπῶς...ἡ ἀνάστασις ἐγίγνετο, Thuc. 2.14.2.

[15] Id. 2.59.1–2.

[16] Cornford, 23.

[17] de Ste. Croix (*supra*, n. 8) 225–89, with accompanying appendixes.

"could not have had a primarily commercial purpose."[18] They were mainly psychological attacks, seeking to humiliate citizens of the nearby state.

I do not wish to support or to reject this analysis here. What is important for Cornford is that the decrees play a large part in sources outside Thucydides: Diodorus (from Ephorus),[19] Aristophanes,[20] and Plutarch.[21] He might have added Andocides, who says that the Athenians went to war διὰ Μεγαρέας.[22] We may reduce the impact of Aristophanes' words (in effect, "the Megarians enlisted the Spartans to insist that the decrees be repealed; when we refused, they went to war") on the usual argument, that his task was always to extract the comic from any situation; Ephorus-Diodorus and Plutarch probably had no such wish. Whatever the real aims of the decrees, they appear several times in the speeches and debates that Thucydides gives us in his first book. Ambassadors from Megara spoke before the Spartan assembly in 432, complaining of their exclusion from the Agora and the ports;[23] the second of three embassies from Sparta to Athens in 432 said that there need be no war if the Athenians would cancel the decree;[24] finally the matter was discussed in an Athenian assembly both by others and by Pericles, who offered to withdraw the decree only if the Spartans would stop excluding others from their territory; the Athenians voted to accept his advice and to send this reply to the Spartans.[25] One might well guess that any controversy that Thucydides mentions three times, and that, according to Andocides, was the cause of the great war, must have been one of the turning points in all the negotiations. Yet Cornford is right to say that "no one, reading the whole story in Thucydides and unacquainted with the other evidence, would gather this impression."[26]

But why was Megara important, and why should anyone propose decrees barring the Megarians from any places whatever? Control over the territory around Megara enabled the Athenians to import and export to and from western Greece. So long as the isthmus of Corinth was the passage to and from the west, "[e]very vase that the Athenian potteries exported to Italy, every cheese that came from Syracuse to the port of Athens, had to pay toll to the keepers of the isthmus."[27] But control over Megara was only a prelude to a far more ambitious program, a western policy with Sicily as the distant objective. The foundation of Thurii in south Italy, in which Athens took part, the alliances with Rhegium in south Italy and Leontini on

[18] de Ste. Croix (supra, n. 8) 284.
[19] 12.39.
[20] Acharnians 524–39; Peace 605–11, 615–18.
[21] Pericles 29–31, especially 29.4.
[22] 3.8. So Aeschines 2.175.
[23] Thuc. 1.67.4.
[24] Id. 1.139.1–2.
[25] Id. 1.145.
[26] Cornford, 29.
[27] Id. 37.

Sicily in 433/2,[28] the alliance with Corcyra in 433,[29] can all be interpreted as testimonies to an active interest in establishing a strong commercial and even political position in the west. The Corcyrean envoys say plainly that their island lies on the coasting route to Italy and Sicily, and they even indulge in the somewhat exaggerated boast that their situation would allow the Athenians to block Peloponnesian ships trying to sail in either direction.[30] Diodorus preserves Ephorus' interpretation (which seems a considerable overstatement), that the Athenians made the alliance with Corcyra because they hoped, after defeating Sparta, to *conquer Sicily*.[31]

Little of this western policy can be connected to Pericles. Thucydides never mentions him during the debate over the alliance with Corcyra; one might deduce that he neither sponsored nor approved such an alliance. It must have been the commercial class in the Piraeus that wanted it. Again, it was Pericles' rival, Thucydides the son of Melesias, who went off to take part in the foundation of Thurii. Pericles' own advice, as given in Thucydides, was that the Athenians should not try to extend their empire;[32] therefore only after his death could "the policy of the Piraeus" come to the surface.[33] The campaigns at the mouth of the Gulf of Corinth, off Naupactus and in Acarnania in 429,[34] the capture of Minoa by Nicias in 427,[35] the expedition to Sicily under Laches in the same year, professedly[36] to help the Leontines against the Syracusans, but actually to estimate Athenian chances of conquering Sicily—all these reveal that Athens had a developing western policy that virtually erupted after Pericles was no longer there to hold it back. Yet at no time, so Cornford, did Thucydides see the connection between the Megarian Decrees and this policy. The drive toward the west reached its climax in 415, when the Athenians were misled into the great, disastrous Sicilian expedition. But by this time Thucydides had long ago formed his opinions about the origins of the war and had written much

---

[28] *IG* I[3] 53–54. The canonical view is that these alliances were first made in the 440s and renewed in 433/2: see R. Meiggs and D. Lewis, *A Selection of Greek Historical Inscriptions* (Oxford, 1969; [2] 1988), commentary to no. 63. If this is so, we have further evidence for an Athenian "western" policy in the 440s. This view of the alliances has been challenged by some scholars, who believe that they were made only once, in 433/2: see H. B. Mattingly, *Historia* 12 (1963) 272; J. D. Smart, *JHS* 92 (1972) 142–46; E. Ruschenbusch, *ZPE* 19 (1975) 225–32. A reply to Ruschenbusch is found in D. M. Lewis, *ZPE* 22 (1976) 223–25.

[29] Thuc. 1.44.

[30] Id. 1.36.2.

[31] Diodorus 12.54.

[32] Thuc. 2.65.7.

[33] Cornford, 51.

[34] Thuc. 2.80–92, 102–103.

[35] Thuc. 2.51. Thucydides calls Minoa an island just off Megara. For its probable location, "the comparatively long and comparatively high range of hills" SE of Megara, see Gomme *ad loc.* In antiquity, these hills will have been separated from the mainland by a marsh crossed by a causeway.

[36] προφάσει, Thuc. 3.86.4.

of his work. The Sicilian expedition had its roots in the policy already foreshadowed in the Megarian Decrees, but the historian assigned this war "to motives which, as he rightly insists, Pericles could not have entertained. Hence he never saw its connexion with the Megarian decrees—a link without which the origin of the Peloponnesian War was an insoluble enigma."[37]

But so far it is not clear why so intelligent a critic as Thucydides could not see the importance of the Megarian Decrees, in other words the motives of the commerical class and the real cause of the war. Cornford finds that the reason for this defect was Thucydides' inability to think critically about causes. In the passage where he tries most clearly to be precise about why the war broke out, 1.23.6, he says that he will record "the complaints and disagreements," τὰς αἰτίας... καὶ τὰς διαφοράς. And, indeed, what follows in the stories of the Athenian alliance with Corcyra and the rebellion of Potidaea[38] is complaints, grievances. But, in the same section of 1.23, Thucydides turns from the "complaints and disagreements" to say that "the truest πρόφασις, although the least discussed," was that the Athenians, by growing more and more powerful,[39] made the Spartans fearful and compelled them to go to war. Cornford first tests here the meaning "pretext" for πρόφασις, a meaning it can certainly have in other places. But, since no historian would speak of "the most genuine pretext" for any action, Cornford jettisons this meaning and concludes that "Thucydides, in fact, throughout his first book used the words αἰτία and πρόφασις interchangeably,"[40] and he approves the translation of Thomas Hobbes, "the truest *Quarrell*, though least in speech."

So the first book "is not an analysis of causes, but the story of a quarrel."[41] In this respect it marks no advance in historical thinking beyond Herodotus. Both historians concentrate on the motives and characters of men and of states. Modern historians, by contrast, "instinctively and incessantly seek for the operation of social conditions, of economic and topological factors, and of political forces and processes of evolution."[42] It is only human will and passions of individual men or cities that drive history in Thucydides' model. "The time for investigating causes, and making hypothetical constructions was not yet."

In Part II, "Thucydides Mythicus," Cornford the Ritualist strides forth. Thucydides' boast, that he has eliminated τὸ μυθῶδες from history, is strongly resisted. In fact, there is a drama in the narrative about Cleon. He is introduced with his uncompromising speech demanding the death penalty

[37] Cornford, 51.
[38] Thuc. 1.24–55; 56–65.
[39] Note the continued action implied in the present participle γιγνομένους.
[40] Cornford, 58–59.
[41] Id. 63.
[42] Id. 66.

for the hostages from Lesbos;[43] the second act is his victory at Pylos;[44] the end is his death at Amphipolis.[45] But in the part of the drama that takes place at Pylos, Thucydides constantly emphasizes the role of luck in the action. It was by chance that a storm came up and drove Demosthenes and his ships there. By further chance, the soldiers conceived the sudden notion of fortifying the place;[46] and there are other interventions of fortune. Yet we may suspect that Demosthenes, the Athenian who led his ships to Pylos, was acting in full knowledge of the strategic advantages of the place; nonetheless, the historian appears unwilling to recognize the element of choice in the events. Why does he ascribe them to luck, Fortune? Cornford proposes that Thucydides was still so firmly in the grip of mythic thinking that he could not rise above this psychological heritage of the Greeks. "Fortune" was not a mere literary device, a flourish of dramatic phrasing, but was *an actual force* in the universe, one that could suddenly strike men and women and influence, even determine, the events in history. Despite what sympathetic modern readers have said, Thucydides has no conception of laws that govern the universe. To a large degree human beings are still vulnerable to the unpredictable interventions of non-human agents. He can describe the symptoms of the sudden terrible plague that devastated Athens in 430, but he specifically leaves it to someone else to say, "be he physician or layman, from what it probably arose,"[47] and to identify whatever agencies had the power to produce such a transformation (μετάστασις).

Mythic narration also informs the story of the last days of Pausanias.[48] The character is insolent and through his arrogance courts his own destruction. He behaves like an oriental dynast, commits treachery, boasts of his power, wants to marry the daughter of the king of Persia, and is betrayed by a messenger at Sparta. The ephors use the ancient trick of hiding behind a screen (we may think of Gyges spying on the wife of Candaules in Herodotus) while Pausanias convicts himself with his own words. In the end of the mini-tragedy, Pausanias is starved to death. There was an original stratum of fact, but "[t]he mould is supplied by drama"; the story of Themistocles' final days is also "rationalised Saga-history, influenced by drama."[49]

In the dramas of Aeschylus we find forces such as Zeus, Nemesis, Ate, Hybris, Peitho; but these forces never appear on the stage—their influence

---

[43] Thuc. 3.37–40.

[44] Id. 4.27–41.

[45] Id. 5.6–11.

[46] Id. 4.4.1, ὁρμὴ ἐνέπεσε...ἐκτειχίσαι.

[47] Cornford, 100.

[48] Thuc. 1.128–35.

[49] Cornford, 137 n. 2.

determines the plot, which is in turn played out by the human agents.[50] Yet not even these are fully developed characters, with complex histories. Agamemnon "is simply Hybris typified in a legendary person....He has not a continuous history: nothing ever happened to him except the conquest of Troy and the sacrifice of Iphigenia."[51]

And in some way such as this Thucydides presents his main actors. Cleon and Pericles are characters without individuality: one is simply "the most violent of the citizens"; the other, "the most powerful man of his time in action and speech." Moreover, the unseen forces irresistibly control history. The Spartans, defeated at Sphacteria, were dismayed by "the many strokes of Fortune (τύχης) coming together within a short time against all calculation."[52] The Athenians, in turn, are misled after their victory here into refusing to make peace, because they had firm hopes that their strength would prevail.[53] Thus Peitho, persuasion, and Elpis, hope, take possession of the Athenians' minds even as they do to characters in Aeschylus. In the Melian Dialogue, in the next book, the Athenians warn the Melians not to trust in Hope, "that consolation in danger," which is "by nature a spendthrift."[54]

The working of such forces as Apate, Elpis, and even Eros[55] is combined in the Sicilian Expedition, to which Alcibiades—notorious for his physical beauty—inflames the Athenians. The people went down to bid farewell to the departing navy "with hope and lamentations."[56] But Hope again reveals itself as extravagant; Nemesis follows self-deception, and another tragic drama is played out. As Aeschylus said of the Persians, "Blossoming Pride has plucked the fruit of Ate."[57]

After the disaster in Sicily, Thucydides' material offered no further scope for dramatic history. Cornford dismisses the rest. "From this point onwards he has little interest in his task; the eighth Book is a mere continuation of the old chronological plan, unfinished, dull, and spiritless. The historian patiently continued his record; but he seems to grope his way like a man without a clue."[58] We might object that, if Thucydides had

[50] We must make an exception for Aeschylus (if he was the playwright), who introduces Kratos and Bia in *Prometheus Bound*.

[51] Cornford, 146.

[52] Thuc. 4.55.3.

[53] Id. 5.14.1: ἐλπίδα τῆς ῥώμης πιστήν.

[54] Id. 5.103.1. Cornford points out that the Athenians' words here are practically paraphrased from Sophocles, *Ant*. 616 ff.

[55] Note ἔρως ἐνέπεσε τοῖς πᾶσιν ὁμοίως ἐκπλεῦσαι, "All alike fell in love with the enterprise" (Crawley), Thuc. 6.24.3, to which cf. Aeschylus, *Ag*. 341 f., ἔρως δὲ μή τις πρότερον ἐμπίπτῃ στρατῷ πορθεῖν ἃ μὴ χρή, "may no mad impulse first come on the army to ravage what they should not." And when the soldiers at Pylos spontaneously decided to wall the place, ὁρμὴ ἐνέπεσε.

[56] Thuc. 6.30.2, μετ' ἐλπίδος...καὶ ὀλοφυρμῶν.

[57] Aeschylus, *Persae* 821 f.

[58] Cornford, 244.

carried his story down to the end, the collapse of Athens would have offered him a tragic climax at which his forces of Hybris and Ate must have been present.   In any case, Cornford now summarizes his perception of Thucydides Mythicus. He inevitably borrowed much of his structure from Aeschylean tragedy. "This unhistoric principle of design came in on the top of his first, chronological plan." But the divine forces in Thucydides are not gods: "he has reverted in a curious way to the *pre*-theological conception of the tragic fact, which existed long before Aeschylus."[59] The mythic, pre-theological conception of the universe was so widely embedded in Greek thought—indeed, it is almost pre-thought—that not even Thucydides could escape it.

III. A View of Cornford

Naturally, so original a book provoked discussion and was variously received by the academic establishment. An unsigned notice in *The Spectator*[60] predicted that "the substantial truth of his position will in the end, we think, appear not less remarkable than its novelty."   Gilbert Murray, too, reviewed the work favorably;[61] he was sympathetic to the search for hidden impulses underneath the apparently Apollonian Greek culture, as he was to show in his *Four* (later, *Five*) *Stages of Greek Religion*. A. Y. Tyrrell also pointed to the difference between Cornford and Theodor Gomperz,[62] who found in Thucydides the modern historian trying to describe human affairs as a process of nature "informed by the light of inexorable causality"; and he predicted that "a perusal of Mr. Cornford's able and brilliant *Thucydides Mythistoricus* will lead [the reader influenced by Gomperz] to modify his opinion considerably."[63]

The American scholar Paul Shorey gently wrote:

> That Thucydides's sense of the moral significance and the dramatic contrasts of history was quickened by reminiscences of Æschylean tragedy, is probable enough. But sober criticism will know how to make a light and tactful use of such suggestions without converting them into a rigid and systematic method of exegesis.[64]

Likewise, the *Saturday Review* found it difficult

> ...to conceive a deliberate conscious historian, with rivals and predecessors, writing of events in which he had been an actor, as subjugated to this extent by the stage....Moreover, allowing that Thucydides' way of regarding events had a tragic tinge—and the strong

[59] Id. 242.
[60] 98 (1907) 862 f.
[61] *The Albany* n.s. 1 (1907) 467–70.
[62] *Greek Thinkers* (English translation) I (London, 1901) 503, quoted by Cornford, 68.
[63] *The Academy* 72 (1907) 311.
[64] *The Dial* 43 (1907) 205.

side of Mr. Cornford's book is as an analysis of Thucydides' mind—we do not thereby grant that he read his mental habit so much into the external universe as to be unaware of plain facts.[65]

Even more severe was Britain's leading periodical in Greek scholarship, which declared that Cornford "has written a most brilliant essay, but cannot be said to have penetrated below the surface of his subject."[66] And M.O.B. Caspari (the later Max Cary) said briefly that the book was "a cogent exposition of Thucydides' shortcomings; but the explanation which it offers hardly seems likely to commend itself."[67]

Cornford had candidly said, "We cannot, of course, *prove* what we have here put forward; it is only the analysis of the impression actually produced on us by Thucydides' story. If the reader does not find that it interprets his own impression, we can do no more."[68] Nor can negative criticism ever be definitive. We are trying to penetrate the mind of a long-dead Athenian, many of whose assumptions must have been different from ours; and the work of the Ritualists, supplemented in our day by the radical studies of E. R. Dodds and Walter Burkert, has surely demolished the idea that the Greeks were wholly emancipated from irrational thought or from action that had its origin in ritual. Cornford's book, the first one on Thucydides in English, is also the most brilliantly written of all books on the historian in our language; yet not even it can quite persuade us that Elpis, Ate, Apate, and others were, for Thucydides, actual forces in the universe, older than the Olympian gods (or at least older than the Greeks' conception of the gods), and that these unseen powers intervene to bring about historical events in the absence of human choice. His mind may have been shaped in this way, but few indeed believe it. Why not? Part of the reluctance to embrace Cornford's daring hypothesis is probably explained by the fact that we—we modern academics, that is, and most people with an average education—do not think in this way. We are quite willing to say that something happened by chance, but by this we mean that two lines of activity crossed, unpredictably. Events happening thus are, for us, accidents. Our language breaks down and we can talk only in synonyms: it was luck, happenstance, even "fate": but we hardly mean by "fate" an effective "outside" force that actually invades our lives. We seem to lack the useful terminology of Aristotle, who could discuss events that took place in harmony with purpose and those that simply "happened." For the latter, he used the verb συμβαίνω, "come together," even "collide." The events thus happening were συμβεβηκότα, about which philosophic discussion was baffled: he

---

[65] *Saturday Review* 104 (1907) 580.
[66] *JHS* 27 (1907) 307 (unsigned).
[67] *YWCS* 2 (1907) 82.
[68] Cornford, 172.

states in the *Metaphysics*[69] that there is no θεωρία that can deal with these "accidents."

Are we, then, forcing our supposedly "rational" way of thought on Thucydides? Perhaps; but again, most of us are willing to consider him "one of us." "If one reckons up the years of the war, one will find that they were 27 years and a few extra days; and, for those who assert anything on the basis of oracles, this prophecy alone turned out in accordance with the facts."[70] Or, after the eclipse of August 27, 413 has persuaded most of the Athenians, who are in mortal danger outside Syracuse, that they must not retreat at this moment even to save their lives, Nicias also refuses to consider leaving until they have waited the "thrice nine days" prescribed by the soothsayers: "he was rather too inclined to divination and that kind of thing."[71] Sentences like this seem informed with cool scepticism and build a cumulative impression of objectivity, fair-mindedness (this tainted only with the historian's obvious dislike for Cleon),[72] and distance from prejudice even against his own state, which he had to leave for twenty years. Arguments can be, and have been, constructed to modify this impression in some details (a modern writer has called him "the least objective of historians"); but even as we discover here and there some prejudice or *Tendenz*, even as we learn to read his emotions (which, admittedly, the philological commentators of the last century hardly tried to do), we remain far from seeing him as a man in the grip of the kind of superstition, even non-verbalized superstition, that Cornford perceived.

It was a great merit of Cornford to draw on his connoisseurship of Greek literature and point out in the historian verbal reminiscences from Aeschylus, Pindar, and Sophocles. Moreover, there is probably a continuum of intensity of meaning, stretching from the Greeks to us, that attends words like "fate" and "hope." It is impossible to pinpoint the moment when such words no longer denoted real entities and became metaphors. But it has always seemed possible to believe that Thucydides could draw on his predecessors' language and could weave ἐλπίς and other such words into his narrative and speeches as a matter of graceful writing, as a way of using and honoring traditions of his literature, without implying that Hope is, like the Furies, "out there," waiting to ensnare and destroy us. We will also agree that he uses dramatic construction, that (for example) the death of Nicias, with its grave, moving epitaph—"of all Greeks, at least in my time, he deserved least of all to reach such a point of misfortune"[73]—

---

[69] 1026 b 3–4.

[70] Thuc. 5.26.3; note ξυμβάν, "turned out," "resulted": a meaning also found in Aristotle.

[71] Id. 7.50.4.

[72] Good discussion: A. G. Woodhead, *Mnemosyne* [4]13 (1960) 289–317; see further H. D. Westlake, *Individuals in Thucydides* (Cambridge, 1968) 60–85.

[73] Thuc. 7.86.5.

would fit perfectly into the final scene of a Greek tragedy.[74] Yet it is not shown, and Cornford did not try to show, that Thucydides' narrative style, with its dramatic tensions and sub-plots, was so indebted to pre-theological motifs as to distort the record of events. Errors and omissions there are, but no unconscious deformation of the truth caused by the historian's being in the grip of "tragic history."[75] A rather obvious nest of mistakes, in my opinion, is Thucydides' acceptance of the letters supposedly sent between Pausanias of Sparta and the king of Persia;[76] but here I think Thucydides was deceived by false documents either shown or summarized to him, rather than by his wish to construct a drama.[77]

The discussion remains closer to reality in Cornford's part I, "Thucydides Historicus." It seems plausible that Thucydides might well have laid more stress on the Megarian Decrees as an important cause of the war—if he had wanted to. We must, however, allow him his judgment about the relative importance of this or that cause. Cornford rather triumphantly proclaims that he has seen what Thucydides did not; yet it is to be doubted whether the decrees against Megara would, in the absence of a more threatening general atmosphere, have provoked a major war between the two systems of city-states. As to his assertion that the anti-Megarian policy was forced on Pericles by the commercial group in the Piraeus, and that Thucydides did not perceive the real significance of this because he concentrated on the large strategic lines of Pericles' planning, all this rests on conjecture. Cornford himself returned to the matter in 1921. He still thought that there was a "whole framework of preconception which the author cannot help bringing with him, because it is the very atmosphere of his mind—in a word, his philosophy of life."[78] But he recognized that "[f]ourteen years ago, writing under the impression of the South African [i.e., the Boer] war, I may have overstressed the financial aspect of imperialism." So perhaps the commercial policy of the Piraeus was less critical than his book maintains. The unfriendly verdict of the reviewer in the *Journal of Hellenic Studies* cannot easily be dismissed: that "it is also difficult to believe that Thucydides was so dense, or so little in the confidence of politicians of his time, as Mr. Cornford's theory presupposes."

---

[74] "Thucydides in his history does undoubtedly dramatize in a sense," J. P. Postgate, *CQ* 1 (1907) 317, in a long discussion of Cornford.

[75] F. W. Walbank, in his admirable paper "History and Tragedy," *Historia* 9 (1960) 216–34, points out (p. 231) that Greeks were especially sensitive to the effects of language. The reading aloud of a vivid historical narrative could lead to the partial confusion between tragedy and history.

[76] Thuc. 1.128 f.

[77] Best discussion: C. W. Fornara, *Historia* 15 (1966) 258–71.

[78] "The Unconscious Element in Literature and Philosophy," a paper read in 1921 and published in his *The Unwritten Philosophy and Other Essays* (Cambridge, 1950) 1–13 (quotations from 1–3). I thank Thomas W. Africa for drawing my attention to this essay.

More productive is Cornford's conclusion that Thucydides had no real conception of cause. He approaches this subject by way of Polybius, who, instructed by Thucydides and perhaps by the ambiguity of his predecessor's language, almost pedantically explains how he proposes to use certain words concerning the causes of war: ἀρχή for the first overt act of hostilities; αἰτία for a decision or resolution that leads to war, and πρόφασις for pretext, alleged (but not actual) cause. Thucydides did not bequeath us such a carefully defined vocabulary.

First we must disagree with Cornford when he says that "There is in Thucydidean Greek no word which even approaches the meaning and associations of the English 'cause' with its correlative 'effect.'"[79] As G. M. Kirkwood pointed out, he overlooked the word αἴτιον, which supplies just the desired meaning at 3.89.5 (an earthquake was the cause of a tidal wave) and elsewhere.[80] Moreover, at 2.48.3 he says he will leave it to others to identify the αἰτίας (here surely "causes") that could bring about a disease like the plague that attacked Athens in 430. Yet Cornford does raise an important point in asserting that Thucydides uses αἰτία and πρόφασις interchangeably in his first book (and, by implication, elsewhere). This is not, I think, true, but the question did lead to some valuable studies of the two words. C. N. Cochrane, influenced by E. M. Walker, pointed out that medical writers use πρόφασις to mean "exciting cause," that is, a stimulus of some kind that brings about the onset of, but still is not the cause of, a disease; if the patient were not already prone to disease, the stimulus would be harmless.[81] He went on to imply that this is the regular meaning in Thucydides. Kirkwood showed, however, that this usage is universal neither in the doctors nor in Thucydides;[82] he and other scholars (especially Pearson) have established the meaning "an explanation that one can put forth" (whether sincerely or not: "pretext" is often possible).[83] αἰτία is a little

---

[79] Cornford, 59.

[80] *AJP* 73 (1952) 37–61; see 1.11.1, 2.65.8, 3.82.8, 3.93.2, 4.26.5, 8.9.3.

[81] C. N. Cochrane, *Thucydides and the Science of History* (London, 1929); for his debt to Walker's lectures on this point, see 17 n. 1. The point was well developed by K. Deichgräber, *Quellen und Studien zur Gesch. der Naturwiss. und der Medizin* 3 (1933) 209–25, esp. 212–17, who translates πρόφασις as "aüßere Ursache."

[82] It is probably to be recognized in Thuc. 2.49.1: apparently healthy people could come down with the plague suddenly, ἀπ' οὐδεμίας προφάσεως, "from no evident inciting cause"; but even in this part of the work, where the historian describes the plague in medical terminology, the translation "without any explanation that one can put forth" could be right. For a more extensive survey of the doctors' usage, see S. Schuller, *RevBelge* 34 (1956) 971–84; he finds it "very uncertain" whether Thucydides knew writings of the Hippocratic school, but his description of the plague makes such knowledge seem highly probable.

[83] Liddell-Scott-Jones derive πρόφασις without hesitation from προφαίνω, but the *Et. Mag.* states: πρόφασις ἀπὸ τοῦ φημί. This latter seems possible in view of προφασίζομαι, "allege, plea." R. Browning, *Philologus* 102 (1958) 60–74, points to some other words in -φασις with two etymologies, one from -φημί and one from -φαίνω (e.g. ἀπόφασις, ἔκφασις, παράφασις); these are formed from the reduced grade of the verb

easier and normally means "grievance, accusation, complaint," a usage that
can shade into "grievance that causes one to act in a certain way," thus
"cause."[84] So in the sentence where Thucydides first summarizes his view
of the cause(s) of the war, 1.23.5–6, Cornford is right to this extent, that
when Thucydides says τὰς αἰτίας προὔγραψα πρῶτον καὶ τὰς
διαφοράς, he means "I have first set forth their grievances and quarrels,"[85]
and that his attention here is on quarrels, not on deeper "causes." But in the
next sentence is the famous phrase τὴν ἀληθεστάτην πρόφασιν, clearly
contrasted with the "grievances and quarrels." Cornford translates this "the
most genuine *pretext*"[86] and then rebukes Thucydides: "We could hardly
have better evidence that Thucydides draws no clear distinction between an
αἰτία and a πρόφασις. No respectable writer who had such a distinction in
his thoughts could speak of a 'most genuine *pretext* (πρόφασις),'" etc. But
here the modern studies of πρόφασις have rendered Cornford's criticism
harmless. Thucydides must here mean "the truest explanation"—but
explanation of what?

The view in fashion today seems to be that Thucydides is giving the
Spartans' motivation for opening the war, that is, they had become afraid of
the Athenians' power because the latter were becoming ever more dominant.
If this is right, we are still near Cornford's theory, according to which
Thucydides was so little a "modern scientific" historian that he could not
think accurately about causes, rather only about motives, complaints, and
emotions. In favor of this view is a point raised by Kurt von Fritz, that
when the phrase ἀληθεστάτη πρόφασις recurs, at 6.6.1, Thucydides is
saying, "the Athenians' most genuine motivation ["das eigentliche, das
wahre Motiv"] was to conquer all Sicily."[87] We are willing to agree that
this was their real motivation, or at least that Thucydides may have thought
so. And yet the basic meaning argued out by Pearson, "explanation that one
can put forth," seems equally possible in both places. At 1.23.6,

---

stem and therefore have short α. H. R. Rawlings III, *Hermes* Einzelschr. 33 (1975),
conjectures that πρόφασις in Thucydides has such a double etymology but that the one
from φημί is the older; thus the meaning would waver between "subjective" and "objective"
explanations (what one puts forth to explain one's own action and the actions of others
respectively). For further discussions of these terms, see Gomme on 1.23.6; L. Lohmann,
Lexis 3 (1952) 5–50, esp. 20–28; Kirkwood (*supra*, n. 80) *loc. cit.*; L. Pearson, *TAPA* 83
(1952) 205–23 and 103 (1972) 381–94; K. Weidauer, *Thuk. und die Hippokratischen
Schriften* (Heidelberg, 1954) 8–20; R. Sealey, *CR* n.s. 7 (1957) 1–12; A. Andrewes, *ibid.*
9 (1959) 223–39; C. Schäublin, *Museum Helveticum* 28 (1971) 133–44; de Ste. Croix
(*supra*, n. 8) 52–58; F. Robert, *RÉG* 89 (1976) 317–42; A. Heubeck, *Glotta* 58 (1980)
222–36; M. Heath, *LCM* 11 (1986) 103–106; J. Richardson in *"Owls to Athens":
Essays...for Sir Kenneth Dover* (Oxford, 1990) 155–61.

[84] Schuller (*supra*, n. 82) arranges all instances of αἰτία and πρόφασις into their
various meanings in Thucydides, but there remains room for differing interpretations.

[85] "Grounds of complaint and points of difference," a typically precise rendering by
Crawley.

[86] Cornford, 58.

[87] *Die Griechische Geschichtsschreibung* I (Berlin, 1967) 625.

Thucydides seems to be saying, "The grievances and quarrels were those I have mentioned; but the truest explanation, though it was least discussed openly, was, I think, that the Athenians were becoming ever more powerful and frightening the Spartans and thus compelled them to go to war." That is, this πρόφασις is one that is being put forth—by the historian: as Raphael Sealey has well observed, it is his own explanation for what happened.[88] So too at 6.6.1, we may translate, "The Athenians offered the fair-sounding purpose of helping their relations and their new allies, but the truest explanation for their action is that they wanted to dominate all Sicily": again, the explanation offered by Thucydides. This explanation naturally includes the "motivation" of the Spartans and Athenians respectively, but there is a difference of approach, of emphasis, between stating a motivation of other people and offering one's own historical explanation.

Whether one accepts this translation or not, it is rather clear that Thucydides is not using πρόφασις as a mere synonym for αἰτία, and that Cornford is not on the most solid ground in asserting that he does.[89] The historian seems to work with two levels of causes. One, as Cornford says, is the level of publicly declared grievances and quarrels; in this respect he follows Herodotus. The other level, which Cornford does not wish to recognize, is that of broad, underlying, long-term causation. The Corcyrean and Potidaean affairs would not have brought about a general war in, say, 450. Thucydides perceived this and wrote the Pentecontaetia[90] to make the broader causes clear. I am willing to believe that he came late, with the perspective of years, to this wider view, and that he was stimulated to write this excursus partly by the publication of Hellanicus' *Atthis* at some time near 400; one can also imagine that conversation among interested people showed him that the true causes of the long war, as well as its essential nature as one single conflict,[91] were not clear to all. But whenever and however he came to see the long-range causes, in the end he did see them.

---

[88] Sealey (*supra*, n. 83) 9. So also Deichgräber (*supra*, n. 83) 220, "Das ist Thukydides' eigene Deutung; in einprägsamer, sorgfältig abgewogener Formulierung legt er hier seine Auffassung dar." Rawlings (*supra*, n. 83) 70 writes "*Prophasis* in this passage…represents Thucydides' own view." I venture, though, to take a different view of Thucydides' word ἀναγκάσαι in 1.23.6 from that of Sealey. In my opinion the Athenians did not (as Sealey holds) intentionally compel the Spartans to fight; the Spartans did, however, finally feel compelled to do so, afraid of further Athenian aggrandizement. So too the British government guaranteed the western frontier of Poland in 1939; the ἀληθεστάτη πρόφασις was that they feared the constantly growing power of Germany and felt compelled to take a stand. But it is not at all clear that Hitler set out to *compel* the *British* to make war: if so, his drive into eastern Europe was a strange way of doing it, and up to a point the British were content to see him going in that direction.

[89] Note the statement of the Mytilenian envoys at Olympia, "we rebelled from Athens τοιαύτας ἔχοντες προφάσεις καὶ αἰτίας," 3.13.1: "explanations and grievances"?

[90] 1.89–118.

[91] A theory that he vigorously sponsors at 5.26.

Cornford has the merit of having provoked discussion about causes in such a way that earlier commentators scarcely approached, probably because as a Ritualist he was determined to probe for the unseen impulses behind events.

Those who publish about Thucydides would like to be seen as having something new to say. The writers sometimes wish to distance themselves from supposed earlier conceptions of Thucydides. They will not, like their imperceptive predecessors, treat him as "a mere quarry for facts" or believe that he sought only a safe reliability in his faithful chronicle. Where the older generation has overlooked emotions, even passions, in Thucydides, they will discover them and redeem the historian as a man of sensitivity. But if any serious students of Thucydides have really held those narrow, old-fashioned views, they have at least had the good taste not to publish them. Even Cochrane, the title of whose book seems to tempt people to see him as an apostle of obsolete positivism, set out to show the critical nature of Thucydides' analysis, not to empty him of all human reactions.[92] Surely we have known for some time that Thucydides was deeply aware of the tragic nature of the great war, saddened by the lamentable events within it, and sensitive to the possibility of the sudden collapse of moral standards. His vocabulary and structure make it certain that tragic drama was immanent in his interpretation of history.

All this does not mean that Cornford's questions should not be asked. If his book were to disappear, we should have lost something. It has been said that the important thing in scholarship is to raise important issues, not necessarily to be "right." If so, we are justified in looking back to Cornford, and to his mentor Jane Harrison, if we would see the issue of Thucydides' relationship to Greek tragedy confronted in challenging and even inspiring form.

University of California, Los Angeles

---

[92] "To suppose that, in his observations either on the fate of Nicias or on that of the unselfish victims of the plague, Thucydides is contemptuous and cynical is to betray complete failure to understand his mind," Cochrane (*supra*, n. 81) 136.

5

Gilbert Murray: Four (Five) Stages of Greek Religion

ROBERT L. FOWLER

Of the major works of the Cambridge Ritualists,[1] Murray's *Five Stages of Greek Religion*[2] is probably the least cited today. This is a paradox, for in its day it was probably the most consulted, certainly by students and non-experts in the field of Greek religion. The eclipse of the book is of a piece with the rest of Murray's scholarship; in spite of his great fame when alive, he might never have written so far as most scholars are concerned today. The reason, broadly speaking, is the complete obsolescence of the Victorian world-view, or, more precisely, the world-view of a Gladstonian Liberal,

[1] The Urbana conference found it very difficult to identify any proposition held by all four of those normally considered as members of the group: Jane Harrison, F. M. Cornford, A. B. Cook, and Gilbert Murray (James Frazer is to be excluded on any reckoning; his work inspired the others but he used anthropology in a quite different way, and distanced himself from the views of the younger scholars). In the end it was concluded that the group was held together more by a powerful attraction to Jane Harrison and her ideas than by a common creed. It also proved difficult to state what exactly the Cambridge school had accomplished. My own judgement is that if accomplishment is measured in terms of facts established, very little; if it is measured in terms of impulse and stimulus imparted, a great deal, even if the response was delayed by a generation or so. The current revival of interest in ritual is bound to produce a wider consultation of Harrison's work in particular. Murray's own verdict is worth quoting in his obituary of F. M. Cornford (*PBA* 29 [1943] 421-432; see p. 422): "[Jane Harrison] showed once and for all how the base of any sound study of Greek religion must no longer be the fictional and largely artificial figures of the Olympian gods, but the actual rites in which the religion expressed itself and, so far as we can divine them, the implications of those rites." This statement need be qualified only to the extent that Harrison was not the first to do so; she was the first in Britain. (I am not forgetting Robertson Smith, Frazer, and other forerunners; but the stress in the statement lies on "once and for all.")

[2] Originally *Four Stages of Greek Religion* (New York/London, 1912); the revised edition with an additional chapter on the philosophical schools was called *Five Stages of Greek Religion* (Oxford, 1925; London, 1935; Boston, 1951; New York, 1955; London, 1977; New York, 1978). Citations in this paper are from the 1925 edition, abbreviated *Five Stages*. An early version of "The Failure of Nerve" (ch. 4 in *Five Stages*) had appeared in the *Hibbert Journal* for 1910, and of "The Last Protest" (ch. 5) in *The English Review* for 1908. The translation of Sallustius in the appendix was made in 1907. Chapters 1 and 2 were then added to make up the original four stages, which were delivered as lectures at Columbia University in April 1912.

which directly inspired all of Murray's work. The idea of progress towards a perfect humanity is nothing more than a historical curiosity now, and the idea of a fearlessly rational Greek society marching calmly forward to the final victory over barbarism seems merely quaint. Of course, influence can take other forms than frequency of citation; Murray's impact as a teacher, both of classical pupils and of the general public, must still be felt in a thousand undetected ways. I have also made the suggestion that J.D. Denniston's surprising judgement that Murray was responsible for the increasing importance of literary criticism in the classics has proven historically correct.[3] The verdict on *Five Stages*, however, must be negative, and in this paper the focus of attention will be placed elsewhere, on the relationship of this book and its author to the Cambridge school. For whatever may be said about the book's afterlife, the stature of its author while alive is undeniable; he played an important role in a major intellectual movement of lasting interest to historians of ideas, even if his role was one of assimilation and communication rather than original creation.[4]

In religion Murray was a rationalist and an agnostic. He disapproved strongly of dogmatism and superstition, both things which Christianity, no matter how liberalized it became in the later nineteenth century, could not claim to have eliminated, if one includes under the heading of "superstition" (as Murray did) such items of faith as the virgin birth and the existence of

---

[3] In my address to the Classical Association of the Middle West and South, March 31, 1989. Denniston's opinion was expressed in a letter to Murray congratulating him on being awarded the Order of Merit in January 1941, quoted by Duncan Wilson, *Gilbert Murray OM* (Oxford, 1987; hereafter "Wilson") 329: "I am sure that we are at the beginning of a new era of classical scholarship, in which people will lose themselves neither in linguistic pedantry nor in pseudo-philosophy and Quellengeschichte, but will look at the great works of Greek literature as Bradley looked at Hamlet and Othello. And I am sure that, when the reckoning is cast up, you will be recognised as the pioneer in this new and better Greek scholarship." I had been accustomed to thinking of Murray's significance exclusively in terms of his example as a humanitarian rather than his lasting scholarly contributions; but on reflection, it seems true that literary criticism of the classics was something new among professional classicists in Murray's day, and that his writings did much to turn the younger generation in this direction (one thinks particularly on C.M. Bowra and Gilbert Highet). J.A.K. Thomson reports in "The Present and Future of Classical Scholarship," *Essays in Honour of Gilbert Murray* (London, 1936) 279-291 (see p. 280): "...by some of his older contemporaries [Sir Richard Claverhouse] Jebb [1841-1905, Regius Professor of Greek in the University of Cambridge and famous editor and commentator of Sophocles] was criticized for asking too often not merely what Sophocles said, but what was the intellectual process which led him to say it."

[4] So much is bluntly stated by the anonymous reviewer of *Four Stages* in *JHS* 33 (1913) 125. S. Peacock, *Jane Ellen Harrison: The Mask and the Self* (New Haven, 1988) 2, writes that although Murray's and Cornford's works "have traditionally been cited as the important work of the Ritualists, Jane Harrison actually stood at the center of the circle." This may be true of scholars in different areas, but it does not correspond to my experience as a classicist and student of Greek religion; there has never been any doubt of Jane Harrison's role.

Heaven and Hell.[5] He did not wish to deny the possibility of religion, of course; that would be to fall into the same error of dogmatism of which he accused his opponents. In any event he had no doubt about the existence of another world, or at least of many unknown factors in human life; he only insisted on an enlightened attitude towards them.

More important than the rightness of one's beliefs was the willingness to make room for others' beliefs. The clearest statement of Murray's own creed is found at the end of *Five Stages*, and is worth quoting at length:

> There is no royal road in these matters. I confess it seems strange to me as I write here, to reflect that at this moment many of my friends and most of my fellow creatures are, as far as one can judge, quite confident that they possess supernatural knowledge. As a rule, each individual belongs to some body which has received in writing the results of a divine revelation. I cannot share in any such feeling. The Uncharted surrounds us on every side and we must needs have some relation towards it, a relation which will depend on the general character of a man's mind and the bias of his whole character. As far as knowledge and conscious reason will go, we should follow resolutely their austere guidance. When they cease, as cease they must, we must use as best we can those fainter powers of apprehension and surmise and sensitiveness by which, after all, most high truth has been reached as well as most high art and poetry: careful always really to seek for truth and not for our own emotional satisfaction, careful not to neglect the real needs of men and women through basing our life on dreams; and remembering above all to walk gently in a world where the lights are dim and the very stars wander.[6]

---

[5] See *Stoic, Christian and Humanist* (London, 1940; 1943; Boston, 1950; rev. ed. London, 1950; Freeport, New York, 1969. Hereafter referred to by title and cited from the 1969 edition) *passim*. On p. 183 Murray remarks: "As for the belief in Hell and Heaven, it is not only not necessary as a basis for morality: it absolutely undermines morality." Unfortunately I have lost the source of a quotation in which Murray says that linking morality to things like the virgin birth is "not only nonsense but pernicious nonsense" because of the evils of dogmatism.

[6] *Five Stages* 205 f. See also *Religio Grammatici. The Religion of a Man of Letters*, Presidential Address to the Classical Association January 8, 1918 (London, 1918) = *Essays and Addresses* (London, 1921) 11-30; *Stoic, Christian and Humanist* 156 f.: "A man who never thinks at all about the Unknown but is confident that outside his approved range of knowledge there is nothing, or at least nothing that matters, is clearly without Religion; I conclude therefore that he is equally without religion whether his approved range is the *Encyclopædia Britannica* or the dogmas of some infallible Church. To be cock-sure is to be without religion. The essence of religion is the consciousness of a vast unknown. Call it Faith or call it Doubt: they are two sides of the same medal"; and *ibid.* 185 f.: "*Deus est mortali iuvare mortalem*: [Pliny, NH 2.7.18] 'God is the helping of man by man'; or should we rather translate it: 'The spirit of mutual help among all mortal beings is the true object of worship?' That, says Comte, is what God is. [This chapter of *Stoic, Christian and Humanist* was originally the Auguste Comte Memorial Lecture of 1939 entitled "What is Permanent in Positivism."] Not an external all-powerful Person, who will show favour to those who obey Him and terrible wrath to those who offend Him; not even

The passage is an eloquent expression of the agnostic's faith and its humanitarian implications. There is a Socratic insistence on the willingness to confess ignorance. The phrase "the real needs of men and women" also reflects the Liberal's concern with problems of political and social organization. The eradication of oppression, unfairness, and prejudice in society were central parts of the Liberal's program for progress. Murray thought that these ideals had been apprehended only once before in human history, in Periclean Athens; but by good fortune they had come to light again in nineteenth-century England. For him, Hellenism and Liberalism were identical causes. It was his job as a Greek scholar not only to know Greek but to further the progress of civilization. It was natural, then, that a great deal of his work was directed towards showing up the strong link, as he saw it, between ancient and modern ideals, and that he saw no incompatability between his two careers as a professor of Greek and an active worker for world peace in the League of Nations.

This constant talk of progress has inevitable moralistic overtones: the worth of anything must be judged according to how it improves individuals and societies. Neither literature nor religion will be excluded from this criterion. In this respect Murray was very sympathetic to the general moral teaching of Christianity; he also liked Stoics more than Epicureans. St. Paul found his constant admiration; the Puritanical side of Paul's teaching (I mean the importance of conscience) was precisely what he found congenial. Murray was happy enough on many occasions to use "Christian" and "Hellenic" as equivalent terms.[7] He did not therefore belong to that anti-Christian school which emphasizes the differences between Greek religion and Christianity in order to prove the former's superiority. In *Five Stages* Murray argued that one of the Olympian religion's higher aspects was its implicit tendency to monotheism; failure to realize this tendency was part of

---

an imaginary Infinitely Good Man whom we must serve out of love for His goodness; but a perfectly real spirit of goodness, which runs in some degree through all life, but finds its highest expression in the best men, the spirit that we can only call *Humanitas*, Humanity."

[7] For example, "Christian or Hellenic civilization" and "Hellenic or Christian standards and moral values" in a letter to Arnold Toynbee quoted by Francis West, *Gilbert Murray: A Life* (London, Canberra and New York, 1984; hereafter "West") p. 235; "[the Greeks] were the one nation that grasped and assimilated the teaching of Christ" in his Glasgow inaugural of 1889, quoted by Wilson p. 44 (although Wilson is right to draw attention to the ironical tone); *Stoic, Christian and Humanist* p. 12: the "Christian spirit" means "the Christian spirit as humanized and liberalized in the nineteenth century, a spirit totally different from that of the hell-ridden persecuting Christianities of various past ages. I would just as soon call it 'a humane spirit' or 'a Liberal spirit'" (the next quotation shows he could easily have added "or a Hellenic spirit"); *Hellenism and the Modern World* (London 1953) 39 f. on Pericles' Funeral Speech: "...but the striking point is the kind of ideal that is aimed at, an ideal not quite like that of any other civilization between that time and our own nineteenth or twentieth century. It was a Liberal civilization: free, tolerant, and unprejudiced; highly cultured; and out of its abundance generous and helpful to the rest of mankind"; ibid. 11 (i.e. the opening words) on what to call European civilization: "We sometimes say 'Christian', sometimes 'Hellenic'."

the reason for its collapse.[8] As regards the influence of Nietzsche, I am unable to find any reference to him in Murray's writings before 1951, by which time the events of the Second World War might be thought to have put a different complexion on things; all the same, the tone of disgust is in my view perfectly predictable from everything he had previously written.[9]

The main question to be asked about Murray and the Cambridge school, therefore, is why he was part of it at all. Their typical fascination with the primitive, even their exaltation of it, one would have thought would repel rather than attract him. A vegetarian who was sickened by the thought of bloodshed—a man who claims to have first taken offense at Christianity because of the implicit cruelty in the miracle of the Gadarene swine[10]— ought to have been horrified by the monstrous savagery of Greek rituals, preferring to forget that they were part of Greek society, as many Victorians forgot about slavery and homosexuality.

There are several answers to this question, none of them far to seek. In the first place Murray was not a member of that classicising and rationalistic school, originating in the eighteenth century and still finding many adherents in the late nineteenth, which saw in Greek art and literature timeless standards of beauty and good taste, in Greek philosophy the founding charter of rationalism, in Greek politics a model of good order in society, and in Greek religion, at least in its symbolic significance, an instance of sane, unsensational, but sublime thinking about the divine. This was the school that found much to admire in the idea of "Olympian calm." Murray rejected these preconceptions together with the rival views of

[8] Pp. 92 f.: "It is curious how near to monotheism, and to monotheism of a very profound and impersonal type, the real religion of Greece came in the sixth and fifth centuries. Many of the philosophers...asserted it clearly or assumed it without hesitation. Aeschylus, Euripides, Plato, in their deeper moments point the same road...But unfortunately too many hard-caked superstitions, too many tender and sensitive associations, were linked with particular figures in the pantheon or particular rites which had brought the worshippers religious peace. If there had been some Hebrew prophets about, and a tyrant or two, progressive and bloody-minded, to agree with them, polytheism might perhaps actually have been stamped out in Greece at one time. But Greek thought, always sincere and daring, was seldom brutal, seldom ruthless or cruel. The thinkers of the great period felt their own way gently to the Holy of Holies, and did not try to compel others to take the same way. Greek theology, whether popular or philosophical, seldom denied any god, seldom forbade any worship. What it tried to do was to identify every new god with some aspect of the old ones, and the result was naturally confusion. Apart from the Epicurean school, which though powerful was always unpopular, the religious thought of later antiquity for the most part took refuge in a sort of apotheosis of good taste, in which the great care was not to hurt other people's feelings, or else it collapsed into helpless mysticism."

[9] *Advance Under Fire*. The Ramsay Muir Memorial Lecture delivered at the Debating Hall, Oxford Union Society, July 22nd, 1951 (London, 1951) 11, 13 f. The speech is a general defence of Liberalism. Nietzsche's worship of strength is denounced together with its political consequences. I do not claim to have read every word of Murray's (his writings in the press were legion), and there may be earlier references which have escaped my notice.

[10] See *Stoic, Christian and Humanist* 7 (i.e. the first page).

the Romantics. Already in the preface of *A History of Ancient Greek Literature* (1897) he rails against misunderstanding the Greeks either as "serene and classical" abstracts or as "fleshly" aesthetes. The new perspective was one of realism, the product of the historicising interpretation fostered particularly in Germany since the days of Friedrich August Wolf. In Murray's time the champion of the historicising school, and a sworn enemy of both Classicism and Romanticism, was Ulrich von Wilamowitz-Moellendorff (1848-1931), whose works transported the young Murray into ecstasies of intellectual excitement.[11] For Murray, as for Wilamowitz, Greek civilization did not happen in an historical vacuum; it is precisely because it did not that one can appreciate its value. The classicising attitude, on the other hand, holds that the value of Greek literature or art is timeless, and can be understood without reference to historical context; the same qualities are exhibited by the classic art of all ages, and must therefore be imbued somehow from without, by contact with the eternal world, presumably that of God, through inspiration or intuition. The advance of historical sensibility by Murray's day predisposed him to finding such an attitude unhistorical and therefore simply untrue. The whole point of the Greek achievement was that they did what they did in the midst of countervailing tendencies. The contrast sets it off. The problems facing Greek artists and writers were those facing every generation, Murray's own not excluded. It is in the nature of humanity that it must always struggle to achieve progress. The thing is not given automatically.[12] Murray's keen awareness of this process in his own society made him think that it was the central problem in ancient society too. Truly "classical" art of lasting value is only understandable as the transcendence of a particular place in time; it cannot achieve such a status without having first struggled with its very real, everyday context, and, even if the end result of such transcendence displays similar qualities from age to age, we cannot understand it in isolation from these ages. The lesson of the necessity of the struggle must be learned if nothing else.

Murray was interested in the primitive aspects of Greek society because he wanted to show where the civilized aspects came from.[13] The main reason he wrote *Five Stages* was to counteract Jane Harrison's exaltation of the chthonic spirits by a vigorous defence of the Olympian deities, who Harrison thought displayed little true religious feeling, but Murray thought

[11] On Wilamowitz and Murray see R.L. Fowler, "Gilbert Murray" and "Ulrich von Wilamowitz-Moellendorff," in *Classical Scholarship: A Biographical Encyclopedia*, edited by Ward W. Briggs, Jr., W.M. Calder III (New York/London, 1990) 321–34; 489–522.

[12] Cf. Frank M. Turner, *The Greek Heritage in Victorian Britain* (New Haven, 1981) 76. (Hereafter "Turner.")

[13] Dr. Renate Schlesier makes the interesting suggestion that Murray's absorption with the contrast of civilized and barbaric may have started as far back as his boyhood in Australia.

belonged to the very best things that Hellenism had to offer. Thus after an opening chapter ("Saturnia Regna") in which the chthonic world of *mana*, *tabu*, and the Year-Daimon—the world of *"Urdummheit,"* "primeval stupidity"—is depicted (though with more sympathy and imagination than this pejorative label would suggest), Murray goes on to argue that the Olympic gods represented a religious "reformation" (p. 80) in the cause of enlightenment or, as he would call it, true Hellenism. The disaster of the Peloponnesian War and the collapse of the polis eventually ensured the demise of Olympianism, but in the fourth century the philosophers tried in various ways to keep the candle burning (the third stage). In the end, however, larger political forces prevented the happy conclusion of these efforts. In the uncertain atmosphere of the Age of the Successors, there occurred a "failure of nerve"[14] in which individuals turned to the mystery religions for salvation (the fourth stage). In accordance with views prevalent at the time, the whole of the Hellenistic period is dismissed as decadent; the view that the Hellenistic mystery religions in particular were unhellenic, and that Christianity was merely a sophisticated form of these, owes much to Richard Reitzenstein, as Murray explicitly acknowledges.[15] The final "stage" in Murray's book is provided by the resurgence of the better kind of paganism in the age of Julian the Apostate; an appendix provides a translation of Sallustius' "On the Gods and the World."[16]

The second "stage" was the pinnacle of Greek civilization, and forms the heart of the book. The character of Murray's ideas will be evident from a summary. The reformation took place in the sixth century, and coincided with the "cardinal moment...when the clear outline that we call Classical Greece begins to take shape out of the mist" (59). In politics, the Greek sense of Greekhood, of Hellenism as a cultural identifier, became fully explicit at this time; it had begun long ago when the emigrant Ionians first encountered Hittites and Semites, but came to maturity during the "first sketch" of the Athenian empire under Peisistratus, in whose time Athens assumed the "leadership of the Ionian race" (63). In literature, the cardinal moment came with Homer, whom Murray dated to the sixth century, again under Peisistratus. In religion, the Homeric gods proved decisive, "radiating" from the Panathenaea (80). In Homer's world the more savage elements of the old religion were eradicated (77). The "royal buccaneers" who were the Olympians in the Heroic Age no longer had much appeal for the bards of "cultivated and scientific Ionia," who saw that they were "meant

---

[14] The phrase was first suggested to Murray in conversation by J. B. Bury (*Five Stages* 8). It is used again as the heading of a sub-section in *Stoic, Christian and Humanist* 64-69.

[15] *Five Stages* 9 where he also acknowledges W. Bousset and P. Wendland. Other authorities cited in the book include F. Cumont, A. Dieterich, W. Warde Fowler, Otto Gruppe, O. Kern, A. Mommsen, M. P. Nilsson, O. Seeck, W. Robertson Smith, and of course Jane Harrison, A. B. Cook, F. M. Cornford, James Frazer, and Andrew Lang.

[16] The five stages, it will be seen, do not go together to make a complete history of Greek religion: *Five Stages*, not *The Five Stages*.

more for romance than for the guiding of life"; but being unable to eliminate them completely owing to popular resistance ("the power of romance is great"), the bards idealized them. What was "intolerable" was "expurgated" or "mysticized and explained away" (79).[17] In Homer's theology: "The world was conceived as neither quite without external governance, nor as merely subject to the incursions of mana snakes and bulls and thunder-stones and monsters, but as governed by an organized body of personal and reasoning rulers, wise and bountiful fathers, like man in mind and shape, only unspeakably higher" (82).[18]

The Olympian movement was moral, intellectual, and political. Under the first heading, it swept away "or at least covered with a decent veil" (83) the basic rites of the chthonic religion, leaving "only a few reverent and mystic rituals, a few licensed outbursts of riotous indecency in comedy and

[17] Cf. *The Rise of the Greek Epic*[4] (Oxford, 1907; 1934, repr. 1960) ch. 5: "The Iliad as a Traditional Book I. The Expurgations: The Homeric Spirit." Chapter I of this book is called "Greece and the Progress of Man." The first words are "These lectures [at Harvard in 1907] form the first part of an attempt to study the growth of Greek poetry from a particular point of view, namely, as the embodiment of a force making for the progress of the human race. By progress I understand some gradual ennobling and enriching of the content of life." If Murray had a specific second part of the attempt in mind, I suppose it was *Five Stages*. On p. 21 after describing some cruelties among Asiatics he says, "These things are in no sense characteristically Greek. They are remnants of the state of things which the highest Greek civilization up to the end of the fifth century B.C., a small white-hot centre of spiritual life in a world of effortless barbarism, tried to transform and perished in the attempt." On p. 15 he speaks of slavery, the subjection of women, and "some startling phenomena of what we should call unchastity in the relations of the sexes" (he cannot say in his day and age "homosexuality") as coming from the East: "And then we imagine that these things are characteristically Greek! They are just the reverse. They are the remnants of that primaeval slime from which Hellenism was trying to make mankind clean." P. 10: "Remnants of savagery lingered on in obscure parts of life, expurgated as a rule and made comparatively innocent, but still bearing the mark of their origin. Such remnants, as a matter of fact, tend to receive undue attention. Our own friends the anthropologists, to whom all true Hellenists owe so much, naturally revel in such things. They search antiquity eagerly for traces of primitive man, for totems, cannibalism, human sacrifice, and the like. The traces which they discover are of the greatest value. But I think they have often mistaken the reverberation of an extinct barbarity for the actual barbarity itself." This is as clear a statement as one could want of how the theories of Jane Harrison fitted into Murray's world-view.

[18] Murray's view of Hesiod (whom he placed two centuries before Homer) is predictable (the Greeks themselves, of course, placed his contribution to theology on a par with Homer's). On p. 65 he allows that he was up to something, but "more timidly." P. 87: "The work of Hesiod as a whole is one of the most valiant failures in literature. The confusion and absurdity of it are only equalled by its strange helpless beauty and its extraordinary historical interest." He is "much more explicit, much less expurgated, infinitely less accomplished and tactful" than Homer. "At the back of Homer lay the lordly warrior-gods of the Heroic Age, at the back of Hesiod the crude and tangled superstitions of the peasantry and the mainland." The final barb is that Homer had the advantage of cultured Athens to work in, but Hesiod had only the pigs of Boeotia. Poor Hesiod! His status as a theological thinker has been completely reappraised since Murray's day, although we must continue to agree that he was inferior to Homer.

the agricultural festivals" (84). It swept away most of the rites of the dead, and "at least for two splendid centuries, the worship of the man-god[19] with its diseased atmosphere of megalomania and blood-lust. These things return with the fall of Hellenism; but the great period, as it urges man to use all his powers of thought, of daring and endurance, of social organization, so it bids him remember that he is a man like other men, subject to the same laws and bound to reckon with the same death" (84).

As an intellectual movement Olympianism brought order to the chthonic world's bewildering variety of half-understood, amorphous spirits. These were crystallized into a finite number of brilliantly distinct anthropomorphic figures (84 f.). Anthropomorphism had this power, but it could not go all the way to monotheism; that final fusion required the hotter furnace of philosophy or mysticism (86).

As a political movement Olympianism sought to provide the gods of the polis. But in this, as in the other spheres, it failed. The Olympians were too universal to be associated with any one city, and too literary to be imposed on a body politic that already had many local divinities available for the purpose (93 f.). In the moral sphere, the lingering barbarism in the countryside eventually proved too strong to stamp out (89). Humanizing the *numina* also brought a dilemma. If you worship a thunderbolt, its moral indifference becomes a problem the moment you regard it not simply as a random shock but as the weapon of a thinking agent. You cannot claim, as you might want to, that such a being is wise and just. You must invent reasons, which are usually bad, for his indiscriminate behaviour, or else acquiesce in the worship of a cruel and capricious god (90). "A being who is the moral equal of man must not behave like a charge of dynamite" (91). Finally, adds Murray, combining the Olympians with all the local gods resulted in a riot of polygamy and polyandry; the Olympians, however, "really aimed at purer morals" (91). The failure in the intellectual sphere has already been commented on above (last paragraph and note 8).

Although the Olympian system failed, it had a few notable achievements. Firstly, it represented progress towards civilization, because "unlike many religious systems, it...encouraged not only the obedient virtues but the daring virtues as well. It had in it the spirit that saves from disaster, that knows itself fallible and thinks twice before it hates and curses and prosecutes. It wrapped religion in Sophrosynê" (95). Secondly, it encouraged "concord and fellow-feeling" in Greece (95). And lastly, one must not forget its sheer beauty. Truth may be greater than beauty, but "in many matters beauty can be attained and truth cannot. All we know is that when the best minds seek for truth the result is apt to be beautiful. It was a great thing that men should envisage the world as governed, not by Giants

---

[19] He means the worship of the king as god incarnate; Murray cites *The Rise of the Greek Epic*[4] 139 f., but the evidence for this belief in Greece before the Hellenistic period is slight.

and Gorgons and dealers in eternal torture, but by some human and more than human Understanding (Ξύνεσις), by beings of quiet splendour like many a classical Zeus and Hermes and Demeter" (95 f.).

As an historical reconstruction this scheme can easily be seen in our day to be wrong on many counts. Few now believe that Homer owes his existence to the Peisistratid redaction. He is rather to be dated to about 700 B.C., contemporary with Hesiod (who was more sophisticated and influential than Murray allows). The gods of Homer are indeed more civilized and sublime than those of peasant belief, but their remaining cruelty and "immorality" are not to be argued away as something Homer was not quite successful in rooting out along with (for example) Hermes' phallicism.[20] They are part of his conception of divinity. Murray assumes without question the Judeo-Christian model; it is revealing that of the two horns of his dilemma, he plainly does not find acquiescence in a cruel god a serious alternative. Yet this was precisely the point of Homeric religion. Again, in the remark about a charge of dynamite, the premise that the gods are moral equals of men is false; they have their own standards. The statement about "purer morals" is in the same vein. Religion for Murray has to be for the "guiding of life." Finally, the statements about what was "swept away" of the chthonic religion are simply untrue; and what was left intact on Murray's own showing is quite a lot (it would include, for example, the Eleusinia and the Thesmophoria). The distinction of Olympic and chthonic is in any event much too sharply drawn, and the insistence on evolutionary progression results in oversimplification and outright distortion of the true historical situation in the different periods. The use of the expression "real religion" in the passage quoted above (note 8) almost admits as much: he knows about the other things, but will not call them "real" or "Hellenic" religion. This will be found only in a few quasi-monotheistic writers like Aeschylus or Plato.

What Murray has done more than anything else is to invest the Olympian system with the attributes of modern Liberalism. This is particularly clear in the sentence on p. 84 (quoted above) containing the words "social organization." It is a truism that every age reinterprets the Classics according to its own lights, and this is well and good. Each time, something new and true is discovered; but much that is untrue is fathered on the Greeks just because it is topical. In the present case, given the fervent, even religious, belief in rationalism and progress in Murray's day, and given the eloquence with which Murray preached this belief, one can see how he

---

[20] *Five Stages* 77; *Rise of the Greek Epic*[4] 125. Professor S. G. Cole remarks that according to recent studies the phallic herms became popular in Athens precisely at the time when Homer was expurgating them according to Murray, and were most popular in the "civilized" fifth century.

so caught the imagination of his contemporaries; but one can see also why his writings became so utterly out of date.[21]

The first reason why Murray wrote his book was his desire to show the correct light in which to place the material unearthed by the Cambridge school. However, Murray's attraction to the primitive aspects of Greek religion cannot be explained purely in negative terms as something that put the "true" Hellenic achievement in perspective. There must have been some positive attraction, too. His deep interest in anthropology throughout his career is well attested.[22] It began, he informs us, with reading Andrew Lang;[23] he contributed chapters to Harrison's books[24] and enthusiastically

[21] Contemporary reviewers found the Olympian chapter refreshingly sensible after the "wild hypotheses" of the first chapter (so W. R. Halliday reviewing *Five Stages* in *CR* 39 [1925] 185; compare J. T. Sheppard on *Four Stages* in *CR* 27 [1913] 197). The morally edifying interpretation of the Olympians was congenial to them, and they admired Murray's popularizing skill in the chapters on Hellenism and the later Greek world. By contrast, A. Lesky, reviewing the 1955 edition in *DLZ* 80 (1959) 798-800, finds it necessary to reject almost everything in the book: he will allow the Year-Spirit in a few instances like Attis and Adonis, but otherwise banishes it, and is critical of Murray's evolutionary approach (particularly in dismissing the whole of the Hellenistic period as a "failure of nerve"). He then adds "Und doch ändert das nichts daran, daß es zu den klassischen Büchern unserer Wissenschaft gehört und diesen Rang behalten wird, mag noch so viel in ihm überholt sein. Der Grund dafür ist, daß diese Darstellung Wert und Würde von der Persönlichkeit ihres Verfassers erhält. Mit der rein wissenschaftlichen, objektiv-historischen Fragestellung hat sich hier aufs intensivste eine andere verbunden, in der eine echt angelsächsische Einstellung eine besondere Sublimierung erfahren hat: die Frage nach Bedeutung und Nutzen der verschiedenen Formen des Religiösen und der einzelnen, Religion verarbeitenden und ersetzenden Denksysteme für den Menschen. Und zwar nicht allein für den griechischen Menschen, sondern für den Menschen schlechtweg, auch den unserer Tage" (799). Detractors of Paul Shorey will find grist for their mill in his review of Murray's *The Classical Tradition in Poetry*, *Saturday Review of Literature* 4 (1928) 608 (quoted with inadequate reference by C. Kluckhohn, *Anthropology and the Classics*[Providence, Rhode Island, 1961] 20): "Professor Murray has done much harm by helping to substitute in the minds of an entire generation for Arnold's and Jebb's conception of the serene rationality of the classics the corybantic Hellenism of Miss Harrison and Isadora Duncan and Susan Glaspell and Mr. Stark Young's 'Good Friday and Classical Professors,' the higher vaudeville Hellenism of Mr. Vachel Lindsay, the anthropological Hellenism of the disciples of Sir James Frazer, the irrational, semi-sentimental, Polynesian, free-verse and sex-freedom Hellenism of all the gushful geysers of 'rapturous rubbish' about the Greek spirit." This is a wildly unfair representation of Murray's position. Lucien Price answered it in the same journal, p. 653. Compare further Shorey's review of *Anthropology and the Classics* (next note) in *CP* 4 (1909) 223 and of *The Rise of the Greek Epic* in *CP* 6 (1911) 238 and 20 (1925) 283.

[22] See apart from the works mentioned here the preface to *A History of Ancient Greek Literature* (quoted below) and "Anthropology in the Greek Epic Tradition outside Homer," in R. R. Marett (ed.), *Anthropology and the Classics. Six Lectures Delivered before the University of Oxford by Arthur J. Evans, Andrew Lang, Gilbert Murray, F. B. Jevons, J. L. Myres, Warde Fowler* (Oxford, 1908) 66-92.

[23]*Five Stages* p. 5. Turner's remark (p. 118) about Lang is interesting in the light of the foregoing discussion: "Lang recognized the savage intellect in order to banish its influence from civilized life. For the anthropologists, religious or irrational social practices existing in the midst of generally rational societies represented dysfunctional

embraced the Year-Daimon (and his influence on Greek drama) to the end of his days.[25] He would not have done so had he not been attracted to these studies in their own right. The reason is to be found once again in Murray's historicism, which would lead him naturally to see something of what Greek society was really like and to find it interesting. This is not so much of a contradiction as it might seem. Murray was full of life as a young man; he was strongly sensitive to every human impulse in his own world and easily transferred this sensibility to the ancient world. His aim was to share his feeling with his contemporaries. As it happened, anthropology came along about the same time and gave him the tools he needed. His political views were also taking shape, and it was not difficult to see how the two could be combined. Progress will most likely be achieved by those who know its real price; Murray's later success as a diplomat showed that he entertained no delusions about the kinds of obstacles thrown up by fools and dogmatics in the practical world. Realism and idealism were simultaneous impulses in Murray's formation as a scholar, as in his character. The combination is already apparent in the preface of his first book, *A History of Ancient Greek Literature*.

But realism is in the eyes of the beholder. Murray saw a great deal more than many Victorians of what Greece was really like; but he saw much less than we do, or think we do. When push came to shove anything primitive was for Murray unhellenic *ex hypothesi*. There was a puritanical element in his make-up which prevented him from fully embracing these barbaric goings-on. For Jane Harrison, on the other hand, the more primitive the better. West quotes a remark of Murray's about Harrison's *Prolegomena to the Study of Greek Religion* (1903) that her views often seemed a bit foolish, "like Aunt Fanny trying to be naughty."[26] Murray's

---

survivals from a previous stage of social evolution." See further below on anthropology's early stress on origins and survivals.

[24] "Critical Appendix on the Orphic Tablets," in J. E. Harrison, *Prolegomena to the Study of Greek Religion* (Cambridge, 1903; [3]1922) 660-674; "Critical Note on Thucydides 2.15.3-6," in *Primitive Athens* (Cambridge, 1906) 159; "Excursus on the Ritual Forms Preserved in Tragedy," in *Themis* (Cambridge 1912; [2]1927) 341-363.

[25] See the "Excursus" in *Themis* (last note); "The Hymn of the Kouretes," *ABSA* 15 (1908-1909) 357-365; *Five Stages* 43-49; *Euripides and His Age* (London, 1913) 61-67 = [2]1946 38-41; *Hamlet and Orestes. A Study in Traditional Types*, British Academy Annual Shakespeare Lecture (London, 1914) =*The Classical Tradition in Poetry*. The Charles Eliot Norton Lectures 1927 (London and Cambridge, Mass., 1927) 206-240; reply to M. R. James (*CR* 31 [1917] 1-4) on Harrison's "The Head of John Baptist" (*CR* 30 [1916] 216-219) in *CR* 31 (1917) 63-64; "Hymn of the Kouretes," in J. U. Powell, and E. A. Barber (eds.), *New Chapters in the History of Greek Literature* [First Series] (Oxford, 1921) 50-53; *The Classical Tradition in Poetry* 64 f.; "Ritual Elements in New Comedy," *CQ* 37 (1943) 46-54.

[26] West p. 133. Harrison's attraction to the primitive was not, however, sexual; see *Reminiscences of a Student's Life* (London, 1925) 81 f. on the difficulty she experienced in first reading Freud: "By temperament I am, if not a prude, at least a Puritan, and at first the ugliness of it all sickened me. I hate a sick-room, and have a physical fear of all

faint criticism of Harrison's provocative ways is slightly hypocritical, giving in to a sense of outraged bourgeois propriety and betraying at bottom an inability to grasp her purpose. Such criticism also seems inconsistent with his own Radicalism in politics: just as Harrison could conceal the unsavoury nature of her subject-matter with a decorous and sincere treatment, Murray (particularly when young) could advocate daring reforms without abandoning the high moral ground. In the study of Greek religion, his attachment to civility kept him from following Harrison all the way; in politics, his conservative personality made him an Establishment Liberal by middle age and an actual Conservative voter in old age.

One might also dwell for a moment on the fascination of Victorians generally with anthropology, and suggest that Murray simply shared a trait of many contemporaries. In this connection I would quote from three places. The first is from the preface of *A History of Ancient Greek Literature* (1897) xi:

> There is more flesh and blood in the Greek of the anthropologist, the foster-brother of Kaffirs and Hairy Ainos. He is at least human and simple and emotional, and free from irrelevant trappings. His fault, of course, is that he is not the man we want, but only the raw material out of which that man was formed: a Hellene without the beauty, without the spiritual life, without the Hellenism.

The two words "of course" are particularly apt to raise a smile; I cannot refrain from commenting either on the very Victorian diction and rhetoric of the closing words, which would not seem out of place on the lips of Dorothea Brooke. Here again is the primitive as "foil" of which we spoke above; but what is more to notice in the present connection should wait until after our other quotations. The next passage is from a letter of 16 October 1897 to William Archer (I include a few words of Wilson's paraphrase, from whom I derive my knowledge of the text). Murray is here speaking of his play *Andromache*, a re-working of the old legend; he finds certain advantages in using the stuff of known saga as the basis of a new work:

> [The] characters needed no careful introduction, but were still highly dramatic—simple well-marked personalities; primitive in a way, but with plenty of room for psychological development, and also "articulate and full of high and delicate sensitivity—with a power of seeing and suffering...elsewhere associated with very advanced and complex stages of society."[27]

Finally, from *Euripides and His Age* (1913) p. 5:

---

obsessions and insanity. Still I struggled on, feeling somehow that behind and below all this sexual mud was something big and real."

[27]Wilson p. 85.

...we have only to exercise a little historical imagination and we shall
find in [Euripides] a man, not indeed modern—half his charm is that he
is so austere and remote—but a man who has in his mind the same
problems as ourselves, the same doubts and largely the same ideals...

There is something about all of these passages that I should like to call
"historical Boswellianism." Boswellianism pure and simple is that pleasure
derived from seeing the high and mighty from close quarters: seeing what
they wore, what they ate, how they comported themselves, when they went
to bed. Historical Boswellianism is the same thing applied to past ages.
One infuses the old ghosts with so much supposititious realism that one
can thrill to their proximity. One eagerly notes the details of ordinary life—
diet, clothes, money, entertainment—and evinces wonder at the similarities
to modern life. These similarities are even found to extend beyond the outer
trappings of daily existence to include beliefs and values. So in the second
and third passages, Murray is careful to emphasize that the ancients are
authentic primitives, just waiting for "development" into moderns; but
already they are "articulate" and "sensitive," early attempts, as it were, at
Jane Austen. The real point of this exercise, however, is not to get truly
close to primitive and ancient peoples, but to heighten the sense of distance.
In this lies "half the charm." The act of historical recreation permits one to
have the kind of awestruck experience that many British travellers had (more
than ever before, since in Victorian England the middle class could also
afford the Grand Tour) when they were able actually to touch the stones of
the Parthenon. The conflicting emotions of affinity and alienation are
simultaneously sharpened and brought into direct contact with each other,
resulting in an exhilarating and piquant experience. I am not an expert on
Victorian Britain by any means, but it seems easy to make the case that this
experience was much sought after by its citizens. It was the age of Great
Exhibitions, of the ubiquitous English tourist, of daring gentlemen's
adventures to hostile climes, and unbounded curiosity in the world's
marvels. And of course, it was the great age of the Empire (note the
"Kaffirs and hairy Ainos" of the first quotation above: British anthropology
was surely spurred by the first-hand contact with primitive societies the
world over). Murray simply shared the common attraction of his
countrymen to these topics. To repeat the essential qualification, however,
Murray—and his countrymen—would only go so far in these vicarious
pleasures; the fascination with the primitive, itself a hangover of Romantic
notions, received a great boost in the late century, but too much realism—a
direct confrontation instead of a vicarious one—would lead to revulsion.
The point of Boswellianism is not to be comfortable in Johnson's presence;
if you are, you are too much like Johnson to have the right experience.
Few Englishmen really wanted to wallow in primitive life; they wanted to
tour it, wearing pith helmets, not loin cloths. Arctic explorers like
Franklin merely moved the ambience of their London clubs to the decks of a

ship when they set out on their expeditions (in this case, Franklin paid the expected price for his lack of preparation). Ultimately the insulating layer between savage and civilized must be maintained. It is very significant that when anthropologists finally went out to live among the natives, the perspective changed at once from one stressing origins and survivals to one stressing functional description of a complete society in situ. It was realized that the so-called "primitive" co-existed right along with the sophisticated in early societies just as it does in our own.[28]

Murray was attracted to the Cambridge Ritualists, we have so far suggested, because he thought that the emergence of civilization must be set off against its primitive background, and because of a natural interest in anthropology which was partly his own and partly typical of his age. A third reason, quickly stated but important nonetheless, is his personal attitude towards religion. The tenets of his faith have already been outlined; here an additional observation needs to be made. Murray was a moralist above all. He also lived in an age when Greek religion was finally beginning to be taken seriously as a working religion. In analysing his own society he always looked first for the moral value of anything; the same held true for Greek society. It is predictable then that a man with this program of study should put Greek religion at the centre of his investigations. His attitude towards religion was also conditioned by his boyhood experiences in Australia. His father was Roman Catholic, his mother was Protestant; to the young Murray the obvious conclusion to be drawn from each group's vilification of the other was that they were both wrong. The issue of religion in society was thus impressed on him from an early age; the merciful absence of dogma in his own home permitted a detached and sane, if keenly interested, view of the phenomenon.

Three further reasons may be added. The first is his warm personal relation with Jane Harrison beginning in 1900, fully documented by both Murray's and Harrison's biographers,[29] and needing no further discussion here. Secondly, Murray was open-minded to a fault, partly out of temperament and partly out of philosophic belief. He was prepared to see the good in anyone's point of view, perhaps especially if it was a radical one. If it was a view repellent to him personally he would make a special effort to suppress his prejudice, one of the world's great evils in his view; as

[28] On this development in anthropology see West 137 f. citing B. Malinowski's and A. R. Radcliffe-Brown's work published in the early 1920's; C. Kluckhohn, *Anthropology and the Classics* (Providence, Rhode Island, 1961) 14; S.C. Humphreys, *Anthropology and the Greeks* (London, 1978) 17-21.

[29] Wilson, index s.v. Harrison, and West, 132-139; S. Peacock, *Jane Ellen Harrison: The Mask and the Self* (New Haven, 1988) ch. 5. For Murray on Harrison see especially his memorial address, *Jane Ellen Harrison. An Address Delivered at Newnham College 27 June 1928* (Cambridge, 1928), reprinted in J. E. Harrison, *Epilegomena to the Study of Greek Religion and Themis, A Study of the Social Origins of Greek Religion* (New York, 1962) 559-577; see also "A Great Scholar," *Listener* 8 March 1951, 373-374; *PBA* 29 (1943) 421-422, 424-425 (part of Murray's obituary of F. M. Cornford).

a rationalist it was his duty to fight the irrational wherever it was found. He was not the kind of scholar who makes up his mind that certain books are worth reading, and others are not; if anything, as J.A.K. Thomson remarked, he suffered fools a little too gladly.[30]

Finally, if we ask what Murray actually contributed to the writings of the Cambridge group, apart from his popularizing of their (especially Harrison's) notions, we should say it was to discuss the presence of ritual forms in Greek literature. This observation may suggest that his attraction to the subject was partly a function of his own artistic instincts. The glory of Greek religion is its ability to inspire great art, and many students of the latter have been led to inquire about the Greek gods in a more or less historical spirit, even before the age of historicism; for if you are sensible that the great artists of the past were flesh and blood, as you are bound to be if you feel an artist's affinity with them, you will take their inspiration as seriously as your own. The case of Winckelmann is sufficient illustration.[31]

Five Stages rivals *The Rise of the Greek Epic* as Murray's best book; certainly it is typical of him in many ways. At bottom it is the work of an amateur, in the best English sense. The humane value of the research counts more in the end than the research itself. Indeed, there is little original research in the book. Murray readily acknowledges his utter dependence on other authorities in the first and the last two chapters. The only personal contribution in the book is his thesis about the Olympians; and it too is not wholly original. On p. 23 Murray calls it "still rather new and unauthorized"; he does not claim simply that it is "new." Similar views are to be found in L. R. Farnell's *The Higher Aspects of Greek Religion*, a course of lectures delivered in 1911 and published in 1912;[32] although parts of Murray's book appeared before this, Farnell's book is a summary of views implicit in his *Cults of the Greek States*, whose first volume appeared in 1896. The whole thesis is in any case easily derived from general notions about the Olympians prevailing in Victorian society, so that one expects to find clear echoes in many places.[33] But although the thesis is not new, it is unmistakably Murray's. He argued it repeatedly and at length, spelled out the implications, and made clear its connection with his own deepest beliefs. He was preaching a gospel in this and in all his books. That was scholarship then. One readily concedes that Murray read an

---

[30] In his obituary, *PBA* 43 (1957) 245-270; see p. 259; cf. Wilson p. 395.

[31] I owe this last suggestion to Ms. Shelley Arlen.

[32] See especially pp. 107-124 of Farnell's book. Cf. Turner p. 130.

[33] Turner (p. 129) quotes two of them: G. Lowes Dickinson's popular *The Greek View of Life* (1896) and especially Edward Caird's *The Evolution of Religion* (New York, ²1894) I, 266: "The gods of Greece are powers that make, perhaps we may not say strictly, 'for righteousness,' but certainly for civilization. They are man's forerunners in the work of taming and subduing nature into his servant; and it is his glory that he can follow them in their labours."

impressive amount; indeed, he was far more learned in European scholarship than many contemporary Englishmen, and as for general culture, one would be hard put to name a more accomplished classicist in all our long annals. But he never displayed the professional attitude towards the evidence that the Germans had, and would not have wanted to. His talent lay in the ability to absorb huge amounts of specialized information and put it in perspective— in his case, the perspective of a Victorian Liberal and moralist. To do it with his verve, insight, and sheer intelligence is a very rare ability indeed, and, even if one has to admit that the learning is derivative at bottom, it ought not to be dismissed as second-rate. It is first rate, often dazzlingly, inspiringly so—or was so, for Victorians. The book no longer speaks to us; whether it is a good or bad thing that we have lost that age's innocent idealism I leave to my readers to decide.

Owing to Murray's great prestige, the old scholarship prevailed longer at Oxford than it should have. Some younger scholars in the 1920s and 1930s like Edgar Lobel and Denys Page were symptomatic of a newer, more professional approach; but the well-known stir created by Eduard Fraenkel's seminars (appointed Corpus Christi Professor of Latin at Oxford in 1935) shows that the old English ways still predominated. Fraenkel was merely doing what his colleagues had been doing for more than a century: professional scholarship. The irony is that Murray fully appreciated the value of men like Fraenkel, and did more than anyone else to bring him and other Jewish refugees from the Nazi nightmare to Oxford. Their presence had a great deal to do with the passing of the kind of scholarship best represented by Murray himself.[34]

University of Waterloo

[34] It is perhaps not well known that Fraenkel published an obituary of Murray in the *Association of Jewish Refugees Information* for July 1957 (I came across it by accident in the Ashmolean Library, to which Fraenkel bequeathed his personal library). Two representative quotations: "But what one primarily felt in his presence was that here was a man who combined the gifts of a supreme mind with the most delicate gentleness and a wealth of humane sympathy." "It was as if in an age of passions, hatred, and persecution the genius of civilized mankind had settled in the elegant frame of this extraordinary old gentleman so that all that is noblest in our European heritage should shine forth with invigorating splendour."

6

La Genèse du Système?
The Origins of Durkheim's Sociology of Religion

ROBERT ALUN JONES

In three successive volumes over the period 1905–7, the Catholic philosophy journal *Revue néo-scolastique* published a series of essays collectively titled "Le Conflit de la morale et de la sociologie." These essays, published as a book in 1911, were written by the Belgian priest and neo-Thomist philosopher Simon Deploige, and contained a sharp attack on the "social realism" of Durkheim and his disciples. "All these views," Deploige observed after summarizing Durkheim's sociology, "pass in France as M. Durkheim's own. But they are of German origin."[1] Durkheim was deeply offended. Had Deploige "wanted to convince people that I have abused my compatriots," he replied on October 20, 1907, "he could hardly have expressed himself in any other way." Deploige's language seemed to imply that Durkheim had made "carefully concealed borrowings among certain German writers." Of course, Durkheim admitted, "I owe much to the Germans, as well as to Comte and others. But the real influence that Germany has exercised on me is quite different from what he says."[2]

Within four days, Deploige replied with explicit references to Durkheim's alleged indebtedness to Schäffle, Wagner, Schmoller, Wundt, Simmel, Lazarus and Steinthal; and a second letter from Durkheim, dated November 8, contained not only a detailed refutation of Deploige's "errors," "inaccuracies," and "insinuations," but what has surely become the most famous (and least understood) autobiographical passage in all of Durkheim's writings: "[I]t was not until 1895," Durkheim observed,

> that I had a clear sense of the central role played by religion in social life. It was in that year that, for the first time, I found the means to approach the study of religion sociologically. This was for me a revelation. That course of 1895 marked a line of demarcation in the development of my thought, so much that all my previous researches

[1] Deploige, 1911: 122.
[2] Durkheim, 1907: 606, 607; my translation.

had to be taken up afresh in order to be placed in harmony with these new views. Wundt's *Ethik*, read eight years earlier, played no role in this change of direction. It was completely due to the studies of religious history that I had just undertaken, and particularly to the reading of the works of Robertson Smith and his school.[3]

Again Deploige replied; and when his essays appeared as a volume in 1911, Durkheim reviewed it savagely in *L'Année sociologique*, alluding again to "all that we owe to Robertson Smith and to the works of the ethnographers of England and America."[4]

The appearance of Durkheim's monumental *Les Formes élémentaires de la vie religieuse* just one year later, with its rich and detailed extensions of the ideas of Smith, Frazer, and the Australian ethnographers, might conceivably have settled the matter. But by 1916, the issue was still further clouded by defenders of a more domestic, Cartesian *provenance*. From Durkheim's earliest days at the École Normale Supérieure, Camille Jullian insisted on the fiftieth anniversary of the publication of *La Cité antique*, he had been deeply affected by the lectures, writings, and example of its author, the great French historian Numa Denis Fustel de Coulanges. "[Durkheim himself] has recognized this," Jullian added, "and proclaims it openly."[5] And Jullian—Durkheim's fellow student at the École, his former colleague at the University of Bordeaux, Fustel's foremost disciple, and the editor of six volumes of his unpublished manuscripts after his death in 1889—was surely in a position to know.

Subsequent scholarship on the origins of Durkheim's sociology of religion has reiterated these early claims on behalf of French, German, and British influences. The French claim, for example, has been particularly championed by Sir Edward Evans-Pritchard, Arnaldo Momigliano, and Steven Lukes.[6] The German position, initially advanced by Deploige, has more recently been resurrected by Wolf Lepenies.[7] And as the final contributor to a colloquium on the Cambridge Ritualists, I might reasonably be expected to reaffirm Durkheim's adamant replies of 1907 and 1911, and thus to insist upon the authenticity of his *révélation* upon reading Smith and Frazer in 1895.

The temptation here is almost irresistible. In fact, it is one to which I have already yielded.[8] More recently chastened by an examination of the evidence in support of both the French and the German claims, however, I will here adopt a more conciliatory posture. First, in roughly chronological

[3] Durkheim, 1907: 613; my translation.

[4] Durkheim, 1913: 326.

[5] See Jullian, "Le Cinquantenaire de *La cité antique*." *Revue de Paris*, 23e année, no. 4 (February 15, 1916), p. 857; cited in Lukes, 1973: 60.

[6] See Evans-Pritchard, 1965: 50–51; Momigliano, 1982: 339–40; and Lukes, 1973: 59–65.

[7] See Lepenies, 1986–87.

[8] See Jones, 1986.

order, and as much detail as space allows, I will consider the case to be made
for each of the alleged influences on Durkheim's sociology of religion. I
will then suggest that these are neither mutually exclusive nor even
alternative interpretations of Durkheim's thought; rather, Durkheim was
attracted to Fustel, German social science, and the Cambridge Ritualists for
the same reasons, so that an understanding of each becomes possible only
through a grasp of the others. Finally, and more tentatively, I will suggest
that this broader, more synthetic grasp of Durkheim's intellectual context
suggests a different—less rationalist and more romantic—conception of his
thought.

I. Fustel and French Historiography

As Jullian observed more than seventy years ago, the suggestion that
Durkheim owed much to Fustel must begin with their association at the
École Normale Supérieure. Born in Paris in the year of the July Revolution
and the Barricades, Fustel had himself attended the École, where he studied
with the historians Victor Duruy, P.A. Chéruel, and J.-D. Guigniaut.
Appointed sub-librarian, Fustel hid himself in the stacks, reading
Montesquieu, Michelet, Tocqueville, Guizot and, above all, Descartes.
When the *coup d'état* of Louis Napoleon (December 2, 1851) led to the
suppression of non-classical studies, Fustel took up the study of Latin,
then Greek, and eventually the history of classical antiquity. For all his
Cartesian spirit, however, Fustel had already embraced the inductive method,
writing an essay in praise of Bacon which shocked his fellow students. In
1853, he joined the newly established École française d'Athènes, moving to
the Lycée Amiens in 1855, the Lycée St. Louis in Paris in 1857 and, in
1860, to the chair of medieval and modern history at the University of
Strasbourg.

During his sojourn in Greece, Fustel collected a number of manuscripts
which provided the foundations for his earliest publications, including his
Mémoire sur l'île de Chios (1856), his highly-praised French thesis,
Polybe, ou la Grèce conquise (1858), and his Latin thesis, *Quid Vestae
cultus in institutis veterum privatis publicisque valuerit* (1858). The Latin
thesis in particular anticipated *La Cité antique* for, according to Fustel, the
goddess Vesta symbolized that domestic, familial religion which became the
official cult of the ancient city, and thus the first phase of Aryan
civilization. But Fustel's masterpiece remains *La Cité antique*, written over
a six-month period at Strasbourg in 1864, comprising lectures given the
two previous years. Initially published at his own expense, it quickly won
Fustel a following at the court of Napoleon III and, by 1890, it had seen its
13th edition. On the recommendation of Duruy (by now the Emperor's
Minister of Public Instruction), Fustel was called to Paris in February,
1870, to give history lectures at the École Normale, and an invitation to

provide a special course to the Empress Eugénie and her suite followed quickly thereafter.

With these associations, the more general French humiliation of 1870–71 was especially acute for Fustel, and it led him from antiquity to the Middle Ages, to an almost romantic attraction for the *ancien régime*, and to that style of scholarship—*de rigueur* among intellectuals of the Third Republic—designed to restore French pride and self-esteem. For more than a century, a central question for European social history had been the institutional origins of feudalism. Arising in Germany, the debate had soon spread to France and gradually resolved into two fiercely defended alternatives, the first insisting that the origins of feudalism lay in Roman civilization, the second equally insistent that its origins were Germanic. By 1870, these two schools of interpretation, fueled by the patriotic sentiments of their respective supporters, confronted one another in a precariously balanced opposition. In 1872, writing in the *Revue des Deux Mondes*, Fustel took up the "Roman" position, insisting that the Germanic invasions of the fifth century had little influence on the history, religion, customs, government, or structure of French society; on the contrary, their arrival merely favored the development of the feudalism already in progress.[9] This article on the early medieval period created a sensation, and by 1874 it had been expanded into a complete volume. Fustel hoped to follow it with several others, bringing the narrative down to recent times; but the storm of criticism which greeted the first installment, and particularly the charge that it was more a product of Sedan than of historical science, led Fustel to return to the initial work and, page by page, tirelessly expose his *apparatus criticus*, conducting a lesson in historical method. The result, which occupied Fustel for the rest of his life and was completed only after his death, was the classic *Histoire des institutions politiques de l'ancienne France* (6 vols.,1874–93).

The *Histoire des institutions politiques* is important for two related reasons. First, it was the project which literally consumed Fustel during the period in which Durkheim was his student at the École Normale.[10] Second, an essential element in the project was the detailed articulation of the method he had followed in writing *La Cité antique* (1864), the same employed by Montesquieu in *L'Esprit des lois* (1734), and the method Durkheim would follow in *De la division du travail social* (1893) as well. Essentially, as Fustel wrote to an admiring critic in 1865, this method relied less on the detailed accumulation of facts (something for which Fustel had

---

[9] See "L'invasion germanique au Ve siècle, son caractère et ses effets," *Revue des Deux Mondes* XCIX (1872). See also Gooch, 1913: 209; Thompson, 1942: II, 360–62.

[10] Fustel lectured at the École Normale from 1870 to 1875, then moved to the Sorbonne, returning to assume the directorship of the École in 1880, shortly after Durkheim had arrived there. He found that administrative duties interfered with his research, and after four years he resigned, again for the Sorbonne, where he remained until his death in 1889.

no more patience than had Durkheim) than on rigorous comparisons (e.g., of the Rig-Veda with Euripides, of the laws of Manu with the Twelve Tables or Isaeus and Lysias) until he had arrived at the conception of a community of beliefs and institutions among Indians, Greeks, and Italic peoples.[11] But if the continuity of ancient belief and practice was thus a premise of *La Cité antique*, so was the radical discontinuity between these and "later peoples"—the last referring unmistakably to Fustel's contemporaries. The naive, idealized comparison of ancient liberties with their modern French counterparts was not simply anachronistic. For Fustel, whose respect for the Church and the *ancien régime* exceeded even that of Durkheim, it was also socially destructive.[12]

So dramatic a contrast between past and present presupposed an explanation for the transition from one to the other; and for Fustel, as for Tylor and Frazer (although certainly not for Durkheim), this explanation was provided by the progress of the human mind.[13] For Fustel, institutions provided no explanation of their associated beliefs; for when we examine the institutions of the Greeks and Romans, they appear obscure, whimsical, and inexplicable. But when we examine the religious ideas of the ancients, these institutional practices become quite transparent. *La Cité antique* thus describes the history of a belief—in particular, the ancient belief that the soul remained associated with the body after death; that the soul must thus be buried with the body; that carefully established ritual precautions were thus to be observed upon such burials; and that, these rituals lacking, the soul was condemned to wander without rest or sustenance, eventually becoming a malevolent spirit and inflicting serious harm on the living.

From this initial, primitive belief, Fustel quite literally derived all the institutions of the ancient world. The *patria potestas*, for example, grew from the authoritative role of the father in the performance of ancient ritual; and it was this authority—not consanguinity—that bound together the members of the ancient family, making it "a religious rather than a natural

[11] Fustel wrote to L. A. Warnkönig, who had written an extremely favorable review of *La Cité antique*, that his type of mind was such that he "could not be content with details," and that his method had thus been "the comparative one." Ignoring Montesquieu, the introduction of the comparative method is frequently ascribed to Henry Sumner Maine's *Ancient Law* (1861); but Fustel was clearly unaware of Maine's work in 1864. Durkheim's dedication of his Latin thesis to Fustel, Momigliano emphasizes, was "more than an act of homage. The link between Montesquieu and Fustel was in everyone's mind during those years . . ." (1982:339; see also 337, 326).

[12] "Having imperfectly observed the institutions of the ancient city," Fustel insisted, "men have dreamed of reviving them among us. They have deceived themselves about the liberty of the ancients, and on this very account liberty among the moderns has been put in peril. The last eighty years have clearly shown that one of the great difficulties which impede the march of modern society is the habit which it has of always keeping Greek and Roman antiquity before its eyes" (1864:11).

[13] See the criticism of this conception in Durkheim, 1893:178–9.

association."[14] To assure the continuous, independent worship of its own ancestors, each family then secured a specific plot of land, which thus acquired "sacred" status; and in this way, *pace* Locke, the institution of private property was born.[15] Similarly, ancient law and morality had their origins in the authority of the father, and were only gradually adapted to the needs of larger, more complex institutions in later centuries.[16]

For the Durkheim scholar, the extent to which this discussion anticipates the arguments of *Les Formes élémentaires* is simply stunning. But no less impressive is the extent to which Fustel's discussion of belief and ritual resembles that of Frazer and Robertson Smith. The ancient city, Fustel observed, was a collective group of those who had the same deities and performed religious ceremonies at the same altar; and nothing in the city was more sacred than this altar, on which the sacred fire was maintained.[17] The earliest religious act was a sacrifice upon this altar, followed by a communal meal in which the god shared.[18] Ritual far exceeded doctrine in importance, for rites were obligatory and unchanging, while doctrine was voluntary and shifted constantly.[19] Political authority was derived from religion, and thus the king was a sacred being, the hereditary priest of the sacred fire;[20] and the city's legal statutes derived, not from ancient ideas of

[14] Fustel, 1864:42.

[15] Fustel, 1864:67.

[16] Fustel, 1864:86–98.

[17] Fustel, 1864:146. See Smith, 1889:114–19.

[18] Fustel, 1864:155. "These old customs," Fustel observed, "give us an idea of the close tie which united the members of a city. Human association was a religion; its symbol was a meal, of which they partook together. We must picture to ourselves one of these little primitive societies, all assembled, or the heads of families at least, at the same table, each clothed in white, with a crown upon his head; all make the libation together, recite the same prayer, sing the same hymns, and eat the same food, prepared upon the same altar; in their midst their ancestors are present, and the protecting gods share the meal. Neither interest, nor agreement, nor habit creates the social bond; it is this holy communion piously accomplished in the presence of the gods of the city" (1864:158; cf. Smith, 1889:313; Durkheim, 1912: 366–92).

[19] To the ancients, Fustel argued, religion meant "rites, ceremonies, acts of exterior worship. The doctrine was of small account: the practices were the important part; these were obligatory, and bound man (*ligare, religio*). Religion was a material bond, a chain which held man a slave. Man had originated it, and he was governed by it. He stood in fear of it, and dated not reason upon it, or discuss it, or examine it" (1864:167). Again: "All these formulas and practices had been handed down by ancestors who had proved their efficacy. There was not occasion for innovation. It was a duty to rest upon what the ancestors had done, and the highest piety consisted in imitating them. It mattered little that a belief changed; it might be freely modified from age to age, and take a thousand diverse forms, in accordance with the reflection of sages, or with the popular imagination. But it was of the greatest importance that the formulas should not fall into oblivion, and that the rites should not be modified" (1864:169; cf. Frazer, 1890:I, 62; II, 245–6; Smith, 1889:18–22; Durkheim, 1912:121).

[20] "It was not force . . . that created the chiefs and kings in those ancient cities," Fustel insisted. Rather, "authority flowed from the worship of the sacred fire. Religion created the king in the city, as it had made the family chief in the house. A belief, an

justice, but from religion.[21]   Citizenship was established entirely on religious grounds; and the stranger, by contrast, was "one who has not access to the worship, one whom the gods of the city do not protect, and who has not even the right to invoke them."[22]

The point toward which all these observations conspired, as I have already indicated, was that ancient peoples, not recognizing any right of opposition to the gods of the city, "had not even the idea" of what we would call "liberty."[23]   So Fustel's account of ancient society, as Durkheim surely recognized and appreciated, stressed the superficiality of "merely political" freedom. Moreover, it was only after the seventh century B.C., when this ancient social organization was attacked by those classes deprived of its advantages and, still later, when the triumph of Christianity introduced the separation of Church and State, that government became free of religious constraint. Henceforth, Fustel concluded, "only a part of man belonged to society," for "in what related to his soul, he was free, and was bound only to God."[24]   Private virtues thus became separated from their public counterparts, and "individual freedom"—previously an oxymoron—became possible.

"There is no doubt about Fustel's influence on Durkheim," Momigliano flatly asserted in 1970.[25]   Quite aside from the testimony of Jullian, Durkheim's studies with Fustel at the École Normale, and associations between the Durkheimians and Fustel's disciples,[26] there is the evidence of Durkheim's own writings. In the opening lecture of his course on the family at Bordeaux (1888), for example, Durkheim suggested that historical studies of early forms of the family be supplemented by more comparative, sociological analyses of societies of the same type—a

---

unquestionable and imperious belief, declared that the hereditary priest of the hearth was the depository of the holy duties and the guardian of the gods" (1864:178; cf. Frazer, 1890:I, 167–71; II, 242–3).

[21] "In order that there should be a legal relation between two men," Fustel observed, "it was necessary that there should already exist a religious relation; that is to say, that they should worship at the same hearth and have the same sacrifices. When this religious community did not exist, it did not seem that there could be any legal relation" (1864:193).

[22] The ancient religion, Fustel observed, "established between the citizen and the stranger a profound and ineffaceable distinction. This same religion, so long as it held its sway over the minds of men, forbade the right of citizenship to be granted to a stranger" (1864:194–5; cf. Smith, 1889:39, 121–24).

[23] Fustel, 1864:223.

[24] Fustel, 1864:394.

[25] Momigliano, 1982:339.

[26] Louis Gernet, for example, was a close friend of the Durkheimians Robert Hertz, Marcel Mauss, and Marcel Granet, and served as general secretary of L'Année sociologique during the last years of his life. The author of L'Approvisionnement d'Athènes en blé au Ve et au IV siècle (1909), Recherches sur le developpement de la pensée juridique et morale en Grèce (1917), and (with A. Boulanger) Le génie grec dans la religion (1932), Gernet was a student of Paul Girard who, in turn, had been a student of Fustel's. Girard was also the biographer of Fustel's biographer, Paul Guirard.

suggestion already partially realized in the work of Montesquieu, Maine, and Fustel. The next step was to extend the field of "useful comparisons" beyond classical antiquity; the domestic law of Australian or American tribes, for example, "helps us better to understand that of the Romans."[27] *De la division du travail social* (1893) remained relatively innocent of ethnography; but Durkheim still praised Fustel for showing, on the comparison of classical texts alone, that "the early organization of [lower] societies was of a familial nature, and that.the primitive family was constituted on a religious base."[28] As we draw close to the pivotal lecture-course on religion of 1894–95, however, the streams begin to merge, and an understanding of Durkheim's interest in Fustel increasingly presupposes an understanding of his interest in German social science and the writings of Smith and Frazer.

II. Wundt and German Social Science

The German victory in the Franco-Prussian War, Ernest Renan observed in 1872, was "the victory of science." Recalling the regenerative role played by the University of Berlin after the Battle of Jena, Renan went on to call for the "radical reform" of French higher education on the model of Protestant Germany.[29] In fact, the French had spent much of the previous thirty years admiring the German educational system,[30] and Renan's concerns had already been reflected in a policy of the *Ministère de l'Instruction Publique* of awarding scholarships to the brightest young French *agrégés* that they might visit Germany to become acquainted with the latest scholarly and scientific advances. It was with this support that Durkheim visited the universities of Leipzig, Marburg, and Berlin in 1885–86.

It was well understood that this German scientific superiority extended to the social sciences. In the first paragraph of his review of Ludwig Gumplowicz' *Grundriss der Soziologie* (1885), Durkheim suggested that the work was further evidence of the German effort to advance sociological studies in every possible direction. "How regrettable it is," he added, that "this interesting movement is so little known and so little followed in France. So it is that sociology, French in origin, becomes more and more a German science."[31] Durkheim's views were shared by Louis Liard, the devout Republican, Renouvierist, and *Directeur de l'Instruction Supérieure*. It was Liard, hoping to reform the philosophy course for the *agrégation* at

---

[27] Durkheim, 1888a:224.

[28] Durkheim, 1893:179.

[29] Renan, 1872:55. For a description of this attitude among intellectuals of the Third Republic, see Claude Digeon's aptly-titled *La Crise allemande de la pensée française* (1959). Steven Lukes has also observed that "it was for long widely held that the 'Prussian Schoolmaster' had triumphed at Sedan" (1973:86n2).

[30] See Gilpin, 1968: esp. ch. 4.

[31] Durkheim, 1885:627.

the École Normale, who encouraged Durkheim to pay special attention to the state of the social sciences during his stay in Germany, in the hope that they might be introduced into French higher education, and provide the basis for a secular, scientific morality for the Third Republic. And upon Durkheim's return, it was again Liard who exerted his considerable influence to create a special position for Durkheim—*chargé de cours* of social science and pedagogy at the Faculty of Letters at Bordeaux—the guise under which sociology officially entered the French university system.[32]

The immediate result of Durkheim's visit were his two "German" essays of 1887—"L'Enseignement de la Philosophie dans les universités allemandes" and "La Science positive de la morale en Allemagne." The essays reviewed an enormous range of German scholarship, providing much of the ammunition for Deploige almost twenty years later; but two of the subjects treated are of special interest for Durkheim's sociology of religion. The first was the German *Völkerpsychologie*, the collective product of a group of anthropologists *cum* psychologists led by Theodor Waitz (1821–64), Hermann Steinthal (1823–99), and Moritz Lazarus (1824–1903), whose works had been introduced to French audiences through Ribot's *La Psychologie allemande contemporaine* (1879). Waitz, the son of a clergyman and seminary director, had studied at Leipzig, published a critical edition of Aristotle's *Organon* (1844) and, in 1846, joined the philosophy faculty at the University of Marburg. Deeply indebted to Herbartian psychology, Waitz's early works sought to reconcile an empirical study of the human mind with his utterly devout religious beliefs. But it was his *Anthropologie der Naturvölker* (6 vols., 1859–72), initially conceived as the empirical foundation for a philosophy of religion, which provided much of the (admittedly rather meager) ethnographic substance of *De la division du travail social* (1893).[33]

The most significant contribution of Lazarus and Steinthal to the social sciences was the *Zeitschrift für Völkerpsychologie und Sprachwissenschaft*. Founded in 1859, the *Zeitschrift* had declared its intention to publish essays concerned with "the discovery of the laws of ethnic psychology," reports of "historical, ethnological, geological, and anthropological facts," and to study language "not as the philologist or the empirical linguist, but in order to discover, with the aid of physiology, the psychological laws of language." Quite aside from the ordinary psychology which deals with individual man, Ribot agreed, "there is room for another science, devoted to social man, or,

---

[32] Lukes, 1973:95.
[33] See Durkheim, 1893: 57n8, 58n11–12, 134n2, 144, 149, 177, 177n7, 184, 244, 244n7, 245n8. In the second edition of *La Psychologie allemande contemporaine* (1886:58–9), Ribot could claim that the volumes devoted to descriptive anthropology "remain still the finest collection that exists, excepting monographs, for the study of the races in a state of nature. Special publications have completed or corrected the work of Waitz in many points; but no work has superseded it as a whole."

more exactly, to groups of men."[34] But Ribot also insisted that the successful realization of such a science depended upon certain theoretical presuppositions. For ethnological psychology to have a "real object," it had to be shown that the study of the individual alone is insufficient; and the essential condition of this proof was the demonstration that "society" is a whole greater than the sum of its individual parts. These, of course, were the central presuppositions of Durkheim's sociology, and they were fully embraced by Ribot in 1886.[35] The "real object" of ethnological psychology was precisely this *Volksgeist*, this "spirit of a people" independent of its individual members.

A "noble program, well-defined," Ribot suggested in 1886, albeit one which remained largely unfulfilled. Admittedly, Lazarus and Steinthal had produced a number of documents on attractive subjects (e.g., the history of religions, literary criticism, linguistics, anthropology, the history of customs, law and politics); but their treatment seemed "as much literary as scientific," "too general for this kind of investigation," and lacking in "exact results."[36] By 1888, Durkheim had reached largely similar conclusions. "In every society," he observed, "there exists a certain number of common ideas and sentiments. These are passed from one generation to another and simultaneously assure the unity and the continuity of collective life. Among these are popular legends, religious traditions, political beliefs, language, and so on. All these phenomena are psychological in nature, but they do not have their source in individual psychology, since they infinitely transcend the individual. They must, therefore, be the object of a special science charged with their description and the investigation of their preconditions. This science could be called social psychology. This," Durkheim added, referring explicitly to Lazarus and Steinthal, "is the Germans' *Völkerpsychologie*." The difficulty for Durkheim, as for Ribot, was that "no results have yet been produced."[37] Like Fustel's treatment of the religious origins of the family, private property, and the state, the *Völkerpsychologie* would have to wait for the *révélation* of 1894–95.

The second development in German social science to attract Durkheim's attention was the experimental psychology of Wilhelm Wundt (1832–1920). Despite a brilliant early career in physiological psychology, Wundt had been passed over as Helmholtz' successor at Berlin, and in 1875 was called to the chair of philosophy at Leipzig. The significance of the appointment, E.G.

---

[34] Ribot, 1886:61.

[35] Ribot, 1886:61–2. "If it be true that the social whole is something else than a simple addition of individuals, if the formation of groups gives birth to new relations, to new forms of development; briefly, if the whole be not an arithmetical sum of units, but a chemical combination differing from its elements, it must be admitted that *Völkerpsychologie* has a province exclusively its own. And this," Ribot concluded, "is the truth."

[36] Ribot, 1886:64–6.

[37] Durkheim, 1888b:63.

Boring has emphasized, cannot be exaggerated: "It brought Wundt formally into the field where psychology was supposed to belong, and it brought him there from physiology. Thus began that paradoxical situation...whereby experimental laboratories grew up as adjuncts to German chairs of philosophy."[38] Indeed, granted space in 1875 for the experimental demonstrations related to his lectures, Wundt established, in 1879, the *Psychologisches Institut*—the world's first laboratory of experimental psychology: "[A] primitive affair of a few rooms, soon increased to eleven," Boring observes, "it was in this first building that experimental psychology actually got its *de jure* independence."[39] Enormously productive, the new laboratory soon required its own medium of publication, and in 1881, Wundt founded the *Philosophische Studien*, the first effective organ of experimental psychology.

Despite the numerical superiority of the Berlin philosophers, Durkheim observed in 1887, "it is always Leipzig that is preferred by foreigners who come to Germany to complete their philosophical education. It is to Wundt and his teachings that this persistent vogue is due. It is this same cause," he added, "which led us to Leipzig, and kept us there longer than anywhere else."[40] The University of Leipzig generally—and the *Psychologisches Institut* in particular—thus became the focus of Durkheim's essay on the teaching of philosophy in Germany, which described the problems under study (e.g., the measurement of reaction time, the estimate of durations, the measurement of sensations of sound, the feeling for musical intervals, the verification of psychological laws by the method of mean graduations, etc.) in considerable detail. "We see how each of these topics is precise and restricted," Durkheim emphasized, "[b]ut however specialized these studies may be, nothing is more capable of raising in young minds the love of scientific precision, to divest them of vague generalizations and metaphysical possibilities, and finally to make them understand how complex are psychological facts and the laws which govern them—all while showing them that, if this complexity is an obstacle, there is nothing in this to discourage the observer."[41]

Wundt thus earned Durkheim's praise as the first German psychologist to break all connections with metaphysics; but simultaneously, Durkheim recognized that Wundt's own countrymen had found it "difficult to forgive him for this," an irony Durkheim attributed to German attachment for the older rationalism: "[E]veryone [in Germany] agrees with Kant," Durkheim complained, by refusing to reduce the higher forms of intelligence to experience—a refusal which removes the life of reason from any conceivable psychological scrutiny. Paradoxically inspired by this unlikely combination

[38] Boring, 1950:323.
[39] Boring, 1950:324.
[40] Durkheim, 1887a:313–4.
[41] Durkheim, 1887a:433.

of German achievement and French reception, Durkheim called for a "scientific philosophy"—i.e., a method which would treat the questions of philosophy according to the procedures of the positive sciences.[42] In fact, the period during which Durkheim visited Leipzig had become Wundt's "philosophische Jahrzehnte," comprising the completion of his *Logik* (2 vols., 1880–83), *Ethik* (3 vols., 1886), and *System der Philosophie* (2 vols., 1889). Not surprisingly, the particular philosophical questions to which Durkheim hoped to apply "the procedures of the positive sciences" were those of ethics.

"It has been my object in the present work," Wundt stated in the first sentence of his *Ethik*, "to investigate the problems of ethics in the light of an examination of the facts of the moral life."[43] Without denying the earlier contributions of metaphysics, psychology, or even utilitarian ethics, Wundt thus declared his own commitment to establishing ethics on an empirical, anthropological foundation. "The straight road to ethics," Wundt added, "lies...through *ethnic* psychology, whose especial business it is to consider the history of custom and of ethical ideas from the psychological standpoint."[44] Like his Romantic antecedents, Wundt was convinced that the development of morality began with language; and like Durkheim, he was equally convinced that this development occurred according to concrete, objective laws, which could be discovered through inductive generalization. But the witness of language, Wundt warned, despite its "complete objectivity," provides only the outward symbol of moral development. To understand the conditions underlying the moral development thus revealed, we must examine two other sources of evidence—religious conceptions and the social norms of custom and law.

Like Fustel, Wundt thought that the first preceded the second. Even among civilized peoples of the present, Wundt answered, most customs are the survivals of primitive ceremonial acts—particularly those of sacrifice[45] and commensality[46]—whose original purpose had been forgotten, and which

---

[42] Durkheim, 1887a:333.

[43] Wundt, 1886:vi.

[44] Wundt, 1886:vi (emphasis in original).

[45] "In its earliest form," Wundt argued, "the funeral feast is a sacrificial feast. Primitive man offers sacrifice to the gods at every important occasion of his life, and will very certainly make an offering at the burial of a kinsman. In part he desires to obtain the divine favour for his dead; but in part—and this is probably the more ancient idea of the two—the dead man is himself an object of worship. The souls of the dead hover over the dwellings of the living, whether to injure or to protect their inmates; so that acts which symbolise adoration or propitiation of the dead always play an important part in primitive worship" (1886:142).

[46] "A second motive," Wundt added, "which came into operation at a later date, but may gradually have ousted the original worship of the dead, lies in the symbolic meaning of a feast eaten in common. The common enjoyment of meat and drink is for primitive man a religious symbol of brotherhood; more especially if the feast have anything of solemnity about it, if it be sanctioned, so to speak, by the presence of the gods. The desire to share the last meal with the dead, to partake oneself of the food given him for his journey to the

had subsequently been pressed into the service of new ends. Custom was always "at first an act of worship, and so owed its obligatory power partly to the universality of religious ceremonial, and partly to the important place that ritual holds in general estimation by reason of its supposed influence on the favour or disfavour of the gods."[47] And the origin of religious worship itself—of the act of sacrifice—lay beyond the reach of scholarly observation.[48]

For Durkheim, Wundt's *Ethik* (1886) represented a "synthesis of all these isolated views, of all these special studies" with which his essay on the positive science of ethics in Germany had been concerned.[49] Moreover, by drawing these more specialized studies together, the *Ethik* had simultaneously become their "philosophical expression," lending "substance" to attempts which, before Wundt, "had remained rather indecisive and unconscious of themselves and of the goal toward which they tended."[50] In certain areas, however, Durkheim felt that Wundt had gone beyond his German colleagues. A typical feature of German philosophical ethics, for example, was its insistence on the role of calculation and will in the evolution of moral ideas, with the related implication that morality and society were, at least in part, "reflective creations" of human reason. Such a view, Durkheim argued, would quickly undermine positive, inductive science altogether, returning us by a short route to the metaphysical deductions of the older rationalism.[51]

What Durkheim particularly admired in Wundt was his steadfast avoidance of this kind of rationalism. For Wundt, the question of the nature of morality was never one of knowing what ought to be, but rather of knowing what is, an approach articulated in his criticism of Rudolf von Ihering's *Der Zweck im Recht* (2 vols., 1877–83). Briefly, Ihering's more utilitarian approach had explained customs as "individual habits" which, once found useful, had gradually been generalized throughout society. Durkheim fully endorsed the criticisms of Wundt. However rational such an explanation might appear, it is observation, not reason, which must decide; and observation tells us that a social custom "is never derived from a private habit." "However strange it might appear," Durkheim insisted, "customs

---

other world, springs, therefore, from a feeling of piety akin to that which impels primitive man to eat of the animal that he has sacrificed to the gods" (1886:142).

[47] Wundt, 1886:134. Again: "Every action of any importance is originally, whatever else it may be, a religious action; and the norms of conduct, which a man feels to be binding upon him in the more serious moments of his life, are soon applied to all the unimportant actions that at all resemble the more critical" (1886:136).

[48] "Of course," Wundt admitted, "religious worship itself must have had an origin. But the time of that origination lies far beyond the reach of our present observation. Even the most primitive form of worship, the cult of the dead, leads us by way of the goods laid out for the dead man straight to the act of sacrifice" (1886:150–1).

[49] Durkheim, 1887b:136.

[50] Durkheim, 1887b:33.

[51] Durkheim, 1887b:136–7.

have always been produced by other customs or, at the origin, by religious practices."[52]

Nevertheless, Durkheim's admiration for Wundt's *Ethik* was not entirely unqualified. As he would argue in *De la division du travail social*, Durkheim felt that the function of morality was "to make society possible," a position with which Wundt agreed. But for Wundt, Durkheim complained, morality performs this essential function *en passant*, "accidentally and as a consequence," almost "without wishing it." Morality results from the efforts man makes to find an enduring object, one to which he can attach himself, and from which he can taste "a kind of happiness which is not passing." The first objects he encounters in this search are his family, his city, and his country. But these things have their value, Wundt insisted, not because of what they are in themselves, but because of the ideal which they imperfectly symbolize. In short, morality maintains societies (as well as the instincts and inclinations which are its condition) because societies constitute the means whereby the moral sentiment is realized; but societies are never more than transitory phases through which morality passes, "one of the forms that it successively goes through."[53]

If we accept Wundt's position, Durkheim warned, one of the essential properties of morality—its obligatory force—becomes utterly inexplicable. Wundt acknowledged this property "in principle," but failed to identify its source, the authority in whose name its commands were uttered. For the religious believer, of course, that name was "God"; but for the agnostic Durkheim, who sought a secular substitute for God, such an explanation was clearly insufficient. For the rationalist, on the other hand, moral commands might be issued in the name of reason, in recognition of the happiness which follows moral behavior; but reason, Durkheim observed, leads only the mind, not the will, and what is desirable for our own happiness is not thereby obligatory upon us. Durkheim did not deny Wundt's fundamental idealist premise: "It is a sure fact," he agreed, that "we need to believe that our actions do not exhaust in an instant all their consequences, that they do not hold completely within the point of time and space where they were produced, but rather that they extend their effects more or less far, in duration as in expanse. Otherwise they would be very small things."[54] But Durkheim did deny that this was the *essential* factor in moral evolution, arguing, on the contrary, that society was not merely "the means whereby the moral sentiment is realized," but its very source; that society secures less ephemeral pleasures for us precisely because it is not "transitory," but rather infinitely outlasts the lifetime of any individual; that morality, in short, was a function of society rather than the reverse.[55]

[52] Durkheim, 1887b:137.
[53] Durkheim, 1887b:138.
[54] Durkheim, 1887b:139.
[55] Durkheim, 1887b:140.

For Durkheim, therefore, the obligatory force of moral rules—the feature which Kant had glorified but utterly failed to explain—was crucial. For all his criticisms of Wundt, however, it was a feature for which Durkheim had no better explanation in 1887 than the rather tentative, indecisive suggestion that it somehow derived from society. The situation had scarcely improved by the appearance of *De la division du travail social* (1893), where Durkheim offered a more detailed definition of moral facts, but where the question of explanation remains unanswered.[56] In the preface to the second, 1902 edition, however, Durkheim announced that he felt "justified in suppressing about thirty pages of the old introduction, which appear useless to us now."[57] And there followed a relatively complete theory of the "religio-moral" authority of the ancient and medieval occupational groups, emphasizing the origin of this authority in the celebrations, banquets, and sacrifices of ancient religious cults.[58] What had intervened, of course, was Durkheim's 1894–95 lecture-course on religion.

III. Smith, Frazer, and the Ritual Theory of Myth

Steven Lukes was quite right to describe Durkheim's earliest writings on religion as "largely formal and rather simpliste."[59] The stage was thus amply set for the famous lecture-course on religion which Durkheim taught at Bordeaux in 1894–95, and the *révélation* it inspired. Unfortunately— besides the oblique reference to his reading of "the works of Robertson Smith and his school"—Durkheim never disclosed the precise nature of this *révélation*, an autobiographical discourtesy which has encouraged a scholarly debate of substantial proportions. Not least among the obstacles to the resolution of this debate is the lack of any sign whatsoever, in works written by Durkheim soon after 1895, that he had seriously embraced the arguments of Smith's *Lectures on the Religion of the Semites* (1889). There is substantial evidence that Durkheim had read *The Golden Bough* (1890), not only in *Le Suicide* (1897), but also in "La Prohibition de l'inceste et ses origines" (1898) and "De la définition des phénomènes religieux" (1899). But of Smith's *Lectures*—and particularly the ritual theory of myth—Durkheim was strangely silent.[60]

As Durkheim's assimilation of the ethnographic literature accelerated in the last years of the 19th century, therefore, the vehicle for this assimilation was Frazer rather than Smith. And when we recall Robert Ackerman's insistence that Frazer "emphatically was not at all a ritualist through most of his career, and [that] it is indeed debatable whether, with the exception of

---

[56] Durkheim, 1893:424–5.

[57] Durkheim, 1893:1n1.

[58] See especially Section II, pp. 9–16.

[59] Lukes, 1973:240.

[60] Durkheim's disciples were less reticent; but in their case, silence was replaced by criticism. See the critical account of Smith's *Lectures* in Hubert and Mauss (1899), as well as Mauss' reviews of works by Jevons (1898), Wellhausen (1898), and Marillier (1899).

a few early years, he might ever have been accurately so identified,"[61] it seems that the alleged influence of the Cambridge Ritualists on Durkheim may have been no more than a mistaken inference drawn from a rare (and thus excessively dramatized) autobiographical passage in Durkheim's writings. Such a conclusion, of course, hardly befits a contribution to a colloquium on the Cambridge Ritualists; and fortunately, it is unwarranted, for Durkheim was deeply influenced both by Smith and by the ritual theory of myth. This influence, however, had to await Durkheim's examination of the pivotal studies of Australian totemism published by Baldwin Spencer and F.J. Gillen in 1899 and 1904, and his subsequent alarm at the thoroughly utilitarian interpretation of these studies embraced by Frazer.

For Robertson Smith, the origin and meaning of sacrifice had been "the central problem of ancient religion." Arguing that communion (in which god and worshipers shared in the consumption of the sacrificial animal) preceded any idea of a sacrificial gift (in which the animal was made over to the god alone), Smith insisted that primitive sacrifice was the periodic reaffirmation of the bonds of kinship—"participation in a common mass of flesh, blood, and bones"—which, among the Arabs, depended on commensality; and since the god was also construed as a kinsman, the communion sacrifice was a primitive, materialistic form of atonement, a periodic reconciliation of man with god.[62] Because these sacrifices were public acts of the clan and forbidden to strangers, and because the only other class of actions thus described was one involving an invasion of the sanctity of tribal blood, Smith suggested that the sacrificial victim was itself a kinsman, was sacred, and was thus a totem. The result of this enormously speculative leap was the single most powerful idea of Smith's *Lectures*—the theory of a primitive totemic sacrament.[63]

Frazer dedicated *The Golden Bough* to Smith, adding that the "central idea" of that work—the conception of the slain god—was derived from Smith's analysis of annual piacular ceremonies.[64] But Frazer immediately added that Smith was not responsible for his explanation of those rites which, indeed, relied heavily on animistic speculations. In fact, what Smith had seen as the unconscious survival of a mystical, theanthropic sacrifice, became in Frazer's hands a rational, utilitarian means to promote the growth and revival of vegetation.[65] As for the mystic, theanthropic sacrifice itself, Frazer described it as one of Smith's most original contributions to the comparative study of religion.[66] But on November 27, 1889, Frazer had already written to J.S. Black that Smith, "influenced probably by his deeply

---

[61] Ackerman, 1975: 115–16. Also see Ackerman's superbly executed study of Frazer's life and work (1987).

[62] Smith, 1889:255.

[63] Smith, 1889:313.

[64] Frazer, 1890:I:x–xi.

[65] Frazer, 1890:I:248.

[66] Frazer, 1894:206.

religious nature," had underestimated the role of fear and overestimated that of the benevolent emotions in molding early religion: "Hence his view of sacrifice as mainly a form of communion with the deity instead of a mode of propitiating him and averting his anger"—of which the latter was, to Frazer, the "substantially correct" view.[67] Where Frazer acknowledged the occurrence of such sacraments, he explained them in a utilitarian manner, as a consequence of the primitive belief that, by "eating the god," one acquires his physical, moral, or intellectual qualities; and of their alleged totemic origin, Frazer simply said "the evidence thus far does not enable us to pronounce decisively."[68]

On July 12, 1897, Baldwin Spencer wrote to Frazer describing his observations among the Arunta of Central Australia the previous summer. In particular, Spencer mentioned the almost complete absence of ritual proscriptions regarding exogamy or the eating of totemic animals.[69] The noteworthy exception was the *intichiuma* ceremony, which clearly involved restrictions on the eating of totemic animals; but the object of these restrictions seemed to be the multiplication of the totemic animal or plant, making it less a religious ceremony than a system of cooperative magic designed to secure a plentiful supply of food.[70] In this utterly utilitarian, economic function, Frazer instantly saw "the original meaning and purpose" of totemism itself. The notion of a system of cooperative magic appeared simple, conformed to the practical necessities of savage life, avoided the "metaphysical haze" some writers had attached to totemism, and was consistent with the traditions related by the Australians themselves.[71] There were also good reasons why the Australians *should* have eaten their totems—the efficacy of sympathetic magic depended heavily on the identification (indeed, the consubstantiality) of the totem and the clan—a belief of which the eating of the totemic animal might be a natural consequence. And this in turn seemed to explain what must have been regarded as Spencer and Gillen's most stunning observation—that among the very groups practicing the alimentary prohibition, a little of the totemic substance had to be periodically, and ritually, consumed—the "totemic sacrament" on whose existence Robertson Smith had speculated in 1889.

For all its plausibility, however, Frazer admitted that his theory faced at least two difficulties. First, while it seemed to explain why men should have once eaten their totems, it failed to explain why they should have ever stopped doing so (i.e., the alimentary prohibition)—a failure not lost on Durkheim (see below). Frazer's rather *ad hoc* solution in 1899 was a

[67] Black and Chrystal, 1912:518.
[68] Frazer, 1890:II, 84–5; 1894:206.
[69] Marett and Penniman, 1932:4–5.
[70] The detailed description of these rites appeared in Spencer and Gillen's *The Native Tribes of Central Australia* (1899), and Frazer's interpretation—developed in the course of his correspondence with Spencer—was published just weeks later (see Frazer, 1899).
[71] Frazer, 1899:836.

speculative appeal to totemic consubstantiality—i.e., "Men may have remarked that animals as a rule, and plants universally, do not feed upon their own kind; and hence a certain inconsistency may have been perceived in the conduct of Grub men who lived on grubs, of Grass-seed men who ate grass-seed, and so with the other animal and vegetable totems."[72] Second, since Australian totemism appeared to exist, in its earliest form, quite independently of exogamy, Frazer's explanation for the first implied no explanation of the second—a hiatus of which he was acutely aware, and which doubtless led to his increasing interest in that subject, and ultimately to his *Totemism and Exogamy* (4 vols., 1910).

Frazer was so enamored of his new theory as to introduce substantial alterations to the second edition of *The Golden Bough* (3 vols., 1900). Between magic and religion, Frazer now introduced "a fundamental distinction and even opposition of principle," arguing that magic, "as representing a lower intellectual stratum, has probably everywhere preceded religion."[73] Second, retaining the animistic foundations of his theory of totemism, Frazer now argued that the phenomenon of "soul transference" had less to do with the protection of the soul than with the control and manipulation of the totemic animal for economic purposes.[74] And third, while Frazer was willing to acknowledge a certain similarity between the *intichiuma* and the totemic sacrament postulated by Smith, he quickly added that it was "a long way" from the Australian rite to its universal practice, and that even the *intichiuma* was not quite what Smith had anticipated: "[W]hat we have found," Frazer concluded, "is not religion, but that which was first the predecessor, and afterwards the hated rival, of religion; I mean magic."[75]

It is difficult to imagine any interpretation of totemism to which Durkheim could have been more opposed. First, Frazer had denied the universality of totemism and its connection with exogamy. Durkheim had committed himself to both just one year earlier.[76] Second, Frazer had

---

[72] Frazer, 1899: 838.

[73] Frazer, 1900:I, xvi.

[74] Frazer, 1899:844. The theory of "soul transference" had provided Frazer's explanation of totemism in 1890. With the publication of Spencer and Gillen's *Northern Tribes of Central Australia* (1904), Frazer discovered a still more primitive form of totemism, and thus introduced still a third theory of totemism. See Frazer (1905:453–6).

[75] Frazer, 1900:I, xix, 202. Frazer was thus understandably irritated upon reading Hubert and Mauss' reference to the "Smith-Frazer system" (1899:5), and sought to set them straight in the Introduction to his second edition: "In an elaborate and learned essay on sacrifice," Frazer observed, "Messrs. H. Hubert and M. Mauss have represented my theory of the slain god as intended to supplement and complete Robertson Smith's theory of the derivation of animal sacrifice in general from a totem sacrament. On this I have to say that the two theories are quite independent of each other. I never assented to my friend's theory, and so far as I can remember he never gave me a hint that he assented to mine" (1900:I, 18).

[76] See "La Prohibition de l'inceste et ses origines" (1898).

suggested that some of society's most powerful interdictions had been rationally and purposefully constructed following an earlier period of permissiveness. That the origin of such interdictions lay in the "collective unconscious," and that primitive societies could hardly be characterized as "permissive," had been among Durkheim's central arguments in *De la division du travail social*. And third, Frazer had suggested that the essential function of totemism was to provide for economic needs, and that this was also its sufficient explanation. The fifth chapter of *Les Règles de la méthode sociologique* had been written explicitly to oppose such "teleological" confusions of the function of a social fact with its cause, and to insist that needs and desires, while they might hasten or retard social development, cannot themselves "create" social facts at all. Finally, to these must be added the undeniable importance of Spencer and Gillen's first volume. As the long-awaited and exhaustively-detailed study of a people more primitive than any hitherto observed, *Native Tribes* was the closest thing to an *experimentum crucis* that Victorian anthropology had to offer; and Spencer repeatedly confirmed and supported Frazer's interpretation through their subsequent extended correspondence.[77]

Durkheim's response appeared in "Sur le totémisme" (1902), a concerted, tendentious effort to rescue the older theory of totemism in both its social (exogamy) and religious (sacrifice) parts. Characteristically, Durkheim began with an appeal to evolution—the insistence that the Arunta, however primitive and isolated, were the result of considerable "indigenous evolution," and that their institutions, including clan endogamy, were the "perversion" of earlier, quite different forms. The obvious objection to this argument—and one of which Frazer was aware— was that it flatly contradicted the traditions of the Arunta themselves, which described their ancestors as practicing endogamy. It was here that Durkheim first appealed to Smith's ritual theory of myth—far from being "accurate historical testimony," these traditions were to be understood as myths invented by the primitive imagination to account for present institutional practices.[78]

But how had this primitive exogamy been transformed into endogamy? Durkheim's answer—again a rather *ad hoc* appeal to the more traditional view of totemism held by McLennan, Smith, and the early Frazer—was that the Arunta had once practiced matrilineal descent combined with patrilocal habitation, an unstable arrangement which required children to live with their fathers only to be separated from them to join their mothers on religious and social occasions. This inherently unstable arrangement

---

[77] Writing to Frazer from Melbourne on July 24, 1903, for example, Spencer complained that "Durkheim writes on sacred groves and caves and spots so sacred that they are only approached by the native in fear and trembling. He talks of 'ce système religieux' and pride in the Achilpa (wild cat) 'une sorte de culte public, commun à toute la tribu...' His whole article is full of misconceptions..." (Marett and Penniman, 1932:84–5).

[78] Durkheim, 1902:95–8.

eventually gave way, in a veritable "revolution," to patrilineal descent.[79] This "revolution" postulated by Durkheim to account for anomalous features of the *social* aspect of Arunta totemism was then extended to account for its equally anomalous *religious* features. The current toleration with respect to the eating of the totem, for example, could be conveniently explained as the consequence of the weakening of the structure of Arunta society, itself a consequence of the shift from matrilineal to patrilineal descent. Interestingly, Durkheim appealed to precisely the same principle appealed to by Frazer (the consubstantiality of clan member and totem) to support precisely the opposite argument (that men could not possibly have killed and eaten their totems in an earlier, more stable social order); and the traditions which described the clan's ancestors as eating their totems with impunity, like those which described them as practicing endogamy, were dealt with through an appeal to the ritual theory of myth—in this case, as the mythological elaboration of that part of the *intichiuma* in which a part of the totem was ceremonially consumed by each member of the clan. This ceremony, Durkheim argued, was indeed the totemic sacrament postulated by Robertson Smith—not in the magical sense proposed by Frazer—but in the genuinely mystical and religious sense originally intended by Smith himself.[80]

Just as the alimentary prohibition had constituted an anomaly within Frazer's theory, however, it was now incumbent upon Durkheim to explain its opposite—the ceremonial eating of the flesh of the totemic animal; and it was here that Durkheim's familiarity with Smith's *Lectures* served him best. Before *Native Tribes*, Durkheim observed, the ethnographic literature on totemism suggested that it consisted almost exclusively of *negative* practices (e.g., taboos, abstentions, interdictions, etc.); but in the *intichiuma*, we have clear evidence of the *positive* aspect of the cult (e.g., prestations, communal sacrifices and feasts, dances, etc). This more positive aspect, Durkheim insisted, was also the more primitive. For Durkheim, like Smith, was convinced that primitive peoples were insufficently rational to coordinate diverse economic activities toward the system of cooperative magic postulated by Frazer. The magical, economic interpretation of the *intichiuma* was a later construction imposed upon a rite whose original meaning and purpose had been religious. At its origin, the totem was sacred because clansmen were periodically required to "revivify their quality" through a communal sacrament, and this alone was the reason the totemic species could not be allowed to die out. The *intichiuma*, Durkheim concluded, agreeing with Smith, was a rite "analogous to those

---

[79] Durkheim, 1902:98–112. The argument presented by Durkheim here is extremely complex, and has been drastically simplified. For the more detailed description, see Jones (1986:614–17). Durkheim's argument is identical to the one he presented in "La Prohibition de l'inceste et ses origines" (1898).

[80] Durkheim, 1902:112–15.

which, in the most developed religions, have for their end the maintenance of the life of the god."[81]

IV. Conclusion

It is tempting to describe Durkheim's successive assimilation of these influences—Fustel, the German *Völkerpsychologie*, Wundt, Frazer, Smith—as "eclectic," and thus as exhibiting the catholicity of Durkheim's theoretical tastes. But this would be to emphasize the differences between them, and as we have seen, the remarkable thing from Durkheim's point of view was how much they had in common—how each was, in some sense, a metaphorical extension of the other, so that collectively they seemed to represent the same idea. In each case, for example, we come face to face with the notion that ritual precedes belief, that practical action precedes rational thought, and that the "unconscious" (considered individually or collectively) plays a powerful role in social behavior. Beyond these more overt similarities, only slightly less audible, we hear the voice of German romanticism and historicism, with their emphasis on experience rather than reason, the organic growth rather than artifical construction of institutions, and concrete, situated meanings rather than abstract, universal ideas.

Far from being "eclectic," therefore, I would rather characterize Durkheim's project as "pragmatic"—a practical project to be understood in terms of his concrete interests and purposes; and whatever sociologists may think, Durkheim's primary goal as a scholar and teacher was not to create a scientific sociology. Rather, it was to construct a secular morality for the Third French Republic, a project for which sociology was a powerful—but by no means the only—tool. Such a morality, Durkheim repeatedly insisted, must have two indispensable features—it must command absolutely, and it must provide ideals for the loftiest human aspirations. For this, there was but one historical precedent—the Judaeo-Christian morality—and Durkheim spent most of his life trying to unlock its secret.

The resources for this purpose became available to Durkheim only gradually, as the rigorous study of classical texts was gradually augmented, first by armchair anthropology, and then by detailed ethnographic observations. And as these empirical and conceptual tools became available, Durkheim clearly perceived and manipulated them analogically. In the *Leçons de sociologie* (1898–1900), for example, Durkheim saw Frazer's concept of *taboo* as the confirmation of Fustel's views on the religious origins of the institution of private property.[82] Again, in "Sociologie et sciences sociales" (1903), Durkheim emphasized that the works of Mannhardt, Tylor, Lang, Robertson Smith, Frazer, Hartland, and Wilken had "annexed at a stroke" that field "which the Germans had observed,

---

[81] Durkheim, 1902:117.
[82] Durkheim, 1898–1900:143–44.

recorded and compared since the beginning of the century."[83] And again, in the preface to the second edition of *De la division du travail social* (1902), Durkheim discovered the answer to the question unresolved in Wundt's *Ethik*—the source of the obligatory force of moral rules—in the "religio-moral" authority of occupational groups, itself founded upon the celebrations, banquets, and sacrifices of ancient religious cults.[84] And finally, in "Sur le totémisme" (1902), appealing repeatedly to the ritual theory of myth, Durkheim conceived the Arunta *intichiuma* on the model of Robertson Smith's ancient Semites.

Far from representing conflicting or even alternative interpretations of Durkheim's thought, therefore, the German, French, and British influences must be seen as expressive of coextensive, analogous ideas, albeit clothed in distinctive cultural metaphors. For the same reasons, it would be wrong to view the Cambridge Ritualists simply as advocates of an idiosyncratic theory of the origins of classical mythology; for the ideas they shared with Fustel, Wundt, Robertson Smith, and Durkheim—historicism, romanticism, irrationality, and the unconscious—were largely those to which the future of European social thought belonged.

Bibliography

Ackerman, Robert. 1975. "Frazer on Myth and Ritual." *Journal of the History of Ideas* 36:115–34.

Ackerman, Robert. 1987. *J.G. Frazer: His Life and Work.* Cambridge: Cambridge University Press.

Black, John Sutherland, and Chrystal, George. 1912. *The Life of William Robertson Smith.* London: Adam and Charles Black.

Boring, Edwin G. 1950. *A History of Experimental Psychology.* 2nd ed. New York: Appleton-Century-Crofts.

Deploige, Simon. 1907. "Réponses aux lettres de M. Durkheim." *Revue néo-scolastique* 14: 607–11, 614–21.

Deploige, Simon. 1911. *Le Conflit de la morale et de la sociologie.* Brussels: De Wit. Translated as *The Conflict Between Ethics and Sociology.* St. Louis and London: Herder, 1938.

Durkheim, Émile. 1885. "Gumplowicz, L., *Grundriss der Soziologie.*" *Revue philosophique de la France et de l'étranger* 20:627–34.

Durkheim, Émile. 1887a. "La Philosophie dans les universités allemandes." *Revue internationale de l'enseignement* 12:313–38, 423–40.

Durkheim, Émile. 1887b. "La Science positive de la morale en Allemagne." *Revue philosophique de la France et de l'étranger* 24: 33–58, 113–42, 275–84. Translated by R.A. Jones as "The Positive Science of Ethics in Germany." *History of Sociology: An International*

---

[83] Durkheim, 1903: 200.
[84] Durkheim, 1902: 10–18.

Review V, 2; VI, 1–2 (Combined Issue: Spring, 1986; Fall, 1986; Spring, 1987), pp. 177–91.

Durkheim, Émile. (1888a) 1978. "Introduction to the Sociology of the Family." Pp. 205–28 in *Émile Durkheim on Institutional Analysis*, edited by Mark Traugott. Chicago and London: The University of Chicago Press.

Durkheim, Émile. (1888b) 1978. "Course in Sociology: Opening Lecture." Pp. 43–87 in *Émile Durkheim on Institutional Analysis*, edited by Mark Traugott. Chicago and London: The University of Chicago Press.

Durkheim, Émile. (1892) 1960. *Montesquieu and Rousseau: Forerunners of Sociology*. Translation by R. Manheim. Ann Arbor, Michigan: University of Michigan Press.

Durkheim, Émile. (1893) (1902) 1933. *De la division du travail social.* Paris: Alcan. Second edition, 1902. Translated by George Simpson as *The Division of Labor in Society*. New York: Free Press.

Durkheim, Émile. 1898. "La Prohibition de l'inceste et ses origines." *L'Année sociologique* 1: 1–70.

Durkheim, Émile. (1898–1900) (1950) 1957. *Leçons de sociologie: Physique des moeurs et du droit*. Paris: Presses Universitaires de France. Translated by Cornelia Brookfield as *Professional Ethics and Civic Morals*. Glencoe, Illinois: The Free Press.

Durkheim, Émile. (1902) 1985. "Sur le totémisme." *L'Année sociologique* 5: 82–121. Translated by Robert Alun Jones as "On Totemism." *History of Sociology* 1: 91–121.

Durkheim, Émile, and Fauconnet, Paul. (1903) 1982. "Sociology and the Social Sciences." Pp. 175–208 in *Durkheim: The Rules of Sociological Method and Selected Texts on Sociology and Its Method* , edited by Steven Lukes. New York: The Free Press.

Durkheim, Émile. 1907. "Lettres au Directeur de *La Revue Néo-scolastique*." *Revue Néo-scolastique* 14: 606–7, 612–14.

Durkheim, Émile. (1912) 1915. *Les Formes élémentaires de la vie religieuse*. Paris: Alcan. Translated by Joseph Ward Swain as *The Elementary Forms of the Religious Life*. New York: Macmillan.

Durkheim, Émile. 1913. "Deploige, Simon, *Le Conflit de la morale et de la sociologie*." *L'Année sociologique* 12:326–8.

Evans-Pritchard, Edward. 1965. *Theories of Primitive Religion*. Oxford: Clarendon.

Frazer, James George. 1890. *The Golden Bough: A Study in Comparative Religion*. 2 vols. London: Macmillan.

Frazer, James George. (1894) 1920. "William Robertson Smith." Pp. 194–209 in *Sir Roger de Coverley and Other Literary Pieces*. London: Macmillan.

Frazer, James George. 1899. "The Origin of Totemism." *The Fortnightly Review* 65:647–65, 835–52.

Frazer, James George. 1900. *The Golden Bough: A Study in Magic and Religion*. 2d ed. 3 vols. London: Macmillan.

Frazer, James George. 1905. "The Beginnings of Religion and Totemism among the Australian Aborigines." *The Fortnightly Review* 84:162–72, 452–66.

Fustel de Coulanges, Numa Denis. (1864) 1956. *The Ancient City: A Study on the Religion, Laws, and Institutions of Greece and Rome*. Garden City, New York: Doubleday.

Gilpin, Robert. 1968. *France in the Age of the Scientific State*. Princeton, New Jersey: Princeton University Press.

Gooch, G. P. 1913. *History and Historians in the Nineteenth Century*. London: Longmans, Green, & Co.

Hubert, Henri, and Mauss, Marcel. (1899) 1964. *Sacrifice: Its Nature and Function* . Chicago: University of Chicago Press.

Jones, Robert Alun. 1977. "On Understanding a Sociological Classic." *American Journal of Sociology* LXXXIII, 2 (September): 279–319.

Jones, Robert Alun. 1984. "Robertson Smith and James Frazer on Religion: Two Traditions in British Social Anthropology." Pp. 31–58 in *Functionalism Historicized: Essays on British Social Anthropology*, edited by George W. Stocking, Jr. Madison: University of Wisconsin Press.

Jones, Robert Alun. 1986. "Durkheim, Frazer, and Smith: The Role of Analogies and Exemplars in the Development of Durkheim's Sociology of Religion." *American Journal of Sociology* XCVIII, 3 (November): 596–627.

Lepenies, Wolf. 1986–87. "Gefährliche Wahlverwandtschaften: Raymond Aron und die deutsch-französischen Beziehungen in der Soziologie." Translated by Robert Alun Jones and Gerd Schroeter as "Dangerous Elective Affinities: Raymond Aron and the German-French Connection in Sociology." *History of Sociology: An International Review* V, 2; VI, 1–2 (Combined Issue: Spring, 1986; Fall, 1986; Spring, 1987), pp. 169–76.

Lukes, Steven. 1973. *Émile Durkheim: His Life and Work: A Historical and Critical Study*. New York: Harper and Row.

Marett, R.R. and Penniman, T.K., eds. 1932. *Spencer's Scientific Correspondence with Sir J.G. Frazer and Others*. Oxford: Clarendon.

Mauss, Marcel. 1898a. "Jevons, F. Byron. *An Introduction to the History of Religions*." *L'Année sociologique* 1:160–71.

Mauss, Marcel. 1898b. "Wellhausen, J. *Reste des arabischen Heidentums*." *L'Année sociologique* 1:183–6.

Mauss, Marcel. 1899. "Marillier, L. *La Place du Totémisme dans l'évolution religieuse*." *L'Année sociologique* 2:202–4.

Momigliano, Arnaldo. 1982. "The Ancient City of Fustel de Coulanges." Pp. 325–43 in *Essays in Ancient and Modern Historiography*, by A. Momigliano. Middletown, Connecticut: Wesleyan University Press.

Renan, Ernest. 1872. *La Réforme intellectuelle et morale*. Paris: Calmann-Lévy.

Ribot, Théodule. 1886. *La Psychologie allemande contemporaine*. Translated from the second edition by James Mark Baldwin as *German Psychology of Today: The Empirical School*. With a Preface by James McCosh. New York: Charles Scribner's Sons.

Smith, William Robertson. (1889) 1894. *Lectures on the Religion of the Semites*. Second Edition. London: Adam and Charles Black.

Thompson, James Westfall. 1942. *A History of Historical Writing. Volume II: The Eighteenth and Nineteenth Centuries*. New York: Macmillan.

Wundt, Wilhelm. (1886) 1897. *Ethics: An Investigation of the Facts and Laws of the Moral Life*. First English, from the Second German ed. Julia Gulliver, translator. London: Swan Sonnenschein and Co. Ltd.; 3 vols.

University of Illinois at Urbana-Champaign

7

Classical Studies in Nineteenth-Century Great Britain as Background to the "Cambridge Ritualists"

P. G. NAIDITCH

The "Cambridge Ritualists" were all educated as classical scholars and all wrote on problems in classical antiquity.[1-5] Their place therefore, in the intellectual history of Great Britain, is at least in part in the history of classical scholarship. To identify that place with precision, and to investigate their reception by British classical scholars of the time, is a task peculiarly difficult. This difficulty has two principal causes.

First, the history of modern classical scholarship is yet in its infancy. Students stand in relation to their subject in much the same way as humanists of the fifteenth century stood to theirs. Every year sees new, significant materials published for the first time, though the critical apparatuses, which would reduce the opportunities for error, have yet to be compiled. No satisfactory biographical dictionaries of classical scholars exist. No single directory, which identifies in good order the various teachers in colleges or schools and professors, readers, lecturers, tutors and coaches in the institutions of higher learning, is available. No book merely listing in convenient form the several British classical periodicals awaits the enquiring student. The result is that, so little has been done, most fail to

Abbreviations

AC	J. Venn/J. A. Venn, *Alumni Cantabrigienses* part II (Cambridge, 1940–1954)
BBA	*British Biographical Archive* (London/München, 1984- [microfiche edition])
BLC	*British Library Catalogue of Printed Books to 1975* (London, 1979–1987)
Boase	F. Boase, *Modern English Biography* (London, 1892–1921; [London 1965])
Clarke	M. L. Clarke, *Greek Studies in England: 1500–1830* (Cambridge, 1945)
PBA	*Proceedings of the British Academy*, London
Sandys	J. E. Sandys, *A History of Classical Scholarship* Vol. 3 (Cambridge, 1908)
**	Not examined

[1] The precise membership of the group is controversial, and its very name potentially absurd; but four names are commonly associated with the title "Cambridge Ritualists": Jane Ellen Harrison (1850–1928), Gilbert Murray (1866–1957), Francis Macdonald Cornford (1874–1943) and Arthur Bernard Cook (1868–1952). All four are treated in Shelley Arlen, *The Cambridge Ritualists: an Annotated Bibliography* (Metuchen/London, 1990).

realise how meagre are the basic reference tools available to them. Classical scholars proper can consult Pauly-Wissowa, Roscher, Daremberg-Saglio, Engelmann-Preuss, the *Bibliotheca Philologica Classica*, Klussmann, Lambrino, and Marouzeau; historians of classical scholarship possess no such equivalent works.

But there is a second reason for there being difficulty in investigating the background of the Ritualists in the history of classical studies in Great Britain. There are false notions abroad about the development of nineteenth century British classical scholarship, and these miscolour the history of the discipline. One can read, for example, that "1855...was...long before English universities had chairs of archaeology," though in point of fact the Cambridge professorship was established before that year.[6] Or one can read

[2] For Harrison, see her *Reminiscences of a Student's Life* (London, 1925) [= *Arion* 4 (1965) 312–46]; *Times* (April 17, 1928), 11c; J. Stewart, *Cambridge Review* 49 (April 27, 1928), 364; F. M. Cornford, *DNB 1922–30*, 408 f.; *Who Was Who* 2, 469; Jessie Stewart, *Jane Ellen Harrison* (London, 1959); J. C. Wilson in J. E. Harrison, *Epilegomena to the Study of Greek Religion and Themis* (New York, 1962), vii–xii, 559–77; S. Peacock, *Jane Ellen Harrison: the Mask and the Self* (New Haven/London, 1988); R. Schlesier in *Classical Scholarship: A Biographical Encyclopedia*, edd. W. W. Briggs and W. M. Calder III (New York/London, 1990) 127–41. Cf. R. Ackerman, *GRBS* 13 (1972) 209–30; *The Diary of A. C. Benson* (New York, 1926) 208; M. C. Bradbrook, *That Infidel Place* (London, 1969), 51; W. M. Calder III, *CW* 74 (1981), 249 n. 11; E. S. Leedham-Green, *A Guide to the Archives of the Cambridge University Press* (Bishops Stortford, 1973), reel 2B: 2.6 for Feb. 5, Feb. 22, May 2, May 29, June 3, July 30, and Nov. 6, 1895 and Feb. 6, Feb. 19 and June 2, 1896; *ibid.* 2.9, 367, 384, 396; Joan Evans, *Prelude & Fugue* (London, 1964), 21; *London and the Life of Literature in Late Victorian England: the Diary of George Gissing* (Sussex, 1978), 497, 578; C. Kluckhohn, *Anthropology and the Classics* (Providence, 1961), index; Mary A. Hamilton, *Newnham* (London, 1936), index; I. Henderson in G. Murray, *An Unfinished Autobiography* (London, 1960), 136; P. Henderson, *Samuel Butler* (Bloomington, Ind., 1954), 171–72; A. John, *Chiaroscuro* (London, 1952), 64; H. M. Kempthorne, *Christ's College Magazine* 60 (May 1968), 80; R. R. Marett, *A Jerseyman at Oxford* (London, 1941), 251–52; G. Murray, *PBA* 29 (1943), 421 f.; P. G. Naiditch, *A. E. Housman at University College, London* (Leiden, 1988), 62 f., n. 22-10; David Newsome, *On the Edge of Paradise* (London, 1980), 212, 245; R. W. Pfaff, *Montague Rhodes James* (London, 1980) 133, 255; E. Raikes, *Dorothea Beale of Cheltenham* (London, 1908) 152, 205; Bertrand Russell, *Autobiography* 1, 1951 (Boston, 1967), 259, 352; F. H. Sandbach, *PBA* 64 (1978), 428; F. C. Steadman, *In the Days of Miss Beale* (London, 1931), 17–19; G. S. Thomson, *Mrs. Arthur Strong* (London, 1949), 24 f.; *Times* (April 20, 1928), 19c; D. Wilson, *Gilbert Murray* (Oxford, 1984), index; L. Woolf, *An Autobiography* 2 (Oxford, 1980) 204; *The Letters of Virginia Woolf*, ed. N. Nicolson, vols. 1–3 (New York, 1975–1978) index.
[3] For Murray, see G. Murray, "Professor at 23," *College Courant* 3.6 (1951) 105–8; C.M.B[owra], *Oxford Magazine* 75 (1957) 478; J.A.K. Thomson, *PBA* 43 (1957) 245–70; idem, *John O'London's Weekly* 2 (1960) 404 f., 427 f., 464, 491, 524, 557, 560, 591, 623; R.L. Fowler in *Classical Scholarship: A Biographical Encyclopedia*, edd. W. W. Briggs and W. M. Calder III (New York/London, 1990) 321–34; G. Murray, *An Unfinished Autobiography* (London, 1960); F. West, *Gilbert Murray: A Life* (London, 1984); D. Wilson, *Gilbert Murray O.M.* (Oxford, 1987); cf. A. Adam, *Arthur Innes Adam* (Cambridge, 1920) 79, 85; R. Ackerman, *J. G. Frazer: His Life and Work* (Cambridge, 1987) 3, 100, 120, 263; idem, *GRBS* 12 (1971) 113 ff.; J. Barnes, *Ahead of His Time* (London, 1979) index; Mrs. Barnett, *Canon Barnett*, Vol. 2 (London, 1918) 218 n.; F. R. Barry, *Period of*

My Life (London, 1970) 42; Lord Beveridge, *Power and Influence* (London, 1953) 182, 266; C. M. Bowra, *Memories 1898–1939* (London, 1966) index; J. Buxton and P. Williams, *New College, Oxford* (Oxford, 1979) 101, 130, 148; M. Clapinson and H. Langley, *Catalogue of the Papers of Gilbert Murray* (Oxford, 1980: unpublished); E. R. Dodds, *Missing Persons* (Oxford, 1977) index; Frank Fletcher, *After Many Days* (London, 1937) 208; J. H. Fowler, *The Life and Letters of Edward Lee Hicks* (London, 1922) 290, 292; G. Glasgow, *Ronald Burrows: a Memoir* (London, 1924) index and 76 f.; J. E. Harrison, *Reminiscences* (London, 1925) 64; M. Hartog, *P. J. Hartog* (London, 1949) 151; R. Helms, "T. S. Eliot on Gilbert Murray," *English Language Notes* 23 (1986) 50–56; H.J.W. Hetherington, *The Life and Letters of Sir Henry Jones* (London, 1924 [1925]) index; Diana Hopkinson, *Family Inheritance: A Life of Eva Hubback* (London, 1954) 50, 54, 114; *The Letters of A. E. Housman*, ed. H. Maas (London, 1971) indexes; T.E.B. Howarth, *Cambridge between Two Wars* (London, 1978) index; *Illustrated London News* 136 (1910) 226 = 306; *ibid.* 138 (1911) 16; *ibid.* 145 (1914) 6; C.E.D. Joad, *Book of Joad* (London, 1932) 14; A. John, *Chiaroscuro* (London, 1952) 64; C. Kluckhohn, *Anthropology and the Classics* (Providence, 1961) index; G. W. Knight, *Jackson Knight* (Oxford, 1975) 323 f.; H. Lloyd-Jones, *Blood for the Ghosts* (London, 1980) 195–214; M. Longson, *A Classical Youth* (London, 1985) 92; A. E. MacNair, *John O'London's Weekly* 2 (1960) 637; Max Mallowan, *Mallowan's Memoirs* (New York, 1977) 25 f.; R. R. Marett, *A Jerseyman at Oxford* (London, 1941) 172, 300; J. H. Muirhead, *Bernard Bosanquet and His Friends* (London, 1935) 166; idem, *Reflections of a Journeyman in Philosophy* (London, 1942) 142, 181; P. G. Naiditch, *The Development of Classical Scholarship* (UCLA, 1991) no. 63; W. Oakeshott, *PBA* 46 (1960) 297, 306; W. Rothenstein, *Since Fifty* (London, 1939) 213; A. L. Rowse, *A Man of the Thirties* (London, 1979) 205; M. Sadler, *Michael Ernest Sadler* (London, 1949) 370; L. Woolf, *Autobiography*, Vol. 2 (Oxford, 1980) 138 f., 167; *The Letters of Virginia Woolf*, ed. N. Nicolson, Vols. 1–2 (New York, 1975/76) indexes.

[4] For Cornford, see *Times* (Jan. 5, 1943) 6f; D. S. Robertson, *Cambridge Review* 64 (1943) 164; R. Hackforth, *DNB1941–50* 177–79; G. Murray, *PBA* 29 (1943) 421–32; D. K. Wood in *Classical Scholarship: A Biographical Encyclopedia*, edd. W. W. Briggs and W. M. Calder III (New York/London, 1990) 23–36; *Who Was Who*, Vol. 4, Third Edition (1964) 253; cf. R. Ackerman, *GRBS* 12 (1971) 113 ff.; idem, *GRBS* 15 (1974) 359, 363 f.; idem, *J. G. Frazer: His Life and Work* (Cambridge, 1987) index; Lord Beveridge, *Power and Influence* (London, 1953) 374; D. C., *Emmanuel College Magazine* 53 (1970/71) 9; K. G., *Times* (Jan. 15, 1943) 7d; C. Hassall, *Ambrosia and Small Beer* (London, 1964) 213, 240; idem, *Edward Marsh* (London, 1959) 632; D. Hopkinson, *Family Inheritance: A Life of Eva Hubback* (London, 1954) 43; G. Keynes, *Henry James in Cambridge* (Cambridge, 1967) 16; W.K.C. Lloyd, *PBA* 68 (1982) 562; G. Murray, *John O'London's Weekly* 2 (1960) 491; J. Stewart, *Jane Harrison* (London, 1959) index; Michael Straight, *After Long Silence* (New York, 1983) 60, 90 f., 97, 99; Gertrude Calton Thompson, *Mixed Memories* (*s.l.*, 1983) 89; *Times* (Jan. 8, 1943) 7b; G. M. Trevelyan, *An Autobiography* (London, 1949) 24; *The Letters of Virginia Woolf*, ed. N. Nicolson, Vol. 1 (New York, 1975) index. For part of his library, see *Heffer* cat. 609, 1944. Some of his papers are preserved in the Frances Cornford collection at the British Library.

[5] For Cook, see P. G. Naiditch, *A. E. Housman at University College, London* (Leiden, 1988) 158 n. 46-1.

[6] H. Lloyd-Jones in Ulrich von Wilamowitz-Moellendorff, *History of Classical Scholarship* (Baltimore, 1982) 137 n. 503. See, for example, *The Cambridge University Calendar for the Year 1855* (Cambridge, n.d.) 154: "DISNEY PROFESSORSHIP OF ARCHAEOLOGY. This Professorship was founded in 1851 by JOHN DISNEY, Esq. of the Hyde, Ingatestone, who also presented to the University a valuable collection of Ancient Marbles." Although it was a difficult professorship to create, the fact is that it was created at this time (cf. G. Daniel, *Some Small Harvest* [London, 1988] 209).

that "Housman was in fact confirming for his period the criteria of excellence which have dominated English classical studies since Bentley."[7] The reasons for the belief that the history of scholarship is chiefly the history of textual criticism are outside the boundaries of the present paper. It is enough here to remark the existence of the idea, and to observe that Housman himself has, perhaps inadvertently, helped foster this belief both by his words and by his actions. Thus, he writes:

> History repeats itself, and we now witness in Germany pretty much what happened in England after 1825, when our own great age of scholarship, begun in 1691 by Bentley's Epistola ad Millium, was ended by the successive strokes of doom which consigned Dobree and Elmsley to the grave and Blomfield to the bishopric of Chester.[8-11]

[7] J. P. Sullivan, *Arion* 1 (1962) 106 (= *A. E. Housman: A Collection of Critical Essays*, ed. C. Ricks [Englewood Cliffs NJ, 1968] 147 f.). It seems to be true enough that Bentley, Porson and Housman are the best known of British classical scholars not only among professional students but among the population at large. See Anon., *Classical Journal* 1 (1810) 17: "One Bentley died, and after a lapse of years a second [*sc.* Porson] rose; a third may yet be hidden in the womb of time." Cf. *CJ* 73 (1828) 21; H. Beveridge, *Athenaeum* 3786 (1900) 62; cp. Anon., *CJ* 78 (1829) 253. See also Anon., *Gentleman's Magazine* 95 (1825) 37: "Elmsley...did not over-value the importance of this very limited province of philology, which the conspicuous success of one great scholar has rendered perhaps too exclusively fashionable among those who aim at a reputation for classical learning." For the popular view, see G. Bernard Shaw, "Misalliance" (1909/10), *The Bodley Head Bernard Shaw*, Vol. 4 (London, 1972) 60: "it is assumed that the schoolmaster has a right to force every child into an attempt to become Porson and Bentley, Leibnitz and Newton, all rolled into one" and "Pygmalion" (1912/13), *ibid.*, 794: "Freddy...knew a little Latin. It was very little, but enough to make him appear to her a Porson or Bentley." For the addition of Housman to form a triumvirate, see e.g. the full title of C. O. Brink's *English Classical Scholarship: Historical Reflections on Bentley, Porson, and Housman* (Cambridge, 1985).

[8] *M. Manilii astronomicon liber primus* (London, 1903) xlii. Housman saw the change as occurring in 1864, a year distinguished by the appearance of H.A.J. Munro's Lucretius. In lecture, Housman affirmed that the book amounted to nothing short of the revival of Latin scholarship in England (University Library, Cambridge, Add. Ms. 6894 6v–7r; cf. *The Confines of Criticism* (Cambridge, 1969) 20–2 (= *Collected Poems and Selected Prose* [London, 1988] 299 f.). That Housman had Munro's Lucretius particularly in mind was thus rightly conjectured by C. O. Brink (*English Classical Scholarship* [Cambridge, 1985] 115). For lives of Housman, see P. G. Naiditch, *A. E. Housman at University College, London* (Leiden, 1988) 26–29.

[9] For Richard Bentley (1662–1742), Master of Trinity College, Cambridge (1700–1742), see Naiditch, "Richard Bentley and the Vice-Master of Trinity College, Cambridge: A Lost Document," *ANQ* (forthcoming).

[10] For Peter Paul Dobree (1782–1825), Professor of Greek at Cambridge (1823–1825), see *Gentleman's Magazine* 95 (Oct. 1825) 372; H. R. Luard, *DNB* Vol. 5 (1885/6) 1039–41; Sandys, 399 f.; cf. *BLC* vol. 84 450 f.; Clarke, index; N. Horsfall, *GRBS* 15 (1974) index; Sandys, index; *Life, Letters and Journals of George Ticknor*, Vol. 1 (Boston, 1877, Sixth Edition) 271.

[11] For Peter Elmsley (1773–1825), Camden Professor of Ancient History at Oxford (1823–1825), see [H. R. Luard?,] *Gentleman's Magazine* 95 (Apr. 1825) 374–77; W. Wroth, *DNB* Vol. 6 (1885/6) 728 f.; Sandys, 394 f.; cf. E. H. Barker, *Literary Anecdotes*, Vol. 1 (London, 1852) 52; *BLC* vol. 94 38; Clarke, index; M. L. Clarke, *George Grote*

England disappeared from the fellowship of nations for forty years: Badham,[12] the one English scholar of the mid-century whose reputation crossed the Channel, received from abroad the praises of Duebner and Nauck and Cobet, but at home was excluded from academical preferment, and set to teach boys at Birmingham, and finally transported to the antipodes: his countrymen, having turned their backs on Europe and science and the past, sat down to banquet on mutual approbation, to produce the Classical Museum and the Bibliotheca Classica, and to perish without a name.[13]

The knowledgeable recognised that Housman was limiting himself strictly to textual criticism.[14] And as a description of the history of textual criticism in Britain Housman's evaluation seems to be not unjust: indeed Wilamowitz, whom he echoes, had come to much the same conclusion.[15] But Housman's remarks disguise the fact that textual criticism was not the sole occupation of British students.

How far from textual criticism British classical scholarship departed, and how far Housman consequently misrepresents the philosophies and sympathies of mid-century Britain, can be clearly seen in a number of ways. One might dwell on the fact that the middle decades of the century saw the

---

(London, 1962) 10–12; G. V. Cox, *Recollections of Oxford* (London, 1868) 107, 149, 179, 393; H. Grote, *The Personal Life of George Grote* (London, 1873) 16 f., 27 f. n.*; J.E.B. Mayor, *Twelve Cambridge Sermons* (Cambridge, 1911) index; N. Horsfall, *GRBS* 15 (1974) 449–77; Sandys, index; J. S. Watson, *The Life of Richard Porson* (London, 1860) index.

[12] For Charles James Blomfield (1786–1857), Bishop of Chester (1824–1828) and London (1828–1856), see *Times* (Aug. 9, 1857) 9d; A. Blomfield, *A Memoir of Charles James Blomfield* (London, 1863); W. Wroth, *DNB*, Vol. 2 (1885) 692–92; Boase 1 c. 315; Sandys, 400 f.; cf. *BLC* vol. 34, 456–63; Clarke, index; N. Horsfall, *GRBS* 15 (1974) 449–77; *Bibliotheca Parriana* (London, 1827) 133; J. Pycroft, *Memories of Oxford*, Vol. 1 (London, 1886) 78; C. Wordsworth, *Annals of My Early Life* (London, 1891) index; idem, *Annals of My Life* (London, 1893) 16; J. Wordsworth, *Times Literary Supplement* (May 8, 1959) 273. I owe this last reference to Ian Jackson, Berkeley.

[13] For Charles Badham (1813–1884), Professor of Latin and Logic at the University of Sydney (1867–1884), see *Times* (April 10, 1884), 7c; *Athen.* 2947 (April 19, 1884), 506; T. Cooper, *DNB* 1 (1885), 857f.; T. Butler in *Speeches and Lectures Delivered in Australia by the Late Charles Badham* (Sydney, 1890); F. Boase, *Modern English Biography*, 1, London 1892 (London, 1965), cols. 122f.; Sandys, 283, 407f.; *The Australian Encyclopaedia* 1 (Sydney, 1958), 387 f.; cf. *BLC* vol. 16, 120 f.; Axel Clark, *Christopher Brennan* (Melbourne, 1980), index; John Cooper, *Wadham College Gazette* no. 14 (Hilary Term 1902) 258; H. D. Jocelyn in *La filologia greca e latina nel secolo XX* 1 (Pisa, 1989) 549–53; H. P. Simpson, *Times* (April 14, 1884), 9f. For his application and testimonials, see University College, London, D.M.S. Watson Library, Appl. Latin 1863.

[14] Cf. R. W. Chambers, *Philologists at University College* (London, 1927) 21; cf. also F. M. Turner, *The Greek Heritage in Victorian Britain* (New Haven, 1981) 7; C. O. Brink, *English Classical Scholarship* (Cambridge, 1985) 117.

[15] The echoes from Wilamowitz's *Herakles* and *Geschichte* have been remarked by D. S. Robertson, *CR* 50 (1936) 114–15, W. M. Calder III, *Ulrich von Wilamowitz-Moellendorff, Selected Correspondence* (Naples, 1982) 288 n. 48, and E. J. Kenney, *The Classical Text* (Berkeley, 1974) 122 n. 2.

first editions of Liddell and Scott's *Greek-English Lexicon*.[16-17] One might observe that it was in this period that Grote's *History of Greece* was first

[16] For Henry George Liddell (1811–1898), Dean of Christ Church (1855–1891), see *Times* (Jan. 20, 1898) 8ab; *Athen.* 3665 (Jan. 22, 1898) 118 f.; *Illustrated London News* 112 (Jan. 29, 1898) 141; H. L. Thompson, *Henry George Liddell* (London, 1899); H. T. Thompson, *DNB*, Vol. 22 (1890) 966–68; Sandys, 418; cf. E. Abbott and L. Campbell, *The Life and Letters of Benjamin Jowett* (London, 1897) index; Anon., *Things I Shouldn't Tell* (London, 1924) 126; A. J. Ashton, *As I Went on My Way* (London, 1924) 79; Mrs. Barnett, *Canon Barnett*, Vol. 1 (London, 1918) 129; A. C. Benson, *The Life of Edward White Benson*, Vol. 2 (London, 1899) 517; E.G.W. Bill and J.F.A. Mason, *Christ Church and Reform* (Oxford, 1970) index; *The Life and Letters of Frederick Lord Blackford* (London, 1896) 26; *Letters of John Stuart Blackie to His Wife* (Edinburgh, 1909) 162; C. M. Blagden, *Well Remembered* (London, 1953) 102; D. H. Blair, *In Victorian Days* (London, 1939) 96; C. and F. Brookfield, *Mrs. Brookfield* (New York, 1905) 353; W. M. Calder III, *Classical Journal* 84 (1989) 265 f.; *The Diaries of Lewis Carroll*, ed. R. L. Green (London, 1953) index; *The Letters of Lewis Carroll*, ed. M. N. Cohen (New York, 1979) index; N. C. Chaudhuri, *Scholar Extraordinary* (London, 1974) index; *Life and Correspondence of John Duke, Lord Coleridge*, Vol. 2 (London, 1904) 233; G. V. Cox, *Recollections of Oxford* (London, 1868) 393, 395 f.; Sir J. Denham, *Memoirs of the Memorable* (New York, n.d.) 196–98; Lady Dilke, *Book of the Spiritual Life* (London, 1905) 49; C. Firth, *Modern Languages at Oxford* (London, 1929) index; G. Faber, *Jowett* (London, 1957) index; J. H. Fowler, *The Life and Letters of Edward Lee Hicks* (London, 1922) 37, 62 f., 68, 78; Mrs. Gell, *Under Three Reigns* (London, 1927) 101; W. Gregory, *An Autobiography* (London, 1894) 38, 45; C. Hayes, *Oxford*, Vol. 39.2 (1987) 68 f.; *Letters of Benjamin Jowett* (London, 1899) index; J. K. Laughton, *Memoir of the Life and Correspondence of H. Reeve* (London, 1898) 379; K. F. Kitchell, Jr., "How the Wrong Parts Wrote Scott and the Right Parts Wrote Liddell," *Classical Journal* 84 (1988) 47–52; idem, *ibid.* 85 (1989) 266–68; *Letters of the Right Hon. Sir George Cornewall Lewis* (London, 1870) 297, 322; L. M. Markby, *Memories of Sir William Markby* (Oxford, 1917) 79; J. Marriott, *Memories of Four Score Years* (London, 1946) 30; Herbert Maxwell, *Evening Memories* (London, 1932) 79; K.M.E. Murray, *Caught in the Web of Words* (New Haven CT, 1977) index; Carola Oman, *An Oxford Childhood* (London, 1976) 93; S. Paget, *Henry Scott Holland: Memoir and Letters* (London, 1921) index; *Memorials of Roundell Palmer*, Vol. 2 (London, 1898) 361; R. Pearsall, *The Worm in the Bud* (Toronto, 1969) 268; J. Pycroft, *Memories of Oxford*, Vol. 1 (London, 1886) 73, 162; *Personal Papers of Lord Rendell* (London, 1931) 147; B. F. Robinson, *Chronicles in Cartoons* (s.l., n.d.) 262; *The Works of John Ruskin*, Vol. 39 (London, 1912) index; *Robert Scott and Benjamin Jowett*, ed. J. M. Prest (Oxford, 1966) 6, 10; Goldwin Smith, *Reminiscences* (New York, 1910) 101, 103; *T. P.'s & Cassell's Weekly* 6 (1926) 614; H. L. Thompson, *Christ Church* (London, 1900) index; *Times* (Jan. 22, 1898) 8e; *ibid.* (Jan. 24, 1898) 10f; W. Tuckwell, *Reminiscences of Oxford* (London, 1900) 117, 151; F. E. Weatherly, *Piano and Gown* (London, 1926) 59; M. V. Woodgate, *Father Benson* (London, 1953) 29; C. Wordsworth, *Annals of My Early Life* (London, 1891) index.

[17] For Robert Scott (1811–1887), Master of Balliol (1854–1870), see *Athen.* 3137 (Dec. 10, 1887) 786; cf. E. Abbott and L. Campbell, *The Life and Letters of Benjamin Jowett* (London, 1897) index; W. M. Calder III, *CJ* 84 (1989) 265 f.; N. C. Chaudhuri, *Scholar Extraordinary* (London, 1974) 219 f.; E. H. Coleridge, *Life and Correspondence of John Duke, Lord Coleridge* (London, 1904) index; K. F. Kitchell, Jr., *CJ* 84 (1988) 47–52; idem, *ibid.* 85 (1989) 266–68; A.G.C. Liddell, *Notes from the Life of an Ordinary Mortal* (London, 1911) 59; F. Meyrick, *Memories of Life at Oxford* (London, 1905) 101; *Robert Scott and Benjamin Jowett* (A Supplement to the Balliol College Record), ed. J. M. Prest (Oxford, 1966); R. G. Tatton, *Selected Writings of Thomas Godolphin Rooper* (London, 1907) xxiv; W. Tuckwell, *Reminiscences of Oxford* (London, 1907) index.

published.[18] Or again one could note that it was at this time William Smith's series of classical dictionaries appeared.[19] But it may be simplest, at once to disprove the false colour which has been given the history of

[18] For George Grote (1794–1871), banker, historian and philosopher, see *Times* (June 19, 1871) 6a; *Athen.* (June 24, 1871) 787; Harriet Grote, *The Personal Life of George Grote*, Second Edition (London, 1873); T. H. Ward, *Men of the Reign* (*s.l.*, 1885 [Graz, 1968]) 378–79; G. C. Robertson, *DNB*, Vol. 18 (1888/9) 727–36; Boase 1 c. 1251; Sandys, 438; M. L. Clarke, *George Grote: A Biography* (London, 1962); K. Christ *Von Gibbon zu Rostovtzeff* (Darmstadt, 1972) index; *BBA* 491:257–82; J. Vaio in *Classical Scholarship: A Biographical Encyclopedia*, edd. W. W. Briggs and W. M. Calder III (New York/London, 1990) 119–26. Cf. *Acad.* 2 (1871) 340 f.; *Athen.* (May 31, 1873) 695; A. Bain, "Bishop Thirlwall's Appointment to St. Davids," *Acad.* 21 (1882) 84; idem, in *The Minor Works of George Grote* (London, 1873) 1–170 (brought to my attention by J. Vaio); *The Letters of John Stuart Blackie to His Wife* (Edinburgh, 1909) index; T. Butler in *Speeches and Lectures Delivered in Australia by the Late Charles Badham* (Sydney, 1890) xvi f.; Clarke, index; **Lady Eastlake, *Mrs. Grote: A Sketch*, Second Edition (London, 1880); F. L. Gower, *Bygone Years* (London, 1905) 104; P. Grosskurth, *John Addington Symonds* (London, 1965) 81 f., 246; F. W. Hirst, *Early Life and Letters of John Morley*, Vol. 1 (London, 1927) 53; W. W. Jackson, *Ingram Bywater* (Oxford, 1917) 7; *Anna Jameson: Letters and Friendships (1812–1860)*, ed. Mrs. Steuart Erskine (London, 1915) index; R. Jenkyns, *The Victorians and Ancient Greece* (Cambridge MA, 1980) index; J. K. Laughton, *Memoirs of the Life and Correspondence of Henry Reeve* (London, 1898) index; *The Letters of the Right Hon. Sir George Cornewall Lewis* (London, 1870) 112 f., 117–20, 125–31, 146–51, 158 f., 160–62, 197–201, 217, 242, 250, 272 f., 320–23, 421 f.; H. Lloyd-Jones, *Blood for the Ghosts* (London, 1982) 103 f.; Harriet Martineau to Mr. Atkinson (Nov. 5, 1871) in *Athen.* (May 31, 1879) 695; J. S. Mill, *Autobiography and Literary Essays*, edd. J. M. Robson and J. Stillinger (Toronto, 1981) appendix 1 (= index); A. Momigliano, *George Grote and the Study of Greek History* (London, 1952) (with additional biographical references) = *Contributo alla storia degli studi classici* (Rome, 1955) 231–33; P. G. Naiditch, *The Development of Classical Scholarship* (UCLA, 1991) no. 40, pl. viii; Janet Ross, *The Fourth Generation* (New York, 1912) 24; Sandys, 166 f., 408; Frank Smith, *The Life and Work of Sir James Kay-Shuttleworth* (London, 1923) 268; Goldwin Smith, *Reminiscences* (New York, 1910) 147; *Later Letters of Lady Augusta Stanley* (London, 1929) 113; W.R.W. Stephens, *The Life and Letters of Edward A. Freeman* (London, 1895) index; *The Letters of John Addington Symonds*, edd. Schueller and Peter (Detroit MI, 1962) index; *Times* (June 22, 1871) 5c; *ibid.* (June 23, 1871) 9f; *ibid.* (June 24, 1871) 5f; *ibid.* (June 26, 1871) 10c; *ibid.* (July 1, 1871) 12a; Sir Richard Temple, *The Story of My Life*, Vol. 1 (London, 1896) 204; L. Tollemache, *Safe Studies* (London, 1900) 131–47; *Letters of the Hon. Mrs. Edward Twisleton* (London, 1928) index.

[19] For Sir William Smith (1813–1893), examiner for the University of London, see *Times* (Oct. 10, 1893) 93; *Academy* 44 (Oct. 14, 1893) 319; *Athen.* 3442 (Oct. 14, 1893) 522–23; Sandys, 430 f.; *BBA* 1018:168–87; cf. E. Abbott and L. Campbell, *The Life and Letters of Benjamin Jowett* (London, 1897) index; *Athen.* 3383 (1892) 290; *ibid.* 3343 (1893) 557; *ibid.* 3515 (1895) 315; T. Butler, in *Speeches and Lectures Delivered in Australia by the Late Charles Badham* (Sydney, 1890) xvii f.; Clarke, index; D. E. Rhodes, *Dennis of Etruria* (London, 1973) 15; Sandys, 420, 439; *Robert Scott and Benjamin Jowett*, ed. J. M. Prest (Oxford, 1966) 6; J.S.T., *Times* (Oct. 13 1893) 6c; perhaps *Times* (June 24, 1871) 5f.

It is worth noting that Smith, especially in the *Dictionary of Greek and Roman Biography and Mythology*, did not limit his contributors to England (London, 1844 [1890]). Bonn supplied Christian A. Brandis, Wilhelm Ihne, Ludwig Ulrichs, whilst Leonhard Schmitz was late of that city; and Adolph Stahl was Professor at the Gymnasium of Oldenburg.

scholarship at mid-century and to identify part of the background of the Ritualists, to examine the despised *Classical Museum*.

To believe Housman, the contributors to the *Classical Museum* were deaf to the work on the Continent. But it was not so.[20] Like its immediate predecessors, the *Classical Journal*,[21] the *Museum Criticum*,[22] and the

[20] The *Classical Museum*, edited by Leonhard Schmitz, appeared in twenty-six seemingly undated numbers. (I have only been able to examine bound sets.) Volumes 1 and 2 each included three numbers; volumes 3–7 each included four numbers; the volumes themselves were each supplied with an extra title page, dated successively 1844 to 1850.
Dating the individual numbers is usually difficult and, sometimes, apparently impossible; and there is little aid to be had from other scholars. J. A. Symonds, in reprinting one of Conington's essays from the periodical, simply gave the number without a year (*Miscellaneous Works of John Conington*, Vol. 1 [London, 1872] 423); John Richmond seems to think that his subject erred in dating his own articles (*James Henry of Dublin* [Dublin, 1976] 24); D. E. Rhodes also confused the year of the volume with the date of the number (*Dennis of Etruria* [London, 1973] 42; more correctly, *ibid.* 176). The problem breaks down into two parts. For the first two volumes, there is a tradition that the opening number belongs to June 1843 (Boase 3 c. 438). There is nothing impossible in this date, and some reason to think it probable: the new periodical is listed, as a quarterly, in *Gentleman's Magazine* 20 (Aug. 1843) 183. That *Neue Jahrbücher für Philologie und Pädagogik* 40.1 (1844) 119, assigns it to "1844" is therefore only a curiosity or a misprint. But it is worth recording that *NJPP* informs its readers where the periodical might be obtained in Leipzig, and summarises the first number at length (119 f.). The second number of the first volume, entirely undated, probably falls between its predecessor and the third number, which should be no earlier than November 1843 (a paper dated Oct. 31, 1843, appears on page 298). With regard to the second volume, the first number apparently belongs to the first quarter of 1844; its only dated entry is, however, "1843" (98). Contemporary references, such as *NJPP* 42 (1844) Verzeichniss, 20; *ibid.* 45 (1845) Verz., 17, are less than helpful. The second number can be no earlier than March 7, 1844 (121); the third and final number presumably belongs to the latter half of 1844.
Scattered through volumes 3–7 are dated entries. First numbers in vols. 4, 5, and 7 are dated respectively Feb. 21, 1846 (100); March 1847 (106); and Feb. 24, 1849 (91). Second numbers in vols. 4, 6 and 7 are dated June 1, 1846 (208); June 14, 1848 (187); and June 4, 1849 (202). Third numbers in vols. 4–7 are dated July (318); Oct. (95); Midsummer (278); and Sept. 11 (319). Fourth numbers in vols. 4–7 are dated Nov. 26 (451); Nov. 16 (469); and Dec. (vol. 7 95); Nov. 13 (431) and Dec. 4 (495). These groupings strongly suggest that the publication appeared in a regular fashion: the first numbers around March; the second around June; the third around September/October; and the fourth, around December. The final volume is prefaced by a note, dated December 1849, announcing the termination of the periodical (see *infra*, n. 48); and Dec. 1849 is also the date of termination given in Boase 3 c. 438.
The *Classical Museum* therefore appeared annually and regularly from 1843 until 1849. During its seven years of existence, some 2930 pages of notes and articles and letters by at least 101 writers were published; reviews, which comprise an additional 148 pages, were generally unsigned. Not all of these scholars were equally productive. The majority of them, indeed, seemingly contributed no more than one or two papers: fifty supplied one, nineteen, two, papers.
[21] So little is known of mid-century British classical periodicals, for even Engelmann-Preuss fail to index most of them, that it is worthwhile to say something about them and to show that their editors also were not indifferent to Continental work. The first number of the *Classical Journal*, a quarterly periodical (March, June, September and December), was dated March 1810. After 80 numbers, at the close of 1829, it was terminated. There is the

Philological   Museum,[23] and indeed like most of its successors,

possibility that another number was planned: *CJ* 80 (Dec. 1828) includes a page numbered
"181-240." This suggests that pages 241 and following had been printed in advance.
Thus, it is clear that *CJ* 62 (June 1825) 209 ff. were prepared before *CJ* 61 (March 1825),
which concludes with pp. *209–*215 (216 is unnumbered), appeared. The former
phenomenon occurs elsewhere in the periodical: see *CJ* 59 (Sept. 1824) 204–208, *CJ* 64
(Dec. 1825) 227–40 (really "227–39") and *CJ* 70 (June 1829) 192–208.

The *Classical Journal* often included works by Continental scholars: e.g., G. Hermann's
De differentia prosae et poeticae orationis disputatio (1794) was reprinted in *CJ* 73 (1828)
79–89, 74 (1828) 185–202 and 75 (1828) 33–40, and his *De Graecae dialectis* appeared in
CJ 76 (1828) 175–87; indeed, *CJ* 73 also included C. A. Brandis's "On Several Passages of
Strabo, Plutarch, and Athenaeus, concerning the Works of Aristotle" (56–63); a
translation of C. O. Müller's review of Rose's *Inscriptiones Graecae uetustissimae* (75–
79); and Thiersch's "On the Homeric Digamma" (118–24). It would be very easy to
multiply examples, and of course there were reviews of Continental publications and,
indeed, notices of foreign books available in a London bookstore. For a list of German
works imported into England, see *CJ* 70 (1827) 345.

[22] For supporters of, and contributors to, the *Museum Criticum*, see the *Gentleman's
Magazine* 201 (July, 1856) 116. In mid-November 1812, C. J. Blomsfield and J. H. Monk
publicised their plans for a new British classical periodical (A. Blomfield, *A Memoir of
Charles James Blomfield* 1 [London, 1863] 24–26; N. Horsfall, *GRBS* 15 [1974] 463).
The journal, whose full title was the *Museum Criticum; or, Cambridge Classical
Researches*, appeared only in eight numbers, whose dates are not always secure: the year
"1826," which is often given, seems to pertain only to the collected edition. How difficult
the problem is may be seen, in brief, from the fact that in the life of Blomfield the author
assigns the seventh number only to "1821 or 1822" (*Memoir* 26). Alone, A. T.
Bartholomew, who makes no reference to nos. 1 and 6 (and probably misdates the final
number), assigns the right years to nos. 2–5 and no. 7 (*Richard Bentley, D.D.: A
Bibliography* [Cambridge, 1908] nos. 283, 192, 195, 187, 281). But Bartholomew
supplies no evidence for his datings.

The first number is cited among new works in the *Eclectic Review* 9 (June 1813) 677;
and Blomfield remarks, in a letter of July 17, 1813, that a thousand copies had been printed
(*GRBS* 15, 464). The second number, announced for October (*MC* 1, 139), presumably
belongs to the same year. Independent evidence, such as the *Quarterly Review* 10 (Jan.
1814) 541, cannot affect the issue. The third number, announced for January or February
1814 (*MC* 2, 281), includes an item dated Jan. 29, 1814 (*MC* 3, 326). The fourth number,
apparently planned for publication around July, was "postponed till October by the advice
of Messrs. Murray and Deighton" (*GRBS* 15, 469). The fifth number, which begins the
second volume, includes a review of a work dated 1815 (*MC* 5, 146), and therefore is
probably no earlier; the sixth number, containing a review of a work dated 1816, is
similarly provided with a probable terminus (*MC* 6, 322). The seventh number belongs to
1821: it includes a rebuttal to E. H. Barker's *Aristarchus Anti-Blomfieldianus*, and this
rebuttal is cited in the *Classical Journal* 48 (Dec. 1821) 43 (cf. *MC* 7, 513). The number is
cited, apparently twice, in lists of new books in the *Quarterly Review* 26 (Jan. 1822) 543;
ibid. 27 (July 1822) 554. The eighth number includes a review of a work dated 1823 (*MC*
8, 643), and therefore should be no earlier than that year. According to an editorial in the
Philological Museum 1 (1831) i: "The *Museum Criticum* came to a close some years ago,
owing to the removal of the distinguished persons, by whom it had been set on foot and
mainly supported, to higher stations and more important cares." Blomfield became
Bishop of Chester in May 1824 (Blomfield, *Memoir* 93). The *Museum Criticum* included
some of Boeckh's *Prolusiones* (*MC* 2:8, 608–36).

[23] When the *Museum Criticum* was terminated, the editors advised their readers that they
had "reason to hope, that another series of Numbers of a similar nature, will issue from the

Terminalia,[24] the *Museum of Classical Antiquities*[25] and the *Journal of Sacred and Classical Philology*,[26] the Classical Museum did give space to Continental labours.

---

press of this University, under the auspices of an able and judicious scholar" (*MC* 8, 698). Presumably, it was the *Philological Museum*, edited by Julius Charles Hare, to which they referred: perhaps by accident, more than one writer referred to this periodical as the *Classical Museum* (*Literary Remains of Henry Fynes Clinton* [London, 1854] 283, 287–90); Sir Gilbert Frankland Lewis, *Letters of the Right Hon. Sir George Cornewall Lewis* [London, 1870] 12).

The earliest clear evidence of an intention to bring out the *Philological Museum* belongs by inference to 1829. On January 1, 1830, on Gaisford's recommendation, G. C. Lewis visited Fynes Clinton to seek contributions for the periodical (*Literary Remains*, p. 283).

The dating of the six numbers of this periodical is secure enough. They were printed, though not therefore actually published, respectively in August 1831, January, April, July and December 1832, and in April 1833 (N. M. Distad, *Victorian Periodicals Newsletter* 18 [Dec. 1972] 29). After the demise of the periodical, there were at least two attempts to start a new classical journal. George Long and William Smith, who had Welcker's promise of support, either abandoned their plan or joined with A. P. Stanley who tried, in 1841, without success, to re-create the periodical (cf. *Robert Scott and Benjamin Jowett*, ed. J. M. Prest [Oxford, 1966] 6; R. E. Prothero, *The Life and Correspondence of Arthur Penrhyn Stanley* 1 [London, 1893] 306; see also *Letters Literary and Theological of Connop Thirlwall* [London, 1881] index). Prest saw Stanley's design as "the origin, presumably, of *The Classical Museum*" (*Scott and Jowett*, 6 n. 20). This thesis is not impossible, since Stanley and Long and Smith were all contributors, but as Schmitz was editor and promoter, it is perhaps unlikely.

It was the declared intention of the *Philological Museum* "to acquaint the English student of classical literature with the new views that have been taken, and the discoveries that have been made, of late years by the scholars upon the continent, that is to say, by a very pardonable synecdoche, the scholars of Germany" (*PM* 1, 150). Its first number contained contributions, reprints, or translations by Savigny (150–73) and Niebuhr (174–76); the second, by Niebuhr (245–79); the third, by Buttmann (439–84), Niebuhr (485–98), and Boeckh (628–31); the fourth, by Boeckh, (101–07), Savigny (117–45), C. O. Müller (227–35), L. Dindorf (241–43); the fifth, by Uhden (308–14); J. E. Biester (329–44), August Boeckh (449–56; 457–67) and F. G. Welcker (468–72); and the sixth by Schleiermacher (438–55, 556–61), Niebuhr (661–70) and Boeckh (694–99, 699–703).

[24] The title *Terminalia; or Notes on the Subjects of the Litteræ Humaniores and Moderation Schools* was changed, on the strength of encouragement "by friends out of Oxford to make this periodical less local," to *Terminalia* for the second and final number (2 [1852] insert). For the spelling "Litteræ," see Naiditch, *A. E. Housman at University College, London* (Leiden, 1988) 35 n. 10-4. Falconer Madan has identified the chief mover as Goldwin Smith (Yale University, G14.76). *Terminalia*, which included only a few articles and notes in its brief existence, had no foreign classical contributors.

[25] The *Museum of Classical Antiquities*, edited by Edward Falkener (1814–1896), likewise did not survive long. Its first number appeared around January 1851; numbers two through eight were dated, respectively, April, July, and October 1851, March, June, and September 1852, and April 1853. In May 1853 there was a Supplement. The work was reissued, in a single volume, in 1855 and in 1860 (cf J. D. Stewart et al., *British Union-Catalogue of Periodicals* 3 [London, 1957] 279; I have only seen the 1860 issue). The *Museum of Classical Antiquities* included Gottfried Semper's "On the Study of Polychromy, and Its Revival" (3 [1851] 228–46) and Carlo Bonucci's "A General Statement of the Excavations of Ancient Monuments in the Kingdom of Naples, from 1830 to 1849" (*ibid.* 285–94); a translation of H. E. Dirksen's "On the Building Act of the Emperor Zeno" (4

With regard to the *Classical Museum*, one need put emphasis neither on the lists of newly published Continental books (e.g., *CM* 1, 139f., 279f., 425f.) nor on reviews of Continental works (e.g., *CM* 7, 320-4, 497-501). Rather, one may observe that many numbers in the *Classical Museum* included English translations of German or Dutch published works. Thus, the German publications include H. W. Voelcker's "On the Signification of ψυχή and εἴδωλον in the Iliad and Odyssey," *CM* 2, 45-54; J. Ch. Voemel's "On the Guardianship Accounts of Demosthenes," *CM* 3, 254-263; C. Wex's "On the *Leges Annales* of the Romans," *CM* 3, 405-416; C. G. Zumpt's "The Religion of the Romans," *CM* 4, 169-192; K. F. Hermann's "On the Date of the Laocoon," *CM* 7, 329-345; and, apparently in whole or in part, E. Platner's "Reminiscences of the Late Gottfried Hermann," *CM* 7, 470-478. The Dutch publications rendered into English include G.P.F. Groshans's "The Zoology of Homer and Hesiod," *CM* 4, 248-75, 374-87; F.A.W. Miquel, "Tentamen florae Homericae" *CM* 5, 42-64; and, perhaps in this category, W H. De Vriese's "Essay on the Papyrus of the Ancients" *CM* 5, 202-215.

More significantly, the *Classical Museum* included original papers and reviews written in, or translated into, English or Latin, by Continental scholars: F. W. Welcker's "On the Sculptured Groups in the Pediments of the Parthenon" *CM* 2, 367-404; G. F Püchta's "Remarks on Professor Long's Paper on the Licinian Law *de Modo Agri*" *CM* 3, 67-77; Theodor Bergk's "On the Age of Babrius" *CM* 3, 115-134; W. Ihne's "The Asylum of Romulus" *CM* 3, 190-193; L. Urlichs's review of Becker's *De Romae Veteris Muris atque Portis* etc. *CM* 3, 194-202; L. Lersch's "On Victorinus. A Contribution to the History of Roman Literature" *CM* 3, 284-290; C. G. Z(umpt)'s review of Welcker's *Wandgemaelde aus Pompeji und Herculanum*, *CM* 3, 448-452; H. Düntzer's "On the Conclusion of the Iliad, from V. 677" *CM* 4, 36-47; J. A. Hartung's "On the Dithyramb" *CM* 5, 373-395; F. W. Welcker's "Further Remarks on the Groups in the Western

---

[1851] 305–52); and A. Schönborn's "On the True Situation of Cragus, Anticragus, and the Massicytus, Mountains of Asia Minor" (6 [1852] 161–66) and G. O. Manara's "Some Observations on the Theatre of Verona" (*ibid.* 201 f.). Presumably foreign as well was Francis Pulszky, who wrote "On the Progress and Decay of Art; and the Arrangement of a National Museum" (5 [1852] 1–15).

[26] The *Journal of Classical and Sacred Philology* appeared in twelve numbers or four volumes, dated respectively: 1.1, March 1854; 1.2, June 1854; 1.3, Nov. 1854; 2.4, March 1855; 2.5, May 1855; 2.6, Nov. 1855; 3.7, March 1856; 3.8, June 1856; 3.9, Dec. 1856; 4.10, March 1857; 4.11, March 1858; 4.12, Dec. 1859. There is apparently no reason to suppose, and some slight reason to believe, that the dates of the numbers reflect the months of publication: in the second number, while one can find references to March 17, 24, 29, 30 and April (262, 210, 224, 278, and 264, respectively), nothing that postdates June 1854 can be found.

JCSP included summaries of foreign journals (e.g. 1.1, 135–38); lists of new foreign books (139–43); "Foreign Announcements" (144); and reviews and notices of foreign publications (105–109, 125 f.). Contributions by foreigners, however, were very rare: cf. R. B. Hirschig of Leiden (3, 388–92; 4, 92–96).

Pediment of the Parthenon" *CM* 6, 279-296; K. H. Funkhänel's "Ordeals among the Greeks and Romans" *CM* 6, 375-387; W. T. Streuber's "On the Earliest Poetry of the Romans" *CM* 7, 140-160; R. Pauli's review of Grimm's *Geschichte der Deutschen Sprache, CM* 7, 161-179; J. Richter's "The Didascalia to Aeschylus' *Septem contra Thebas*" *CM* 7, 312-317 and his review of Bekker's edition of Dio Cassius, *CM* 7, 320-324. Likely enough also foreign was B. Gäbler, who wrote "The English Language Considered as a Practical Basis for the Study of Other Indo-European languages" *CM* 6, 141-151, and a series called "On the Relation between the Consonantal Systems of the English and Sanscrit Languages" *CM* 6, 361-75; 7, 44-70, 126-40. Not improbably Pauli was "R. P.," who wrote the "Chaunsun del Secle" *CM* 6, 466-70 and reviewed J. de Wal's *Mythologiae septentrionalis, CM* 6, 188-194. In addition, it is to be remembered that the editor, Leonhard Schmitz, himself was born near Aachen.[27]

Finally, one should notice that, aside from the ordinary membership, the *Classical Museum* included Foreign Correspondents.[28] No list appears in the first volume, but thereafter it is a regular feature; and the names included are Theodor Bergk (Marburg, *CM* 2-7); Emil Braun (Rome, *CM* 2-7); H. Düntzer (Bonn, *CM* 3-7); Lorenz Lersch (Bonn, *CM* 2); Julius Richter (Berlin, *CM* 7 only); Ludwig Urlichs (Bonn, *CM* 2-7); W. Vischer (Basel, *CM* 2 only); F. G. Welcker (Bonn, *CM* 2-7); and C. G. Zumpt (Berlin, *CM* 2-6). The Chevalier Bunsen was a member of the large Management Committee. It is probably no accident, since the editor was educated there, that so many of the scholars (H. Düntzer, L. Lersch, L. Urlichs, and F. G. Welcker) were associated with Bonn. Thus did Badham's countrymen turn their backs on Europe.

But it is true that the *Classical Museum* included very few papers on textual criticism. And although a memoir of Hermann might be published and although critical editions might be reviewed, the first portion of Ritschl's *T. Macci Plauti Comoediae*, Bonn/London 1848, was given a very

---

[27] For Leonhard Schmitz (1807–1890), Headmaster of the High School, Edinburgh, tutor to the Prince of Wales (later Edward VII), see *Times* (May 30, 1890) 7f; *Athen.* 3267 (June 7, 1890) 739; *Boase* 3 c. 438; *BBA* 973: 373–75; cf. *The Letters of John Stuart Blackie* (Edinburgh, 1909) 128; N. M. Distad, *Guessing at Truth* (Shepherdstown, 1979) 113, 220 n. 31; D. E. Rhodes, *Dennis of Etruria* (London, 1973) 102; Sidney Lee, *King Edward VII: A Biography* 1 (New York, 1925) 73 n.; P. Magnus, *King Edward the Seventh* (London, 1964) 29; *Times* (June 3, 1890) 9e; *Letters Literary and Theological of Connop Thirlwall* (London, 1881) 400 (index). Testimonials (British Library, London 8366 bb 33 [16]; fragment pp. 17–31, Glasgow, Coll. Coll. B3 box 6).

[28] This feature was fairly unusual. Thus, although the Association in Paris, whose membership numbered above 700, had more than a score of members in Great Britain, all save three were Greek businessmen, Greek educators, or Frenchmen: the exceptions were J. S. Blackie, John Stuart Mill and a certain businessman named Sugdury (*Annuaire de l'association pour l'encouragement des études grecques* 3 [Paris, 1869] xvii, xxx, xxxvi respectively). None of the members dwelt in Germany, though a Richard Koenig lived in Egypt (*ibid.* xxxiii).

long notice (R.H.S.,[29] *CM* 7, 346-371). The merits and defects of texts which interested Housman were not those which usually intrigued the reviewers of this periodical. Instead, the pages of the periodical were given chiefly to other kinds of scholarship. The twenty-five longest works should serve to illustrate this statement:

162.35 pages: E. H. Bunbury, "On the Topography of Rome" *CM* 3, 319-81; 4, 1-35, 117-135,427-444; 5, 215-244.[30]

85.41: James Henry, "Commentaries on, and Illustrations of, the Eneis of Virgil" *CM* 6, 32-56, 127-141,220-252; 7, 180-195.[31]

54.20: B. Gäbler, "On the Relation between the Consonantal System of the English and Sanscrit Languages" *CM* 6, 361-375; 7, 44-70, 126-140.

47:20: W. Watkiss Lloyd, "Explanation of the Groups in the Western Pediment of the Parthenon" *CM* 5, 396–443.[32]

45.65: W. Watkiss Lloyd, "Homer and his Art" *CM* 6, 387–431.

45.50: M. G., rev. George Grote's A History of Greece, v. 1-2. *CM* 5, 125-170.[33]

44.25: G. C. Lewis, "The Hellenics of Xenophon, and their Division into Books" *CM* 2, 1-144,146.[34]

[29] Not known to me. Probably not Richard Horton Smith (afterwards, Richard Horton-Smith, K.C., 1831–1919), fourth classic (1856), and classical lecturer at King's College, London (1857–1859): the author of the review seems too learned to have been at most eighteen years of age.

[30] For Sir Edward Herbert Bunbury, baronet (1811–1895), see *Times* (March 8, 1895) 10c *Athen.* 3516 (March 16, 1895) 346; Boase 4 c. 539; *BBA* 168:347–49; cf. perhaps *Athen.* 1881 I 751; *BLC* vol. 47, 280; H. G. Schlichter, *Times* (March 9, 1895) 12b; for his library, see *Sotheby, Wilkinson & Hodge*, July 2–17, 1896. Perhaps it should be noted that "Bunbury" in *The Importance of Being Earnest* was not he, but Henry S. Bunbury (R. Ellmann, *Oscar Wilde* [New York, 1988] 37).

[31] For James Henry (1798–1876), physician and author of *Aeneidea*, see Sandys, 436; John Richmond, *James Henry of Dublin* (Dublin 1976); *BBA* 541:238–43; cf. W. B. Stanford, *Ireland and the Irish Tradition* (1975 [Totowa, 1977]) index; W. B. Stanford and R. B. McDowell, *Mahaffy* (London, 1971) 170; J. S. Starkey, *Hermathena* 64 (Nov. 1944) 19–31; R. D. Williams, *ibid.* 116 (1973) 27–43.

[32] For William Watkiss Lloyd (1813–1893), see *Times* (Dec. 27, 1893) 3e; cf. Anon, *Athen.* 3453 (Dec. 30, 1893) 916; M. B.-E., *Athen.* 3453 (1893) 916.

[33] Probably William Maxwell Gunn, who taught under Schmitz at the High School at Edinburgh (*A Dictionary of Greek and Roman Biography and Mythology*, London 1890). For Gunn, perhaps see **T. Guthrie, *A Sermon...On the Occasion of the Death of W. M. Gunn* (Edinburgh, 1851); perhaps cf. *BLC* vol. 135, 309.

[34] For Sir George Cornewall Lewis (1806–1863), politician, see *Times* (April 15, 1863) 9e; *Letters of the Right Hon. Sir George Cornewall Lewis* (London, 1871); Boase 2 c. 413; Sandys, 439; *BBA* 684:304–32; cf. E.G.W. Bill and F.J.A. Mason, *Christ Church and Reform* (Oxford, 1970) index; *BLC* vol. 191, 201 f.; N. M. Distad, *Guessing at Truth* (Shepherdstown, 1979) index; *Dear Miss Nightingale: A Selection of Benjamin Jowett's Letters to Florence Nightingale* (Oxford, 1987) index; A. Momigliano, *Contributo alla storia degli studi classici* (Rome, 1955) 249–62 (brought to my attention by John Vaio); *Times* (Apr. 18, 1863) 11d.

43.90: J. S. Blackie, "On the Theology of Homer" *CM* 7, 414-458 (= Blackie, *Horæ Hellenicæ*, London 1874, pp. 1-59).[35]

43.65: H. Bonnycastle, "An Attempt to Restore the Text and the Scansion of Homer, upon an Entirely new System and Principle" *CM* 7, 15-33, 289–299,378–394.[36]

41.75: G.P.F. Groshans, "The Zoology of Homer and Hesiod" (translated by William Bell Macdonald) *CM* 4, 248-275, 374-387.[37]

41.00: J. S. Blackie, review of fifteen works on the Prometheus Bound. *CM* 5, 1-41 (= Blackie, *Horæ Hellenicæ*, London 1874, pp. 60-110).

40.75: A. P. Stanley, review of Colonel Leake's *Topography of Athens*. *CM* 1, 41-81.[38]

[35] For John Stuart Blackie (1809-1895), then Professor of Latin in Aberdeen (1842–1851), later Professor of Greek at Edinburgh (1852–1882), see *Times* (March 4, 1895) 10e; *The Day-Book of John Stuart Blackie* (London, 1902); *The Letters of John Stuart Blackie to His Wife* (Edinburgh, 1909); *Athen.* (March 9, 1895) 312 f.; *Illustrated London News* 106 (March 9, 1895) 285; J. G. Duncan, *The Life of John Stuart Blackie* (Glasgow, 1895); H. A. Kennedy, *Professor Blackie, His Sayings and Doings: A Biographical Sketch* (London, 1896); Anna M. Stoddart, *John Stuart Blackie* (London, 1895); A. Gordon, *DNB* 22, 204–07; Sandys, 427; *BBA* 112:194–224. Cf. E. Abbott and L. Campbell, *The Life and Letters of Benjamin Jowett* 1 (London, 1897) 399; *Athen.* (Sept. 9, 1882) 340; *ibid.* (March 9, 1895) 315; *ibid.* (Nov. 12, 1898) 678; *BLC* vol. 33, 443–45; *The Memoirs of John Macmillan Brown* (Christchurch, 1974) 23–25, 73–74; P. Corder, *Life of R. S. Watson* (London, 1914) 48; R. A. Falcone, *T.P.'s and Cassell's Weekly* 4 (Aug. 1, 1925) 482, 489; R. Farquharson, *In and Out of Parliament* (London, 1911) 33, 59; G. L. Gower, *Years of Content* (London, 1940) 199; Annie Grey, *More About People* 2 (Feb. 11, 1899) 126; *ILN* 104 (1894) 347, 587; B. H. Jackson, *Recollections of T. G. Jackson* (London, 1950) 40; *John O' London's Weekly* 2 (Dec. 13, 1919), 244; Sir Henry Jones, *Old Memories* (New York, ca. 1922) 219 f.; R. J. MacKenzie, *Almond of Loretto* (London, 1905) 44; Isabella Mayo, *Recollections* (London, 1910) 245; "Our Portrait Gallery," *Dublin University Magazine* 87 (April 1876) 404–16; F. Petrie, *Seventy Years in Archaeology* (London, n.d.) 131; H. J. Rose, *PBA* 23 (1937) 489; *Memoirs of Lord Salvesen* (London, 1949) 13 f.; W. B. Selbie, *The Life of Andrew Martin Fairbairn* (London, 1914) 11, 177; C. Stewart, *Haud Immemor* (London, 1901) 46; *Times* (March 7, 1895) 7e; L. B. Walford, *Recollections of a Scottish Novelist* (New York, 1910) 150–52; G. Wyld, *Notes of My Life* (London, 1903) 17–19. See also *Testimonials in Favour of John Stuart Blackie*, 1851, First, Second, Third series (British Library, London, 8366 bb 33/1).

[36] Not known to me.

[37] For William Bell Macdonald (1807–1862), who also wrote "Aristophanica" for *CM* (4, 100–02, 204–06; *ibid.* 7, 92 f.), see *BBA* 716:258–61; *Gentleman's Magazine* 214 (March 1863) 390; G.C.B., *DNB* 12 (1887) 491 f.

[38] For Arthur Penrhyn Stanley (1815–1881), Dean of Westminster (1863–1881), see R. E. Prothero, *The Life and Correspondence of Arthur Penrhyn Stanley, D.D.* (London, 1893); *Letters and Verses of Arthur Penrhyn Stanley*, ed. R. E. Prothero (New York, 1895); *A Victorian Dean*, edd. The Dean of Windsor and H. Bolitho (London, 1930); cf. E. Abbott and L. Campbell, *The Life and Letters of Benjamin Jowett* (London, 1897) index; G.K.A. Bell, *Randall Davidson* (New York, 1935) index; A. C. Benson, *The Life of Edward White Benson* (London, 1899) index; *Letters of Dr. John Brown* (London, 1907) index; Frances Baroness Bunsen, *A Memoir of Baron Bunsen* (London, 1868) I 591, II 449; N. C. Chaudhuri, *Scholar Extraordinary* (London, 1974) 232; N. M. Distad, *Guessing at Truth* (Shepherdstown, 1979) index; G. Faber, *Jowett* (London, 1957) index; *The Letters of Mrs.*

40.33: F. W. Newman, "On the Intrusive Elements of Latin" *CM* 6, 321-361.[39]

40.25: G. Long, rev. Von Savigny's *System des Heutigen Römischen Rechts* (German and French). *CM* 5, 290-330.[40]

39.33: John Robson, "On the Comparative Advantages of Some Methods of Teaching Latin and Greek" *CM* 4, 388–427.[41]

37.00: F. G. Welcker, "On the Sculptured Groups in the Pediments of the Parthenon" *CM* 2, 367-404 (transl. by L. Schmitz).

35.00: William James Hickie, "Contributions towards a Metaphysics of Greek Syntax" *CM* 7, 219–253.[42]

Gaskell (Cambridge, Mass., 1967) index; *Letters of John Richard Green* (New York, 1901) index; A.J.C. Hare, *The Life and Letters of Frances Baroness Bunsen* (London, 1879) index; idem, *The Story of My Life* (London, 1896) index; *Dear Miss Nightingale; A Selection of Benjamin Jowett's Letters to Florence Nightingale*, edd. V. Quinn and J. Prest (Oxford, 1987) index; *Letters of Benjamin Jowett* (London, 1899) index; S. Lee, *King Edward VII* 1 (New York, 1925) index; V. P. Lipman, *Palestine Exploration Quarterly* 120 (Jan.–June 1988) 47–49; **Letters of Matthew Arnold*, ed. G.W.E. Russell (London, 1896) index; *The Works of John Ruskin* 39 (London, 1912) index; G. St. Aubyn, *Edward VII* (London, 1979) index; *Letters Literary and Theological of Connop Thirlwall* (London, 1881) 400, 402 (index); L. A. Tollemache, *Old and Odd Memories* (London, 1908) index; C. Wordsworth, *Annals of My Early Life* (London, 1891) index; idem, *Annals of My Life* (London, 1893) index.

[39] For Francis William Newman (1805–1897), Professor of Latin at University College, London (1846–1863), see *Times* (Oct. 6, 1897) 4c; *Athen.* 3650 (Oct. 9, 1897) 489–90; I. G. Sieveking, *Memoir and Letters of Francis W. Newman* (London, 1909); *BBA* 813: 75–94; cf. *Athen.* 3650 (1897) 492; H. H. Bellot, *University College, London* (London, 1929) index; *The Letters of John Stuart Blackie to His Wife* (Edinburgh, 1909) 126; Agnes Fry, *A Memoir of the Rt. Hon. Sir Edward Fry* (Oxford, 1921) 43–44; T. P. Hallett, *Times* (Oct. 7, 1897) 7f; Charles Kingsley, *His Letters and Memories of His Life* (New York, 1977) 117; R. Pearsall, *The Worm in the Bud* (London, 1969) index; Sir H. Roscoe, *Life & Experiences* (London, 1906) 26; H. S. Salt, *Memories of Bygone Eton* (London, n.d.) 62; L. A. Tollemache, *Old and Odd Memories* (London, 1908) 261, 264 f.; P. Venables, *Athen.* 2946 (April 12, 1884) 475.

[40] For George Long (1800–1879), Professor of Greek (1828–1831) and Latin (1842–1846) at University College, London, see J. S. Cotton, *Academy* 46 (Aug. 23, 1879) 140; W. B. Philpott, *Athen.* 2704 (Aug. 23, 1879) 239 f.; **H. J. Mathews, *Brighton College Magazine* (1879); idem, *In Memoriam George Long* (1879); *AC* 4 (1951) 204; Sandys, 430; *BBA* 699: 227–39; cf. *Athen.* 1871 II 18; *ibid.* 1880 II 257, 289; H. H. Bellot, *University College, London* (London, 1929) index; P. A. Bruce, *History of the University of Virginia* (New York, 1922) index; idem, "Professor Key and Professor Long" *University of Virginia Alumni Bulletin* 17 (1924) 273–78; G.M.E[dwards?], *Cambridge Review* 1 (1879) 37; *Letters of George Long*, ed. T. Fitzhugh (Charlottesville, 1917); J. Glucker, *Pegasus* (Exeter, 1981) 120–23; R. H. Hutton in *The Works of Walter Bagehot* 1 (Hartford, 1891) xxix; S. Piercy, "George Long in His Old Age: Some New Letters," *University of Virginia Alumni Bulletin* 17 (1924) 427–79; Sandys, 436; *Robert Scott and Benjamin Jowett*, ed. J. M. Prest (Oxford, 1966) 6; J. Thorne, *Athen.* 2305 (Aug. 30, 1879) 273.

[41] For John Robson (1815–1876), Master, University College School, London, see *Athen.* 2530 (Apr. 22, 1876) 568; *BBA* 941: 102.

[42] For William James Hickie (ca. 1830–?), second Master at Lynn Grammar School, see *AC* 3 (1947) 358; cf. *BLC* vol. 47, 355 f.

34.50: W. F. Ainsworth, A Memoir Illustrative of the Geography of the Anabasis of Xenophon" *CM* 2, 170-185, 299-317.[43]

34.50: Thomas Dyer, "On the Chronology of the Horatian Poems" *CM* 2, 187-221.[44]

34.20: Thomas Dyer, "Sophocles, and his Dramatic Art" *CM* 5, 65-99.

33.25: George Grote, rev. Boeckh's *Metrologische Untersuchungen.* *CM* 1, 1-34.

32.00: J. S. Blackie, rev. of Conington and Sewell's translations of the Agamemnon. *CM* 6, 432-463.

31.50: J. S. Blackie, "On the Rhythmical Declamation of the Ancients" *CM* 1, 338-369

31.50: Charles Newton, "On the Sculptures from the Mausoleum at Halicarnassus" *CM* 5, 170-201.[45]

30.00: George Long, "The Licinian Rogation, *de Modo Agri* or *Agrorum*," *CM* 2, 254-284.

Not unexpectedly, several of these scholars were amongst the chief contributors to the *Classical Museum*. But the mainstays are to be judged not on the number of their signed papers—by that standard George Dunbar[46] would be the most important contributor (78 pages/fifteen papers)—but by the size of their writings: T. H. Dyer (213 pages/twelve papers), F. W. Newman (206 pages/fourteen papers), E. H. Bunbury (202 pages/six

[43] For William Francis Ainsworth (1807–1896), naturalist and traveller, see *Times* (Nov. 30, 1896) 12c; *Athen.* 3606 (Dec. 5, 1896) 799 f.; Boase 4 cc. 51 f.; E. I. Carlyle, *DNB* 22 (1901) 20–21; *BBA* 11: 373–86; cf. S. M. Ellis, *William Harrison Ainsworth and His Friends* (London, 1911) index.

[44] For Thomas Henry Dyer (1804–1888), clerk, India House, writer, see *Acad.* 33 (Feb. 11, 1888) 97; *Athen.* 3146 (Feb. 11, 1888) 180; G. B. Smith, *DNB* 6 (1888/89) 289 f.; Boase 1 c. 947; *BBA* 355: 360–65.

[45] For Sir Charles Thomas Newton (1816–1894), archaeologist and Keeper of Greek and Roman Antiquities, British Museum, see P. Gardner, *Acad.* 46 (Dec. 8, 1894) 473; *Athen.* 3502 (Dec. 8, 1894) 797; E. Gardner, *Papers of the British School at Athens* 1 (1894/95) 67–77; *Nature* 51 (Jan. 10, 1895) 250 f.; R. C. Jebb, *CR* 9 (1895) 81–85; idem, *JHS* 14 (1894) xlix–liv; Boase 2 cc. 1127 f.; Sandys, 443–45; *AC* 4 (1951) 540; *BBA* 813:424–30. Cf. *Athen.* 3218 (June 29, 1889) 809; E.G.W. Bill and J.F.A. Mason, *Christ College and Reform* (Oxford, 1970) 20 f.; *BLC* vol. 236 41; E.A.W. Budge, *By Nile and Tigris* 1 (London, 1920) 36, 73; W. M. Calder III and D. A. Traill, edd., *Myth, Scandal and History* (Detroit 1986) index; *Classical Review* 3 (1889) 423; G. Daniel, *Some Small Harvest*(London, 1988) index; Joan Evans, *Time and Chance* (London, 1943) 220–22, 261; P. Gardner, *Autobiographica* (Oxford, 1933) 31–34, 39; A. Gudeman, *Imagines Philologorum* (Leipzig, 1911) 29; T.G.H. James, ed., *Excavating in Egypt* (Chicago, 1982 [1984]) index; [W. P. Maunsell,] *Blackwood's Magazine* 157 (April 1895) 596–613; J. H. Middleton, *CR* 3 (1889) 186–87; S. Peacock, *Jane Ellen Harrison* (New Haven, 1988) index; F. Petrie, *Seventy Years in Archaeology* (London, n.d.) 56, 73; D. E. Rhodes, *Dennis of Etruria* (London, 1973) index; *The Works of John Ruskin* 39 (London, 1912) index; J. Stewart, *Jane Ellen Harrison* (London, 1959) 10; G. S. Thomson, *Mrs. Arthur Strong* (London, 1949) 21–24, 32, 42, 100; *Times* (Dec. 5, 1894) 9f; G.C.W. Warr, *Acad.* 46 (1894) 473; idem, *CR* 9 (1895) 85.

[46] For George Dunbar (1774–1851), Professor of Greek at Edinburgh, see L. C. Sanders, *DNB* 6 (1888/89) 153; Boase 1 c. 928; Sandys, 426; *BBA* 348:418–26; cf. *BLC* vol. 89, 101; Sandys, 418.

papers), J. S. Blackie (171 pages/seven papers), George Long (157 pages/nine papers), G. Cornewall Lewis (108 pages/five papers), C. K. Watson (154 pages: 48 of articles, 106 of translations/five papers and six translations),[47] and W. Watkiss Lloyd (139 pages/four papers). These few writers, making up barely seven percent of the contributors, were responsible for over forty percent of the text; and none of them worked much on editions of classical texts. The departure of many of these scholars marks the end of the *Classical Museum*.[48]

Blackie, Bunbury, Dunbar, Grote, Henry, Long, Newman, Schmitz, Stanley and the rest: certain British scholars are conspicuous by their absence. One cannot perhaps put emphasis on Gaisford,[49] who generally

[47] For Christopher Knight Watson (ca. 1824–1901), Secretary, Society of Antiquaries (1860–1885), see *AC* 6 (1954) 368; cf. *BLC* vol. 346, 100; *Times* (June 3, 1890) 9e.

[48] The final volume of the *Classical Museum* is prefaced by an announcement from the Committee of Management and the Editor. They say that "owing to the slender support which the Journal has met with from the Scholars of this country, whose interest in the Museum has of late rather decreased than increased, it has been found expedient for the present to discontinue the publication" (*CM* 7, prelim. p. 1, Dec. 1849). It is difficult, if not impossible, to determine precisely what led to the failure of the *Classical Museum*. Of the eight writers who supplied the most text, Dyer and Bunbury had had nothing published since the fifth volume, and Lewis nothing since the second, whilst Newman's sole contribution to the seventh was only five pages long. Thus, of the first three chief contributors, all had seemingly abandoned the journal. But Blackie, Long, Watson and Lloyd continued loyal and productive; and Lloyd, indeed, was relatively a new contributor, for his first paper appeared in the fifth volume. Without the relevant correspondence, in particular the archives of the editor, Leonhard Schmitz, and the publishers, no real conclusion about the failure of the periodical can be reached.

[49] For Thomas Gaisford (1779–1855), Regius Professor of Greek (1812–1855) and Dean of Christ Church, Oxford (1831–1855), see *Times* (June 4, 1855) 9a; ***Literary Churchman* (June 16, 1855) (= *Journal of Classical and Sacred Philology* 2 [Nov. 1855] 343–48); Boase 1 c. 1116; H. R. Luard, *DNB* 7 (1886/7) 810–12; Sandys, 395 f.; *BBA* 437:76–84; cf. E. H. Barker, *Literary Anecdotes* 1 (London, 1852) 51 f.; E.G.W. Bill and J.F.A. Mason, *Christ College and Reform* (Oxford, 1970) index; *Letters of Frederick Lord Blackford* (London, 1896) 25; N. C. Chaudhuri, *Scholar Extraordinary* (London, 1974) 94 f.; Clarke, index; *Literary Remains of Henry Fynes Clinton* (London, 1854) 21 f., 82 f., 211, 214–16, 222 f., 227, 230, 242, 245–47, 281–84, 294 f., 299, 301, 306, 308, 311, 332, 339 f., 343; *BLC* vol. 118 365 f.; G. J. Cowley, *Oxford Magazine* 34 (1915) 40–42; G. V. Cox, *Recollections of Oxford* (London, 1867) 166 f., 313, 369, 392 f.; F. L. Gower, *Bygone Years* (London, 1905) 8; A. Gudeman, *Imagines Philologorum* (Leipzig, 1911) 20; N. Horsfall, *GRBS* 15 (1974) index; R. C. Jebb, *JHS* 14 (1894) xlix; H. Lloyd-Jones, *Blood for the Ghosts* (London, 1982) 81–102; H. R. Luard, *JSCP* 3 (1856) 123 f.; Max Müller, *My Autobiography* (New York, 1901) index; *Bibliotheca Parriana* (London, 1827) 626; Mark Pattison, *Memoirs* (London, 1885) 246 f.; *The Correspondence of Richard Porson*, ed. H. R. Luard (Cambridge, 1867) 107; J. Pycroft, *Memories of Oxford* (London, 1886) I 108, 295, 418; II 77; Sandys, index; *Times* (June 11, 1855) 12e; H. L. Thompson, *Christ Church* (London, 1900) index; L. Tollemache, *Old and Odd Memories* (London, 1908) 167; W. Tuckwell, *Reminiscences of Oxford* (London, 1900) index; idem, *Oxford Magazine* 31 (1913) 320; W. W. Vernon, *Recollections of Seventy-Two Years* (London, 1917) 93; C. Wordsworth, *Annals of My Early Life* (London, 1891) index; idem, *Annals of My Life* (London, 1893) 119. For part of his library, see *Maggs* cat. 779 (1948) nos. 6, 23, 39, 59, 94, 109, 142 (cp. *Athen.* 3261 [1890] 533).

wrote books, not articles, but there are a good many scholars of the period who did not so limit themselves. Thus, *Terminalia*, which existed in 1851 and 1852, included contributions principally from Goldwin Smith,[50] John Conington[51] and F. A. Paley.[52] Thus, too, the *Journal of Classical and*

[50] For Goldwin Smith (1823–1910), educational reformer, see *Times* (June 8, 1910) 8abc; Goldwin Smith, *Oxford Magazine* 28 (June 16, 1910) 392 f., 393; *A Selection from Goldwin Smith's Correspondence* (New York, 1913); S. Lee, *DNB 1901–11* 328–40 (with additional bibliography); *Who Was Who* 1 (1966) 659; cf. E. Abbott and L. Campbell, *The Life and Letters of Benjamin Jowett* 1 (London, 1897) 176; B. B. Batty, *Oxford Magazine* 28 (1910) 393; R. Berry, *Behind the Ivy* (Ithaca, NY, 1950) index; M. Bishop, *A History of Cornell* (Ithaca, NY, 1962) index; H. Charlesworth, *Candid Chronicles* (Toronto, 1925) 110–22; idem, *More Candid Chronicles* (Toronto, 1928) index; P. Dorf, *The Builder: A Biography of Ezra Cornell* (New York, 1952) index; A.J.C. Hare, *The Story of My Life* 1 (London, 1896) 415, 448; W. T. Hewett, *Cornell University: A History* 2 (New York, 1905) index; *Illustrated London News* 104 (1894) 298; *Dear Miss Nightingale: A Selection of Benjamin Jowett's Letters to Florence Nightingale* (Oxford, 1987) index; *Letters of Benjamin Jowett* (London, 1899) index; W. F. Monypenny and G. E. Buckle, *The Life of Benjamin Disraeli* 2 (New York, 1929) 506; J. Morley, *The Life of William Ewart Gladstone* (London, 1922) index; K. C. Parsons, *The Cornell Campus* (Ithaca, NY, 1968) index; W. P. Rogers, *Andrew D. White and the Modern University* (New York, 1942) index; *The Annual Index to the Times 1910* (London, n.d.) 1281; H. S. White, *Willard Smith* (New York, 1925) 101, 319–34.

[51] For John Conington (1825–1869), Corpus Professor of Latin at Oxford (1854–1869), see *Acad.* 1 (Nov. 13, 1869) 58; *Athen.* (Nov. 13, 1869) 560 f.; H.A.J. Munro, *Journal of Philology* 2 (1869) 334–36; H.J.S. Smith in *Miscellaneous Writings of John Conington* 1 (London, 1872) ix–lxxi; H. Nettleship, *DNB* 4 (1885/6) 938–42; Boase 1 c. 691; Sandys, 422 f.; *BBA* 257:84–92; cf. E. Abbott and L. Campbell, *The Life and Letters of Benjamin Jowett* 1 (London, 1897) 176, 249; *The Letters of Matthew Arnold to Arthur Hugh Clough* (London, 1932) index; A. J. Ashton, *As I Went on My Way* (London, 1924) 76; *BLC* vol. 68 51 f.; G. C. Brodrick, *Memories and Impressions* (London, 1900) 86 f., 101; T. Butler, in *Speeches and Lectures Delivered in Australia by the Late Charles Badham* (Sydney, 1890) xix f.; L. Campbell, *CR* 7 (1893) 474; A. J. Church, *Memories of Men and Books* (London, 1908) 145;L. C. Collins, *Life and Memoirs of John Churton Collins* (London, 1912) 159 f.; G. Faber, *Jowett* (London, 1957) 32, 90; **T. Fowler, *The History of Corpus Christi College, Oxford* (London, 1893) 211; *Letters of Mrs. Gaskell*, edd. Chapple and Pollard (Cambridge, MA, 1967) 380, 384, 461; F. Gribble's *The Romance of Oxford Colleges* (London, 1910) in *Oscar Wilde: Interviews & Recollections*, ed. E. H. Mikhail (London, 1979) I 24; P. Grosskurth, *John Addington Symonds* (London, 1964) index; A.J.C. Hare, *The Story of My Life* 2 (London, 1896) 4; C. Hayes, *Oxford* 39.2 (1987) 64, 67; *Henry Scott Holland: Memoir and Letters*, ed. S. Paget (London, 1921) index; C. Hollis, *The Oxford Union* (London, 1965) 73 f.; A. E. Housman to E. H. Blakeney, April 25, 1932 (*Kenneth W. Rendell* cat. 67 [Dec. 1971] no. 107); W. W. Jackson, *Ingram Bywater* (Oxford, 1917) 180; idem, *PBA* 2 (1905/6) 521; *Dear Miss Nightingale: a Selection of Benjamin Jowett's Letters to Florence Nightingale*, edd. Quinn and Prest (Oxford, 1987) 180; *Letters of Benjamin Jowett*, edd. Abbott and Campbell (London, 1899) 212; *Reminiscences of Lord Kilbracken* (London, 1931) 58–60; H. Lloyd-Jones, *Blood for the Ghosts* (London, 1982) 15 f., 102; P. G. Naiditch, *The Development of Classical Scholarship* (UCLA, 1991) no. 44, pl. ix; M. Nettleship in H. Nettleship, *Lectures and Essays* 2 (Oxford, 1895) xvii; R. L. Nettleship, *Memoir of Thomas Hill Green* (London, 1906) 12 f.; *Memorials of Roundell Palmer, Earl of Selborne* (London, 1898) I 130, II 464; Mark Pattison, *Memoirs* (London, 1885) 245–52; L. Ragg, *A Memoir of E. C. Wickham* (London, 1911) 56, 142; J. Richmond, *James Henry of Dublin* (Dublin, 1976)

Sacred Philology, which began in March 1854, only a few years after the demise of the *Classical Museum*, included amongst its contributors scholars such as Benjamin Hall Kennedy,[53] Richard Shilleto,[54] H.A.J. Munro,[55]

63; Sandys, 434 f.; *The Letters of John Addington Symonds*, edd. Schueller and Peters (Detroit, 1967–69) index; *The Memoirs of John Addington Symonds* (New York, 1984) index; *Times* (Oct. 23, 1869) 8d; *ibid.* (Oct. 25, 1869) 9c; L. A. Tollemache, *Benjamin Jowett* (London, n.d.) 17, 19; idem, *Old and Odd Memories* (London, 1908) index; W. Tuckwell, *Reminiscences of Oxford* (London, 1900; ed. 2 1907) index; M. L. West, *CQ* 38 (1988) 555.

[52] For Frederick Apthorp Paley (1816–1888), at the time a private tutor, see *Times* (Dec. 12, 1888) 9f; *Athen.* 3190 (Dec. 15, 1888) 813 f.; G. W. Cox, *Acad.* 34 (Dec. 22, 1888) 406 f.; *Eagle* 15 (1889) 366–68; D.B.S., *CR* 3 (1889) 80–82; E. C. Marchant, *DNB* 15 (1888) 99–101; Sandys, 409 f.; M.R.P. McGuire, *The New Catholic Encyclopedia* 10 (New York, 1967) 925; cf. M. de la Bedoyère, *The Life of Baron von Hügel* (London, 1951) 36; M. L. Clarke, *Paley* (London, 1974) 136; N.G.L. Hammond, *Sir John Edwin Sandys* (Cambridge, 1933) 37, 76; **A. Peel, *Letters to a Victorian Editor* (London, 1929) 204–13 (brought to my attention by W. M. Calder III); F. M. Turner, *The Greek Heritage in Victorian Britain* (New Haven, 1981) 102; N. Wedd, *The University, King's College, Cambridge* (MS.: King's College, Cambridge) 12–13; cp. W. Everett, *On the Cam* (Cambridge, 1865) 43.

[53] For Benjamin Hall Kennedy (1804–1889), Headmaster of Shrewsbury School (1836–1865) and Regius Professor of Greek in the University of Cambridge (1867–1889), see *Times* (April 9, 1889) 12 ab; *Acad.* 35 (April 13, 1889) 255; *Athen.*3207 (April 13, 1889) 473; *Saturday Review* 7 (April 13, 1889) 442 f.; G. H. Hallam, *Journal of Education* 21 (May 1, 1889) 239–41; *Oxford Magazine* 7 (May 1, 1889) 279; W. F. Smith, *Cambridge Review* 10 (May 2, 1889) 298 f.; J.E.B. Mayor, *CR* 3 (May, 1889) 226 f.; *ibid* 3 (June, 1889) 278–81; *Eagle* 15 (1889) 475–77; J. E. Sandys, *Jahresbericht über die Fortschritte der klassischen Altertumswissenschaft* 61 (1890) 22–24; T. E. Page, *DNB* 10 (1891/92) 1302–04; Boase 2 c. 195; Sandys, 403 f.; *BBA* 640:164–72. Cf. J. Adam, *Emmanuel College Magazine* 7/1 (1895) 5; *Athen.* 3333 (1891) 356; C. M. Blagden, *Well Remembered* (London, 1958) 70; E. H. Blakeney, *Times* (April 18, 1889) 3c; (with J.E.B. Mayor, *ibid.* [April 23, 1889] 10c); *BLC* vol. 2 449–51; M. R. Bobbitt, *With Dearest Love to All* (London, 1960) index; C. W. Bowling in C. Whibley, *In Cap and Gown* (London, 1889) 330 xii; L. Campbell, *CR* 7 (1893) 374; *CR* 3 (1889) 237; G. G. Coulton, *A Victorian Schoolmaster* (London, 1923) 46; idem, *Fourscore Years* (Cambridge, 1944) index; P. Cowbury, ed., *A Salopian Anthology* (London, 1964) index; H. A. Dalton, *Oxford Magazine* 7 (1889) 374; R. H. Elliott, *Athen.* (April 27, 1889) 540; J. D'E. Firth, *Rendall of Winchester* (London, 1954) 22; G. W. Fisher, *Annals of Shrewsbury School* (London, 1989) 325 f.; G. H. Hallam, *Eagle* 38 (June, 1917) 287 f.; M. A. Hamilton, *Newnham* (London, 1936) index; A. E. Gathorne Hardy, ed., *Gathorne Hardy, First Earl of Cranbrook: A Memoir* 2 (London, 1910) 19 f.; T. R. Glover, *Cambridge Retrospect* (Cambridge, 1943) 34, 68; G. L. Gower, *Mixed Grill* (London, 1947) 81; E. Graham, *The Harrow Life of Henry Montagu Butler* (London, 1920) 373; Sir William Gregory, *An Autobiography* (London, 1894) 31–34; N.G.L. Hammond, *Sir John Edwin Sandys* (Cambridge, 1933) 76; J. F. Harris, *Samuel Butler* (London, 1916) index; W. E. Heitland, *Eagle* 15 (1889) 448–60; P. Henderson, *Samuel Butler* (Bloomington, IN, 1954) 150 f.; C. F. Hillyard, *Oxford Magazine* 7 (1889) 406; F. D. How, *Six Great Schoolmasters* (London, 1904) 89–137; M. R. James, *Eton and Kings* (London, 1926) 182–84; C. Jebb, *Life of Sir Richard Claverhouse Jebb* (Cambridge, 1907) 133, 266; H. M. Kempthorne, *Christ's College Magazine* 60 (May, 1968) 81; B. H. Kennedy, *Between Whiles*, Second edition, (London, 1882) v–x, 389–401; F. A. Keynes, *Gathering Up the Threads* (Cambridge, 1950) 38; *Reminiscences of Lord Kilbracken* (London, 1931) 37; J. B. Langstaff, *Oxford – 1914* (New York, 1965) 202; E. S. Leedham-Green, microfilm of Archives of the

John Eyton Bickersteth Mayor,[56] and John Conington. Of these scholars, Mayor, Munro, Paley, Shilleto, and Smith seemingly did not contribute at all to the *Classical Museum*. Kennedy, however, though he published only a single note, and that in reply to criticism (*CM* 6, 312f.), was a member of the Management Committee. But Conington was a contributor: he published a letter of enquiry about Escorial manuscripts of Aeschylus, a note on Sophocles, and perhaps a review of an edition of the *Iphigenia in Aulis*, the last under the initials "J. C." (*CM* 1, 410; 6, 473-5; 2, 98-110). Since Mayor and the others published in other periodicals about the same time as the *Classical Museum*, it follows not that the scholars of Oxbridge

Cambridge University Press (Chadwyck-Healey: microfilm) II.1 index, V 123; *Letters of Edward Lear*, ed. Lady Strachey (New York, n.d.) 163; E.J.B. MacAlister, *Sir Donald MacAlister* (London, 1935) 84; Mary P. Marshall, *What I Remember* (Cambridge, 1947) 16–17, pl. 5; J.E.B. Mayor, *The Latin Heptateuch* (London, 1889) lxvii–lxvix; I.R.D. Morgan, *Memoirs of Henry Arthur Morgan* (London, ca. 1927) 77–94; Mrs. Moss, *Moss of Shrewsbury* (Shrewsbury, 1932) 85, 149, 188 f., index; Sandys, index; *School World* 1 (July, 1899) 272; H. F. Stewart, *Twelve Cambridge Sermons by John E. B. Mayor* (Cambridge, 1911) xiv, xx–xxiii; C. A. Stray, "Paradigms of Social Order: The Politics of Latin Grammar in 19th Century England" (unpublished?); J. Stuart, *Reminiscences* (London, 1912) 177, 200; J. Waite in T. S. Evans, *Latin and Greek Verses* (Cambridge, 1893) x–xii.

[54] For Richard Shilleto (1809–1876), Cambridge coach, see *Times* (Sept. 25, 1876) 9f; *Athen.* 2553 (Sept. 30, 1876) 434; Boase 3 c. 553; Sandys, 406; *AC* 5 (1953) 497; cf. A. J. Ashton, *As I Went on My Way* (London, 1924) 76 f.; *BLC* vol. 301, 170; G. F. Browne, *Recollections of a Bishop* (London, 1915) 118; Oscar Browning, *Memories of Sixty Years* (London, 1910) index; *Cambridge Review* 15 (1894) 206; R. Duckworth, *A Memoir of the Rev. James Lonsdale* (London, 1893) 58, 82; T. S. Evans, *Latin and Greek Verse* (London, 1893) viii; P. Gardner, *Autobiographica* (Oxford, 1933) 13; W. E. Heitland, *After Many Years* (Cambridge, 1926) 129–31, 137 (brought to my attention by W. M. Calder III); E. V. Lucas, *The Colvins and Their Friends* (New York, 1928) 10; E. Graham, *The Harrow Life of Henry Montagu Butler* (London, 1920) index; N.G.L. Hammond, *Sir John Edwin Sandys* (Cambridge, 1933) 11 f., 14 f., 119 f.; P. Henderson, *Samuel Butler* (Bloomington, IN, 1952) 17; Mrs. Moss, *Moss of Shrewsbury* (Shrewsbury, 1932) 47 and index; R. St. J. Parry, *Henry Jackson* (Cambridge, 1926) 13–15, 17, 25, 138, 150, 228; A. Quiller-Couch, *Memoir of Arthur John Butler* (London, 1917) 47, 61; H. Stewart, *Twelve Cambridge Sermons by John E. B. Mayor* (Cambridge, 1911) xvi, xx; G. M. Trevelyan (London, 1932) 37–43, 200 f., 204; G. O. Trevelyan, *The Ladies in Parliament and Other Pieces* (Cambridge, 1869) 73. For his library, see *Athen.* 2587 (1877) 673.

[55] For Hugh Andrew Johnstone Munro (1819–1885), first Professor of Latin in the University of Cambridge (1869–1872), see P. G. Naiditch, "A. E. Housman and H.A.J. Munro," *AN&Q* 21.1/2 (1982) 16–19. To the sources for his life listed there, add R. Ackerman, *J. G. Frazer* (Cambridge, 1987) 29; S. H. Butcher, *Proceedings of the Classical Association of Scotland* (1906) 11; G. G. Coulton, *St. Catharine's Society Magazine* (Sept. 1937) 43 f.; W. W. Fowler, *Oxford Magazine* 18 (1900) 298; J. Glucker, *Pegasus* (Exeter, 1981) 104 f.; R. R. Marett, *A Jerseyman at Oxford* (London, 1941) 294; P. G. Naiditch, *The Development of Classical Scholarship* (UCLA, 1991) no. 42; *Oxford Magazine* 3 (1885) 170 f.; J. A. Spender, *Oxford* 2 (Spring 1936) 50; L. Stephen, *Life of Henry Fawcett* (London, 1886) 129; H. M. Stewart, *Francis Jenkinson* (Cambridge, 1926) 14.

[56] For J.E.B. Mayor (1825–1910), Professor of Latin at Cambridge (1872–1910), see P. G. Naiditch, *A. E. Housman at University College, London* (Leiden, 1988) 204 f. n. 62–1.

were indifferent to scholarship or uncommonly indolent but that their contributions to classical periodicals were controlled by factors such as friendship with the editors or the editors' acquaintances. The editors and chief contributors to the *Classical Museum* were associated more with Bonn, University College, London, and Thomas Arnold's Rugby than with Kennedy's Shrewsbury.

There is another element in all of this which wants emphasis. Kennedy, Shilleto, Munro and, in a way, Mayor were particularly known for verbal scholarship. Art and archaeology, though not entirely foreign to the *Journal of Classical and Sacred Philology*, were, given its title, less noticeable in this periodical. Yet the investigation of art and archaeology was not therefore out of fashion in the older universities. There had, however, been a change in the background of those who pursued such studies. In the eighteenth century, scholars were perhaps evenly divided between academically trained and privately or school trained writers. Similarly, those born in the first quarter of the nineteenth century, who interested themselves in these subjects, were less likely to have attended Oxford or Cambridge than those born afterwards.

John Yonge Akerman (1806–1873), the numismatist, had no academic background at all.[57] Samuel Birch (1814–1898), who spent his career in the British Museum, had had five years at Merchant Taylor's.[58] George Dennis (1814–1898), the author of *Cities and Cemeteries of Etruria*, only spent about a year at Charterhouse.[59] Francis Cranmer Penrose (1817–1903), architect and archaeologist, was educated at Winchester but not at Oxford or Cambridge.[60] John Turtle Wood (1821–1890), the excavator of the Temple of Artemis at Ephesus, likewise had no academic training.[61] Sir John Evans

[57] For Akerman, see *Athen.* 2405 (Nov. 29, 1873) 696; *Numismatic Chronicle (Proceedings)* n. s. 14 (1874) 13–19; cf. *Athen.* 2406 (Dec. 6, 1874) 733; G. Daniel, *Some Small Harvest* (London, 1988) index; W.S.W. Vaux, *Athen.* 2409 (Dec. 27, 1874) 871. Cp. *Revue de la numismatique belge* 5th ser. 6 (1874) 227.

[58] For Birch, see *Times* (Dec. 29, 1885) 8c; *Acad.* 29 (Jan. 2, 1886) 10; *Athen.* 3036 (Jan. 2, 1886) 34 f.; Boase 1 c. 283; **E.A.W. Budge, *Trans. Soc. Bibl. Arch.* 9, 1–41; idem, *DNB* 22 (1890) 199–202; *BBA* 108:128–38; cf. *Athen.* 2580 (April 7, 1877) 449; *ibid.* 3036 (Jan. 2, 1886) 34–35; *ibid.* 3103 (April 16, 1887) 515; *BLC* vol. 32 499–502; E.A.W. Budge, *By Nile and Tigris* (London, 1920) index; E. Hawkins, *Proceedings of the Numismatic Society* 1 (1840) 1–6; D. I. Heath, *Athen.* 2391 (Aug. 23, 1873) 242; T.G.H. James, ed., *Excavating in Egypt* (Chicago, 1982 [1984]) index; "Our Portrait Gallery," *Dublin University Magazine* 90 (July 1877) 53–60; *Times* (Dec. 31, 1885) 10a; *ibid.* (Jan. 13, 1886) 10b.

[59] For Dennis, see *Times* (Nov. 17, 1898) 10a; Boase 5 cc. 75 f.; Sandys, 443; D. E. Rhodes, *Dennis of Etruria* (London, 1973); *BBA* 319:94–95; cf. *BLC* vol. 8,0 466 f.; Sandys, 445 f.; G. Waterfield, *Layard of Nineveh* (New York, 1963 [1968]) 26, 397.

[60] For Penrose, see *Times* (Feb. 17, 1903) 8f; G., *Athen.* 3930 (Feb. 21, 1903) 249; D'A. Power, *DNB* 15 (1888) 788; *AC* 5 (1953) 87; cf. *BLC* vol. 25,1 188; Dillon, *Times* (Feb. 19, 1903) 8b; Joan Evans, *Time and Chance* (London, 1943) 301; *JHS* 23 (1903) 1; C. B. Oldfield, *Times* (Feb. 20, 1903) 9f.

(1823–1908),[62] despite his eminence in the field, never attended college. Reginald Stuart Poole (1832–1895), who eventually headed the Department of Coins and Medals in the British Museum and held the position of Yates Professor of Archaeology at University College, London, was privately educated.[63] Other archaeologists can be easily added to this list.

The chief exceptions of whom I am conscious are Anthony Rich (1803–1891), the author of a *Dictionary of Roman and Greek Antiquities*,[64] who took his degree at Cambridge; Sir Charles Thomas Newton (1816–1894), the excavator of the Mauseoleum and first Keeper of the Department of Greek and Roman Antiquities in the British Museum; and Churchill Babington (1821–1889), editor of the papyrus speeches of Hyperides and Disney Professor of Archaeology in the University of Cambridge.[65] The long-lived Walter Copland Perry (1814–1911), who wrote *Greek and Roman Sculpture*, had studied at Manchester College, York, and taken a doctorate at Göttingen. He had, however, no connexion with Oxbridge.[66]

But then there is a change. It becomes the rule, not the exception, for students of *Realien* to have attended institutions of higher education. Sir Henry Fanshawe Tozer (1829–1916), who wrote the *History of Ancient*

---

[61] For Wood, see R. S. Poole, *Acad.* 37 (April 12, 1890) 257; *Proceedings of the Society of Antiquaries* 13 (1890) 183 f.; Boase 3 c. 1472; cf. *BLC* vol. 355, 70; Hyde Clarke, *Athen.* 3390 (1892) 518; J. C. Francis, *Notes by the Way* (london, 1909) 115; D. E. Rhodes, *Dennis of Etruria* (London, 1973) index. A collection of some of his papers, including two notable letters from Schliemann, survives at the Archives of the History of Art, in the Getty Center for the History of Art and the Humanities, Santa Monica, California, Collection 860962.

[62] For Evans, see *Times* (June 1, 1908) 13ab; W. R., *Nature* 78 (June 11, 1908) 131 f.; Joan Evans, *Time and Chance* (London, 1943); cf. A. C. Benson, *The Life of Edward White Benson* 2 (London, 1899) 132; C. Bigham, *The Roxburghe Club* (Oxford, 1928) 141, 165 f.; C. T. Currelly, *I Brought the Ages Home* (1956 [Toronto, 1976]) 58, 65, 126, 141, 165 f.; G. Daniel, *A Hundred Years of Archaeology* (London, 1950) index; Lady Charlotte Guest, *Extracts from Her Journal* (London, 1950) index; Sir Edward R. Harrison, *Harrison of Inghtam* (London, 1928) index; H. G. Hutchinson, *Life of Sir John Lubbock, Lord Avebury* (London, 1914) index; *Illustrated London News* 111 (1897) 221; Mrs. Donald Macalister, *Sir Donald Macalister* (London, 1935) 141; *Letters of Alexander Macmillan*, ed. G. A. Macmillan (privately printed, 1908) 165 f.; R. R. Marett, *A Jerseyman at Oxford* (London, 1941) 189, 305; *Times* (June 5, 1908) 13b.

[63] For Poole, see P. G. Naiditch, *A. E. Housman at University College, London* (Leiden, 1988) index. Cf. also T.G.H. James, ed., *Excavating in Egypt* (Chicago, 1982 [1984]) index.

[64] For Rich, see Boase 6 c. 465; W. P. Courtney, *Notes and Queries* 112 (Dec. 9, 1905) 461 f.; *AC* 5 (1953) 286; *BBA* 926:42 f.; cf. F. Darwin, *Charles Darwin* (London, 1892) 285, 293.

[65] For Babington, see *Times* (Jan. 14, 1889) 9e; *Nature* 39 (Jan. 17, 1889) 281; *Athen..* 3195 (Jan. 19, 1889) 84; *CR* 3 (1889) 133–34; *Journal of Botany* 27 (1889) 110 f.; Sandys, 411; cf. *Letters of John Richard Green* (New York, 1901) 278 f.; T. D. Rogers, *Sir Frederic Madden at Cambridge* (Cambridge, 1980) index; Sandys, index; J. E. Sandys, *CR* 3 (1889) 135. For his library, see *Sotheby, Wilkinson & Hodge*, Nov. 27–29, 1889.

[66] For Parry, see A. Gordon, *DNB 1901–11* 109–11; *BBA* 869:69 f.

Geography, was educated at Oxford.[67] Alexander Stuart Murray (1841–1904) combined in himself interests in mythology and art and wrote *A Manual of Classical Mythology* and *A Handbook of Archaeology*. He had studied at the Universities of Edinburgh and Berlin and succeeded Newton as Keeper of the Department of Greek and Roman Antiquities in the British Museum.[68] Edward Lee Hicks (1843–1919), the author of *A Manual of Greek Historical Inscriptions*, had received his education at Oxford.[69] Sir John Edwin Sandys (1844–1922), who wrote a book called an *Introduction to Latin Epigraphy* and jointly edited Seyffert's *Dictionary of Classical Mythology, Religion, Literature, Art, and Antiquities*, had studied at Cambridge.[70] Archibald Henry Sayce (1845–1933), a commentator on Herodotus, was educated at Oxford.[71] Percy Gardner (1846–1937), Professor

[67] For Tozer, see *Times* (June 3, 1916) 6b (= *The Stapledon Magazine* 5 [1919] 5–6); *Oxford Magazine* 34 (1916) 356; G. B. G[rundy], *Geographical Journal* 48 (1916) 176 f.; *Alpine Journal* 30 (1916) 330–31; W. W. Jackson, *PBA* 7 (1915–16) 455–74; cf. *BLC* vol. 328 311; L. R. Farnell, *Bibliography of the Fellows and Tutors of Exeter College* (Oxford, 1914) 64–66; G. Glasgow, *Ronald Burrows* (London, 1924) 72; N.G.L. Hammond, *Sir John Edwin Sandys* (Cambridge, 1933) 101 f.; *Later Letters of Edward Lear*, ed. Lady Strachey (New York, 1911) 307; R. R. Marett, *A Jerseyman at Oxford* (London, 1941) 112, 114, 128; Janet Ross, *The Fourth Generation* (New York, 1912) 292–93; *Times* (June 8, 1916) 11b.

[68] For Murray, see *Times* (March 7, 1904) 10d; *ibid.* (March 10, 1904) 6a; *Athen.* 3985 (1904) 345–46; *Proceedings of the Society of Antiquaries of London* ser. 2 20 (1903–05) 112–13; E. M. Thomson, *PBA* 1 (1903-04) 321-23; Sandys, 446; *Who Was Who* 1 (1966) 515; cf. *BLC* vol. 230, 372 f.; E.A.W. Budge, *By Nile and Tigris* 2 (London, 1920) 117 n.; C. T. Currelly, *I Brought the Ages Home* (1956 [Toronto, 1976]) 246; J. H. Fowler, *The Life and Letters of Edward Lee Hicks* (London, 1922) 79; T.G.H. James, ed., *Excavating in Egypt* (Chicago, 1982 [1984]) 15; F. Petrie, *Seventy Years in Archaeology* (London, n.d.) 133; *Times* (March 10, 1904) 6a.

[69] For Hicks, see *Times* (Aug. 16, 1919) 13c; J. H. Fowler, *The Life and Letters of Edward Lee Hicks* (London, 1922); cf. *BLC* vol. 147, 366 f.; *ILN* 136 (1910) 562; *Reminiscences of Lord Kilbracken* (London, 1931) 106; E. A. Knox, *Reminiscences of an Octogenarian* (London, ca. 1935) 80; J. B. Lancelot, *Francis James Chavasse, Bishop of Liverpool* (Oxford, 1929) 37–38, 40; *Times* (Aug. 18, 1919) 13c; *ibid.* (Aug. 19, 1919) 19c; *ibid.* (Aug. 20, 1919) 13c; *ibid.* (Sept. 19, 1919) 6c. A small collection of letters to Hicks is at the Honnold Library, Claremont, Ox/MSS Bx 5199 H529.

[70] For Sandys, see P. G. Naiditch, *A. E. Housman at University College, London* (Leiden, 1988) 209 n. 63–1. Cf. P. G. Naiditch, *The Development of Classical Scholarship* (UCLA, 1991) no. 51, pl. xi.

[71] For Sayce, see his *Reminiscences* (New York, 1923); *Times* (Feb. 6, 1933) 14c; L.H.D.B., *Nature* 131 (1933) 296 f.; F. L. Griffith, *Journal of the Royal Asiatic Society* (1933) 497–99; cf. Mrs. Barnett, *Canon Barnett* 1 (London, 1918) 241; *BLC* vol. 291 214–17; E.A.W. Budge, *By Nile and Tigris* (London, 1920) I 12, 14–15, II 25; C. T. Currelly, *I Brought the Ages Home* (1956 [Toronto, 1976]) 123, 153; G. Daniel, *A Hundred Years of Archaeology* (London, 1950) 215, 291; G. B. Grundy, *Fifty-Five Years at Oxford* (London, 1945) 202 f.; *Illustrated London News* 138 (1911) 230; M. R. James, *Eton and Kings* (London, 1926) 193; T.G.H. James, ed., *Excavating in Egypt* (Chicago, 1982 [1984]) index; S. Langdon, *Journal of the Royal Asiatic Society* (1933) 499–503; Matt, *T.P.'s & Cassell's Weekly* 7 (1926) 82; M. Pope, *The Story of Archaeological Decipherment* (New York, 1975) index; D. Rhodes, *Dennis of Etruria* (London, 1973)

of Classical Archaeology at Oxford, had received his education in the same University.[72] E. S. Roberts (1847–1912), who wrote *An Introduction to Greek Epigraphy*, studied at Cambridge.[73]

Sir William Mitchell Ramsay (1851–1939), Professor of Classical Archaeology at Oxford, was a product of Aberdeen and Oxford.[74] Sir Arthur John Evans (1851–1941), the discoverer of the Minoan Civilisation, was an Oxonian.[75] James Theodore Bent (1852–1897), the traveller and

index; D. Roll-Hansen, *The Academy* (Copenhagen, 1957) index; *Times* (Feb. 8, 1933) 10c; *ibid.* (Feb. 8, 1933) 15cd; *ibid.* (Feb. 9, 1933) 17c; *ibid.* (Feb. 21, 1933) 8c.

[72] For Gardner, see his *Autobiographica* (Oxford, 1933); *Times* (July 19, 1937) 16de; J. L. M[yres], *Nature* 140 (1937) 267 f.; *Oxford Magazine* 21 (Oct., 1937) 50 f.; *Christ's College Magazine* 44 (Dec., 1937) 21; G. F. Hill, *PBA* 23 (1937) 459–69; cf. R. Ackerman, *J. G. Frazer* (Cambridge, 1987) 140, 162; *BLC* vol. 120, 63; P. A. Blunt, *Oxford Magazine* 4 (1963) 112; Joan Evans, *Time and Chance* (London, 1943) index; L. R. Farnell, *An Oxonian Looks Back* (London, 1934) 277 and index; G. B. Grundy, *Fifty-Five Years at Oxford* (London, 1945) 159; T.G.H. James, ed., *Excavating in Egypt* (Chicago, 1982 [1984]) 15; P. E. Matheson, *Life of Hastings Rashdall* (London, 1928) index; Carola Oman, *An Oxford Childhood* (London, 1976) 168; S. Peacock, *Jane Ellen Harrison* (New Haven, 1988) 120, 148, 215 f.; W. B. Saltie, *The Life of Andrew Martin Farbairn* (London, 1914) 399; *Times* (Aug. 28, 1937) 13c; F. M. Turner, *The Greek Heritage in Victorian Britain* (New Haven, 1981) index and plate opp. 15; T. P. Wiseman, *A Short History of the British School at Rome* (London, 1990) 2, 4.

[73] For Roberts, see *Times* (June 17, 1912) 11d; Onlooker, *School World* 14 (Aug., 1912) 294; *Cambridge Magazine* 2 (Oct. 19, 1912) 8; J. Foster, *Alumni Oxonienses: The Members of the University of Oxford 1715–1886* 5 (Oxford, 1891) 314; cf. F. Alex. Barton, *MAP: More About People* 13 (1904) 297; *BLC* vol. 277, 323; D.H.S. Cranage, *Not Only a Dean* (London, 1952) 95, 154; *Granta* 5 (1892) 219–20; F. A. Keynes, *Gathering Up the Threads* (Cambridge, 1950) 112; E. S. Leedham-Green, *A Guide to the Archives of the Cambridge University Press* (Bishops Stortford, 1973) reel 2B: April 26 and May 10, 1894, May 14 and June 3, 1895; Max Pemberton, *MAP: More About People* 5 (1900) 513; *Times* (June 18, 1912) 11b; *ibid.* (June 19, 1912) 11b; *ibid.* (June 20, 1912) 9b.

[74] For Ramsay, see *Times* (Apr. 22, 1939) 14b; J. L. M[yres], *Nature* 143 (1939) 752; **J. Fraser, *Aberdeen University Review* (1939) 243–46; J.G.C. Anderson, *DNB 1931–40* 727 f.; *AC* vol. 5 238; cf. *BLC* vol. 270, 158–60; D.H.S. Cranage, *Not Only a Dean* (London, 1952) 87; L. R. Farnell, *An Oxonian Looks Back* (London, 1934) index; idem, *Bibliography of the Fellows and Tutors of Exeter College* (Oxford, 1914) 48–54; J. H. Fowler, *The Life and Letters of Edward Lee Hicks* (London, 1922) 91; D. G. Hogarth, *Accidents of an Antiquary's Life* (London, 1910) 3, 5–7, 11 f., 151–57; *Illustrated London News* 138 (Feb. 11, 1911) 191; D. E. Rhodes, *Dennis of Etruria* (London, 1973) index. For his library, see *Blackwell's* 455 (1939).

[75] For Sir Arthur John Evans, see *Times* (July 12, 1941) 6f; J. L. M[yres], *Nature* 148 (1941) 106–08; J. L. Myres, *PBA* 27 (1941) 323–57; J. L. Myres, *Obituary Notices of Fellows of the Royal Society* 3 (1941) 941–68; E. T. Leeds, *Oxford* 8.1 (1942) 90–96; Joan Evans, *Time and Chance* (London, 1943); **D. B. Harden, *Sir Arthur Evans 1851–1941: A Memoir* (Oxford, 1983); J. L. Myres, *DNB 1941–50* 240–43; Sylvia L. Horwitz, *The Find of a Lifetime* (New York, 1981); cf. A. M. Adam, *Arthur Innes Adam* (Cambridge, 1920) 87; *Letters of Frederic Lord Blackford* (London, 1896) 374; C. M. Bowra, *Memories 1898–1939* (London, 1966) 247–48; Ann Brown, *Arthur Evans and the Palace of Minos* (Oxford, 1989); **J. S. Candy, *A Tapestry of Life: An Autobiography* (Braunton, Devon, 1984); C. T. Currelly, *I Brought The Ages Home* (1956 [Toronto, 1976]) 63–65, 77; G. Daniel, *A Hundred Years of Archaeology* (London, 1950) index; L. R. Farnell, *An Oxonian*

archaeologist, also had attended Oxford.[76] Sir William Ridgeway (1853–1916), Professor of Archaeology at Cambridge, was a student at both Trinity College, Dublin and Cambridge.[77] Sir James George Frazer (1854–1941), commentator on Pausanias and author of *The Golden Bough*, had studied at Glasgow and Cambridge.[78] Walter Scott (1855–1925), who wrote

---

Looks Back (London, 1934) 116, 123, 178 and index; *Letters of John Richard Green* (New York, 1901) 422; D. B. Harden, *Sir Arthur Evans: Centenary Exhibition* (Oxford: Ashmolean Museum, 1951); idem, *Sir Arthur Evans, 1851–1941: A Memoir* (Oxford: Ashmolean Museum, 1983); W. A. McDonald, *Progress into the Past: The Rediscovery of Mycenaean Civilization* (Bloomington, IN, 1967 [1969]) index; R. R. Marett, *A Jerseyman at Oxford* (London, 1941) index; Carola Oman, *An Oxford Childhood* (London, 1976) 91, 127–28, 153; *Oxford Magazine* 25 (1907) 296–97; R. W. Pfaff, *Montague Rhodes James* (London, 1980) 80; Dilys Powell, *The Villa Ariadne* (London, 1973); W.R.W. Stephens, *The Life and Letters of Edward A. Freeman* (London, 1895) index; P. Sutcliffe, *The Oxford University Press* (Oxford, 1978) 176; H. Waterhouse, *The British School at Athens* (London, 1986) index; *Times* (July 9, 1941) 4e; *ibid.* (July 19, 1941) 6b; J. J. Wilkes, "Arthur Evans in the Balkans 1875–81," *Bulletin of the Institute of Archaeology* (1976) 25–56. For his library, see *Blackwell's* cats. 492 and 493 (1943). The references to Harden, Candy and Powell were brought to my attention by W. M. Calder III.

[76] For Bent, see *Times* (May 7, 1897) 11f; *Athen.* 3629 (1897) 657; *Geographical Journal* 9 (1897) 670 f.; Boase 4 cc. 369–70; W. Carr, *DNB* 22 (1890) 179–80; cf. *BLC* vol. 25, 296; J. H. Fowler, *The Life and Letters of Edward Lee Hicks* (London, 1922) 91; Sir C. Markham, *Geographical Journal* 9 (1897) 674.

[77] For Ridgeway, see *Times* (Aug. 13, 1926) 12bc; **Near East* 30 (Aug. 19, 1926) 185; A. C. Haddon, *Nature* 118 (Aug. 21, 1926) 275 f.; *Spectator* 137 (Aug. 21, 1926) 267; *London Mercury* 14 (Sept. 1926) 453; D. S. Robertson, *Cambridge Review* 43 (Oct. 15, 1926) 12 f.; *CQ* 20 (1926) 208; R. S. Conway, *Caian* 34 (1926–27) 143–55; idem, *PBA* 12 (1926) 327–36; *American Journal of Archaeology* 31 (1927) 359; R. S. Conway, *DNB 1922–30* 720–22; *Who Was Who* 2, 891; *AC* 5 (1953) 301; cf. R. Ackerman, *GRBS* 12 (1971) 117, 124–25; J.R.L. Anderson, ed., *C. K. Ogden: A Collective Memoir* (London, 1977) 37 f.; *BLC* vol. 276 42 f.; W. Blunt, *Cockerell* (New York, 1965) 139; D.H.S. Cranage, *Not Only a Dean* (London, 1952) 95, 148; C. T. Currelly, *I Brought the Ages Home* (1956 [Toronto, 1976]) 66 f., 108, 134, 159, 164, 178, 184, 205, 227 f.; G. Daniel, *A Hundred Years of Archaeology* (London, 1950) 192; idem, *Some Small Harvest* (London, 1988) 69, 209, 211; J. D. Dickson, *Times* (Aug. 16, 1926) 6g; Joan Evans, *Time and Chance* (London, 1943) 347; C. Kluckhohn, *Anthropology and the Classics* (Providence, RI, 1961) 6; A.S.F. Gow, *Outline of My Life* (Ts.: Trinity College, Cambridge, Gow Papers) 16; *The Letters of A. E. Housman*, ed. H. Maas (London, 1971) 427; T.E.B. Howarth, *Cambridge between Two Wars* (London, 1978) index; *Illustrated London News* 169 (Aug. 21, 1926) 342; E. S. Leedham-Green, *A Guide to the Archives of the Cambridge University Press* (Bishops Stortford, 1973) reel 2B: May 18 and Oct. 19, 1894, Nov. 6, 1895, Nov. 13, 1896 and March 5, 1897; *Nature* 118 (1926) 538; R. St. J. Parry, *Henry Jackson* (Cambridge, 1926) 72; S. C. Roberts, *Adventures with Authors* (Cambridge, 1966) index; H. D. Skinner, *Christ's College Magazine* 60 (1967) 40; H. F. Stewart, *Francis Jenkinson* (Cambridge, 1926) 15, 47, 84; *Times* (Aug. 13, 1926) 14; *ibid.* (Aug. 17, 1926) 13a; H. G. Wood, *Terrot Reavely Glover* (Cambridge, 1953) index; *Testimonials of William Ridgeway*, Cambridge 1889 (Glasgow University, Coll. Coll. B3 box 7). For part of his library, see *Blackwell's* cat. 220 (1927) nos. 1–895.

[78] For obituaries of Frazer, see R. Ackerman, *J. G. Frazer* (Cambridge, 1987) 315 n. 4, whose book also includes references to many published and unpublished sources; see also *Who Was Who* 4 409 f.; cf. *The Selected Letters of Robert Bridges*, ed. D. E. Stanford

on the Herculaneum papyri, had taken his degree at Oxford.[79] Lewis Richard Farnell (1856–1934), University Lecturer in Classical Archaeology at Oxford and author of *Cults of the Greek States*, took his degree at Oxford.[80] William Roger Paton (1858–1921), who dwelt in Greece and wrote on Greek epigraphy, had studied at Oxford, though without conspicuous success.[81]

Eugénie Sellers, afterwards Strong (1860–1943), author of *Roman Sculpture from Augustus to Constantine* and Assistant Director of the British School at Rome, had studied at Cambridge.[82] Ernest Arthur Gardner

(Newark, 1983–84) index; N. C. Chaudhuri, *Scholar Extraordinary* (London, 1974) 364 = 380; E. Clodd, *Grant Allen* (London, 1900) 144–46 J. D'E. Firth, *Rendall of Winchester* (London, 1954) 26; C. Hassall, *Edward Marsh* (London, 1959) 230–31; T.E.B. Howarth, *Cambridge between Two Wars* (London, 1978) index; H. G. Hutchinson, *Life of Sir John Lubbock, Lord Avebury* 2 (London, 1914) 146–48, 189; G. W. Knight, *Jackson Knight* (Oxford, 1975) index; R. R. Marett, *A Jerseyman at Oxford* (London, 1941) index; K. Pearson, *The Life, Letters and Labours of Francis Galton* 3a (Cambridge, 1914–30) 239; D. Wilson, *Gilbert Murray* (London, 1984) index; cp. *Nature* 146 (1940) 515. In addition, see T. Besterman, *A Bibliography of Sir James George Frazer* (1934 [London, 1968]), supplemented by R. Ackerman, 309 f. To these may be added A. Platt, *CR* 5 (1891) 339, and Frazer's English translation of Matius ap. Cic. fam. XI 28 (*Trinity College [Cambridge] Lecture Room* [Nov. 18, 1901]).

[79] For Scott, see *The Australian Encyclopaedia* 8 (Sydney, ca. 1958) 41 f.; cf. *BLC* vol. 296, 270; I. Elliott, *Balliol College Register* (Oxford, 1934) 88; George Houstoun Reid, *My Reminiscences* (London, 1917) 26. Cf. A. J. Ashton, *As I Went on My Way* (London, 1924) 73 f. For his testimonials, see Yale University, Sterling Library G4.1 Sc.0.8.

[80] For Farnell, see his *An Oxonian Looks Back* (London, 1934); *Nature* 133 (1934) 713; R. R. Marett, *PBA* 20 (1934) 285–96; E. A. Barber, *DNB 1931–40*, 269; cf. C. M. Bowra, *Memories 1898–1939* (London, 1966) 252; W. M. Calder III in Calder/D.A. Traill, *Myth, Scandal, and History* (Detroit, 1986) 46 n. 80; O.G.S. Crawford, *Said and Done* (London, 1955) 69; F. W. Dillistone, *C. H. Dodd* (London, 1977) 45; Joan Evans, *Time and Chance* (London, 1943) index; L. R. Farnell, *Bibliography of the Fellows and Tutors of Exeter College* (Oxford, 1914) 10–12; C. Firth, *Modern Languages at Oxford* (London, 1929) 133; G. Gabell, *Oxford Magazine* (May 2, 1969) 264; T. F. Gailor, *Some Memories* (Kingsport, TN, 1937) 116; P. Gardner, *Autobiographica* (Oxford, 1933) 38; G. B. Grundy, *Fifty-Five Years at Oxford* (London, 1945) 97, 138, 154, 159, 215; C. Hollis, *Oxford in the Twenties* (London, 1976) 44; G. W. Knight, *Jackson Knight* (Oxford, 1975) 64; J. D. Mabbott, *Oxford Memories* (Oxford, 1986) 39–40; R. R. Marett, *A Jerseyman at Oxford* (London, 1941) 112, 155, 209 and index; idem, *The Stapledon Magazine* 7 (June, 1928) 205–07; J. C. Masterman, *On the Chariot's Wheel* (Oxford, 1975) 141 ff.; N. M. Murray, *Across the Busy Years* 2 (New York, 1940) 36–37; W. Oakenshott, *PBA* 46 (1960) 304; D. Wilson, *Gilbert Murray* (Oxford, 1987) 129, 148, 301–02; E. M. Wright, *The Life of Joseph Wright* (London, 1932) 488, 519. For his library, see *Blackwell's* cat. 351 (1934).

[81] For Paton, see *Times* (June 2, 1921) 12e; cf. Ian Anstruther, *Oscar Browning* (London, 1983) 138; *BLC* vol. 249, 75; W. M. Calder III, *CP* 84 (1989) 234 f.; J. H. Fowler, *Life and Letters of Edward Lee Hicks* (London, 1922) 90–92; W. R. Paton, *CR* 1 (1887) 176 f.; *The Letters of Oscar Wilde* (New York, 1962) index.

[82] For Strong, see J.R.B., *Girton Review* 123 (1943) 13 f.; J.M.C. Toynbee, *Antiquaries Journal* 23 (1943) 188 f.; idem, *DNB 1941–50* 848 f.; J. L. Myres, *Nature* 152 (1943) 441; Gladys Scott Thomson, *Mrs. Arthur Strong* (London, 1949); cf. *Girton Review* 146 (1951) after p. 14; N.G.L. Hammond, *Sir John Edwin Sandys* (Cambridge, 1933) 116; *More About*

(1862–1939), a Director of the British School at Athens and brother of Percy Gardner, had studied at Cambridge.[83] David George Hogarth (1862–1927), also a Director of the British School at Athens, was a graduate of Oxford.[84] Francis John Haverfield (1862–1919), an authority on Roman Britain and Camden Professor of Ancient History, had been educated at Oxford.[85] Sir Frederic George Kenyon (1863–1952), papryologist and Director and Principal Librarian of the British Museum, likewise was an Oxonian.[86] Henry Beauchamp Walters (1867–1944), Keeper of the

People 19 (1907) 99; S. Peacock, *Jane Ellen Harrison* (New Haven, 1988) 58, 259 n. 4; E. Sharp, *Hertha Ayrton* (London, 1926) index; T. P. Wiseman, *A Short History of the British School at Rome* (London, 1990) 5, 8–13; 15 f., 18, 20, 35 f.

[83] For Gardner, see *Times* (Nov. 29, 1939) 4a; J.M.C. Toynbee and H.D.A. Major, *DNB 1931–40*, 307 f.; *Who Was Who* 3 493; cf. *BLC* vol. 150, 233 f.; C. T. Currelly, *I Brought the Ages Home* (1956 [Toronto, 1976]) 45, 230; P. Henderson, *Samuel Butler* (Bloomington, IN, 1954) 192 *Illustrated London News* 136 (1910) 1020; M. R. James, *Eton and Kings* (London, 1926) 148, 191; T.G.H. James, ed., *Excavating in Egypt* (Chicago, 1982 [1984]) 40; F. Petrie, *Seventy Years in Archaeology* (London, n.d.) 57, 62, 66; *Times* (Dec. 4, 1939) 9b.

[84] For Hogarth, see his *A Wandering Scholar in the Levant* (London, 1896) and *Accidents of an Antiquary's Life* (London, 1910); *Times* (Nov. 7, 1927) 19bcd; J. L. M[yres], *Nature* 120 (1927) 735–37; C.R.L. Fletcher, *Geographical Journal* 71 (1928) 321–44; H. R. Hall, *Journal of Egyptian Archaeology* 14 (1928) 128–30; A. H. Sayce, *PBA* 13 (1927) 379–83; *Who Was Who* 2 505; cf. *Correspondence of Robert Bridges and Henry Bradley* (Oxford, 1940) 152; Joan Evans, *Time and Chance* (London, 1943) index; L. R. Farnell, *An Oxonian Looks Back* (London, 1934) 150, 184, 276; C. Firth, *Modern Languages at Oxford* (London, 1929) index; W. Goodenough, *Times* (Nov. 8, 1927) 17d; T.G.H. James, ed., *Excavating in Egypt* (Chicago, 1982 [1984]) 58, 162, 177; G. Macmillan, *Times* (Nov. 9, 1927) 16e; Max Mallowan, *Mallowan's Memoirs* (New York, 1977) 28; R. R. Marett, *A Jerseyman at Oxford* (London, 1941) 220; *Times* (Nov. 7, 1927) 14b; *ibid.* (Nov. 9, 1927) 17d; *ibid.* (Nov. 24, 1927) 11b.

[85] For Haverfield, see *Times* (Oct. 2, 1919) 11d; *Nature* 104 (1919) 117; D. G. H[ogarth], *Oxford Magazine* 38 (Oct. 17, 1919) 6–7; *Yorkshire Post* in *Oxford Magazine* 38 (Nov. 28, 1919) 128–29; *Geographical Journal* 54 (1919) 395; G. Macdonald, *PBA* 9 (1919–20) 475–91; idem, *DNB 1912–21* 244 f.; cf. *BLC* vol. 142, 197 f.; P. A. Blunt, *Oxford Magazine* 4 (1963) 112; J. D'E. Firth, *Rendall of Winchester* (London, 1954) 62; J. H. Fowler, *The Life and Letters of Edward Lee Hicks* (London, 1922) 148; G. B. Grundy, *Fifty-Five Years at Oxford* (London, 1945) 156; F. W. Hirst, *In the Golden Days* (London, 1947) 137–38; Sir J. Marriott, *Memories of Four Score Years* (London, 1946) 40, 114; J. C. Masterman, *On the Chariot's Wheel* (Oxford, 1975) 260; *Nature* 104 (1919) 266; *Times* (Oct. 3, 1919) 11b; *ibid.* (Oct. 6, 1919) 11b; L. Wickert, *Theodor Mommsen* 4 (Frankfurt am Main, 1980) index.

[86] For Kenyon, see *Times* (Aug. 25, 1952) 8a; H. I. Bell, *PBA* 38 (1952) 269–94; F. G. Randall, *Nature* 170 (1952) 560 f.; E. G. Turner, *Gnomon* 24 (1952) 527–28; *Who Was Who* 5, 612 f.; cf. *Letters of P. S. Allen* (London, 1939) 105; C. Bigham, *Roxburghe Club* (Oxford, 1928) 109; T. S. Blakeney, *The Private Library* ser. 2 8 (1975) 120–21; *BLC* vol. 173, 127–29; D.H.S. Cranage, *Not Only a Dean* (London, 1952) 203; H. Cushing, *Life of Sir William Osler* (Oxford, 1925) index; P. Gardner, *Autobiographica* (Oxford, 1933) 49; Sir J. Marriott, *Memories of Four Score Years* (London, 1946) 40; R. W. Pfaff, *Montague Rhodes James* (London, 1980) 366, 389; E. D. Ross, *Both Ends of the Candle* (London, 1943) 116; *Robert Ross: Friend of Friends* (London, 1952) 212; C. Webster, et al., *Times* (Aug. 28, 1952) 6be; Lady Worsley, *Times* (Sept. 11, 1952) 8e.

Department of Greek and Roman Antiquities in the British Museum, studied at Cambridge.[87] Sir George Francis Hill (1867–1948), Keeper of the Department of Coins and Medals at the British Museum, was educated at University College, London and Oxford.[88] Sir John Linton Myres (1869–1954), Lecturer in Classical Archaeology in the University of Oxford, had taken his degree at Oxford.[89] Bernard Pyne Grenfell (1869–1926), a papyrologist, had studied at Oxford.[90]

Also from Oxford was Grenfell's colleague, the papyrologist Arthur Surridge Hunt (1871–1934).[91] Robert Carr Bosanquet (1871–1935), both Director of the British School at Athens and Professor of Classical Archaeology at the University of Liverpool, was educated at Cambridge.[92] Richard MacGillivray Dawkins (1871–1955), Director of the British School

[87] For Walters, see *Who Was Who* 4, 1198.

[88] For Hill, see P. G. Naiditch, *A. E. Housman at University College, London* (Leiden, 1988) 54 n. 15–1.

[89] For Myres, see **T. J. Dunbabin, *PBA* 41 (1955) 349–65; J.N.L. Myres, *Commander J. L. Myres, R.N.V.R.: The Blackbeard of the Aegean* (London, 1980); *Who Was Who* 5 805 f.; cf. A. M. Adam, *Arthur Innes Adam* (Cambridge, 1920) 88, 99–100; *BLC* vol. 231, 208–10; *Correspondence of Robert Bridges and Henry Bradley* (Oxford, 1940) index; P. A. Blunt, *Oxford Magazine* 4 (1963) 112; J. Buxton and P. Williams, *New College, Oxford* (Oxford, 1979) 101, 141; G. Daniel, *Some Small Harvest* (London, 1988) index; E. R. Dodds, *Missing Persons* (Oxford, 1977) 39; Joan Evans, *Time and Chance* (London, 1943) index; T. Kelly, *For Advancement of Learning* (Liverpool, 1981) index; G. W. Knight, *Jackson Knight* (Oxford, 1975) index; R. R. Marett, *A Jerseyman at Oxford* (London, 1941) index; B. C. Trigger, *Gordon Childe* (New York, 1980) index; H. Waterhouse, *The British School at Athens* (London, 1986) index; E. L. Woodward, *Short Journey* (New York, 1946) 41. For his library, see *J. Thornton & Son* cat. 333 (ca. 1955).

[90] For Grenfell, see U. Wilcken, *Gnomon* 2 (1926) 557–60; J. G. Milne, *Journal of Egyptian Archaeology* 12 (Oct., 1926) 285 f.; **P. S. Allen, *Oxford Magazine* (June 3, 1926) 531 f.; **A. S. Hunt, *PBA* 12 (1926) 357–64; cf. *Letters of P. S. Allen* (London, 1939) 112–15, 123 f., 137, 145; N. Barker, *Bibliotheca Lindesiana*, Second edition (London 1978) index; *BLC* vol. 132, 253 f.; C. T. Currelly, *I Brought the Ages Home* (1956 [Toronto, 1976]) 69; T.G.H. James, ed., *Excavating in Egypt* (Chicago, 1982 [1984]) index; R. W. Pfaff, *Montague Rhodes James* (London, 1980) 163.

[91] For Hunt, see U. Wilcken, *Gnomon* 10 (1934) 446–48; J. G. Milne, *Journal of Egyptian Archaeology* 20 (Nov., 1934) 204 f.; cf. N. Barker, *Bibliotheca Lindesiana*, Second edition (London 1978) index; *BLC* vol. 155, 467; T.G.H. James, ed., *Excavating in Egypt* (Chicago, 1982 [1984]) index; R. W. Pfaff, *Montague Rhodes James* (London, 1980) 163.

[92] For Bosanquet, see *Times* (April 23, 1935) 12c; *Nature* 135 (1935) 817 f.; Ellen S. Bosanquet, *Robert Carr Bosanquet* (Gloucester, 1938); idem, *DNB 1931–40*, 90 f.; cf. **N. H. Baynes, *PBA* 13 (1927) 371; *BLC* vol. 38, 256; C. T. Currelly, *I Brought the Ages Home* (1956 [Toronto, 1976]) 45–47, 79; A. C. Deane, *Time Remembered* (London, 1945) 84; Maisie Fletcher, *The Bright Countenance* (London, 1957) 48, 62–63, 89; G. Glasgow, *Ronald Burrows* (London, 1924) 141, 171; *The Lyttelton Hart-Davis Letters* 5 (London, 1983) 115; J. H. Muirhead, *Bernard Bosanquet and His Friends* (London, 1935) index; R. W. Pfaff, *Montague Rhodes James* (London, 1980) 101; *Times* (April 24, 1935) 12c; *ibid.* (April 27, 1935) 14b; G. M. Trevelyan, *An Autobiography* (London, 1949) 44; H. Waterhouse, *The British School at Athens* (London, 1986) index; T. P. Wiseman, *A Short History of the British School at Rome* (London, 1990) 33 n. 28.

at Athens, had attended Cambridge.[93] Thomas Ashby (1874–1931), Director of the British School at Rome, was an Oxonian.[94] This list also could be easily extended.

Here the exceptions are Barclay Vincent Head (1844–1914), who left school at seventeen to work in the British Museum;[95] Warwick William Wroth (1858–1911), who went from the King's School, Canterbury, to the British Museum;[96] and Sir Cecil Harcourt-Smith (1859–1944), who worked in the British Museum, helped found the *Classical Review*, and eventually headed the Victoria and Albert Museum, had gone to Winchester but not to University.[97]

Merely to list these students in this way suffices to indicate the truth of the matter. Too many contemporary scholars devoted themselves to non-verbal studies, without harm to their reputations, for a bias against *Realien* to be the sole or even the chief explanation for such negative reactions as the Ritualists' labours occasioned. Accordingly, if one design to evaluate the reception of the Ritualists, it will be necessary to reject the commonplace notion that their investigations were entirely outside the

[93] For Dawkins, see *Times* (May 6, 1955) 13e; **R.J.H. Jenkins, *PBA* 41 (1955) 373–88; W. R. Halliday, *DNB 1951–60*, 287 f.; cf. A. M. Adam, *Arthur Innes Adam* (Cambridge, 1920) 120; M. J. Benkovitz, *Frederick Rolfe: Baron Corvo* (London, 1977) index; J. Betjeman in A. Thwaite, *My Oxford* (London, 1977) 69–70; *BLC* vol. 78, 229; Ellen S. Bosanquet, *Robert Carr Bosanquet* (Gloucester, 1938) 135, 152; C. T. Currelly, *I Brought the Ages Home* (1956 [Toronto, 1976]) 46 f.; *They Stand Together: The Letters of C. S. Lewis and Arthur Greeves*, ed. W. Hooper (London, 1979) 341; Joan Evans, *Time and Chance* (London, 1943) 372, 395; *In Memoriam Archie 1904–64* (s l., 1966) 12; Fr. Rolfe, *Letters to R. M. Dawkins* (London, 1962); A. L. Rowse, *A Man of the Thirties* (London, 1979) 26; G. Stephenson, *Times* (May 18, 1955) 13d; A.J.A. Symons, *The Quest for Corvo* (London, 1934 [1935]) index; *Times* (May 16, 1955) 10b; H. Waterhouse, *The British School at Athens* (London, 1986) index; D. Weeks, *Corvo* (London, 1971) index.

[94] For Ashby, see A.H.S[mith]., *PBA* 17 (1931) 515–41; cf. R. Keaveney, *Views of Rome from the Thomas Ashby Collection in the Vatican Library* (Rome, 1988; brought to my attention by R. H. Rouse, UCLA); G. M. Trevelyan, *An Autobiography* (London, 1949) 33; G. Thomson, *Mrs. Arthur Strong* (London, 1949) 93–95, 105; T. P. Wiseman, *A Short History of the British School at Rome* (London, 1990) 3, 5–13, 15 f., 19 f., 33, 35 f., pl. 1b, 2.

[95] For Head, see *Athen.* 4521 (1914) 861 (= *Numismatic Chronicle* 4th ser. 14 [1914] 249–52); E. B[abelon], *Revue numismatique* 4th ser. 18 (1914) 519–20; G. F. Hill, *Revue belge de numismatique* 71 (1919) 183–86; cf. *BLC* vol. 143 95 f.; P. Gardner, *Autobiographica* (Oxford, 1933) 27; T.G.H. James, ed., *Excavating in Egypt* (Chicago, 1982 [1984]) 15; *Numismatic Chronicle* 4th ser. 14 (1914) 168, 252–55 (= *Revue numismatique* 4th ser. 18 [1914] 520–22).

[96] For Wroth, see *Times* (September 28, 1911) 9 f.; G. F. Hill, *Numismatic Chronicle* 4th series 12 (1912) 107–109; A. Blanchet, *Revue numismatique* 4th series 6 (1912) 295 f.; W. B. Owen, *DNB 1901–11*, 713 f.; *Times* (October 4, 1911) 11b; (October 18, 1911) 11b; cf. J. Allan, *Numismatic Chronicle* 12 (1912) 109 f.

[97] For Harcourt-Smith, see *Times* (March 29, 1944) 7d; J. Layer, *DNB 1941–50*, 354 f.; *Who Was Who* 3, 1066; cf. E. S. Bosanquet, *Robert Carr Bosanquet* (Gloucester, 1938) 51, 53, 56–58, 66, 73; H. Waterhouse, *The British School at Athens* (London, 1986) index.

mainstream of scholarly work, for to do otherwise is to falsify the history of classical scholarship.[98]

University of California, Los Angeles

[98] I am grateful to Interlibrary Loan, University Research Library, UCLA, for arranging for a set of the *Classical Museum* to be lent to me.

8

A Ritualist Odyssey:
Victorian England to Soviet Russia

J. K. NEWMAN

> As a matter of fact, literature has
> borrowed far more from the people than
> the people have borrowed from
> literature, though both processes have
> been at work in the course of history.

Andrew Lang, *Myth, Ritual and Religion* (1887), II, p. 290

In the era of Gorbomania, the most valuable contribution to be made by the philologist is to remind the Russians that they belong to Europe—and the Europeans that they have much to learn from Russia. The study of the Cambridge—and more than Cambridge—Ritualists and their reception in the Soviet Union is well calculated to secure this end.

Victorian Cambridge, Victorian Oxford—these are names redolent of an ordered world unlikely to be recreated, and threatened by change even when apparently most secure. The very Empire that guaranteed this domestic tranquillity had led Britons into the furthest corners of the world. Some returned, like Cambridge-educated Darwin, with unsettling news about the origin of species. Others, like Andrew Lang (1844–1912), early in his career (1868–75) Fellow of Merton College, Oxford, were struck by the extraordinary similarities between the familiar stories of the classical authors and the tales of peoples recorded by explorers and missionaries who could have had no direct contact with each other, and least of all with any book-learning, yet whose myths showed strange resemblances to those of the Greeks.

This is already to reveal a secret of empire, *posse ritualistam alibi quam Cantabrigiae fieri*. Ritualism was more than a Cambridge phenomenon. Can this be surprising? Matthew Arnold spoke of Oxford's towers as breathing the last enchantments of the Middle Ages, and the Oxford Movement, at its height in mid-century, was often called "ritualistic." In a letter preserved in the University Library at St. Andrews Lang wrote: "My heart is Catholic, but my head is Protestant." In spite of his recalcitrant head, this was an amazing statement for the son of Scottish Calvinists to make, and its warring members are characteristic of the scholarly œuvre.

Tradition persists. Even in modern Oxford, Merton Street, though so close to the High, retains a somnolent charm. It was to lodgings there, granted by Merton College, that J. R. R. Tolkien, once a professor of Anglo-Saxon and then world-famous as the new Ariosto, retired after the death of his wife. He had a predecessor in the young Scots Fellow of Merton already mentioned, Andrew Lang, also famous with a wide public in late Victorian Britain both for his fairy tales and of course as joint translator of the *Iliad* and *Odyssey*.

Just like Professor Tolkien, who would later memorialize him in a lecture at St. Andrews University, Lang also raised more serious claims as a student of his medium. He was a prolific author in many fields, but his books relevant here were:

Custom and Myth (1884, but containing papers written and printed
  much earlier);
Myth, Ritual and Religion (1887);
The Making of Religion (1898);
Myth, Ritual and Religion (second revised edition, 1899).

His work on totemism is cited sixteen times by Freud in his *Totem und Tabu* (1913). Freud's is the second name to be mentioned here (Darwin's was the first) among that triad whose hammer blows shook to pieces the Victorian world. The teller of fairy tales kept company with Titans.

This is not the place even to sketch all that Lang had to say[1] as part of the Oxford School that included such scholars are R. R. Marett and L. R. Farnell, both Rectors of Exeter College. He married in 1875 and, in later life, blamed his failure (as he saw it) to become a major scholar of anthropology on his need to go off and earn his living at a time when Oxford appointments were hardly available except to the celibate. Always uneasily aware that he was a devotee of *belles lettres*, and therefore academically suspect, he represents a Romantic and quirky sensibility far removed from the formal training that might have seemed appropriate on the Continent (although he found early recognition in France). But his background had its strengths. He was a veteran of anthropological fieldwork without any conscious planning. Because he was born in relatively backward and undeveloped Scotland, in fact in Walter Scott country, and because his old nurse (like Pushkin's) filled his head with folktales while he was still a young boy, he had an empirical knowledge of the untidy, odd, irrational, "peasant" side of life that made him instinctively reject clever ideas invented in the study. His first quarrel as a young don was with his

---

[1] The dissertation of A.P.L. de Cocq, *Andrew Lang, A Nineteenth Century Anthropologist* (Tilburg 1968), is basic.

Oxford colleague, the German-born and educated Professor Max Müller, deputy Taylorian Professor of Modern Languages and Fellow of All Souls.

Müller, an expert in Sanskrit, believed that myth was a "disease of language,"[2] the result of an excessive fondness for metaphorical expression. At some stage an original and quite natural observation by the Aryans about the dawn followed by the sun, for example, had been corrupted, thanks to confusion engendered by masculine and feminine grammatical noun-endings, into the story of female Daphne (Sanskrit *ahana* or *dahana*, "dawn") pursued and eventually destroyed by male Phoebus Apollo (φοῖβος, "the shining one"). It is clear how much anthropology of this kind could be concocted without ever leaving the confines of the ivory tower.

Lang, however, argued that myth is not a misunderstanding by uncouth and woolly-minded barbarians of the pristine Aryan language and culture from which Western civilization was thought to stem. The very resemblances between the myths of peoples who could not have misunderstood the Aryans because they could never have known anything about them showed that myth must play a far more necessary—although similar—role in the primitive apprehension of the world. Myth is also too important for primitive man to be content with something crude and wrong-headed, any more than the hunter could be content with a spear that would not pierce. It is true that Lang tended to be too patronising of the primitive mentality, and to vacillate over whether similar tales had an independent origin or alternatively owed their diffusion to borrowing, but at least he established the point that primitive man is not stupid when he does not work with categories and concepts developed millennia after his time, and projected onto an idealized *Urkultur* so that, by its fictitious standards, he may be found wanting.

Lang always remained *homo ludens*, a Celt, a poet and author of fairy tales who ultimately lost contact with Oxford. He may have been refused a professorship, and later (1903) even kept out of the Wardenship of his old College, by the influential opposition of the philosopher F. H. Bradley. Whether he actually wanted to lead a rationalist revolution is open to doubt, since as a poet, he accepted that the imagination could be the vehicle of a larger truth, and this explains Tolkien's interest in him.[3] In *The Making of Religion*, for example, he maintained that one cannot simply reject paranormal or psychic phenomena. But his anthropological theory, which he never denied to be evolutionary, may provoke two reactions. One is to reduce, to emphasize the surviving element of the primitive, and to demand that this element be purged. If there is an origin of biological species, a movement from the lower to the higher in which many traces of the lower still linger, is there a corresponding evolution of the spirit? If it is our duty to control the lower in the interests of the higher, how can we shirk the

---

[2] See R. Lancelyn Green, *Andrew Lang* (London 1962), pp. 40–41; de Cocq, p. 61.
[3] Obviously a major comparative study of Lang and Tolkien is due.

same duty in the spiritual sphere?   If religion shows elements of superstition, must it not be right to purge it of the old, so that the pure spirit is left?   And, if the old cannot be purged, do we not need a different sort of religion, or perhaps no religion at all?

Crudely put, this is the attack on Christianity implicit, if not always consciously so, in these nineteenth-century speculations. The discovery of a misunderstood ritual now fossilized and surrounded with a new and more palatable gloss of rationalizing respectability threatened the very foundation of belief, once that gloss was stripped away. In particular, it lent fresh weaponry to those questioning the basis of society on economic grounds— and here we come to the third of our destructive Titans, Karl Marx. Just as capital was nothing more than theft, religion, the opium of the people, was the vestige of a once living belief now grown irrelevant and hypocritical, preserved by the exploiting class as an elaborate charade in order to bamboozle its victims. Both should be jettisoned in favour of a new order, in which a man's reward corresponded to his labour, his beliefs to the scientific explanation of the way the world both works and is controllable in man's interest.

Certainly Marxism is discredited as a political system in our time, since the rational ordering of society has proved impossible to attain by the fostering of class consciousness. But in the field of religion and art? It comes as a shock to the reader who opens the pages of Russian literary history and criticism in our century—for example, I. Tronsky, История й Литературы (Leningrad 1951)—to find a degree of sophistication in the appreciation of literary texts which makes the French look superficial and the British antiquated. Indeed, the tragedy of English scholarship in our century has been to turn its back on its own best insights, so that while Gilbert Murray is made fun of in Oxford lecture-rooms, the английская школа (i. e. of the Ritualists) is something one first hears about in Cyrillic:

> Английская наука показала, что трагедия имеет остов страстей разрываемого на части бога, а комедия с её сценами жертвоприношения, варки и еды—перепетию перехода из смерти в реновацию. По Murray ...[4]

> English scholarship has shown that tragedy preserves the outline of the passion of a dismembered god, while comedy, with its scenes of sacrifice, cooking and eating, shows the peripeteia of the passage from death to renewal. According to Murray...

There then follows a sketch of the theory of the ἐνιαυτὸς δαίμων. I hold no brief in this court for him, but, to speak generally, it seems extraordinary that this kind of thinking and these sorts of theories had to pass from Britain to Russia, and from Russia to Paris, before they eventually—fifty years

---

[4] O. M. Freudenberg, Поетика Сюжета и Жанра (Leningrad 1936), p. 187.

on—came back to Britain via Lévi-Strauss[5] and others as the *dernier cri*. What is wrong with the British system of education?

What happened is evidently that English (Classical) scholarship had what elsewhere (in his book on the stages of Greek Religion) Murray (an Australian) describes as a failure of nerve—with certain honourable exceptions, such as E. R. Dodds[6]—who was an Irishman. Perhaps the influence of A. E. Housman turned Classicists back to the linguistic and textual, and there is much to be said for understanding the text. But texts have contexts, and to forget that is to forget what Classical scholarship is for.

My remarks here will be based on the reading chiefly of the following works:

Texts of the Russian Formalists (especially B. Tomashevsky, Yu. Tynyanov, V. Shklovsky, B. Eichenbaum).[7]

V. Propp, Морфология сказки (Leningrad 1928) (=*Types of the Fairy Tale*).

M. Bakhtin, Проблемы Поетики Достоевского (Moscow 1963) and Творчество Франсуа Рабле и народная культура средневековья и ренессанса (Moscow 1965) (= *Problems of Dostoevsky's Poetics* and *The Literary Creation of François Rabelais and the Popular Culture of the Middle Ages and Renaissance*).

O. Freudenberg, Поетика Сюжета и Жанра (Leningrad 1936) and Миф и Литература Древности (Moscow 1978) (= *The Poetics of Subject and Genre* and *The Myth and Literature of Antiquity*).

S. M. Eisenstein, Избранные Произведения в шести томах (= *Selected Works in six volumes*, Moscow 1964).

Yu. Lotman, Структура Художественного Текста (Moscow 1970) (= *The Structure of an Artistic Text*).

This is a galaxy of critical thought, and the notion that the history of ancient literature can be written even in Cambridge without reference to it is absurd, not least perhaps if it is based on the idea that literary prose is a simpler and more easily intelligible medium than verse.

---

[5] *The Structural Study of Myth and Totemism*, A. S. A. Monographs 5, ed. E. Leach (London 1967), offers a useful critique for the English-speaking reader.

[6] If Farnell's work on Pindar had shown a more fruitful relation to his study of the *Cults of the Greek States* things might have been different.

[7] Everyone has read V. Erlich, *Russian Formalism* (4th ed., The Hague—Paris—New York 1980). Ignazio Ambrogio, *Formalismo e Avanguardia in Russia* (Rome 1968), provides a different perspective.

Some of this sophistication has nothing directly to do with English Ritualism. The debt of Marxism to Hegel[8] needs no emphasis. In his *Aesthetik*, Hegel, though ultimately interested in a work of art as an expression of the Spirit, had emphasized, following the Classicist and theologian F. Schleiermacher, that all works of art are grounded in historical reality. Though ultimately it may be of no interest that Petrarch's mistress was called Laura, there is an earlier point at which that information is rightly made available by and to the scholar.   Hegel, again like Schleiermacher, was also aware that formal works of art may owe their genesis to popular roots.

If, with Marx, history unfolds not as the self-manifestation of the Spirit (*Phänomenologie des Geistes*) but as the revelation of the iron laws of deterministic materialism, the interest in popular roots is if anything made stronger, for now, in a theory where matter and the labour needed to change it hold pride of place, it is no longer the "higher" manifestation to which attention is directed but precisely the vulgar, less hypocritical, less disguised and pretentious.   Ritualism therefore, as a theory which saw the structure even of works of art as determined by the survival of half understood religious and superstitious practices, if not at the basis of Marxist aesthetic theory, was bound to seem consonant with Marxism, and F. M. Cornford, though no Marxist, wrote in "The Marxist View of Ancient Philosophy": "Now that I have made some study of that doctrine [Marxism], I can see further light to be gained from that quarter."[9]

We owe Marxism a great deal.   Even the Formalist treatment of the work of art as self-contained and as determined by its own inner laws, though apparently so alien to materialism, was in fact akin to the theory that art is essentially something divorced from spirit, and the work of art is something made (a вещь = a "thing") just like any other product. In this respect, the polemic conducted by L. Trotsky[10] with the Formalists which led to their suppression was quite mistaken, and the more elaborate polemic attributed variously to Bakhtin and "P. N. Medvedev" (Формальный Метод в литературоведении = *The Formal Method in the Study of Literature*) should be treated as conditioned by the time and place of its publication

---

[8] Although Lang did blame himself for too great dependence on Hegel at one stage (de Cocq, p 73).—Immer wieder erstaunt man darüber, daß die modernen deutschen Altphilologen nichts mit ihren eigenen Philosophen und Metaphysikern zu tun haben wollen. Ob das aus Wilamowitzens Streit mit Nietzsche hervorgeht? Aber wenn es der wichtigste Auftrag der heutigen Wissenschaft ist (wie einst Eduard Fraenkel bemerkt haben soll), sich mit Nietzsche auseinanderzusetzen?

[9] *The Unwritten Philosophy and Other Essays* (Cambridge 1967), p. 118. His poet-son John was actually killed (1936) in the Spanish Civil War fighting for the Communist cause.

[10] Литература и Революция (= *Literature and the Revolution*, Moscow 1924).   Erlich suggests (*op. cit.*, p. 102) that Trotsky was helped by Lang's hypothesis of literary self-generation when he attacked the Formalist notion of "homeless plots."

(Leningrad 1928), rather than as the last word on its theme. On the other side, precisely because of the irrelevance of this quarrel, it is not surprising to find Formalist terms freely used by both Bakhtin and Eisenstein. The more recent work of Lotman appears to be quite eclectic.

A great deal turns on the nature of the primitive reality from which art grows, and of which it is the reflection. How material is matter? The truth that the most primitive tribes have a use for art has been re-emphasized by Lotman. Art is not dispensable unless man is denatured. This is a big discovery in a society where the drably utilitarian (Moscow University) has been thought to be more working-class and therefore more "honest" than the ornate—not of course where the peasantry (народ) has to be impressed, as the Moscow Underground proves.

The first problem therefore which Russian Marxism encounters in its exploration of primitive society is that the primitive is not outgrown. There is not a peasant society, close to the soil, where everything is explicable in terms of rational tribal need, which may now be replaced by a proletariat with better and more enlightened explanations. Stalin tried this in his collectivization war of the 1930s. But, as he found, "rationality" is not a concept which at this level makes sense.[11] If one thinks of the ordered symmetry of peasant art, of its colours and designs, it is clear that the primitive mind is certainly logical, but logical in terms of its peculiar perceptions of the forces at work in the universe. The educated mind, in rejecting the larger awareness possessed by the primitive, so often does not so much expand as impoverish its world-view. One already seems to echo themes that fascinated Euripides. They certainly recur in Tolstoy and Turgenev.

This explains both the incommensurability of myth with the rational, and its inevitably fragmentary and even self-contradictory nature. If myth is what Eliot called a "raid on the inarticulate," the prisoners brought back from these raids into no man's land will not always give a coherent account of what is happening over on the other side. The educated rationalist also risks losing contact with his base. In Russia, the народ is held in contempt by Party intellectuals for precisely this reason. Of course it returns the compliment.

We spoke of two possible responses to Lang, and mentioned only the reductionist, which sees the survival of myth and ritual as something negative and even shameful. We omitted the second response, more and more insistent in our time, which sees the survival of myth as something precious and positive, to be neglected only at the price of impairing and diminishing our world-view. It is self-centred in the extreme to imagine that "the West"—which usually means "the modern professoriate"—has a

---

[11] And Eisenstein's contribution to the struggle in his agricultural film Старое и Новое (1929) was, as he himself freely admits (Избр. Произв. III, pp. 72 ff.), not wholly rational.

monopoly on the perception of the way things are. A given time, a given place of course have their own significance. But we "canonize" (to use a Formalist term) and freeze those moments of significance at our peril. If we are concerned with the universal, all experience has its role to play in defining what that universal is. The student of Aristotle must learn again why poetry is more philosophical than history, and why the myth is the ψυχή or soul of tragedy.

Aristotle was open to the comic in a way that Aristotelians have often found offensive, for example in arguing that tragedy originated from the satyr-play or in attributing even the *Margites* to Homer. But Cicero himself, who in a famous and damaging remark[12] (*De Opt. Gen. Or.* I. 1) urged that *et in tragoedia comicum vitiosum est et in comoedia turpe tragicum*, also notes that the material which may supply the ethical and tragic may also at another level supply the comic. The discussion of laughter in the second book of the *de Oratore* is germane. Himself a master of witty repartee, he points out that the given material *per se* may be quite ambiguous (II. 61. 248):

> Sed hoc mementote, quoscumque locos attingam, unde ridicula ducantur, ex eisdem locis fere etiam gravis sententias posse duci: tantum interest, quod gravitas honestis in rebus severisque, iocus in turpiculis et quasi deformibus ponitur....

> It should be borne in mind that more or less all my evidence for the laughable may also serve for the expression of the serious. The only difference is that seriousness rests on matters of strict morality, while the rather discreditable and even misshapen is material for joking.

Here, the move towards what Bakhtin calls the "grotesque body" (гротескное тело) in *deformibus* may be noted. It is an instinctive part of the Roman sense of humour, as names like "Strabo" and "Naso" attest.

This insight into the undifferentiated primitive constitutes one of the chief attractions of Olga Freudenberg's books.[13] Primitive man is not blasphemous or unfeeling when he confounds what later sensibility keeps so carefully separate, when he keeps his money, for example, in the temple of Juno Moneta (ambiguity of χρῆσθαι: cf. χρέος, χρηστήριον,

---

[12] It would of course eliminate Homer's δακρυόεν γελάσασα (mentioned below), Virgil's Dido (*paene comicus stilus est* says Servius in his introduction to Book IV); and Shakespeare's *Merchant of Venice* or Molière's *L'Avare*, to go no further.

[13] She was Professor of Classics at Leningrad University. Though she is sometimes called "Friedenberg" (for which the Russian would be Фрийденберг), her name (Фрейденберг in Russian orthography, by the well-known Russian inability to represent more directly the German *eu*) is anglicized as "Freudenberg" in the English summary on pp. 598–603 of her Миф и Литература Древности. Her many fruitful ideas must excuse a certain wildness and indiscipline in their presentation—an excuse that must be used for more Russians than her! On dira du génie russe ce qu' a dit Baudelaire du poète: *Ses ailes de géant l'empêchent de marcher.*

χρηματιστής). There is a level at which these later distinctions are not yet felt. It is modern puritanism that is too nice about the wearing of a transvestite Greek reveller's eastern cap at a metamorphosing, comic symposium by a Christian bishop. For the more discerning student of culture, all this is a reassuring token that modern puritanism and compartmentalization are being forced by ritual into some sort of contact with a lasting reality.

Freudenberg particularly emphasizes the continuing influence of the primitive conventions of genre, even on so-called contemporary works. This is a truth lost sight of by those who are too concerned, for example, with "Roman poetry and the life of luxury":

> задача науки—показать, что и современная буржуазная реальность, находящая отражение в литературе, является примитвно-условной.[14]

> The task of scholarship is to show that even contemporary bourgeois reality, finding its reflection in literature, is in debt to the primitive and conventional.

It is often tempting for the student of the Classics, preoccupied with the image of literature as a mirror of society, and forgetful of the ambiguities of this metaphor (δι' ἐσόπτρου ἐν αἰνίγματι), to take the post-classical satirists at their word, and conclude that, with the death of Augustus, Roman literature became the reflection of a decadent and immoral society, best forgotten, and conveniently enabling a curtailment of the reading list. Freudenberg points out that satire finds immorality for the same reason that the visitors to the Emerald City of the Wizard of Oz saw everything green. In the age of Aristotle and Alexander the Great, Theophrastus notes only oddities because oddities are what he is looking for. Suppose Homer had described only Thersites.

But if we are able in this way to bring together our political perceptions of the lasting achievement of the Roman Empire and our literary appreciation of its authors, the terms "Silver" and "Golden" Ages must be replaced by simple chronological designations, and talk about "decadence" will now become the sign of a failure of understanding. Incidentally, this will help us to see the courts of Nero and Domitian as brilliant centres of artistic achievement, not least in the encouragement they gave to the pantomime, for which both Lucan and Statius wrote. Was this any more discreditable than the now-vanished operas written by Racine and Boileau for the Sun-king? It will also give respectability back to Byzantium, where an ex-mime-actress was the consort of the great Justinian.

---

[14] Поетика Сюжета и Жанра, p. 242.

It is Mikhail Bakhtin,[15] however, who has torpedoed the Marxist hope of finding a primitive and potentially godless world which might be the reality needed to underpin the now old-fashioned demand by Trotsky and Stalin for Socialist Realism. In his picture of society, the primitive lives on even today in the age-old celebrations of the peasant year, its unfolding seasons, its unity of opposites, its eternal recurrences, what he calls весёлое время. As the tribe celebrates its times of plenty and fears its times of dearth, certain repeated elements make themselves felt: the most important of these is laughter, and the ambivalent expression of laughter in double entendre (*inversa verba*). To this tribe, primitive though it may be, we all belong, honouring its rituals every time we say our prayers, attend a wedding or a funeral, rejoice at a birth or grieve at a departure, δακρυόεν γελάσαντες. It will be seen how little likely this awareness of a kinship with the past is to encourage a univocal literature of propaganda.

Bakhtin was no classical scholar—a fact which it is dangerous to overemphasize—but, in the wake of the anthropological movement of the nineteenth century he sets a new agenda for literary historians in our time. The following areas in particular will need attention:

1. The comprehension of the conventions of the dialogue. Principally here, laughter (one version of which is the Socratic irony) and indecisiveness (ἀπορία) are key characteristics, so that texts so disparate as the end of Tacitus' *Dialogus* (*cum adrisissent, discesserunt*) and Pilate's conversation with Christ (τί ἐστιν ἀλήθεια;) now become canonical. Here, I would say that first tasks might be the evaluation of the Melian Dialogue and the *Octavius* of Minucius Felix.

2. The other-directed nature of language, and the survival in it of many different levels, especially of religious vocabulary.

3. The understanding of the place of laughter in the sacred (*risus paschalis*). What a study of the serio-comedy of the *Bacchae*, for example, remains to be written (and how much it would have to contradict Cicero's *in tragoedia comicum vitiosum est*). As our age becomes more and more secularized, more and more dimensions of religious experience are becoming lost: for example, the proper description of the reaction to a miracle, so beautifully caught by Pindar in the first *Nemean* (55–56).

4. The importance of metamorphosis, already noted in the primitive mentality by Lang. Ovid's poem has rightly been praised, but so often for the wrong reasons. For the first time, it will be possible both to admit the extraordinary influence which it has had on all subsequent European

---

[15] Evidently Bakhtin is a controversial figure. A (not wholly satisfactory) introduction to one who has been called (avec justesse, à mon avis) "le plus grand théoricien littéraire de notre ère" is afforded by K. Clark and M. Holquist, *Mikhail Bakhtin* (Harvard U. P. 1984).

literature, not least on Shakespeare and Milton, and to know why that has been the case.

5. The polyphonic nature of artistic language (Virgil's *vox et os et hypocrisis*), its parodies, *inversa verba* and so on. Here, it may be possible for the first time to do justice to the linguistic theories of, for example, Gorgias.[16]

6. The nature of ancient satire. Since satire is the peculiarly Roman genre, the question of the genuine originality of Roman literature may now be broached with some hope of a reasonable answer.

7. The relationship of the work of art to time. The suspension of the clock, the elasticity of the whole concept of serial time have been long known to literary scholars. But some of the conventional *monumentum aere perennius* may now be reinterpreted as less trite.

8. Anachronism. This whole question is bound up with this elasticity not only of time but also of place (they are both special cases of metamorphosis). With appropriate software, it is possible on a modern computer screen to switch and change, enlarge and diminish, colour and uncolour and recolour the dimensions of a drawing so that it may be explored from every point of view. What the microchip does now "out there," the artist has been doing for centuries on the screen of his mind. The sophistication of response to a literary text by classical scholars cannot remain at the blackboard level of chalk and talk.

9. The theory of the genres. This will also need overhaul—and here we touch on the old Marxist and reductionist hope that everything could be brought back to a sort of *Urliteratur*, the "work-cry" or something similar, chanted by the tribal collective as it pulled on the communal rope. But the primal experience is death and resurrection, in crude terms, hunger and eating, and already Homer, who ends the *Iliad* with a funeral feast, shows how early these notions are, at least for the Greeks, and how they persist into literature.

Particularly therefore the social ambience of the genres will demand attention: in the first instance, the religious occasion, at which games play so important a part, but then also the funeral, the symposium, the komos, the wedding. The ancients, for example, had a defined social etiquette, and questions about the proper conduct of guests unite such otherwise unlikely companions as Pindar and Catullus. If Tantalus stole from his hosts, if

---

[16] Cf. "Protagoras, Gorgias, and the Dialogic Principle," *Illinois Classical Studies* XII (1986), pp. 43 ff. See also the next note.

Ixion actually had the impudence to assail his host's wife,[17] then Marrucine Asinius and Thallus were their descendants.

If the "higher" genres do not have priority, neither do the lower, since such distinctions are too complex for primitive thought. When they emerge, the genres alternate in a perpetual quest for what the Formalists call остранение, "estrangement." Perhaps in fact it must be recognized what traces of their motley, undifferentiated origins the genres retain, the highest making concessions to the lowest (again Shakespeare comes to mind, but he has a good ally in Dante), and the lowest already showing their affinity to and striving towards the highest.

This also implies a new relationship to "rhetoric." Too often the problems of interpretation are thought to be solved by looking in the handbook left by Menander. But there is a popular rhetoric generated by the emotional pressure and dialectic of the given situation, by what Eisenstein would call its "music," of which assonance and alliteration, but also recurrence and balance are tokens (it is why poetry is perfected before prose). It is foolish to look for mechanical rules to explain an art still living. The history of the genre comes first![18]

10. The nature of the classical tradition. This is something else demanding overhaul, since if the common feature of different literary works is their relationship to what Lang calls "the people," it will no longer be necessary to make *Quellenforschung* depend simply on showing that later X "knew" or alternatively "could not have known" earlier Y. Earlier and later authors converge,[19] not necessarily because one read the other, or both read a common literary source, but because they were drawing on the same primitive and popular wells of inspiration. To name yet again an author who keeps cropping up in the discussion, Shakespeare's classicism will I think be proved quite profoundly by this new line of investigation.

11. The concept of scholarship. This must change. So often the role-model persisting from classroom to study in the professor's mind has been that of the severe taskmaster, who in moving from his group of undergraduates to his books has felt obliged to keep knocking heads together

---

[17] Ἤισχυνε ξενίαν τράπεζαν κλοπαῖσι γυναικός, Aesch., *Aga.* 401–02, of Paris. The metre is "Priapean."

[18] The use of σοφιστής (e.g. Pindar, *Isth.* 5. 28) in the sense of "lyric poet," "musician," has perhaps some importance for the interest of the Sophists in persuasive language.

[19] Curiously, Lang did not like "convergent evolution": de Cocq, p. 74. According to de Cocq, convergence was defined by Paul Ehrenreich in his *Allgemeine Mythologie* as: "Konvergenzähnlichkeiten, dh. daß Dinge verschiedenen Ursprungs, unter Einfluß der gleichen Umgebung und gleicher Kulturverhältnisse ähnliche Formen annehmen." When Tolstoy begins *Anna Karenina* with an aphorism, he is obeying the injunction of the medieval *poetriae* about *ordo artificialis*. Are we not to make this point because we cannot show that he had read the authors collected by Faral?

even when their owners were now no longer Smith and Jones but Virgil, Lucan—or Dante. Bentley's strictures on Milton are an obvious example. But if there is no longer a set of rationalist prescriptions that authors must obey or perish, but rather a connection to a pre-rational reality, the judgment about a given author's success in making this connection will no longer be so easy. It will be necessary to sit at the feet of great authors—great precisely because they are seen to have made this connection—rather than to deal out grades on a scale that always tends to magnify the past and diminish the present. This will be difficult, but I believe it will be one method of again making the Classics seem relevant to our own day. If "literature has borrowed far more from the people than the people have borrowed from literature," can the study of "the people" and its aesthetic be avoided by the scholar?

12. If the nature of scholarship changes, so must the preparation which students are offered in our courses. To speak paradoxically, it is easy to emphasize the "hard" disciplines, those where there is—or appears to be—a right or wrong answer immediately knowable. But, if we now stress knowledge of, and the ability to use, the Latin and Greek languages, what they mean, how they fit together; knowledge of how great authors have received their predecessors, including authors not normally considered "classical"; knowledge of structure and rhetoric, of topoi and their estrangement, this is not to exalt subjectivity and looseness. It is rather to demand skills so refined that only long preparation and careful cultivation will foster them.[20] I would say in fact that it is to demand the skills of an Erasmus, and that, as so often, we are really talking here about a return, in this case to the Humanism of the Renaissance.[21] Their practitioners will no longer be in the rough and ready—to be frank, arrogant—business of knocking heads together. They will be there not as the masters, but as the servants of the Muses.

These are large conclusions to draw from Soviet scholarship, or even from the whimsical, academically suspect Lang, with uncomfortable implications. But no one, for example, would think of writing the history of European literature while omitting Pushkin or Pasternak. Pushkin was greatly influenced by the Greco-Roman Classics, and to the Formalists seemed far more the culmination of the neo-classicism of the eighteenth century than the harbinger of the Romanticism of the nineteenth. And Pasternak was Olga Freudenberg's cousin.

University of Illinois at Urbana-Champaign

---

[20] *Vagliami 'l lungo studio e'l grande amore / che m'ha fatto cercar lo tuo volume.*

[21] As expounded by Machiavelli, for example, in his letter to Francisco Vettori of December 10, 1513.

9

An Awful Warmth About Her Heart: The Personal in Jane Harrison's Ideas on Religion

SANDRA J. PEACOCK

Along with the works of her close colleagues in the Ritualist Circle, Gilbert Murray and Francis Cornford, Jane Harrison's *Prolegomena to the Study of Greek Religion* (1903) and *Themis: A Study of the Social Origins of Greek Religion* (1912) helped break new ground in the study of ancient religion and thought. Although Harrison produced her two great works comparatively late in her life, there is a good deal of continuity from her earliest writings in the 1880s to the full-blown exposition of Ritualist theory in *Themis*. This is not surprising, for her scholarly activity always mirrored the personality and life experiences of this remarkable woman.

It is difficult to trace the origins of Harrison's specific interest in ancient Greece and the Classics. She professed to have longed to study Greek in her childhood, only to be stopped in her tracks by a conservative and conventional aunt. In her essay "Scientiae Sacra Fames," Harrison recalled that

> Some half-century ago a very happy little girl secretly possessed herself of a Greek grammar. A much-adored aunt swiftly stripped the gilt from the gingerbread with these chill, cutting words: "I do not see how Greek grammar is to help little Jane to keep house when she has a home of her own."...the child understood: she was a little girl, and thereby damned to eternal domesticity; she heard the gates of the temple of Learning clang as they closed.[1]

She seems to have had a fairly typical middle-class education as a young woman, with a series of governesses to tend and educate her—after a fashion. According to Harrison, these women were "grossly ignorant,"

---

[1] Jane Ellen Harrison, "Scientiae Sacra Fames," in *Alpha and Omega* (London: Sidgwick and Jackson, 1915), p. 117.

though "good women, steadily kind to me."[2] She particularly liked one governess, whom she described as "a woman of real intelligence, ignorant but willing and eager to learn anything and everything I wanted" (RSL, 26). They tackled German and Latin, but this interlude ended abruptly when the "kind governess was...removed to a lunatic asylum" (RSL, 27). Harrison spent three years (1868-71) at Cheltenham Ladies' College, but nothing in those years seems to relate to her interest in the classics. In fact, her Cheltenham education instilled in her "a dislike for history which has lasted all my life" (RSL, 35).   However, Harrison's recollection in her "Reminiscences" of her first encounter with Aristotle at Newnham suggests that she was drawn to Classics because she wanted to escape the religious training of her youth. She recalled that

> the *Ethics* was among the set books for my year at Cambridge. To realise the release that Aristotle brought, you must have been reared as I was in a narrow school of Evangelicalism—reared with sin always present, with death and judgment before you, Hell and Heaven to either hand. It was like coming out of a madhouse into a quiet college quadrangle where all was liberty and sanity, and you became a law to yourself. The doctrine of virtue as the Mean—What an uplift and revelation to one born in sin! The notion of the *summum bonum* as an "energy," as an exercise of personal faculty, to one who had been taught that God claimed all, and the notion of the "perfect life" that was to include as a matter of course friendship. I remember walking up and down in the College garden, thinking could it possibly be true, were the chains really broken and the prison doors open. (RSL, 80–81)

Although somewhat stylized and written from the vantage point of age, this description sheds light on Harrison's motives for a career in Classical Studies.

Though her mature work reflects a rapidly strengthening commitment to the ritual origin of religion and mythology, even Harrison's earliest books show her fascination with the primacy of emotion, which became the central tenet of ritual theory as she defined it. As early as her *Myths of the Odyssey in Art and Literature* (1881) and *Introductory Studies in Greek Art* (1885), Harrison toyed with the ideas which later became the backbone of her theory. However, she articulated the ritual viewpoint distinctly in *Mythology and Monuments of Ancient Athens* (1890): "*ritual practice misunderstood* explains the elaboration of myth....Some of the loveliest stories the Greeks have left us will be seen to have taken their rise, not in poetic imagination, but in primitive, often savage, and, I think, always *practical* ritual." "In regarding the myth-making Greek as a practical savage rather than a poet or philosopher," Harrison claimed kinship with

---

[2] Jane Ellen Harrison, "Reminiscences of a Student's Life" (London: Hogarth Press, 1925), p. 22. Subsequent references throughout the paper are cited in parentheses in the text, preceded by the abbreviation "RSL."

"Eusebius, Lobeck, Mannhardt, and Mr. Andrew Lang."[3] She devoted her life to honing and refining this theory, eventually drawing on the evidence of archaeology, anthropology, and comparative religion.

Harrison produced these early works during a period of nearly twenty years spent studying ancient art and archaeology in London, with frequent trips to the Continent and visits with European scholars. She augmented a private income by giving public lectures. In 1898, having failed in two bids to secure the Yates Professorship at University College, London, Harrison returned to Newnham College as a research fellow. Bitter over her failure to secure the Yates chair, she accepted Newnham as a "second-best" post, but it was also a locale with many pleasant associations for her. There, Harrison settled into the friendships that guided the course of her future life and work. A. W. Verrall, who had married Harrison's good friend Margaret Merrifield, introduced her to Gilbert Murray in 1900, and at about the same time Harrison met Francis Cornford at one of her Cambridge lectures. Soon, this dynamic and persuasive woman created the Ritualist Circle with Murray and Cornford (and sometimes A. B. Cook), but she always stood at its center. Harrison believed the most ardently of the three in the principles of Ritualist theory, and unlike Murray and Cornford she embraced all of its implications. Behind ritual lay the religious impulse, which Harrison saw as the most fundamental component of human experience. "The religion of Orpheus," she claimed in the *Prolegomena*, "...is the worship of the real mysteries of life, of potencies (*daimones*) rather than personal gods (*theoi*); it is the worship of life itself in its supreme mysteries of ecstasy and love."[4] While Murray and Cornford applauded the triumph of Olympian "rationality" and "serenity" over the unbridled emotionalism of orgiastic religious practice, Harrison mourned the loss of kinship with the religious impulse and the natural world. She sometimes invoked Nietzsche and later Bergson to reinforce her intuitive belief in the primacy of emotion and the significance of the religious impulse. Simply noting Harrison's scholarly citations, however, begs the question of the motivations underlying her ideas about religion. As Robert Ackerman pointed out in his recent biography of J. G. Frazer, "no intellectual project...is undertaken for purely intellectual reasons, although *post facto* justifications are frequently offered to make it all seem a selfless struggle for Truth."[5] Harrison herself, describing the unconscious but irrepressible need

---

[3] Jane Ellen Harrison and Margaret Merrifield, *Mythology and Monuments of Ancient Athens* (London: Macmillan, 1890), p. iii. Cf. Robert Ackerman, "Jane Ellen Harrison: The Early Work," *Greek, Roman, and Byzantine Studies* 13 (Summer 1972), p. 225.

[4] Jane Ellen Harrison, *Prolegomena to the Study of Greek Religion*, 2nd edition (Cambridge: Cambridge University Press, 1907), p. 657. Subsequent references throughout the paper are cited in parentheses in the text, preceded by the abbreviation "PSGR."

[5] Robert Ackerman, *J. G. Frazer: His Life and Work* (Cambridge: Cambridge University Press, 1987), p. 55.

to release energy through work, wrote in her autobiography that "one reads round a subject, soaks oneself in it, and then one's personal responsibility is over; something stirs and ferments, swims up into your consciousness, and you know you have to write a book....It leaves you spent, washed out, a rag, but an exultant rag" (RSL, 64). Intellectual and personal influences must be studied together in order to flesh out the full picture of the scholar at work.

The figures of Nietzsche and Bachofen cast long shadows over the *Prolegomena* and *Themis*. In the *Prolegomena*, Harrison refers only once to Nietzsche's *Birth of Tragedy*, drawing attention to his "contrast, beautiful and profoundly true, between the religion and art of Apollo and Dionysos." Apollo's "watchword is limitation," while Dionysos "breaks all bonds; his motto is the limitless Excess" (PSGR, 445). Nietzsche sensed the supreme importance of the irrational, as did Harrison. He also perceived the terror that lay under the veneer of civilization: "Philosophical men even have a presentiment that the reality in which we live and have our being is also mere appearance, and that another, quite different reality lies beneath it." To Nietzsche and Harrison, the Olympian pantheon served a far more essential function than that of a mere group projection: "The Greek knew and felt the terror and horror of existence. That he might endure this terror at all, he had to interpose between himself and life the radiant dream-birth of the Olympians."[6] In *Themis*, Harrison again contrasted Apollo and Dionysos:

> a difference, the real significance of which was long ago, with the instinct of genius, divined by Nietzsche. The Olympian has clear form, he is the '*principium individuationis*' incarnate; he can be thought, hence his calm, his *sophrosyne*. The mystery-god is the life of the whole of things, he can only be felt....The Olympians are of conscious thinking, divided, distinct, departmental; the mystery-god is the impulse of life through all things, perennial, indivisible.[7]

Duncan Wilson overstated the case in calling Harrison "a student of Nietzsche," without considering her statement on the subject: "Disciple as I am *on that matter* of Nietzsche"—*that matter* being the need to balance the Apollonian and the Dionysian in life.[8]

Harrison's attack on the Olympians reached its peak in *Themis*, but with the *Prolegomena* she had already begun to strip away their veneer and to explore their chthonic predecessors. She attributed the triumph of the Olympians to the victory of patriarchy over matriarchy. The Olympians

---

[6] Friedrich Nietzsche, *Die Geburt der Tragödie*, ed Elisabeth Förster-Nietzsche (Leipzig: Kröner, 1917), Vol. I, 21, 31; trans. Walter Kaufmann (New York: Random House, 1967), pp. 34, 42.

[7] Jane Ellen Harrison, *Themis: A Study in the Social Origins of Greek Religion*, second edition (Cambridge: Cambridge University Press, 1927) 476.

[8] Duncan Wilson, *Gilbert Murray, OM* (Oxford: Clarendon Press, 1987), p. 119; Jane Ellen Harrison, *Themis*, p. viii. Italics added.

reflected the social structure that created them: patriarchal, civilized, hierarchical, with great distance between worshiper and gods. However, she argued, worship of the Olympians was preceded by chthonic cult practices marked by worship of the mother and other female deities. This religion also reflected the society which created it: a matriarchal social order where mothers ruled. She credited Eduard Gerhard with first noting in 1849 "the fundamental unity of all the Greek goddesses" in the image of a mother figure; "his illuminating suggestion has been obscured for half a century by systems...that see in ancient deities impersonations of natural phenomena" (PSGR, 263, n. 1). For further evidence, Harrison relied on Johann Bachofen's *Mutterrecht*, which she described, "spite of the wildness of its theories," as "the fullest existing collection of ancient facts" (PSGR, 262, n. 1). Bachofen believed that, for the ultimate good of society, matriarchy must give way to patriarchy—fond though he was of the reign of the mothers. Though Bachofen knew that matriarchy must perish, he treated it with the same reverence that Harrison showed in both the *Prolegomena* and *Themis*—and for similar reasons. The significance of the mother-child bond had a strong personal appeal to both scholars; they differed over matriarchy's role in the development of civilization, not over its embodiment of deeply felt longings for love and nurturance. To Bachofen, the triumph of patriarchy signaled the beginning of law, order, and civilization, despite the regrettable end of matriarchy; to Harrison, however, the triumph of patriarchy brought a sense of loss and separation from nature, the divine, and one's own emotional connectedness with the rest of the world.

Many scholars' names fill the footnotes in Harrison's books, but they influenced her less than they struck a sympathetic chord. J. G. Frazer, Andrew Lang, William Ridgeway, E. B. Tylor, Wilhelm Mannhardt and various continental archaeologists and classicists, later Emile Durkheim and Arnold van Gennep, even Henri Bergson and William James, parade across the pages, serving mainly to substantiate Harrison's claims. Like Engels and Freud, she ranged widely over time and space in the search for supporting evidence and willingly drew on any source that offered proof of her theories. Even Ridgeway, her nemesis, occasionally offered insights that agreed with hers or at least led in a similar direction. Perhaps William Robertson Smith exerted the most fundamental influence, for his *Religion of the Semites*, with its use of comparative religion and emphasis on ritual, probably served as an early inspiration to Harrison.[9] She also saw Smith as a heroic figure, "exiled for heresy" (RSL, 83). However, the most compelling evidence in Harrison's eyes was the vast amount of visual evidence (vase paintings, statuary, and artifacts) that she had examined and offered in proof of her theories. While an ancient text may be incomplete or

[9] Robert Ackerman, *Frazer*, Chapter 5, "Mythography and Ambivalence," offers a thorough summary and analysis of the state of anthropological and classical debates at the time.

obscure, flawed by poetic exaggeration or anti-pagan bias, the artistic remains of the past seem to show what the Greeks actually did in religious matters, and Harrison's books are characterized, not only by overimaginative prose, but a wealth of visual data.

However, reading alone cannot account for a scholar's intellectual trajectory. As Robert Ackerman notes, "it is simplistic to imagine that the effects of a book or a theory are straightforward or unequivocal in any of its readers."[10] In "Alpha and Omega," Harrison described her odyssey from student of Hellenic art to scholar of Greek religion. Her description illustrates the inseparable connection between her own life experience and her perceptions of the past. Justifying her rather lengthy "lapse into autobiography," she states that she does "not think one's view or attitude can be understood without the statement of how it grew up," for "Thought, to be living, does and must arise straight out of life."[11] Not all scholars agree with her, preferring to think of their work as an objective search for truth unaffected by personal factors. Recognizing that scholarship invariably reflects the writer's own experience means confronting one's past; a task many scholars, it seems, would rather not undertake. Natalie Davis has candidly explored the relationship between her life and her work;[12] Harrison's case too shows that work and life cannot be examined separately. Judging by her own words, two factors directly influenced her thought: an unassuaged sense of loss that can be traced back to her mother's death in Harrison's infancy, and the Evangelical religion of the stepmother that replaced Harrison's mother.

Harrison traces her "religious life" to her "rather violently Protestant" religious upbringing in a mid-Victorian family she describes as "Evangelical, almost, though not quite, to the point of Calvinism." She later "reacted into rather extreme High Churchism," as she "was always a ritualist at heart." After this rebellion, she "lapsed into Broad Churchism, and finally...into complete Agnosticism": all before the age of twenty-four. At Newnham, though "a complete Agnostic," she admits that "whenever I had the chance I went to hear Mass or the nearest High Church simulation of it." Religion—as a vital force, an impulse, not as creed—still exerted a compelling influence over her. Yet "having tried all the theologies open to me, I came to the conclusion that religion was not for me, that it said

---

[10] *Ibid.*, p. 245.

[11] Jane Ellen Harrison, "Alpha and Omega," in *Alpha and Omega*, pp.183–84.

[12] "I wrote 'The Reasons of Misrule' about youth groups and festivals because of the Yippies....I wrote the 'Rites of Violence'...because of Vietnam...and the riots I was seeing....Did you ever read my piece 'Ghosts, Kin, and Progeny'? It had a lot of mourning. I wrote it when I was mourning my mother." Natalie Zemon Davis, "Interview," *Radical History Review* 24 (Fall 1980), pp. 115-39. For a similar account of the connection between personal experience and scholarly creativity, see Lucien Febvre, "How Jules Michelet Invented the Renaissance," in *A New Kind of History* (New York: Harper, 1975), pp. 258-67.

nothing to my spiritual life, and I threw myself passionately into the study of literature and art." During her London years in the 1880s and 1890s, she avoided churches and "lived with artists and literary people," devoting herself to art, literature, and archaeology.[13]

Over the years, however, religion still beckoned to her.

> And then within my own professional work it happened rather oddly that I became slowly aware that what I really was interested in was, not Greek art, but Greek religion, and even Greek literature held me largely for its profoundly religious content. So, gradually I worked and lectured more and more on Greek mythology, and less and less on Greek art; and then, again, I found it was not mythology really that interested me and drew me, save for its poetry, but ritual and religion. I was always hankering after that side of things, wanting to understand it, excited about it.

She presented her growing fascination with religion less as a conscious turn toward a specific field of study than as an irresistible force pulling her; rather like the religious impulse itself. She denied feeling drawn toward religion because she felt "spiritually lonely or 'seeking for the light'"; in any case, she "plunged into comparative religion." Her study "confirmed my own agnosticism as to all the theology" and she believed that "as a personal question, religion...had no longer any interest to me." She attributed her lack of interest to the "religious satiety" of her early years.[14] Aware of the contradictory picture she presented, Harrison conjectured that

> Possibly outsiders saw a certain absurdity in an avowed—quite openly avowed—Agnostic passionately studying religion. I never thought about it at all till I came back to Cambridge about 1900. It was then part of my normal official duty to say grace on occasions and to read prayers in the morning. I did this a few times, and then some lingering sense of truth and decency rose up in me, and said: You are an Agnostic; you can't, you mustn't. As you value your spiritual life, you mustn't use words you don't believe. So I didn't.
>
> Then I began to think, was I really devoting my life to the study of a number of pernicious superstitious errors? Of course, some people can and have done that. I felt absolutely certain that it was not so with me; that I was studying a vital and tremendous impulse—a thing fraught indeed with endless peril, but great and glorious, inspiring, worth all a lifetime's devotion.
>
> And then bit by bit I came to see that the thing I loved, that beckoned to me and drew me irresistibly, was religion; the thing that hampered and thwarted me and even disgusted me was theology.[15]

[13] Harrison, "Alpha and Omega," pp. 184-85.
[14] *Ibid.*, p. 185.
[15] *Ibid.* ,pp. 185-86.

This brief chronicle of her intellectual journey reminds us that we cannot understand the development of Harrison's ideas about religion in terms of intellectual influence alone. Work and life are inextricably bound, and few writers have been as self-revelatory as Jane Harrison. Her early affinity for ritual theory dictates that scholars examine her intellectual pedigree in a circumspect fashion. One cannot attribute her theory only to the influence of some school of thought, for she began to formulate her ideas about the origins of religion before she had read the works she credited as influential.[16] If the intellectual threads cannot adequately explain the path of development, where are we to turn?

In addition to the *Prolegomena*, two other works contain evidence of the source and growth of her ideas about religion. Her brief autobiography, "Reminiscences of a Student's Life," is an entertaining yet unexpectedly revealing piece. Her 1915 collection of essays, *Alpha and Omega*, also contains crucial data. Unlike the "Reminiscences," written near the end of her life, these essays date from Harrison's most productive period, just before the outbreak of World War I. Most of them appeared around the time of *Themis* and reflect Harrison's preoccupation with understanding the mystery of ancient religion. Her constant weaving together of past and present, her own experience with that of the Greeks, helps to explain why her works appealed more to readers than those of rival scholars. Harrison had an astonishing empathy with her subjects, for she could feel and think in the way she believed they had, and her works conveyed this empathy to her readers. In order to understand this capacity, one must follow her back and forth between childhood and adulthood, between past and present.

The outline of Harrison's childhood experience is fairly straightforward. She was the third daughter born to the prosperous Hull timber merchant Charles Harrison and Elizabeth Hawksley Nelson Harrison, daughter of a gentry family. Her mother died soon after Harrison's birth in 1850, and five years later her father married a Welsh Evangelical woman whom he had recently hired to serve as governess to his daughters. Jane Harrison's life changed immediately, for several reasons. First, the second marriage proved enormously fertile, eventually producing nine children. Second, and most

---

[16] For example, in the introduction to *Themis*, Harrison credited Bergson with showing her the light on "the real distinction between the mystery-god Dionysos and the Olympians" (543). But his influence only provides the name—*durée*—for a notion she had already developed and celebrated in her versions of Dionysian and Orphic religion. Cf. Harrison, *Themis*, 473, 477. In an even more revealing passage in the preface to the second edition of *Themis*, Harrison lauded the work of younger scholars whose findings had validated her own insights. She says that "the real delight was to find that these notions [of gods as a reflection of social order, early existence of matriarchal goddesses, etc.] which for me, with my narrow classical training, had been, I confess, *a priori* guesses had become for the new school matter of historical certainty, based on definite facts, and substantiated by a touch-and-handle knowledge and a sort of robust common-sense to which I could lay no claim" (ix).

important for the question at hand, Harrison's religious upbringing became much more stringent.

Her father was a Nonconformist not given to strict observance of the Sabbath. Jane Harrison believed him "incapable of formulating a conviction," but felt "he really would have sympathised with the eminent statesman who 'had a great respect for religion as long as it did not interfere with a gentleman's private life.'" He "attended church with fair regularity," although "on what used to be called 'Sacrament Sundays' he was apt to have a slight attack of lumbago" (RSL, 19). Father and daughters often spent Sundays visiting Charles' brother and his stable of racehorses. Gemimi Harrison, however, soon put an end to such laxity. She halted the Sunday visits, a move which her stepdaughters viewed as an attempt to separate them from their father. It is more likely that Mrs. Harrison simply believed strongly in the tenets of her faith; nevertheless, to the young girls (especially Jane, who had been the closest to her father), religious observance became associated with the loss of a pleasant family tradition. Charles Harrison could sometimes escape his wife's clutches through the occasional attack of lumbago, but the girls were trapped.[17]

Decades later, Harrison reflected on her religious upbringing in an essay titled "Unanimism and Conversion," originally delivered in 1912 as a lecture to the Cambridge Society of Heretics. After declaring that "the very word Conversion has a strange, old-world, superstitious sound in our ears today," Harrison offered her "hope and trust that no young child's life is embittered nowadays by being told that he must 'flee from the wrath to come,' that he must 'look not behind him,' that the 'old Adam in him must die,' that he must 'lay hold on salvation and the cross of Christ,' and that if he neglect so great salvation he will go 'into outer darkness, where shall be wailing and gnashing of teeth'—'where their worm dieth not.'" It was, she points out, "a grim and awful thing to tell a child," and "only shows what a tough thing a healthy child's mind is that any of us emerged into even tolerable sanity, though we carry, I think, always the scars, in a certain ferocity of mind, a certain intolerance in conviction."[18] Sixty years after receiving these admonitions Harrison wrote as if she were still hearing them.

In the 1912 essay "Heresy and Humanity," Harrison remarked on the strength of the societal demand for religious conformity. If she should "deny the law of gravitation, no one will worry me about it." They may "think me a fool; but they will not come and argue at, and browbeat, and socially ostracize me. But if I doubt the existence of a God, or even, in the days of my childhood, if I doubted the doctrine of eternal damnation—well, I become a 'moral leper.' The expression has now gone out; its mild, modern

---

[17] For a detailed discussion of Harrison's childhood, see Sandra J. Peacock, *Jane Ellen Harrison: The Mask and the Self* (New Haven: Yale University Press, 1988), Chapter 1.

[18] Jane Ellen Harrison, "Unanimism and Conversion," in *Alpha and Omega*, p. 59.

substitute is looking at you sadly."[19] In "Scientiae Sacra Fames," Harrison revealed the true motive behind her hatred of Victorian religion; one currently being revived, in a different guise, by some feminist scholars. Harrison says she "noticed with amusement at a recent discussion at the Heretic Society at Cambridge that 'Deity' is a man's word; women don't talk of 'the Deity.' And this 'Deity,' this man's god, is one of two things—either a gigantic, overgrown, impossible man, or that thing still remoter from experience, that utter Abstraction remote from all reality, the Absolute. Man, in a word, has made of religion, *theology*, an intellectual abstraction, divorced ever more and more from life" (italics added). Thus, she says, "I have never met with a woman who was interested in theology."[20] Theology took all the life and emotion out of religion, leaving it a purely intellectual exercise. She saw this battle initially played out between the chthonic deities of the archaic period and the classical Olympians. The chthonic deities represent religion; the Olympians, rationality and theology.

Harrison rebelled against theology—both the theology of her upbringing and that of the hated Olympians—by becoming passionately engaged in the study of primitive religion. Throughout her work, she buttressed her arguments with references to personal experience too numerous to mention. In "The Influence of Darwinism on the Study of Religions," she told a story obviously drawn from her own past to illustrate the close connection between children and primitives. "To children," she says, "animals are always people. You promise to take a child for a drive. The child comes up beaming with a furry bear in her arms. You say the bear cannot go. The child bursts into tears. You think it is because the child cannot endure to be separated from a toy. It is no such thing. It is the intolerable hurt done to the bear's human heart—a hurt not to be healed by any proffer of buns. He wanted to go, but he was a shy, proud bear, and he would not say so."[21] Children and primitives sensed and appreciated the living spirit within every aspect of the natural world. Thus, to Jane Harrison, childhood perceptions of relations among living things are a survival of primitive thought patterns, undefeated by rationality.

Once she accepted the primacy of emotion and the urgency of the religious impulse, Harrison turned her attention to primitive religion. The trauma of her mother's death contributed most profoundly to the development of another component—perhaps the most important—of Harrison's vision of ancient religion: her interest in the cults of female deities and her insistence that this phenomenon proved the historical

[19] Jane Ellen Harrison, "Heresy and Humanity," in *Alpha and Omega*, p. 30.

[20] Harrison, "Scientiae Sacra Fames," in *Alpha and Omega*, p. 135.

[21] Jane Ellen Harrison, "The Influence of Darwinism on the Study of Religions," in *Alpha and Omega*, p. 173. Harrison's obsession with bears is discussed in Peacock, *Harrison*, pp. 109-16, 164.

existence of matriarchy. Her theories about chthonic cults shifted slightly between the *Prolegomena* and *Themis*. In the years before she wrote the *Prolegomena*, several forces converged to draw her to the importance of matriarchy and the cults of female deities. The underlying factor was Harrison's longstanding grief over her mother's death from puerperal fever. She had lost her mother in infancy, too early even to have memories of her. She worshiped the image of her mother, however, as transmitted to her by family tradition and in contrast to her stepmother. Harrison idealized her mother as "a silent woman of singular gentleness and serenity," as opposed to her garrulous stepmother, who could "talk the hind leg off a donkey" (RSL, 28). In Harrison's eyes, the Olympian pantheon symbolized patriarchy and male oppression of women, and ultimately stood for the force of sexual desire that had deprived her of her mother. Had her parents not mated, she would not have been born and her mother need not have died. But her mother did die, and Harrison was—through no fault of her own—responsible. Late in her life, Harrison used a revealing phrase to describe her mother's death. Writing to her friend, the Russian aristocrat Dmitri Mirski, to console him on his mother's death, she said, "I have always wondered what it was like to have a mother for *I sent mine out of the world*—but one has to pay the price in losing her."[22] Harrison's words indicate an assumption of responsibility for her mother's death, even though by then she would have been aware of the prevalence of puerperal fever. Harrison signed many of her letters to Gilbert Murray with the designation "Ker," which connotes a death-daimon. Renate Schlesier perceptively interprets Harrison's use of this term as an indication that Harrison viewed herself as a death-demon, on whose account her mother had died.[23]

Such a burden of guilt would be very heavy for a child to bear, and Harrison devised a way to blame her father rather than herself for the deed. Her father's sexual impulse had killed her mother, not Harrison's birth itself. That same sexual impulse had ruined her own life as well, for instead of having a loving mother, a savage twist of fate had provided her with an unwelcome stepmother. A passage in "Homo Sum," too lengthy to be cited here, clearly depicts Harrison's father trying to justify his wish to remarry without directly mentioning the real reason implicit in his arguments: sexual desire.[24] In the young Jane's eyes, the stepmother had stolen her father from her.

[22] Jane Ellen Harrison to Dmitri Mirski, May 6, 1926 (italics added), Jane Ellen Harrison Papers, Newnham College Archive, Cambridge. Cf. Nancy Fix Anderson, "No Angel in the House: The Psychological Effects of Maternal Death," *Psychohistory Review* 11, no. 1 (Fall 1982) 20-46.
[23] Renate Schlesier, "Jane Ellen Harrison," in *Classical Scholarship: A Biographical Encyclopedia*, edd. W. W. Briggs Jr. and W. M. Calder III (New York/London: Garland Publishing Co., 1990) 127.
[24] Jane Ellen Harrison, "Homo Sum," in *Alpha and Omega*, pp. 95-97.

Once Harrison turned to the study of religion, she was drawn to the evidence of mother goddesses and a pre-patriarchal world where mothers ruled. "The mythology of Zeus, patriarchal as it is through and through, lays no stress on motherhood....But the bull-divinity worshipped in Crete was wholly the son of his mother..." (PSGR, 496). She turned to Cretan evidence to illustrate the primacy of the mother, citing Arthur Evans' discovery of a Cretan seal depicting the "Mountain Mother." The *Prolegomena* features a drawing of the seal of a signet ring found at Knossos, "a veritable little manual of primitive Cretan faith and ritual" (PSGR, 496-97) The seal depicts a female figure standing on top of a pedestal of some kind, flanked by two lions, with a stylized figure off to the side. Harrison brings the drawing to life, attributing the creation of the image (if not the ring itself) to "the Mycenaean women of Cnossos" who "made their goddess in their own image, clad her, wild thing though she was, in their own grotesque flounced skirt," giving her also "her own fierce mountain-ranging lions, tamed into solemn heraldic guardians." The Mother "stands with sceptre or lance extended, imperious, dominant...before her in rapt ecstasy of adoration stands her Mystes." (497) Triumphantly, Harrison concludes that "the little seal impression is a standing monument of matriarchalism" (PSGR, 497). In a footnote, she recalled that when she "first saw a drawing of the seal" she thought "it was 'too good to be true'"; as well she may have (PSGR, 497). However, examination of the original fragments convinced her of the truth of her insight. In *Themis*, she noted that "to the mythologist, it is sufficient evidence of a matrilinear state of society in Greece...that such a social structure is seen thus clearly reflected in mythology," though she admitted that "to the mind trained rather in historical method...such evidence may seem less convincing."[25]

Regrettably, this happy state of affairs in Minoan Crete and prehistoric Greece could not withstand the pressure of patriarchal forces invading from the north. In her discussion of Pandora in the *Prolegomena* ("in ritual and matriarchal theology the earth as Kore"), Harrison explained the changing images of female figures. She cites Hesiod's story of "the Making of Pandora," which he shaped "to his own *bourgeois*, pessimistic ends" (PSGR, 284). His version reveals "the ugly malice of theological animus. Zeus the Father will have no great Earth-goddess, Mother and maid in one, in his man-fashioned Olympus, but her figure *is* from the beginning, so he re-makes it; woman, who was the inspirer, becomes the temptress; she who made all things, gods and immortals alike, is become their plaything, their slave, dowered only with physical beauty, and with a slave's tricks and blandishments. To Zeus, the archpatriarchal *bourgeois*, the birth of the first woman is but a huge Olympian jest..." (PSGR, 285). Having outgrown the "belief in the magical potency of women," her natural connection with the earthy and mysterious powers of sexuality and fertility, man "proceeded

---

[25] Harrison, *Themis*, p. 498.

by a pardonable practical logic to despise and enslave her as the weaker."
Only later would it be understood "that the stronger had a need, real and
imperative, of the weaker"; for the moment, patriarchy triumphed over
matriarchy (PSGR, 285). Furthermore, man not only displaced woman in
the hierarchy of power; he also revised her history.

Life on Olympus did not resemble the gracious relations that marked
the matriarchal world. In fact, the Olympians looked suspiciously like
Harrison's own family.

> In the Homeric Olympus we see mirrored a family group of the ordinary
> patriarchal type, a type so familiar that it scarcely arrests attention.
> Zeus, Father of Gods and men, is supreme; Hera, though in constant and
> significant revolt, occupies the subordinate place of a wife; Poseidon is
> a younger brother, and the rest of the Olympians are grouped about Zeus
> and Hera in the relation of sons and daughters. These sons and
> daughters are quarrelsome among themselves and in constant
> insurrection against father and mother, but still they constitute a
> family, and a family subject, if reluctantly, to the final authority of a
> father. (PSGR, 260)

A similar passage can be found in *Themis*;[26] both sketches reflect the
quarrels between Jane and her sisters with Gemimi's children over cash and
property.

In addition to Harrison's grief over her mother's death, she had to cope
with the death of her father, to whom she had been very close, in 1894.
Two reminiscences in her autobiography attest to the nature of their
relationship. As a child, she fell in love with Russia because of her father's
extensive business dealings with Russian timber merchants, and one of her
fondest memories was of a Russian sledge in which he sometimes took her
for drives. Describing their outings, Harrison remarked, "thank God it held
only one, so I could dream undisturbed of steppes and Siberia and bears and
wolves" (RSL, 10). Thank God too, no doubt, that it allowed her time with
her father by herself. Much later in her life, she tried to share her work with
him.

> I always sent a copy of every book I wrote to my father, and he always
> acknowledged them in the same set words: "Thank you for the book
> you have sent me, your mother and sisters are well. Your affectionate
> father." I am sure he never read them, and I suspect his feeling towards
> them was what the Freudians call *ambivalent*—half shame, half pride.
> Years after his death I learnt, and it touched me deeply, that, on the rare
> occasions when he left home, he took with him a portmanteau full of
> my books. Why? Well, after all, he was a Yorkshireman, it may have
> been he wanted a "bit o' coompany." (RSL, 39)

[26] *Ibid.*, pp. 490-91.

After his death, she had only her stepmother and many half-siblings, along with two full sisters; none of whom shared her passion for the past and from whom she felt alienated.

Harrison developed the idea of matriarchy in part out of a desire to reconstruct her dead mother; her father's death in 1894 also influenced the *Prolegomena*. Having established her belief in the superiority of matriarchy and its associated cults, Harrison moved on to Dionysos worship as a survival of primitive (matriarchal) ritual into the Classical period. She then devoted four chapters to Orpheus and Orphic mysteries, portraying Orpheus as a northern religious reformer, "a dissenter, a prig" (PSGR, 516). Harrison dissects Orphic mythology and ritual to prove that Orpheus and Dionysos represent the same duality as Nietzsche's Apollo and Dionysos, yet underneath it all she seems to link Orpheus with her father.

Like Charles Harrison, Orpheus was a widower, though Harrison downplayed the story of his great love for Eurydice as a late mythological addition. It is important to her that the love story be a late corruption, for in one version of the myth Orpheus risked his life to rescue Eurydice from Hades. In Harrison's view, "anyone who realizes Orpheus at all would feel that the intrusion of desperate emotion puts him out of key" (PSGR, 603). The mythical Orpheus she preferred fell somewhere in between: he possessed the virtue of fidelity, unlike her father, for he "refuses to reveal his mysteries to women, whom since the loss of his own wife he had hated *en masse*" (PSGR, 468). In return, the Maenads, jealous of the men's privileged participation in Orphic mysteries, tore him to pieces and threw his limbs into the sea. Just as the Great Mother represents Harrison's ideal mother, this Orpheus represents the ideal father: the father who comes to loathe all women when he loses his wife, rather than the father who takes a beautiful and fecund second wife. Orpheus is taciturn, unemotional, like her father, whom she described as "remote and solemn" (RSL, 13). Orpheus is also "a reformer, a protestant; there is always about him a touch of the reformer's priggishness" (PSGR, 461). Her anger at what she perceived as her father's abandonments—his remarriage and, more important at this time, his death—may have led her to remark that "it is impossible not to sympathize a little with the determined looking Maenad who is coming up behind to put a stop to all this sun-watching and lyre-playing" (PSGR, 461). Mourning always includes elements of ambivalent feelings—sorrow over the loss of a loved one, anger over his or her flaws, despair over abandonment. Ultimately, the sense of loss dominates, and Harrison's Orpheus is a noble figure who she insists actually lived (PSGR 469, 471).

Around this same time, Harrison also experienced an unhappy romance with the art historian and critic Dugald Sutherland MacColl.[27] Harrison and

---

[27] For a discussion of Harrison's relationship with MacColl, see Peacock, *Harrison*, Chapter 3, especially pp. 68-75, 83-89. The topic of folk survivals was "in the air" at the time, and Harrison surely discussed the "primitive" elements of Greek religion with

MacColl met through mutual friends in 1886, and before long they were exchanging lively letters and sharing each other's work. He frequently lectured at Oxford and other places on folk songs, ballads, and dances. In 1888 they traveled together to Greece. Even before this trip, though, MacColl had influenced Harrison greatly by denouncing her work as too aesthetic and introducing her to his own interests: the study of myth, ritual, and folklore. He took credit for introducing her to the work of Wilhelm Mannhardt and J. Theodore Bent. Mannhardt's massive evidence for survivals of primitive religion in European peasant cultures greatly influenced Frazer, and his concept of "corn-spirits" ultimately affected Harrison's Year Daimon. Bent's travels in the Cyclades led him to write on picturesque survivals of ancient beliefs in nineteenth-century Greek culture.[28] After an agonizing period of self-doubt and self-evaluation (well documented by some of her letters to MacColl), Harrison followed MacColl's intellectual lead, perhaps because she was by then in love with him. According to Hope Mirrlees, Harrison's companion in her later life, MacColl proposed to Harrison but she turned him down, citing a fibrous tumor that made it dangerous for her to have children. It is equally likely that Harrison demurred out of fear of MacColl's intellectual power over her. She had, after all, completely altered her lecturing style and her view of the ancient world in response to his criticisms. In any case, they remained close friends, travel companions, and collaborators until MacColl married in 1897—another loss.

The decade of the 1890s was a tumultuous one for Harrison. In some ways she viewed her return to Newnham in 1898 as a defeat, but in light of the tragedies of the previous years she probably welcomed it as well. Upon her return to Cambridge, she met and became very close to the Pembroke philologist Robert A. Neil. In her autobiography, she described him as the friend whose "sympathetic Scotch silences made the dreariest gathering burn and glow" (RSL, 55), and his "Sunday luncheons were to me the best intellectual thing in Cambridge."[29] In fact, they agreed to marry. In light of her refusal of MacColl's proposal years before, one cannot help but

---

interested scholars. In her review of Rohde, she defends Dionysian exultation against the "common sense" of "the thoroughly British Pentheus." (Jane Ellen Harrison, "Rohde's *Psyche*, Part II," *Classical Review* 8 [1894], p. 165). Her commitment to orgiastic religion is already evident.

[28] Though much of Mannhardt's work was not directly relevant to Harrison's interests, he is cited in the *Prolegomena* on pp. 51, 79, 81, 96, 117, 271. In 1885, J. Theodore Bent published both "Researches Among the Cyclades" (*Journal of Hellenic Studies* 5 [1885]: 42-58) and *The Cyclades, or Life Among the Insular Greeks* (London, 1885). Frequently in his entertaining book, Bent cites picturesque customs that illustrate his contention that "nowhere is one brought so clearly face to face with the connecting links between heathendom and Christendom as one is in Greece" (482). Many of Bent's examples of antique survivals are cited by John C. Lawson in his *Modern Greek Folklore and Ancient Greek Religion* (Cambridge: Cambridge University Press, 1910).

[29] Jane Ellen Harrison to Jessie Stewart, November 1901, Jane Ellen Harrison Papers.

wonder why she accepted Neil. Perhaps her view of the matriarchal goddesses reflected her hopes for their relationship. These goddesses stood in a more noble relation to the male figures surrounding them than the later patriarchal gods would allow female figures. "The relation of these early matriarchal, husbandless goddesses...to the male figures that accompany them is one altogether noble and womanly, though perhaps not what the modern mind holds to be feminine. It seems to halt somewhere half-way between Mother and Lover, with a touch of the patron saint" (PSGR, 273). At age fifty, most likely beyond the possibility of pregnancy (and therefore less prey to worries about sexuality), perhaps Harrison saw a chance to recreate the "noble and womanly" relation between woman and man, based on shared intellectual interests. However, her description of the fate of matriarchy belied her optimism: "With the coming of patriarchal conditions this high companionship ends. The woman goddesses are sequestered to a servile domesticity, they become abject and amorous" (PSGR, 273). She still may have feared that she herself would suffer the same fate. Unfortunately, Neil died suddenly in 1901 after an attack of appendicitis. She admitted that "every scrap of my present work [the *Prolegomena*] has been discussed with him and simply aches with remembrance."[30] She felt genuine sorrow, but given her ambivalence about love and marriage, one wonders if their marriage would have been a happy one.

The wrenching events of the previous few years undoubtedly combined to increase Harrison's sense of loneliness and to turn her thoughts to the matriarchal world, which promised (in her view) unqualified love and nurturance. It seems likely that her passionate defense of matriarchy and the superiority of chthonic deities reflects her lifelong mourning for her lost mother; a sense of loss that flared in intensity with every succeeding loss. Faced with abandonment—by MacColl, her father, and Neil—Harrison fell back on the figure of the good mother for support and nurturance. She had never known her mother as a real human being, with faults and shortcomings, so she could create her in the image of the all-loving, all-caring mother figure she craved. Harrison transformed her dead mother into the Great Mother, who "is mother of the dead as well as the living" (PSGR, 266). In the words of the *Prolegomena*, "the Mother herself keeps ward in the *metro*polis of the dead, and therefore the Athenians of old called the dead 'Demeter's people'" (PSGR, 267).

By the time of *Themis*, Harrison's vision of the mother goddess had changed. In the *Prolegomena*, the figures were Demeter and Kore, Mother and Maid. In *Themis*, the circle became the mother and son—Semele and Dionysos, or the mother goddess and the *kouros*. What accounts for the change? Probably her vision shifted as a result of a change in the configuration of her immediate circle. Evidence from Harrison's papers

---

[30] Jane Ellen Harrison to Jessie Stewart, 1901, Jane Ellen Harrison Papers. For more discussion of Harrison's relationship with Neil, see Peacock, *Harrison*, pp. 107-08.

shows clearly that she was very much in love with Francis Cornford, twenty-five years her junior, and that she fell into a deep depression when he married Frances Darwin, the daughter of Harrison's best friend, in 1909. Augustus John's portrait of Harrison, painted in the summer of the Cornford-Darwin wedding, reflects the sorrow she could not hide. Harrison was ill and unable to work for some time after the marriage, and it is significant that *Themis* was the major work to emerge from that period.[31] The connection between her experience and her work is irrefutable. The figures in the circle changed—mother and son became the projection of the group, just as they were the projection of Harrison's views of herself and Cornford. Regardless of Harrison's wide-ranging discussion of comparative religion, two ideas remain at the center of her theory: that the mother goddess is supreme, and that the circle, whatever its composition, revolves around her. Harrison had revered the mother goddess as a substitute for her own mother. Now Jane Harrison was the supreme female figure, and she could be happy and productive only when the Ritualist Circle revolved around her. The world of *Themis* was the Ritualist Circle projected into Greek prehistory with Harrison as Themis.

The other major innovation in the book was the Year Spirit, who leaves but always returns, unlike Francis Cornford. Most scholars vehemently rejected the concept of an Eniautos Daimon, which Harrison insisted lay behind every dying-and-resurrected god. Only Gilbert Murray became a devoted champion of the year daimon and remained so to the end of his life. If the once and future year spirit meant Cornford to Harrison, Murray's attachment to the concept was rooted in a more universal concern—he suffered from what his son-in-law Arnold Toynbee called "a painful fear of death....His rationalist belief could not dispel the irrational anxiety in his heart."[32]

Harrison's middle years were marked by heights of happiness alternating with despair. When she wrote her *Epilegomena to the Study of Greek Religion* in 1921, she strove to put the buffeting of the previous twenty years behind her. Rather than continue to praise the primacy of emotion and the significance of the religious impulse, she advocated asceticism. "Asceticism is then not only resistance to the descending wave, it is also, it is chiefly, the rising on the upward wave, buoyant, triumphant. To the Greek asceticism is 'the attuning of an instrument,' not the mortification of the flesh....Is this asceticism a thing cold and dead? Hear Keats again: 'There is an awful warmth about my heart—like a load of immortality.' An

[31] See Peacock, *Harrison*, Chapters 6 and 7, for an analysis of Harrison's relationship with Cornford and its connection with her work.
[32] Arnold Toynbee, *Experiences* (New York and London: Oxford University Press, 1969), pp. 117-18.

awful warmth about his heart. Yes, and an awful light about his head."[33] The poignant prose of the *Epilegomena* cannot match the drama of either the *Prolegomena* or *Themis*. One senses, too, that Harrison had finally relinquished her position in the center for a more reflective view on the sidelines. Her critics blasted her earlier works for their emphasis on the irrational and the emotional. Many of her theories have been proven wrong, and much of her work stands in danger of being misinterpreted in the current revival of interest in her, particularly by feminist scholars. Still, her work absorbs readers in a way that few scholars can equal. Harrison wrote so unguardedly about herself that the reader must engage with her books on two levels: as studies of ancient religion and as almost autobiographical texts. She left us two invaluable gifts: a reminder akin to Freud's, that the works of civilization cannot be achieved without discontent; and an admonition to keep alive as much of our natural selves as possible. She learned these lessons from her own experience, not from books.

Emory University

[33] Jane Ellen Harrison, *Epilegomena to the Study of Greek Religion* (Cambridge: Cambridge University Press, 1921; repr. New Hyde Park: University Books, 1962), pp. lv-lvi. Her views on asceticism were considerably influenced by Solovier.

10

Prolegomena to Jane Harrison's
Interpretation of Ancient Greek Religion*

RENATE SCHLESIER

Ancient Greek religion and its history continue to the present day to offer numerous puzzling questions for research. Even to apply the term "religion"[1] to the complex picture of ancient Greek cult practices and mythic narratives is not unproblematical, in view of the evolving signification of the term over the centuries. This is true also of such terms as faith, piety, holiness, spirituality, mysticism, irrationality, anthropomorphism,[2] etc., terms whose meanings have been shaped, within the interpretative tradition

---

* Translated from the German by Michael Armstrong. For the purposes of the Conference, Dr. Scott Scullion had translated an earlier summary.

[1] On the hermeneutic problem of the term "religion" and its history in scholarship, and on the study of religion, cf. J. Waardenburg, *Religionen und Religion. Systematische Einführung in die Religionswissenschaft* [= Sammlung Göschen 2228] (Berlin and New York 1986); see also H. Cancik, B. Gladigow, and M. Laubscher (eds.), *Handbuch religionswissenschaftlicher Grundbegriffe*, vol. 1 (Stuttgart/ Berlin/ Köln/ Mainz 1988), "Kultur und Religion" 43–58 (D. Sabbatucci), "Religionssoziologie" 59–86 (G. Kehrer), "Religionspsychologie" 87–107 (H. Zinser), "Religionsethnologie" 157–94 (G. Schlatter), and "Geschichte der Religionswissenschaft" 217–62 (K.-H. Kohl). On the history of the term (in connection with Varro and Cicero, *De Natura Deorum*), cf., from a Christian point of view: M. Despland, *La religion en occident: Evolution des idées et du vécu* (Montreal 1979); E. Feil, *Religio: Die Geschichte eines neuzeitlichen Grundbegriffs vom Frühchristentum bis zur Reformation* [= Forschungen zur Kirchen- und Dogmengeschichte 36] (Göttingen 1986). On the Roman concept: W. F. Otto, "Religio und Superstitio," *Archiv für Religionswissenschaft* 12 (1909) 533–54 and 14 (1911) 406–22, reprinted in *Aufsätze zur Römischen Religionsgeschichte* [= Beiträge zur Klassischen Philologie 71] (Meisenheim am Glan 1975) 92–130. Jane Harrison refers to Otto's "excellent analysis of *religio*" in her discussion of religion as an "inextricable relation" of *mana* and *tabu* in *Themis: A Study of the Social Origins of Greek Religion* (1912; second edition: Cambridge 1927) 90.

[2] For criticism of the term "faith," see A. Henrichs, "'Der Glaube der Hellenen:' Religionsgeschichte als Glaubensbekenntnis und Kulturkritik," in W. M. Calder III, H. Flashar, and Th. Lindken (eds.), *Wilamowitz nach 50 Jahren* (Darmstadt 1985) 263–305; see also W. Fahr, *ΘΕΟΥΣ ΝΟΜΙΖΕΙΝ.: Zum Problem der Anfänge des Atheismus bei den Griechen*, Diss. Tübingen 1969. On the term "anthropomorphism," cf. K. Heinrich, *Anthropomorphe: Zum Problem des Anthropomorphismus in der Religionsphilosophie* [= Dahlemer Vorlesungen 2] (Basel and Frankfurt am Main 1986).

of the Occident, by the course of philosophical and of Christian thought. That these and many comparable terms are to be employed with caution—or that it might perhaps be better to avoid them and to replace them with others—is an insight that has been gaining ground only gradually among scholars in Altertumswissenschaft; so far, it has been more readily accepted by historians of religion[3] than by philologists and archaeologists.

The time-honored complications that arise when historically evolving terms are applied to ancient Greek religion are exacerbated by a contradiction arising from the history of scholarship, a contradiction that has characterized the modern study of Greek religion since its beginnings approximately two hundred years ago. This study was inaugurated during the Enlightenment as a criticism of religion,[4] but it received its strongest impetus from scholars who, inspired by Romanticism, were critical of the Enlightenment.[5]

Since then, historians of Greek religion, on the basis of the literary tradition and the evidence of ancient art as it has gradually come to light, have systematically analyzed two questions:

1) In what did cult-practices consist (where, beginning when, how long)?

2) In what did religious conceptions consist (bearing in mind that they too were temporally and geographically differentiated)?

The resulting problem of the relationship between rituals and myths is still theoretically and methodologically unsolved. Dispute continues,

---

[3] On the specificity of the source materials for ancient Greece and the resulting terminological problems, cf. J. Rudhardt, *Notions fondamentales de la pensée religieuse et actes constitutifs du culte dans la Grèce classique* (Genève 1958); W. Burkert, *Griechische Religion der archaischen und klassischen Epoche* [= Die Religionen der Menschheit 15] (Stuttgart/Berlin/Köln/Mainz 1977), especially 27–33; see also *ibid.*, 402–12 on "piety," "holy," etc. [English translation: *Greek Religion* (Cambridge, MA and Oxford 1985)]. Against a restrictive use of the term "holy" in respect to Greek polytheism: J.-P. Vernant, "Religion grecque, religions antiques" (1975) in *Religions, histoires, raisons* (Paris 1979) 11: "il y a des formes et des degrés divers du sacré plutôt qu'une polarité sacré-profane. L'insertion du religieux dans la vie sociale, à ses divers étages, ses liens avec l'individu, sa vie, sa survie, ne prêtent pas à une délimitation précise du domaine de la religion."

[4] Criticism of customs and myths was of prime importance; see chiefly B. Le Bovier de Fontenelle, *De l'origine des fables* (1724); J.-F. Lafitau, *Moeurs des sauvages amériquains comparées aux moeurs des premiers temps*, two volumes (1724); Ch. de Brosses, *Du culte des dieux fétiches ou Parallèle de l'ancienne religion de l'Egypte avec la religion actuelle de la Nigritie* (1760); Chr. G. Heyne, *Quaestio de causis fabularum seu mythorum veterum physicis* (1764). Cf. M. Detienne, *L'invention de la mythologie* (Paris 1981) 9–25; F. Graf, *Griechische Mythologie. Eine Einführung* [= Artemis Einführungen 16] (München and Zürich 1985) 15-21.

[5] Interest in the Orient, especially in reference to the mystery cults and Indian priestly wisdom, was predominant here, above all in G. F. Creuzer (note 24, below); the precursor in this field was J. G. von Herder, *Ideen zur Philosophie der Geschichte der Menschheit* (1784), book 13, chapter 2 (the Greek language came from the Caucasus). Cf. Graf (above, note 4), 17 f., 26 f.

although on many individual points modern scholars tread on firmer ground than was possible one hundred years ago, when three scholars, all either living in Cambridge or educated there, came forward almost simultaneously with an ahistorical, anthropological concept of religion that dislodged myth from its previously unchallenged position of primacy: William Robertson Smith (1846–94), in *Lectures on the Religion of the Semites* (1889),[6] James George Frazer (1854–1941), in *The Golden Bough* (first edition 1890),[7] and Jane Ellen Harrison (1850–1928), in *Mythology and Monuments of Ancient Athens* (1890).[8]

The conviction held by all three scholars was summarized by William Robertson Smith in a lapidary formula: "in almost every case the myth was derived from the ritual, and not the ritual from the myth."[9] That Frazer was led to this idea by Robertson Smith can be regarded as certain.[10] It remains uncertain whether Jane Harrison had read Robertson Smith's work before she formulated her similar ritualistic views.[11]

---

[6] Cf. Morton Smith, in this volume.

[7] See R. Ackerman, *J. G. Frazer: His Life and Work* (Cambridge 1987) 95-110.

[8] *Mythology & Monuments of Ancient Athens. Being a translation of a portion of the "Attica" of Pausanias by Margaret de G. Verrall. With introductory essay and archaeological commentary by Jane E. Harrison* (London and New York 1890). Cf. R. Ackerman, "Jane Ellen Harrison: The Early Work," *GRBS* 13 (1972) 225 f., and Renate Schlesier, "Jane Ellen Harrison," in W. W. Briggs, Jr., and W. M. Calder III (eds.), *Classical Scholarship: A Biographical Encyclopedia* (New York 1990) 130.

[9] William Robertson Smith, *The Religion of the Semites. The Fundamental Institutions* (1889; second edition: 1894; reprint: New York 1956) [= The Methuen Library] 18.

[10] On the meeting of Smith and Frazer in Cambridge (January 1884) and Frazer's turning to anthropology under Smith's influence, see Ackerman (above, note 7) 58-63.

[11] Robertson Smith gave his "Lectures on the Religion of the Semites" beginning in October 1888 (published in book form, 1889) for the Burnett Fund in Aberdeen. Between 1880 and 1898 Harrison was in London, and she seems to have become acquainted with Smith's work only after her return to Cambridge as Newnham Research Fellow; it was probably Frazer who introduced her to the work. Cf. Harrison, *Prolegomena to the Study of Greek Religion* (Cambridge 1903; third edition: 1922; reprint: New York: Arno Press, 1975) 126 n. 1. "Robertson Smith, exiled for heresy, had seen the Star in the East; in vain; we classical deaf-adders stopped our ears and closed our eyes; but at the mere sound of the magical words 'Golden Bough' the scales fell—we heard and understood," she writes in her *Reminiscences of a Student's Life* (London 1925) 83. The first reference (so far as I am aware) to her knowledge of Smith's book and to the high esteem in which she held it is her recommendation in 1901 to her student Jessie Graham Crum (later Mrs. Hugh F. Stewart) to read the book in preparation for the Classical Tripos; see J. Stewart, *Jane Ellen Harrison: A Portrait from Letters* (London 1959) 14. Not until *Themis* (1912) is Robertson Smith cited in support of decisive theoretical premises, especially on matters in the sociology of religion; cf. (above, note 1) 28 f., see also 136, 329. In *Prolegomena* 111 n. 1 she hails him as the first to explain the Bouphonia correctly as "ox-*murder*," noting that she had independently come to the same conclusion in *Mythology & Monuments* (above, note 8) 424 ff. The ritualism in this book seems actually to have been influenced not by Robertson Smith but chiefly by E. B. Tylor and Andrew Lang; cf. notes 39 and 20, below.

The three scholars' ritualistic outlook was motivated by opposition to the Christian referential system—explicitly in Jane Harrison,[12] primarily implicitly in Robertson Smith and Frazer.[13] An anti-Christian polemical undertone, however, is audible only in Frazer and Jane Harrison, in contrast to Robertson Smith, who adhered to a theological perspective.[14] They all support the primacy of ritual over myth by adducing comparative material from so-called primitive cultures; only Harrison and Robertson Smith, though, reveal overt sympathy with the material significance of the rituals,[15] whereas Frazer, with his Enlightenment sympathies, tends to emphasize that the rituals are ineffectual.[16] Ancient Greek religion supplied decisive evidence to Robertson Smith and Frazer,[17] but it stood at the very center of Jane Harrison's life-work.[18] How (and perhaps why) this is so is the subject of this investigation.

[12] In her autobiographical lecture "Alpha and Omega" (given in 1910 before the Sunday Essay Society of Trinity College, Cambridge) Harrison admits, "I was always a ritualist at heart (that form of Churchmanship still holds me by sentiment), but there was too much Protestant blood in my veins for it to take real possession; so I lapsed into Broad Churchism, and finally, as I thought, into complete Agnosticism" (*Alpha and Omega* [London 1915] 184). Cf. *ibid.*, 205: "To be an Atheist, then, to renounce eikonic theology, is to me personally almost an essential of religious life." On Harrison's relation to Christianity see also notes 18, 31, 54, 114, 125, below.

[13] The *interpretatio christiana* is especially visible in Smith's sacramental interpretation of the sacrificial meal—implicitly modeled on the Eucharist (cf. Smith [above, note 9] 312 ff.: Lecture IX) and in Frazer's universalization of the "Dying God"— implicitly modeled on the Christ-figure; cf. J. G. Frazer, *The Golden Bough: A Study in Magic and Religion* (third edition, Part III, London 1911).

[14] In his obituary for Robertson Smith (who was a life-long Christian), Frazer stated that the comparative method of religious research that his best friend had followed leads to the undermining of religion; see Ackerman (above, note 7) 83.

[15] For Smith the holiness of "primitive" rites is justified by their reverence for physically fixed times and places; cf., e.g., Smith (above, note 9) 140–42. Sharing this persuasion, Harrison indulges in polemic against religions which, removed from this original naturalism and possessing a "full-blown theology," no longer deserve the name of "religion;" cf., e.g., Harrison, *Alpha & Omega* (above, note 12) 179 ff. See also *Reminiscences* (above, note 11) 84: "When I say 'religion', I am instantly obliged to correct myself; it is not religion, it is ritual that absorbs me." Cf. the contrary position of W.K.C. Guthrie, *The Greeks and Their Gods* (1950; reprint: London 1977) xiii: "I find that my confession would be the opposite of Jane Harrison's. It is not ritual that absorbs me, it is the state of mind of the people who performed the ritual."

[16] According to Frazer, the rituals of "vegetation cults" are based on the erroneous belief that man can use "sympathetic magic" to influence the course of nature; cf. especially *The Golden Bough,* third edition, Part I: "The Magic Art and the Evolution of Kings" (London 1911) I, 220 ff.

[17] For example, Smith attempts to make his thesis of "primaeval vegetarianism" "quite plain" by means of an interpretation of the Bouphonia: Smith (above, note 9) 303–6; see also above, note 11. For Frazer, who was a classical philologist by trade, the ancient field of reference always remains explicit; the most important gods for him, as for Harrison, are Dionysos and Demeter.

[18] On the reasons for Harrison's shifting from Christianity to Greek religion via Greek art, cf. Harrison, *Alpha & Omega* (above, note 12) 184 f.

I. *On the Genesis of Jane Harrison's Ritualism*

Jane Harrison first explicitly expressed a ritualistic view in 1890 in the Foreword to her third book, a detailed commentary, enriched with archaeological material, on excerpts from Pausanias' *Attica* (which was translated by her friend from student days, Margaret de G. Verrall).

> My belief is that in many, even in the large majority of cases *ritual practice misunderstood* explains the elaboration of myth. . . . Some of the loveliest stories the Greeks have left us will be seen to have taken their rise, not in poetic imagination, but in primitive, often savage, and, I think, always *practical* ritual. In this matter—in regarding the myth-making Greek as a practical savage rather than a poet or philosopher—I follow, *quam longo intervallo*, in the steps of Eusebius, Lobeck, Mannhardt, and Mr. Andrew Lang.[19]

The last-named ally, Andrew Lang (1844–1912), a countryman of Robertson Smith and Frazer, whose attitudes were influenced by the Scottish Enlightenment, can be described as an immediate forerunner of the Ritualists. At the center of the books he had published a few years earlier, *Custom and Myth* (1884) and *Myth, Ritual, and Religion* (1887), stood the concept of "survival,"[20] which Edward Burnett Tylor (1832–1917) had introduced in his work *Primitive Culture* (1871)[21] and which Robertson

---

[19] *Mythology & Monuments* (above, note 8) iii. Harrison's definition of myth here contains echoes of the Oxford scholar of comparative religion Friedrich Max Müller (1823-1900) from Dessau, son of the lyric poet Wilhelm Müller (1794-1827), whose works became popular in the settings of Franz Schubert. Max Müller defined myth as a "childhood disease" of language, as a "dialect" that produced "mythological misunderstandings" on the basis of "polyonymy and synonymy:" *Griechische Sagen* (1867) 144 f.; see also *Introduction to the Science of Religion: Four Lectures Delivered at the Royal Institution with Two Essays on False Analogies and the Philosophy of Mythology* (London 1873) 355; on "mythological infection," see 359. Harrison, in *Prolegomena* (above, note 11) 263 n. 1, opposes "systems" like Müller's "that see in ancient deities impersonations of natural phenomena;" in *Themis*, however, she herself returns to a similar system; cf. note 102, below.

[20] Cf. A. Lang, "The Myth of Cronus," in *Custom and Myth* (1884; second edition: London 1885; reprint: Oosterhout N.B. 1970) 63: "The survival we explain as, in a previous essay, we explained the survival of the bull-roarer, by the conservatism of the religious instinct." Cf. also, in a vivid image, *ibid.*, 53: "Like the erratic blocks in a modern plain, like the flint-heads in a meadow, the story is a relic of a very distant past." On Harrison's first meeting with Lang, see *Reminiscences* (above, note 11) 62. On the Scottish Enlightenment, cf. note 46, below. The standard life of Lang is R. L. Green, *Andrew Lang: A Critical Biography* (Leicester 1946).

[21] See E. B. Tylor, *Primitive Culture: Researches into the Development of Mythology, Philosophy, Religion, Language, Art, and Custom*, two volumes (1871; London and New York 1920) I, 16: "Among evidence aiding us to trace the course which the civilization of the world has actually followed, is that great class of facts to denote which I have found it convenient to introduce the term 'survivals.' These are processes, customs, opinions, and

Smith, Frazer, and Harrison adopted as one of the fundamental concepts of their ritualism.

The Germanist Wilhelm Mannhardt (1831–80), whose work *Wald- und Feldkulte* (1875–77) interpreted Greek religion as the outgrowth of agricultural practices, supplied to the Ritualists' emphasis on folklore the fundamental interpretative model and a slogan to go with it: the so-called "vegetation god," or vegetation-daimon and -spirit.[22]

Christian August Lobeck (1781–1860) was one of the foremost exponents of that rationalism in German Altertumswissenschaft which sought to slay Romanticism with its own weapons. In his erudite work *Aglaophamus* (1829) he assembled the ancient evidence relative to the mystery cults and strictly distinguished them from mythical fables; he thus destroyed the foundations of that mystification of myth[23] which Georg

---

so forth, which have been carried on by force of habit into a new state of society different from that in which they had their original home, and they thus remain as proofs and examples of an older condition of culture out of which a newer has been evolved." Cf. also 21; 70–159 (chapters 3–4: "Survival in Culture"). Tylor already figures in Harrison's first book, *Myths of the Odyssey in Art and Literature* (London 1882) 218, as a decisive "authority;" cf. note 39, below. See also *Reminiscences* (above, note 11) 83. On Tylor as Harrison's and Frazer's "guiding star," cf. A. Henrichs, *Die Götter Griechenlands: Ihr Bild im Wandel der Religionswissenschaft* [= Thyssen-Vorträge. Auseinandersetzungen mit der Antike 5, edited by H. Flashar] (Bamberg 1987) 13.

[22] See W. Mannhardt, *Wald- und Feldkulte*, vol. 1: *Der Baumkultus der Germanen und ihrer Nachbarstämme. Mythologische Untersuchungen;* vol. 2: *Antike Wald- und Feldkulte aus nordeuropäischer Überlieferung erläutert* (1875–77; second edition: 1905; reprint: Darmstadt 1963); on Mannhardt's appreciation of Tylor, cf. vol. 2, xxii f.; cf. also *Mythologische Forschungen* (Berlin 1884). Frazer emphasizes that his *Golden Bough* was dependent on Mannhardt's work: "I have made great use of the works of the late W. Mannhardt, without which, indeed, my book could scarcely have been written," he writes in the foreword to the first edition (1890; third edition: I, ix); cf. R. Ackerman, "Frazer on Myth and Ritual," *Journal of the History of Ideas* 36 (1975) 121. Harrison refers approvingly to Mannhardt's interpretations of ritual in *Prolegomena* (above, note 11) 51 n. 2 [Lupercalia]; 79 n. 2; 81 n. 1; 96 n. 2 [Thargelia: Eiresione and Pharmakos]; 117 n. 3 [Argei]; 271 n. 2 [etymology of Demeter].

[23] See Chr. A. Lobeck, *Aglaophamus sive de theologiae mysticae Graecorum causis libri tres*, two volumes (Königsberg 1829; reprint: Darmstadt 1961), a rationalistic defense of the uniqueness of Greek religion and philosophy; he explicitly (vol. 1, ix) followed J. H. Voß and his two-volume *Antisymbolik* (1824–26), which was directed against Creuzer. Lobeck, a theologian and schoolman and a student of the great "Wort-Philologe" Gottfried Hermann, names his main target Creuzer only once, at the beginning of the book 1 ("Eleusinia"), in the laconic remark, "Creuzerum, qui in omnibus Sancrucium pedetentim sequitur, in hac causa postea non nominabo" (vol. 1, 8 n. 1). On Lobeck's quarrel with "mythologi nostri," cf. A. Horstmann, "Der Mythosbegriff vom frühen Christentum bis zur Gegenwart," *Archiv für Begriffsgeschichte* 23.1 (1979) 32. Lobeck's useful collection of materials was later of service even to authors whose intentions were by no means in agreement with his own; cf., e.g., Harrison, *Prolegomena* (above, note 11) 107 n. 1; 147 n. 3; 150 n. 1; 161 n. 2.

Friedrich Creuzer (1771–1858) had propagated in his monumental work *Symbolik und Mythologie der alten Völker* (1810–12).[24]

The Church Father Eusebius (260–339), bishop of Caesarea and the most important historian of the early Christian centuries prior to Constantine, may be the most surprising name in Harrison's list. But Eusebius has in common with the other forerunners of Harrison's ritualism a rationalism based on a theory of development. Eusebius' history of the Church postulates an historical period of savagery and barbarism which lasted from the Fall of Man until the Advent of Christ and during which the divine Logos was progressively revealing itself.[25]

Robertson Smith's name is missing from Harrison's list, and another name is unmentioned that one might especially have expected to see in a list of the sources that inspired her ritualistic theory of myth: Karl Otfried Müller (1797–1840). In his works one already finds the idea (which goes back to ancient interpretations) that the myths recount, interpret, and re-shape local customs and historical events.[26] Harrison expressly names him

---

[24] G. F. Creuzer, *Symbolik und Mythologie der alten Völker, besonders der Griechen*, four volumes (1810–12; third edition: 1837–42; reprint: Hildesheim and New York 1973) [= Volkskundliche Quellen. Neudrucke europäischer Texte und Untersuchungen V: Sitte und Brauch, edited by H. Brausinger]. On the controversy surrounding Creuzer, his opponents and supporters, cf. E. Howald (ed.), *Der Kampf um Creuzers Symbolik. Eine Auswahl von Dokumenten* (Tübingen 1926); see also above, note 23; Graf, *Griechische Mythologie* (above, note 4) 26. As far as I am aware, there is no indication that Harrison read Creuzer, although she certainly did not otherwise shrink from "heavy volumes of German;" cf. Gilbert Murray, *Jane Ellen Harrison: An Address* (Cambridge 1928) 4 [= Harrison, *Epilegomena* and *Themis*, ed. J. C. Wilson (New York 1962) 560]. But Harrison often followed in the footsteps of Creuzer's most loyal supporter among the archaeologists, Theodor S. Panofka (1800–58); cf. O. Gruppe, *Bericht über die Literatur zur antiken Mythologie und Religionsgeschichte aus den Jahren 1898–1905* [= *Jahresbericht über die Fortschritte der klassischen Altertumswissenschaft*, founded by C. Bursian, edited by W. Kroll, *Supplementband* vol. 137] (Leipzig 1908) 280, an annihilating discussion of Harrison's *Prolegomena*: "seit Gerhard und Panofka ist wohl niemand die Wege gewandelt, die sie einschlägt. Sie setzt voraus, daß die Künstler, besonders die Maler der Vbb. [Vasenbilder] nicht allein die Geschichte der Kulte genau kannten, sondern auch sie symbolisch darzustellen versuchten." Gerhard and Panofka, like Tylor, were already among the "authorities" cited in Harrison's first book *Myths of the Odyssey* (above, note 21) 215, 218. On Gerhard's importance for Harrison, see note 67, below. On Panofka, see A. Rumpf, *Archäologie I: Einleitung. Historischer Überblick* [= Sammlung Goschen 538] (Berlin 1953) 86 f., and on Eduard Gerhard (1795–1867) *passim*. On Gerhard and his friend and colleague Panofka see also A. Borbein, "Klassische Archäologie in Berlin vom 18. bis zum 20. Jahrhundert," in Willmuth Arenhövel and Christa Schreiber (eds.), *Berlin und die Antike. Aufsätze* (Berlin 1979) 119–33. On Creuzer, Gerhard, and Panofka, cf. R. Lullies and W. Schiering (eds.), *Archäologenbildnisse* (Mainz am Rhein 1988) 14 f.; 20–22; 25 f.

[25] Cf. Eusebius' *Historia Ecclesiastica* I, 1–4. On Eusebius' church history as a pioneering work, see P. Meinhold, *Geschichte der kirchlichen Historiographie*, Vol. 1 [= Orbis Academicus III/5] (Freiburg and München 1967) 95–110.

[26] See K. O. Müller, *Geschichte hellenischer Stämme und Städte*, vol. 1: *Orchomenos und die Minyer* (Breslau 1820); vols. 2–3: *Die Dorier* (Breslau 1824); *Prolegomena zu einer wissenschaftlichen Mythologie* (Göttingen 1825; reprint: Darmstadt 1970). Müller's work *Die Etrusker* (four volumes, 1828) and his *Handbuch der Archäologie der Kunst* (1830)

in connection with the thesis that the Olympian gods had become detached from their original connection to local cults—though she does so in a peripheral passage, in the Foreword to the English edition of A. H. Petiscus's compendium *Der Olymp oder Mythologie der Griechen und Römer* (1863), translated by Katherine Raleigh as *The Gods of Olympus* (New York 1892). Every theorist of mythology, according to Harrison, must take his lead from Müller.

> . . . what he must do, or fail, is to trace each Saga to its local home, to carry out the work that the great H. D. [i.e., K. O.] Müller began before his time, to disentangle the "confederacy of local cults" from which the ultimate Olympian assembly was formed.[27]

Jane Harrison's knowledge of Karl Otfried Müller's works is already documented in her first book, *Myths of the Odyssey in Art and Literature* (1882). The bibliography lists two of his books, and the Foreword paraphrases (without mentioning Müller's name) the central insight of his *Prolegomena zu einer wissenschaftlichen Mythologie* (1825), an insight which also occurs in his works on archaeology and his histories of the several Greek peoples: "both Homer and the artist drew their inspiration from one common source, local and national tradition."[28] The title of Müller's epoch-making introductory book probably also inspired the title of Harrison's own pioneering work, *Prolegomena to the Study of Greek Religion* (1903).[29] Karl Otfried Müller indirectly influenced even Harrison's repudiation of her strict Anglican upbringing, for David Friedrich Strauss, whose two-volume work *Das Leben Jesu, kritisch bearbeitet* (1835–36) she read in 1869–70 in her twentieth year[30] and which initiated her conversion to agnosticism, had modelled his historical and mythological interpretation of

---

were among Harrison's essential reference works since her first book, *Myths of the Odyssey* (above, note 21) 215, 218. As support for one of the fundamental theses of her *Prolegomena*—that "primitive" and "matriarchal" tribes had been subjugated, and their culture absorbed, by conquerors from the north—Harrison cites Müller (though with incorrect citation of author's name and the place and date of publication) on the "compulsory marriage of Hera to Zeus," *Prolegomena* (above, note 11) 315 n. 1; cf. *ibid.*, 316 n. 3. On Müller as one of the chief sources for Harrison's interpretation of the Erinyes, cf. note 78, below.

[27] I have unfortunately not seen this edition with Harrison's introduction; I quote from Ackerman (above, note 8) 229.

[28] Harrison, *Myths of the Odyssey* (above, note 21) ix.

[29] It is possible that even the interpretation of the chief figure of Harrison's "central work" *Themis* (*Reminiscences* [above, note 11] 73) was inspired by Müller; he seems to set Themis, as an impersonal power, above Zeus; cf. *Prolegomena zu einer wissenschaftlichen Mythologie* (above, note 26) 356.

[30] Cf. Sandra J. Peacock, *Jane Ellen Harrison: The Mask and the Self* (New Haven and London 1988) 28.

the New Testament on Karl Otfried Müller's interpretation of Greek traditions.[31]

Thus the novelty of Harrison's first book (as was later the case with the works of Robertson Smith and Frazer) consisted primarily in the fact that English readers now became acquainted for the first time with the historical-critical analysis of cult and myth, the earliest exponent of which in Altertumswissenschaft had been Karl Otfried Müller.[32] Beyond this, Harrison (unlike Robertson Smith and Frazer) profited from contemporary German classical archaeology's eager interest in questions of religious history.[33] Lessing, citing Plutarch, had already demonstrated in *Laokoon* (1766) that myths are not mere poetic fictions and that the evidence of literature and the visual arts is of equal importance.[34] Many scholars, to be sure, clung to idealistic views and continued to maintain that ancient art works were nothing but illustrations of myths as treated by the poets.[35] But

[31] Cf. Horstmann (above, note 23) 41 with note 14. His reading of Strauss in February 1865 had a similar effect on the twenty-year-old Nietzsche: he gave up the study of theology and decided to concentrate on classical philology; cf. C. P. Janz, *Friedrich Nietzsche Biographie* (1978) (München 1981) vol. 1, 146. Eight years later, as a professor of classical philology in Basel who had begun to distance himself from the profession, Nietzsche castigated David Strauss in the "Erste Unzeitgemäße Betrachtung" as an opponent of Wagner and a fanatic for religious reform.

[32] On Müller's far-reaching influence, cf. W. Burkert, "Griechische Mythologie und die Geistesgeschichte der Moderne," in W. den Boer (ed.), *Les études classiques aux XIXe et XXe siècles: Leur place dans l'histoire des idées* [= Entretiens sur l'antiquité classique 26, Fondation Hardt] (Vandoeuvres-Genève 1980) 164 f.; Graf, *Griechische Mythologie* (above, note 4) 27–29; *Archäologenbildnisse* (above, note 24) 23 f. Müller left his mark on the most influential innovators in the field of the history of ancient Greek religion, above all (in addition to Harrison) Erwin Rohde (1845–98) and his friend Friedrich Nietzsche (1844–1900) as well as the latter's opposite Ulrich von Wilamowitz-Moellendorff (1848–1931). On Müller's influence on Wilamowitz, cf. also Henrichs (above, note 2) 275, 292 n. 135. On Rohde see also notes 60, 74, 78, 93, 122; on Nietzsche see notes 31, 47, 48, 102, 118, 122. John Leitch's translation of Müller, *Introduction to a Scientific System of Mythology* (London 1844) should be noticed.

[33] Here too Müller was a pioneer (cf. especially note 26). Harrison was probably introduced to Müller's work (as well as to the works of other, predominantly German, archaeologists interested in the history of religion, e.g., Heinrich Brunn, Alexander Conze, Eduard Gerhard, Wolfgang Helbig, Otto Jahn, Johannes Overbeck, Theodor Panofka, and Friedrich Gottlieb Welcker) by Wilhelm Klein (1850–1924), a scholar her own age whom she met in 1880 while he was staying in London; Klein was later Professor Ordinarius for Classical Archaeology in Prague. Cf. *Myths of the Odyssey* (above, note 21) xiv; 215–19; on Klein see *Archäologenbildnisse* (above, note 24) 98 f.

[34] See G. E. Lessing, *Laokoon oder die Grenzen der Malerei und Poesie* (1766), especially chapters VI–XXV. The motto of this essay on the specific methods of imitation by painters and poets is from Plutarch, *Moralia* 347 a: ὕλῃ καὶ τρόποις μιμήσεως διαφέρουσι. Cf. K. Borinski, *Die Antike in Poetik und Kunsttheorie von Ausgang des klassischen Altertums bis auf Goethe und Winckelmann* [= Das Erbe der Alten 10] vol. 2 (Leipzig 1924) 228–32.

[35] Otto Jahn (1813–69), for example, was of this opinion; see Renate Schlesier, "Mythenwahrheit versus Aberglaube: Otto Jahn und der böse Blick," in W. M. Calder III, H. Cancik, and B. Kytzler (eds.), *Otto Jahn (1813–1869): Ein Geisteswissenschaftler*

Jane Harrison belonged from the beginning to that school of archaeologists (unfortunately, they remain even today in the minority) who see in works of art independent "commentaries" or "variants" of myths[36] and even consider it possible that a large portion of vase paintings, in particular, depict specific rituals[37]—an insight which is found in Harrison's first book:

> It appears that at the festival of the Attic Aiora the women of Athens were wont to swing themselves, in memory of an Attic heroine, Erigone, who died the death of Phaedra. . . . Vase pictures with female figures swinging occur not unfrequently; they may have some reference to this ceremony.[38]

---

zwischen Klassizismus und Historismus (Stuttgart 1990, in press). Ludwig Ross (1806–59) maintained, *contra* Jahn, the thesis that certain representations of the Trojan War are older than the epic; cf. *Archäologische Aufsätze*, Erste Sammlung (Leipzig 1855) especially viii.

[36] Harrison, *Myths of the Odyssey* (above, note 21) viii; cf. *ibid.* ix: "the ancient artist was no *illustrator* in the modern sense of the term. The words of Homer may or may not have sounded in his ears as he wrought: the text of the last edition of the poet's works was certainly not before his eyes. Frequently we have plain evidence that it is not the artist who is borrowing from Homer, but that both Homer and the artist drew their inspiration from one common source, local and national tradition. Nothing perhaps makes us realise more vividly that the epics of Homer are embodiments, not creations, of national Sagas, as this free and variant treatment of his mythology by the artist." Once again, Harrison's argument is here in line with that of K. O. Müller (the modern tendency to trace the Homeric epics back to "oral tradition" and "folk-tale" also goes back to Müller). The "archäologische Hermeneutik" of Carl Robert (1850–1922) leads in the same direction in granting that works of visual arts are independent representations of myths and of rituals. See *Bild und Lied. Archäologische Beiträge zur Geschichte der griechischen Heldensage* [= Philologische Untersuchungen 5] (Berlin 1881; reprint: New York 1975); *Archaeologische Hermeneutik* (Berlin 1919). On Robert, cf. *Archäologenbildnisse* (above, note 24) 96 f. Robert introduced the term "bildliche Tradition," cf. W. Geominy, "Die Welckersche Archäologie," in W. M. Calder III, A. Köhnken, W. Kullmann, and G. Pflug (eds.), *Friedrich Gottlieb Welcker. Werk und Wirkung* [= Hermes Einzelschriften 49] (Stuttgart 1986) 232. On Robert's adoption of Harrison's "year-daimon," cf. note 115, below.

[37] This is the position taken today especially by the collaborators of Jean-Pierre Vernant in Paris, although they generally do not acknowledge Harrison's status as a pioneer; cf., e.g., J.-L. Durand, *Sacrifice et labour en Grèce ancienne* (Paris and Rome 1986) 4, who describes Harrison simply as an adherent of "frazérisme." But for a critical acknowledgement of Harrison's importance, see Nicole Loraux, "L'autochtonie: une topique athénienne" (1979) in *Les enfants d'Athéna: Idées athéniennes sur la citoyenneté et la division des sexes* (Paris 1981) 35–73. On the methodological problem of the relationship between reality and "imaginaire" in vase-paintings, cf. also J.-P. Vernant et al., *La cité des images. Religion et société en Grèce antique* (Lausanne and Paris 1984).

[38] Harrison, *Myths of the Odyssey* (above, note 21) 122 n. 2. This interpretation of vases portraying swinging women as depictions of the Aiora festival at the Athenian Anthesteria is today *opinio communis* (among historians of religion, if not among archaeologists); see (though he does not mention Harrison in this context) W. Burkert, *Homo necans: Interpretationen altgriechischer Opferriten und Mythen* [= Religionsgeschichtliche Versuche und Vorarbeiten 32] (Berlin and New York 1972) 266–69; *Griechische Religion* (above, note 3) 363 f.

The anthropological approach that characterized Harrison's comparative methodology from her first book on was also pioneering. Myths and customs of "primitive" peoples are adduced from Tylor's *Primitive Culture* as analogies to those of the Greeks.[39]

The reasons why the originality of Harrison's *Myths of the Odyssey* was generally overlooked cannot here be analyzed in detail. That the innovations that appear in the book were later expressed more clearly and more consistently is certain. Methodologically, of course, Harrison remains true to herself, and the question arises whether this can be said of her theory of the history of religion as well. To anticipate my results: Harrison's life-work, in my view, develops a coherent model of the history of ancient Greek religion, the fundamental conceptions of which remain consistent; only the nuances and emphases vary.

This model is sketched out and applied in the two early books already mentioned as well as in the numerous papers and reviews published chiefly in the *Journal of Hellenic Studies* and the *Classical Review*.[40] It is also fundamental to the relatively schematic summary treatments, intended for a wider audience, among her later works: *The Religion of Ancient Greece* (1905), *Ancient Art and Ritual* (1913), *Mythology* in the series "Our Debt to Greece and Rome" (1924), and *Myths of Greece and Rome* (1927). Her essayistic, often autobiographically colored works, especially the collection *Alpha and Omega* (1915), also bear witness to her consistent use of this model. An instructive exception is the conventional handbook *Introductory Studies in Greek Art* (1885), Harrison's second book, which, because it rates the Olympians so positively, seems odd among her works yet does not invalidate the system that she elsewhere embraces. But Harrison's basic ideas for the history of religion are most clearly visible in her two chief works, *Prolegomena to the Study of Greek Religion* (1903) and *Themis: A*

---

[39] Cf. Harrison, *Myths of the Odyssey* (above, note 21) e.g., 97 f.: for the wide dissemination of the "longing, swiftly changed to a conviction, that somewhere, by some desolate lake or darkly yawning cavern, a way led to the world below, by which the living might pass to revisit the dead, the dead the living" Harrison cites appropriate references to Greeks, Romans, Teutons, Celts, Aztecs, "South African savages," and Egyptians, and then quotes Tylor on a myth and a custom of the "Fijians." Cf. also, *ibid.* 202 n. 1, the parallel she draws between the story of Scylla and a belief (reported by Tylor) found among the Delaware Indians. On Harrison's anticipations in her first book of later motifs, see also Peacock, *The Mask* (above, note 30) 75–81.

[40] The bibliography in Stewart, *J. E. Harrison* (above, note 11) 203–8 is incomplete and inaccurate. For a complete bibliography of the works of the Cambridge Ritualists (including Harrison) see Shelley Arlen, *The Cambridge Ritualists: An Annotated Bibliography* (Metuchen/London, 1990). Among Harrison's most important papers and reviews are: review of Erwin Rohde, *Psyche. Seelencult und Unsterblichkeitsglaube der Griechen*, CR 4 (1890) 376–77 ("first half") and CR 8 (1894) 165–66 ("second half"); "Delphika.—(A) The Erinyes. (B) The Omphalos," JHS 19 (1899) 205–51; "Pandora's Box," JHS 20 (1900) 99–114; "Mystica Vannus Iacchi," JHS 23 (1903) 292–324 and 24 (1904) 241–54.

Study of the Social Origins of Greek Religion (1912), and in her final theoretical work, the psychological and philosophical essay *Epilegomena to the Study of Greek Religion* (1921).

II. *A Few Basic Religious-Historical Concepts in Harrison's Work*

1. *Evolution*

Charles Darwin's theory of evolution was for Jane Harrison a new credo, which she adopted at about the age of twenty. (*The Descent of Man* appeared in 1871). In a pamphlet published in 1909, *The Influence of Darwinism on the Study of Religions*,[41] she emphasized that the "doctrine of evolution" not only robbed of its validity the Christian doctrine she had till then accepted but also taught her above all that religion could not be understood if it was regarded as absolute truth, namely as "what we should now call Theology and what the ancients called Mythology."[42] It is precisely the study of ritual, not the study of myth, which teaches us that every religion is subject to "development." According to Harrison, it is thanks to Darwin that the genesis and evolution of religious phenomena can finally be studied, like other phenomena, in a scientific way, that is, as an anthropological process, following natural laws, progressing from simple, primitive, barbaric and savage, sensual, low beginnings to complex, developed, civilized, spiritual, higher goals.[43] Through her choice of these adjectives, which she often employs as synonyms or alternatives, Harrison insinuates a moral judgement, according to which the primitive stage of development is negative, the "higher stratum" positive.

It is typical of Harrison that she applies this Credo in contradictory ways. Her unquestioned—indeed, her explicitly emphasized—ethical stance is opposed by an emotional countercurrent. Her emotional sympathies, which are just as clear and unambiguous as her ethical commitment, lie with the primitive stratum and with the emotions, ideas, and actions that (in

---

[41] Reprinted in Harrison, *Alpha & Omega* (above, note 12) 143–78.

[42] *Ibid.*, 144.

[43] Darwin himself, however, was a child of his times in religious matters, Harrison felt (cf. *ibid.*, 147 f.). The movement toward anthropology and comparative religion, which had been stimulated by the theory of evolution, had been realized by other scholars, among whom Harrison especially emphasizes Tylor and Frazer (151), in addition to Wilhelm Wundt (1832–1920) and Henri Bergson (1859–1941); cf. notes 49 and 122, below. Despite her adherence to the theory of evolution and its idea of progress (cf., in summary, 177 f.), Harrison's sympathies with the rituals of savage peoples, e.g., "magical dances," are unmistakeable (162–66). For Bergson's influence on Harrison, especially his concept of "durée" in *L'évolution créatrice* (1907), cf. *Themis* (above, note 1), xii, 477; see also 86 (man as *homo faber*), 473, 479.

her conception) belong to that stratum, though they live on as "survivals" even in the "higher" stages of development.[44]

2. *Origin*

Since Darwin's *On the Origin of Species* (1859) at the latest (though the Romantics had already brought it into fashion), the search for the origin— the origins of all phenomena in human society and in nature—was one of the obsessions of nineteenth-century scholars.[45] Jane Harrison had not a moment's doubt that the origin was something that could be reconstructed in every case and that all later developments could only be deciphered by tracing them back to their origins. Here again it is clear that Harrison opts for a Romantic and a positivistic position at the same time. The idea that rationality is a gain and is part of the progress towards a higher and better state is congruent with positivism.[46] The conviction that the irrational is

[44] See e.g., Harrison, *Alpha & Omega* (above, note 12) 160: "We still say 'Holy, Holy, Holy,' and in some mystic way feel the holier." Or *ibid.*, 166: "We shall best understand this primitive state of mind if we study the child 'born in sin.' If a child is 'playing at lions,' he does not *imitate* a lion—i.e., he does not consciously try to be a thing more or less like a lion: he *becomes* one." On totemism, cf. also notes 61, 73, and 129, below.

[45] From the point of view of the development of linguistics, cf. M. Olender, *Les langues du paradis. Aryens et Sémites: un couple providentiel* (Paris 1989). For a religious-philosophical criticism of the notion of origin in mythological thought, cf. K. Heinrich, "Die Funktion der Genealogie im Mythos," in *Parmenides und Jona. Vier Studien über das Verhältnis von Philosophie und Mythologie* (Frankfurt am Main 1966) 9–28, 163–67 [= *Vernunft und Mythos. Ausgewählte Texte* (Frankfurt am Main 1983) 11–26, 89–93].

[46] On the early history of positivism within the Enlightenment's criticism of religion, see above, note 4. The formation of Harrison's theories was less influenced by the French and German Enlightment than by the Scottish. The Scottish thinkers, taking their cue from David Hume's *Of the Populousness of Ancient Nations* (1752), used predominantly ancient evidence to develop the idea of universal progress in social history as a process proceeding by stages: Adam Smith, *Lectures on Jurisprudence* (1762), Adam Ferguson, *An Essay on the History of Civil Society* (1767), and John Millar, *The Origin of the Distinction of Ranks* (1771); see H. Schneider, "Schottische Aufklärung und antike Gesellschaft," in P. Kneißl and V. Losemann (eds.), *Alte Geschichte und Wissenschaftsgeschichte* [= Festschrift Karl Christ] (Darmstadt 1988) 431–64. Nineteenth-century scholars particularly influenced by the Scottish Enlightenment included Henry Maine, *Ancient Law, Its Connection with the Early History of Society, and Its Relation to Modern Ideas* (1861), John Ferguson McLennan, *Primitive Marriage: An Inquiry into the Origin of the Form of Capture in Marriage Ceremonies* (1865), and Lewis Henry Morgan, *Systems of Consanguinity and Affinity of the Human Family* (1870); *Ancient Society, or Researches in the Lines of Human Progress from Savagery through Barbarism to Civilization* (1877). These works, along with those of Tylor (above, note 21), laid the foundations for positivistic anthropology; cf. W. E. Mühlmann, *Geschichte der Anthropologie* (1948; third edition: Wiesbaden 1984) 102–7; G. W. Stocking, Jr., *Victorian Anthropology* (New York and London 1987) especially 295–305; A. Kuper, *The Invention of Primitive Society: Transformations of an Illusion* (London and New York 1988). Harrison dealt (implicitly, as a rule) above all with the epoch-making hypotheses of McLennan (totemism) and Morgan (matriarchy) as well as with Maine's theory of an original patriarchy, an element in the development of which, however, was the increasing

the original, that it contains a deeper truth than rationality, and that its rejection is a process of decadence and loss, is preconditioned by Romantic thinking.[47]

Harrison's cyclic harmonization of religion, as it is dramatized in her central book *Themis*, is also simultaneously Romantic and positivistic. Again and again "the social origins of Greek religion" are newly revealed and repeated on all levels, in all periodic rituals: "the origin is the goal."[48] To the missionary zeal that Harrison never abandoned, it is self-evident that this goal is to be sought not only in Greek religion; it must be realized "here and now," "for us," "consciously."[49] Harrison does not hesitate to use Christian

equality of women. In 1901 Harrison recommended the reading of Maine ("Themistes") as preparation for philological exams; cf. Stewart, *J. E. Harrison* (above, note 11) 14; cf. also Stocking 206: Maine's book "was circulated (with his permission) by feminist groups."

[47] Cf. R. Haym, *Die romantische Schule. Ein Beitrag zur Geschichte der deutschen Geistes* (1870; reprint: Darmstadt 1977), especially book 2 (on August Wilhelm and Friedrich Schlegel): "Das Entstehen einer romantischen Kritik und Theorie," 143–286; H. Freier, *Die Rückkehr der Götter. Von der ästhetischen Überschreitung der Wissensgrenze zur Mythologie der Moderne* (Stuttgart 1976); see also E. Behler, "Die Auffassung des Dionysischen durch die Brüder Schlegel und Friedrich Nietzsche," in *Nietzsche-Studien* 12 (1983) 335–54.

[48] This sentence, which summarizes in lapidary fashion the theoretical obsessions of the nineteenth century (cf. also Olender [above, note 45]), and is anticipated by Heraclitus (22 B, frg. 103, Diels-Kranz), is from K. Kraus, "Der sterbende Mensch," in *Worte in Versen* I (second edition: Leipzig 1919) 69. It is cited as a motto by Walter Benjamin, "Über den Begriff der Geschichte" [Geschichtsphilosophische Thesen], in *Gesammelte Schriften*, edited by R. Tiedemann and H. Schweppenhäuser, I.2 (Frankfurt am Main 1974; second edition: 1978) 701. On Nietzsche's use of ancient cyclic theories of history (though he differed from Harrison in being non-sociological), see K. Löwith, *Nietzsches Philosophie der ewigen Wiederkehr des Gleichen* (1935), in *Sämtliche Schriften* 6 (Stuttgart 1987) especially 238–56. On the problem of the difference and sameness of "alpha" and "omega," cf. Harrison, *Themis* (above, note 1) 535; *Alpha & Omega* (above, note 12) 179–208.

[49] The modernizing gesture is a consistent characteristic of Harrison's scholarly ethos. In her first book she writes, "I believe the educational value of a study of archaeology," and considers that not the least component of this value lies in "well-balanced emotion;" see *Myths of the Odyssey* (above, note 21) xii–xiii. The anthropological emphasis that grows ever stronger in her works seems to serve this ethical aim even more consistently; cf. *Themis* (above, note 1) 23: "we offer to the humanist the mysteries of Zagreus made harmless, humanized by anthropology;" or 118 on "*omophagia* or *Eating of Raw Flesh*": "our moral repugnance disappears, or at least suffers profound modification, when the gist of the rite is understood." On the transformation of the religious view of life into conscious philosophical thought, cf. *ibid.*, xxii: "I have come to see in the religious impulse a new value. It is, I believe, an attempt, instinctive and unconscious, to do what Professor Bergson bids modern philosophy do consciously and with the whole apparatus of science behind it, namely to apprehend life as one, as indivisible, yet as perennial movement and change." (On Bergson see above, note 43.) The final station of Harrison's "pedagogically" intended modernization (see also note 127, below) is the third and last part of her *Epilegomena to the Study of Greek Religion* (Cambridge 1921) 35–40 [= *Themis*, ed. Wilson (above, note 24) li–lvi]: "The Religion of To-Day," with its motto: "*Via Crucis, Via Lucis*."

analogies: "Themis like *Doom* begins on earth and ends in heaven."[50] For her, individualism and intellectualism are comparable with the Fall, since they result in abandonment of the religious origins of society, namely the unanimity that is sanctioned by Themis and that solemnly revolves around her.[51]

3. *Reality*

Reality consists for Harrison above all in the actions, not the thoughts, of human beings, or more precisely in actions that are "still" indissolubly linked with thought and feeling. Thus only rituals have religious reality; myths do not.[52] Nevertheless, Harrison distinguishes different grades of

[50] Harrison, *Themis* (above, note 1) 483. On the *interpretatio christiana*, see also note 114, below.

[51] Although in *Prolegomena* (above, note 11) 261 Themis was for Harrison "but another name for Gaia" (cf. Aeschylus, *Prometheus* 209 f.), the word is exalted, in *Themis* (above, note 1) 533 f. to a religious name for "social order;" see also the definition, *ibid.*, 485 f.: "In a word Themis is not religion, she is the stuff of which religious representations are made. . . . She is the substratum of each and every god, she is in a sense above as well as below each and every god, but herself never quite a full-fledged divinity." For Harrison, Themis represents the origin of religion, an origin which she defines as "not spiritual and individual, but social and collective;" cf. *ibid.*, 28. Individualism, for Harrison, includes theology (the development of individual anthropomorphic gods) and the accompanying rationalism that suppresses the emotional, ritual impulses of art and religion; cf. *ibid.*, 42–48. After the outbreak of World War I, however, she bids a disappointed farewell, in the "Epilogue on the War: Peace with Patriotism," to her glorification of collectivism: "For five long years, in season and out, I have preached collectivism—its relation to life and religion, its inspirations, its perils. . . . With collectivism, for argument's sake, I have ceased to conjure;" *Alpha & Omega* (above, note 12) 234 f.

[52] Harrison retains this conception through all the variations in her understanding of the relationship between ritual and myth, from the definition of myth as "ritual practice misunderstood" (cf. above, note 19) to the idea, introduced in *Themis* (above, note 1) 331 that "the myth is the plot of the δρώμενον." The latter idea does not merely equate ritual and myth (thus Burkert, "Griechische Mythologie" [above, note 32] 175) but constitutes a yet more emphatic elevation of ritual over myth; according to Harrison, ritual has no need whatever of such a "plot." Harrison consistently assumes the priority of ritual, as she sometimes assumes the possibility that the myth may have arisen simultaneously; see *Themis* 13 and 16. For agreement with Harrison's ritualism, cf. S. E. Hyman, "The Ritual View of Myth and the Mythic," in T. A. Sebeok (ed.), *Myth: A Symposium* (Bloomington and London 1965) 136–53; against this: J. Fontenrose, *The Ritual Theory of Myth* (Berkeley/Los Angeles/London 1967) 26–35. Cf. also C. Kluckhohn, "Myths and Rituals: A General Theory," *Harvard Theological Review* 35 (1942) 60 n. 61; S.G.F. Brandon, "The Myth and Ritual Position Critically Considered," in S. H. Hooke (ed.,) *Myth, Ritual, and Kingship: Essays on the Theory and Practice of Kingship in the Ancient Near East and in Israel* (Oxford 1958) 262 f. For pro-ritualistic "second thoughts" (with the help of ethology), see W. Burkert, *Structure and History in Greek Mythology and Ritual* [= Sather Classical Lectures 47] (Berkeley/Los Angeles/London 1979) 36 ff. Burkert, like Harrison, assumes that ritual is older than myth; but cf. his even-handed definition, *ibid.*, 57: "'Myth' means telling a tale with suspended reference, structured by some basically human action pattern; ritual is stereotyped action redirected for demonstration. Thus both are dependent on action programs, both are detached from pragmatic reality, both serve

reality according to her evolutionistic model of religion, which favors the origins: the older a ritual, the more authentic is its relation to reality.[53] In her autobiography she confesses the subjective preference that underlies her theoretical interests: "A thing has little charm for me unless it has on it the patina of age. Great things in literature, Greek plays for example, I most enjoy when behind their bright splendours I see moving darker and older shapes. That must be my *apologia pro vita mea*."[54]

Jane Harrison's sympathy with the "dark" and "older"[55] entities that lie behind the surface of things, texts, pictures, and scenes is not to be confused with an interest in the past and in history *per se*; the contrary is true. The old things that interest her are exactly the things that are not yet past, that are still operative in the present, and that shine through the new and emerge

---

communication." Cf. also H. S. Versnel, "Gelijke monniken, gelijke kappen: Myth and Ritual, oud en nieuw," *Lampas* 17.2 (1984) 194–246, English version now in L. Edmunds (ed.), *Approaches to Greek Myth* (Baltimore/London, 1990) 25-90. On Harrison's definition of ritual as "re-done or pre-done" (in *Themis*) see below, note 116; cf. *Alpha & Omega* (above, note 12) 175: "ritual deadens the intellect and stimulates will, desire, emotion;" on the analogy between theology and mythology; *ibid.*, 202: "mythology is only, like eikonism, the attempted expression of the unknown in terms of the known; it usually obscures rather than illuminates religion;" *ibid.*, 186: "Theology is the letter that killeth, religion the spirit that maketh alive." Cf. also above, note 42.

[53] According to Harrison, the oldest rituals are derived from the "life-impulse," as it is expressed in the magic of "primitive" peoples, and survive in "mystery-cults and sacraments;" cf., e.g., Harrison, *Alpha & Omega* (above, note 12) 174 f.

[54] Harrison, *Reminiscences* (above, note 11) 86 f.; cf. *Alpha & Omega* (above, note 12) 201. Harrison here refers to the book written by John Henry Newman (1801–90), the Anglican theologian who converted to Catholicism in 1845 and later became a Cardinal, *Apologia pro vita sua: Being a History of His Religious Opinions* (1864). Harrison's paraphrase seems to allude to her similar revulsion from her Anglican background and to her own "conversion"—to the anthropology of Greek religion. On conversion experiences in her life, cf. (on her relinquishing the classicistic attitude toward art) Harrison, "Unanimism and Conversion," in *Alpha & Omega* 42 ff. (see also above, note 18); Stewart, *J. E. Harrison* (above, note 11) 115; Ackerman, "Early Work" (above, note 8) 223; Peacock, *The Mask* (above, note 30) 70 ff. (letters to Donald Sutherland MacColl, whom Harrison describes as her "paraclete," "Convincer of Sin and Consoler in my miracle play," *ibid.*, 74). After a dream which she regarded as a spiritual rebirth comparable to a mystic communion, she wrote to Murray in 1912, " Do you think a blasphemous Ker could be converted?" (Stewart 113). (Harrison, whose mother died four weeks after her birth, often signed her letters "Ker," a Greek spirit of death.) On Harrison's "apologia" cited in the text, cf. also the introduction to *Themis* (above, note 1) xxv: "I . . . still confess, that I have little natural love for what an Elizabethan calls 'ye Beastly Devices of ye Heathen.' Savages, save for their reverent, totemistic attitude towards animals, weary and disgust me, though perforce I spend long hours in reading of their tedious doings. My good moments are when, through the study of things primitive, I come to a better understanding of some song of a Greek poet or some saying of a Greek philosopher." On "ye Beastly Devices of ye Heathen," see also *Reminiscences* (above, note 11) 83; Murray, *Five Stages of Greek Religion* (1925; third edition: New York 1951; reprint: 1955) 2; Guthrie, *The Greeks and Their Gods* (above, note 15) 19; C. Segal, *Tragedy and Civilization: An Interpretation of Sophocles* (Cambridge MA and London 1981) 14.

[55] These are the "some neglected aspects of Greek religion" of which Harrison speaks in the first sentences of *Prolegomena* (above, note 11) vii.

into the light.[56] Harrison conforms to Enlightenment values insofar as she tries to assist the old things in this process of emergence—but her intention is to conserve them. At school she developed an insurmountable "dislike for history,"[57] in particular for revolutions and other wars and especially for the "rulers" and "conquerors" who, as great men, make history.[58]

On the other hand, this hostility to history seems to contradict her historicizing and often even euhemeristic approach to mythical figures and stories. For Harrison, it is beyond question that Orpheus, Theseus, or Minos actually lived.[59] And because the "development" to the status of a god is for Harrison a late stage of religious history,[60] it is not difficult for her to see, even in gods and in cultic heroes, "original" spirits, primarily in

[56] Implicitly Harrison here places herself in the universal-historical tradition of German idealism (Schiller, Wilhelm von Humboldt). Cf. Renate Schlesier, "Religion als Gegenbild. Zu einigen geschichtstheoretischen Aspekten von Eduard Meyers Universalhistorie," in W. M. Calder III and A. Demandt (eds.), *Eduard Meyer: Leben und Leistung eines Universalhistorikers* (Leiden 1990) 368–416. Harrison explicitly takes over Tylor's concept of "survivals" (cf. above, note 21), but unlike him she does not wish to eliminate them but rather to emphasize their worth and to become their ally, as the Romantics did.

[57] Harrison, *Reminiscences* (above, note 11) 35.

[58] Cf. Harrison, *Alpha & Omega* (above, note 12) 221–59; see also her letter to Gilbert Murray (June 1922): "my hatred of history, newspapers, politics, and politicians," in Stewart, *J. E. Harrison* (above, note 11) 47.

[59] On Orpheus, see Harrison, *Prolegomena* (above, note 11) 469: "Orpheus was a real man, a mighty singer, a prophet and a teacher, bringing with him a new religion, seeking to reform the old one. He was martyred and after his death his tomb became a mantic shrine"; see also 455. But on the reality of Minos and other heroes, cf. *Themis* (above, note 1) 261 f. On Harrison's criticism of Euhemerism, cf. also notes 62 and 115, below.

[60] On Harrison's position, cf. *Prolegomena* (above, note 11) 322–62, chapter VII: "The Making of a God;" *Themis* (above, note 1) 260–340, chapter VIII: "Daimon and Hero," 364–444, chapter IX: "From Daimon to Olympian." A similar view on the priority of hero to god was held by Creuzer (above, note 24, vol. 3, 749 ff.), Rohde, *Psyche. Seelencult und Unsterblichkeitsglaube der Griechen* (1890/1894, [cf. above, note 40], second edition: Freiburg im Breisgau/Leipzig/Tübingen 1898; reprint: Darmstadt 1974); and Ulrich von Wilamowitz-Moellendorff, *Euripides. Herakles* (1889), vol. 2 (second edition: Berlin 1895; new edition: Darmstadt 1959; reprint: 1984). In *Prolegomena* Harrison agrees with Rohde's explanation of hero-cult as an outgrowth of the cult of the dead, but in *Themis* she opposes to Rohde's view (and to her own views in her earlier works) her new thesis of the hero as year-daimon; cf., e.g., 374 n. 1. On Rohde's importance for Harrison, see notes 74, 78 93, 122, below. Hermann Usener (1834–1905), on the other hand, viewed the hero as a demoted god: *Götternamen. Versuch einer Lehre von der religiösen Begriffsbildung* (1896; third edition: Frankfurt am Main 1948); cf. also "Göttliche Synonyme" (1898), in *Kleine Schriften*, vol. 4: *Arbeiten zur Religionsgeschichte* (Leipzig and Berlin 1913) 259–306. On Usener see R. Kany, *Mnemosyne als Programm. Geschichte, Erinnerung und die Andacht zum Unbedeutenden im Werk von Usener, Warburg und Benjamin* [= Studien zur deutschen Literatur 93] (Tübingen 1987) 13–128; J. Bremmer, "Hermann Usener," in *Classical Scholarship* (above, note 8) 462–78. On Harrison's agreements and disagreements with Usener, cf., e.g., *Themis* 425 n. 1; *Alpha & Omega* (above, note 12) 161 (on the "Augenblicksgötter," an expression of Usener's); see also a letter (1908/09) to Frances Darwin, in Ackerman, "Some Letters of the Cambridge Ritualists," *GRBS* 12 (1971) 123. Against the thesis of the hero as a "faded god," but also against Harrison's

plant or animal form,[61] or embodiments of social experience.[62] Like
Heinrich Schliemann,[63] with whose co-worker Wilhelm Dörpfeld[64] she

assumption of a (totemistic) "polydaimonism" previous to (anthropomorphic)
"polytheism," see L. R. Farnell, *Greek Hero Cults and Ideas of Immortality* [= Gifford
Lectures 1920] (Oxford 1921) 19–52; 280 ff. On this controversy today, cf. Burkert,
Griechische Religion (above, note 3) 314: "Sowohl-Als auch."

[61] In *Prolegomena* the hero (as originally bound to a local cult) is conceived of as a
transitional stage between "ghost" and god; the shape in which he prefers to manifest
himself is the snake (see also note 67, below), in contrast to the anthropomorphism of the
individualized and universalized Olympians. In *Themis* this idea is expanded and
systematized. Here the generic term for the postulated pretheistic stage and its "survivals"
is the *daimon*, who can assume the most varied shapes—animal (preferably, once again,
the snake), plant, stone, etc.—and represents, in tribal rites, fertility and the seasonal
rhythms of life. Totemism is for Harrison now the religious phenomenon—religious
because it is magical!—*par excellence*; it is the identification of man with animal (see also
above, note 44), which requires no god. Theoretically she is here less close to Robertson
Smith and Frazer than to Durkheim (cf. below, note 62) and to Lucien Lévy-Bruhl (1857–
1939), from whom she borrows the term "participation" from *Les fonctions mentales dans
les sociétés inférieures* (1910). Cf. *Themis* (above, note 1) especially 122, 128–31.

[62] Cf. Harrison, *Themis* (above, note 1) 315: "The *daimon* proper, we have seen, was a
collective representation expressing not a personality so much as a function, or at least a
functionary, the eponym of a gens, the *basileus* of a state." *Ibid.*, 478: "a god is a real
thing—a real thing because he is the utterance of a real collective emotion." On the choice
of terminology: Harrison speaks of "representation," of "utterance" and "incarnation"
(e.g. 154, 156), not of "symbolism" (cf., against this term, *ibid.*, 262, 264). Shallow
rationalistic Euhemerism has also become suspect in Harrison's eyes; cf. *ibid.*, 261 f. In
her terminology (especially the term "representation") and to some extent in her thought
(cf. above, note 61), Harrison is now being influenced by contemporary French sociology
of religion, particularly Émile Durkheim (1858–1917) and the essays he published in
L'Année Sociologique and in the *Revue de Métaphysique et de Morale* (cf. especially
Themis 476 f., 486 n. 3; see also 29 n. 2, 63 n. 1, 390 n. 5, and note 110, below).
Durkheim's chief work, *Les formes élémentaires de la vie religieuse*, appeared in 1912, the
year in which *Themis* was published. Cf. also Harrison, *Epilegomena* (above, note 49) 6
f., 12, 15. According to G. H. Hartman, "Structuralism: The Anglo-American Adventure,"
in *Beyond Formalism: Literary Essays* 1958–70 (New Haven and London 1970) 3–23,
Harrison was just as much a predecessor of Northrop Frye's anthropological interpretation
of literature as was Durkheim of Lévi-Strauss's structural anthropology; Hartman (7)
considers Harrison one of "our first modern and inspired structuralists." Cf. also F. M.
Turner, *The Greek Heritage in Victorian Britain* (New Haven and London 1981) 127 f.

[63] Harrison saw in the work of Schliemann (1822–1890) proof that visions can become
real: "We Hellenists were, in truth, at that time 'a people who sat in darkness', but we were
soon to see a great light, two great lights—archaeology, anthropology. Classics were
turning in their long sleep. Old men began to see visions, young men to dream dreams. I
had just left Cambridge when Schliemann began to dig at Troy" [i.e., in 1870—but
Harrison did not move from Cambridge to London until 1880], *Reminiscences* (above,
note 11) 82 f. On Schliemann cf. *Archäologenbildnisse* (above, note 24) 45 f.; W. M.
Calder III and Justus Cober (editors), *Heinrich Schliemann nach Hundert Jahren*
(Frankfurt/Main 1990). On moving to London and beginning to lecture at the British
Museum, Harrison formed and maintained close ties with (chiefly German) archaeologists;
see above, note 33; cf. also *Reminiscences* 64: "All my archaeology was taught me by
Germans."

[64] On Wilhelm Dörpfeld (1853–1940) and Schliemann, cf. Rumpf, *Archäologie* (above,
note 24) 94 f.; *Archäologenbildnisse* 112 f. On Harrison and Dörpfeld, see *Reminiscences*

maintained close scholarly ties for decades, Harrison (until she turned to the sociology of religion) considered all non-divine figures of ancient mythology to have been real persons of the remote past. At bottom she thereby adopts the attitude of one of her favorite ancient authors, Pausanias. But Pausanias' methods cannot distinguish critically between history and fiction.[65]

4. Anthropomorphism

Jane Harrison regarded anthropomorphism as a universal religious phenomenon, which, however, harmonized particularly well with the Greek tendency to clarity and rationality.[66] True, in Greece as in all other parts of

---

(above, note 11) 65; Calder (above, n. 63).   The most important result of their collaboration was the two books *Mythology & Monuments* (above, note 8; see especially xiv) and *Primitive Athens as Described by Thucydides* (Cambridge 1906), in which Harrison augmented Dörpfeld's topographical researches with detailed comments on the history of cult.

[65] Harrison is most influenced by Pausanias' Euhemerism and accepts it most uncritically in *Mythology & Monuments* (above, note 8).   But in later books she continues to cite Pausanias constantly as a reliable authority; Harrison supplies his "customary vagueness" (*Prolegomena* [above, note 11] 68) with her own conjectures and speculations.   On the possibility of preserving Euhemerism and simultaneously maintaining a critical distance from it by ritualistic interpretation of vase-paintings, cf. *ibid.*, 283 n. 3; on Euhemerism see also above, note 62, and note 115, below.   On the trustworthiness of Pausanias, cf. C. Habicht, *Pausanias' "Guide to Greece"* [= Sather Classical Lectures 50] (Berkeley/Los Angeles/London 1985).

[66] Such an idea of Greek anthropomorphism remains constant in Harrison's work (see also note 70, below), but she judges anthropomorphism positively only in passing, in *Introductory Studies in Greek Art* (1885; fifth edition: London 1902) 180 f.; on the primarily aesthetic quality of anthropomorphism, cf. *ibid.*, 175 ff. Harrison conceives of religious development as a process of "gradual anthropomorphism," as a "passage from sprite and ghost and demon to full-fledged divinity": *Prolegomena* (above, note 11) 240. In *Themis* (above, note 1) xi, she explicitly describes this process as an accelerating departure from specifically religious characteristics, and concludes that the Olympians are "*non*-religious;" cf. *ibid.*, 447: "We think and write of the gods of the Greeks as anthropomorphic, 'of human form' or 'shape.' The clumsy word is too narrow; its associations are rather of art than of religion. The word used by Herodotus ἀνθρωποφύης 'of human growth' or 'nature' is wider and better." Cf. *Alpha & Omega* (above, note 12) 198 f. See also Harrison's association of anthropomorphism with sexuality, *Themis* 371: "Because Eros is human there is excess and ugliness waiting to shadow and distort nature's lovely temperance" [sic!].   On Harrison's ambivalent autobiographical remarks on sexuality, cf., e.g., the letter to Frances Darwin (later Mrs. F. M. Cornford) 1908/09, in Ackerman, "Some Letters" (above, note 60) 123: "Yes the world *is* a ruthless place & sex the most ruthless thing in it." See also the letter to Murray, 28 August 1909, in Stewart, *J. E. Harrison* (above, note 11) 119: "sex . . . I think it *the* wonder and beauty of the world— only apt to go all wrong and ugly." See also the letter to Murray, January 1914, *ibid.*, 141: "one would think sex was more sublimated in woman." In *Reminiscences* (above, note 11) 34, she mentions her own "sixty years of sex-subservience," and mentions also (88–90) her life-long tendency to fall in love again and again; cf. also notes 73 and 94, below.

the world spirits of the dead, demons, specific animals (especially snakes[67] and birds) were worshipped; but the oldest literary sources, the Homeric epics, already attest unambiguously anthropomorphic gods, the Olympians, whom Harrison understood as sublime but no longer genuinely religious figures:

> We are apt to regard the advance to anthropomorphism as necessarily a clear religious gain. A gain it is in so far as a certain element of barbarity is softened or extruded, but with this gain comes loss, the loss of the element of formless, monstrous mystery. The ram-headed Knum of the Egyptians is to the mystic more religious than any of the beautiful divine humanities of the Greek. Anthropomorphism provides a store of lovely motives for art, but that spirit is scarcely religious which makes of Eros a boy trundling a hoop, of Apollo a youth aiming a stone at a lizard, of Nike a woman who stoops to tie her sandal. Xenophanes put his finger on the weak spot of anthropomorphism.[68]

[67] The snake was, if not Harrison's favorite animal—that was probably the bear, above all the "she-bear," cf. Peacock, *The Mask* [above, note 30] 109–15—at least the animal whose "demonism" most fascinated her (see also above, note 61) and spoke most personally to her. Cf. the letter to Murray, December 1900, in Stewart, *J. E. Harrison* (above, note 11) 32, in which she describes herself as a "particular Eve" with a "fell curiosity;" she would only too gladly let herself be seduced by the "bad serpent" (here an ironic description of her former teacher A. W. Verrall). The snake is already a leitmotiv in Harrison's "Delphika" (above, note 40), the most important preliminary study for *Prolegomena*; the association of female divinities with snakes is there interpreted as a "survival" of the cult of the "earth genii" in serpent form. Harrison here follows Eduard Gerhard (cf. above, note 24), who, "with an insight extraordinary for his time, divined that practically nearly all the women goddesses of Greece are but modifications of one primitive goddess—Mother Earth" ("Delphika" 220 f.); the quotation that follows, from Gerhard's *Über Metroon und Göttermutter* (1849) (cf. *Prolegomena* 263 n. 1), in which Themis is mentioned, among others, and the "serpent symbol" appears as a chief attribute of goddesses, seems almost an anticipatory summary of Harrison's life-work—except that (in contrast to Gerhard) even at that time she would understand the serpent not only as "merely the symbol of the primitive earth daemon, but her [sic!] actual supposed vehicle;" cf. also *ibid.*, 235: "the snake is the symbol and vehicle of the earth oracle" (*contra* Crusius' interpretation as a "Raumausfüllung"). The equation of serpent and phallus is not, in Harrison's view, something original, cf. *Themis* (above, note 1) 266 n. 2: "Probably at first the snake was the totemistic vehicle of reincarnation and only later, when the true nature of parentage was known, identified with the φάλλος." In the last text published in her lifetime, the Foreword to the second edition of *Themis* (viii), she hails the serpent/dragon (the Delphic Python), killed by the Olympians, as "still unreasonably dear to me." Cf. Francis M. Cornford in the obituary note for Harrison in the *Newnham College Newsletter*, January 1929: "Her intuitive sense that snakes and Gorgons lurk at the root of true religion" (quoted by Stewart, *J. E. Harrison* [above, note 11] 87).

[68] Harrison, *Prolegomena* (above, note 11) 258. Knum is "more solemn, more religious than any human Zeus the Greeks have left us;" see *Themis* (above, note 1) 114. On the motives for Harrison's condemnation of the god Eros, see above, note 66.

Following in the footsteps of Xenophanes—though without reference to his moralistic criticism of the (to him) by no means "lovely" gods[69]—and in explicitly heretical opposition to the account of Creation in the Jewish and Christian scriptures, Harrison repeatedly postulates (it virtually becomes a leitmotiv) that man made the gods in his own image.[70] The problem of how all these different forms of anthropomorphism could arise is easily solved: Harrison applies the evolutionary model as a sort of bed of Procrustes. But the constructions that she contrives to this end are not necessarily consistent or tenable.

For example, she states that the completely anthropomorphic gods reflect the "gentler affections"[71] of civilized people, who have become conscious of their humanity, while evil spirits correspond to barbaric states of development. Of course Harrison is aware that this comforting evolutionary model does not come off without a hitch: "to be human is not necessarily to be humane."[72] The explanation of the animal form of gods and ghosts by anthropomorphism presents even fewer difficulties to Harrison: primitive man, according to her, simply did not yet distinguish strictly between himself and the animals.[73]

[69] See Xenophanes, 21 B, frg. 11–12 (Diels-Kranz). Harrison refers chiefly to frg. 14–16. Cf. W. Jaeger, *The Theology of the Early Greek Philosophers* [= Gifford Lectures 1936] (Oxford 1947) 38–54, especially 47–50.

[70] See, e.g., Harrison, *Prolegomena* (above, note 11) 363: "So far the formula for Greek theology has been, 'Man makes the gods in his own image.'" Cf. 476: "The old orthodox anthropomorphic religion of Greece made the gods in man's image, but, having made them, kept them aloof, distinct. It never stated in doctrine, it never implied in ritual, that man could become god. Nay more, against any such aspiration it raised again and again a passionate protest. To seek to become even *like* the gods was to the Greek the sin most certain to call down divine vengeance, it was 'Insolence.'" See also, as a general pronouncement on the psychology of religion, *ibid.*, 257, 561, 564, and *Alpha & Omega* (above, note 12) 172: "We are all of us born in sin; in that sin which is to science 'the seventh and deadliest,' anthropomorphism, we are egocentric, egoprojective. Hence necessarily we make our gods in our own image." Cf. also notes 72 and 127, below.

[71] Harrison, *Prolegomena* (above, note 11) 258.

[72] *Ibid.*, 72, with the addition of a characteristic variant: "Man is cruel and implacable, and he makes the ghost after his own image." See also (*ibid.*, 564) the variation (which points ahead to *Themis*): "Man makes the rites of the gods in the image of his human conduct. The mysteries of these man-made gods are but the eternal mysteries of the life of man." On anthropomorphism, cf. above, notes 66 and 70.

[73] Harrison started here from one of the basic assumptions of evolutionistic anthropology, the equation of the "primitive" and the child (see above, note 44). The procedure of Sigmund Freud (1856–1939) was comparable, based as it was on a similar analogy between "phylogenesis" and "ontogenesis;" cf. R. Schlesier, *Konstruktionen der Weiblichkeit bei Sigmund Freud. Zum Problem von Entmythologisierung und Remythologisierung in der psychoanalytischen Theorie* (Frankfurt am Main 1981) [second edition 1990: *Mythos und Weiblichkeit bei Sigmund Freud*] 22, 127. Freud spoke of the child as "der kleine Primitive": *Abriß der Psychoanalyse* (1938) in *Gesammelte Werke*, vol. 17 (fourth edition: Frankfurt am Main 1966) 111. In 1912–13 (that is, in the same period as Harrison's *Themis* and Durkheim's *Formes élémentaires de la vie religieuse*) Freud published *Totem und Tabu*, in which he refers primarily to the work of the English

The situation becomes more complicated for Harrison in the case of the Satyrs, with their equine attributes, since she considers them a late religious phenomenon. In this case, she admits, the general rule of progress from animal form to human form is broken. But Harrison is not at a loss for a rational explanation of this "reverse case" of the Satyrs. They are not "powers of fertilization" but distorted representations of an "actual primitive population," the Thracian Satrai; they have been transformed into monsters by the "malign imagination of the conquerors."[74]

---

anthropological school—Tylor, Lang, Robertson Smith, and Frazer (he seems not to have known of Harrison's work). Freud's works repeatedly influenced Harrison (see also below, note 100), though more often implicitly than explicitly. She refers to him especially after reading *Totem und Tabu*. The chapter "Totem, Tabu and Exogamy" in her *Epilegomena* (above, note 49) "is based on Durkheim and Freud" (7 n. 1) and directed against Frazer's separation of exogamy and totemism. She enthusiastically adopts Freud's theory of *ambivalence* (a term coined by Bleuler) as an explanation of the double character of taboo and holiness (*ibid.*, 10 f.) and refers, in the Foreword to the second edition of *Themis* (above, note 1) viii, to Freud's theory as the basis for her "half reluctant palinode" in *Epilegomena*: "the psychology of Freud has taught me that the full-blown god, the Olympian, has a biological function which could never be adequately filled by the *daimon*." On the other hand, she felt repelled by Freud's theories of sexuality and the therapy based on them; the "obscenities" in James Joyce's *Ulysses*, she remarks indignantly, "made me feel as though I were in a psycho-analyst's consulting room with a patient forced to unburden himself of every thought, every impression, however feeble and seemingly irrelevant:" *Reminiscences* (above, note 11) 25; cf. also *ibid.*, 81 f.: "By temperament I am, if not a prude, at least a Puritan, and at first the ugliness of it all [i.e., Freud's topics] sickened me. . . . Still I struggled on, feeling somehow that behind and below all this sexual mud was something big and real. Then fortunately I lighted on *Totemism and Taboo*, and at once the light broke and I felt again the sense of release. Here was a big constructive imagination; here was a mere doctor laying bare the origins of Greek drama as no classical scholar had ever done, teaching the anthropologist what was really meant by his *totem and taboo*, probing the mysteries of sin, of sanctity, of sacrament—a man who, because he understood, purged the human spirit from fear." See also (*ibid.*, 39) her description of the attitude of her father (a timber merchant) toward her books, which she regularly sent him as soon as they appeared: "I am sure he never read them, and I suspect his feelings towards them was what the Freudians call *ambivalent*—half shame, half pride." On Freud's importance for Harrison, cf. Stewart, *J. E. Harrison* (above, note 11) 3, 181, 184; Ackermann, "Early Work" (above, note 8) 215 f.; Peacock, *The Mask* (above, note 30) 182, 201, 203, 236 f. On Harrison's attitude toward sex, see above, note 66, and note 99, below.

[74] Harrison, *Prolegomena* (above, note 11) 386, cf. 379–88, *passim*. In her thesis of the Thracian origins of Dionysos and his circle Harrison was following P. Kretschmer, "Semele und Dionysos," in *Aus der Anomia* (Berlin 1890) 17 ff. (cf. *Prolegomena* 403 n. 2; 411 n. 1), and Rohde, *Psyche* (above, note 60) vol. 2, 1 ff. Dodds too accepted the theory of a non-Greek origin (despite the archaeological findings that clearly contradict the idea): *Euripides. Bacchae*, ed. E. R. Dodds (Oxford 1944; second edition: 1960) xx ff. Against the Thracian origin and on the motivation behind this theory, see now Susan G. Cole, "Mail-Order Maenads" (*sub prelo*). On Harrison's *interpretatio thracica* of Dionysos, see note 122, below; on the Maenads, see note 129, below.

But when in *Themis* Harrison finally styles the Satyrs "fertility-daimones"[75]—as she describes, incidentally, almost all other male figures of ancient Greek religion—she replaces the historicizing interpretation with a naturalistic one, but she maintains substantially unchanged the thesis that anthropomorphism is a higher and later stage of religious history in which primitive and earlier stages are contained or negated.

5. *Daimon Versus God*

Among the most constant elements in Harrison's conception of religion is the conviction that the *daimon* belongs, in comparison with the god, to an earlier, more original stage of evolution.[76] For her the terms *"daimon,"* "ghost," "spirit," and "sprite" are largely interchangeable. Nevertheless the *daimones* were differently evaluated in Harrison's two main works. In *Prolegomena* the *daimones* are classified mainly under the rubric of the apotropaic[77] and are viewed as something evil to be averted—though the

[75] Satyrs are discussed in *Themis* (above, note 1) especially on page 14 (as *daimones*, like Silenoi, Kuretes, Bakchoi, and Tityroi, with reference to Strabo); cf. 25, 59, 182, 200, 372. The connection of Satyrs with "fertility" (a term which for Harrison refers not primarily to sexuality but to agriculture) is anticipated in *Prolegomena* (above, note 11) 420 f.; here by an etymological construction she sees the Satyrs as originally barley-juice drinkers: "Tragedy I believe to be not the 'goat-song,' but the 'harvest-song' of the cereal τράγος, the form of spelt known as 'the goat.'" On this controversial point, cf. H. Patzer, *Die Anfänge der griechischen Tragödie* [= Schriften der wissenschaftlichen Gesellschaft an der Johann Wolfgang Goethe-Universität Frankfurt am Main, Geisteswissenschaftliche Reihe 3] (Wiesbaden 1962) especially 57–67, 114–20 (where, on 115, the concept of Satyrs as "daimons of fertility" is adopted—though without mention of Harrison's name). A. W. Pickard-Cambridge, *Dithyramb, Tragedy, and Comedy* (Oxford 1927) 164–66 [cf. second edition, edited by T.B.L. Webster (Oxford 1962) 123 f.] agrees with Harrison in rejecting the "goat-song" theory (from τράγος, he-goat) but opposes her and Murray's theory of the year-daimon (*ibid.*, 185–206; cf. Webster, more positively, second edition 126–29) and cautiously refrains from interpretation. But cf. R. Seaford (ed.), *Euripides. Cyclops* (Oxford 1984) 5–16, who, however, refers not to Harrison but to the adoption of her ritualistic position by Cornford (16 n. 48) and George Thomson (14 n. 44).

[76] The priority of the *daimon* over the god was Harrison's fundamental conception in *Prolegomena* as well as in *Themis* (cf. above, note 60). The religious-historical basis for this idea was the thesis that the monsters of Greek mythology, like the Gorgon Medusa, "beyond all doubt were borrowed from the east" (*Introductory Studies* [above, note 66] 157 f.) and thus originally were part of the older oriental religions. Cf. now Burkert, *Die orientalisierende Epoche in der griechischen Religion and Literatur* [= Sitzungsberichte der Heidelberger Akademie der Wissenschaften, Philosophisch-Historische Klasse, 1984, Bericht 1] (Heidelberg 1984); "Oriental and Greek Mythology: The Meeting of Parallels," in J. Bremmer (ed.), *Interpretations of Greek Mythology* (London and Sidney 1987) 10–40.

[77] See, e.g., Harrison, *Prolegomena* (above, note 11) 190. On the problem of the term, cf. R. Schlesier, s.v. "Apopompe," s.v. "Apotropäisch," in H. Cancik, B. Gladigow, and M. Laubscher (eds.), *Handbuch religionswissenschaftlicher Grundbegriffe*, vol. 2 (Stuttgart/Berlin/Köln/Mainz 1990) 38–45. For Harrison, the Gorgon is apotropaic *par excellence*; she is "a sort of incarnate Evil Eye" (*Prolegomena* 196; 197 n. 1, with reference to Jahn's pioneering work of 1855; cf. Schlesier, "Jahn und der böse Blick"

Erinyes/Eumenides are of course a significant exception.[78] But in *Themis* the positive side of the *daimones* is stressed, that is, their tendency to promote fertility and to renew social unity by the feasts of the annual cycle.[79] The male gods and the heroes were all originally *"Eniautos-daimones,"*[80] *daimones* of the year-beginning, who were worshipped

[above, note 35]). Jahn was one of the "authorities" cited in Harrison's *Myths of the Odyssey* (above, note 21) 217.

[78] In 1899, in "Delphika" (above, note 40), Harrison had already undertaken to vindicate the Erinyes, whom she interpreted as originally Eumenides, the "Kindly Ones." Aeschylus' conception of these figures was, she insisted, a "misrepresentation;" "the hideous form given to the Erinyes" was a novelty which was to be ascribed to the tragedian (*ibid.*, 247). See also *Mythology & Monuments* (above, note 8) 560–62 (against Jebb). Harrison develops this position in *Prolegomena* (above, note 11), especially 213–56. As a matter of fact, Harrison there follows the interpretation of K. O. Müller (on his importance for Harrison, see above, section I) in his *Aeschylos Eumeniden. Griechisch und Deutsch. Mit erläuternden Abhandlungen über die aüssere Darstellung und über den Inhalt und die Composition dieser Tragödie* (Göttingen 1833); cf. "Delphika" 206 (Harrison quotes the second revised English edition of 1853): "C. O. Müller states distinctly that the Erinyes 'were neither more nor less than a particular form of the great goddesses who rule the earth and the lower world and send up the blessings of the year, namely Demeter and Cora.'" With this interpretation she combines, in agreement with Rohde's *Psyche* (above, note 60), "this fundamental truth, that the Erinyes are angry souls," and amalgamates the two interpretations as follows (*ibid.*, 213): "This snake form brings together the views of C. O. Müller and Rohde; it is a connecting link between ancestral ghosts and earth genii." Cf. *ibid*, 220, on the connection between Maenads and Erinyes (without reference to Aeschylus, *Eumenides* 500): "Maenads in mythology and Erinyes are only differenciations of the same fundamental idea." On Harrison's interpretation of the Maenads, cf. also notes 126 and 129, below. Harrison's sympathy with the Erinyes probably cannot be separated from her predilection for snakes (see above, note 67) and her emotional interest in the fate of murdered mothers (cf. above, note 54). See also "Delphika" 239: "All mother earth is polluted by the blood of a mother. There is no possible release from this physical fact, no atonement."

[79] That this interpretation is owing to a need for innocuous rationalization and an idealization of mythical "ugliness" is clear in many passages of *Themis*; see, e.g., 368 on Herakles, who is interpreted as a "fertility-daimon:" "So understood, the monstrosities of the story become real and even beautiful." On Harrison's attempts at harmonization, cf. also above, notes 49 and 80. On her glorification of the supposedly harmonious nature of collectivism and her later renunciation of this view (and incidentally her turning away from research on the history of religions altogether) after the outbreak of the First World War, see above, note 51.

[80] This term is an artificial blending of two terms found in a hymn to the Megistos Kouros (the Dictaean Zeus), an inscription discovered in Palaikastro on Crete and dating from the second or third century A.D.; the excavator R. C. Bosanquet had published it together with Harrison and Murray in 1908–09 in the *Annual of the British School at Athens* 15, 339–56; cf. Burkert, *Griechische Religion* (above, note 3) 168 f. and note 37; M. L. West, *The Orphic Poems* (Oxford 1983) 132. In *Themis* (above, note 1) 1–29, Harrison discusses the hymn, the last word of which, the name of the goddess, she chooses as the title of her book. On her interpretation of the word κοῦρος as "he of the Shorn-Hair" (paradigmatically Hippolytos), cf. *ibid.*, 337 and note 1; (see also in this sense, on the festival of Apatouria, P. Vidal-Naquet, "Le cru, l'enfant grec et le cuit," (1974), reprinted in: *Le chasseur noir. Formes de pensée et formes de société dans le monde grec* (Paris 1981) 190. Harrison considers the bull one of the original forms in which the

particularly in snake-form.[81] This announcement of Harrison's received the approbation of Gilbert Murray, who contributed a chapter to *Themis* on the ritual forms preserved in tragedy,[82] and of Francis Cornford, who attempted, in the chapter that he contributed, to apply the system sketched out in *Themis* to the origin of the Olympic games.[83]

The contrast of *daimon* and god that is typical of Harrison's work from the start rests on her never-questioned assumption that the terms *daimon* and *theos*, wherever they occur in Greek texts, always express two radically opposed religious ideas. But for this assumption, and for the suggestion that the *daimones* were intermediary beings or powers of evil, Harrison can

---

eniautos- ("year-") daimon was incarnated, and thus she is enabled to reconstruct a pre-theistic justification for and sublimation of animal sacrifice, the Christian implications of which cannot be overlooked (*Themis* 156): "This holy vehicle of the year's *mana*, this ἐνιαυτός-daimon who died for the people, became at Delphi and in many other places a bull-god, a divinity born of his own sacrifice, i.e. of his own sanctification. . . . To us the sacrifice of a god seems a miracle or a blasphemy, but when the god is seen to be begotten of the sacrifice the anomaly is softened." Harrison sees a mitigation of blood sacrifice particularly in the fact that it is (she assumes) an "annual ritual" that was connected with the belief in the "resurrection" of the slaughtered creature and thus subserved the spiritual participation and "communication" of the festival community. On the universality of the Eniautos-daimon, cf. 374: "Once the Eniautos-daimon comes to his own, and once it is recognized that it is his mask which each and every individual dead man eventually puts on, once it is seen that he, not the individual dead man, is the real 'Strong One,' 'Venerable One,' the essential 'Hero,' on whom the luck and life of the year depend . . . ;" cf. the reconstruction of the typical "life-history" of an Eniautos-daimon, a history which in Attic drama is constantly repeated and does not become monotonous only because of variations in name and "plot," *ibid.*, 331–40. For Harrison, the prototypical Eniautos-daimon is Dionysos (cf. note 122, below), as well as Zeus, Apollo, and Hermes; among the heroes it is particularly Herakles. With reference to Kretschmer (cf. above, note 74) she assumes that "Zeus-Young-Man, Zeus Kouros" and Dionysos are one and the same (*Themis* 48).

[81] Cf. above, note 67, and note 91, below.

[82] G. Murray (1866–1957), "Excursus on the Ritual Forms Preserved in Greek Tragedy," in *Themis* (above, note 1) 341–63. Eric Robertson Dodds (1893–1979), a student of Murray and in 1936 his successor as Regius Professor in Oxford, in his commentary on the *Bacchae* (above, note 74) xxvii, interprets the story of Pentheus as a reflection of "primitive sacrificial ritual," though he does not refer to Harrison's *Themis* or to Murray's contribution to Harrison's book. But cf. the Foreword (vii): "I must thank Professor Murray, to whose lectures on the *Bacchae* I, like so many others, owe my first real understanding of the play's greatness and of its religious background." On Harrison's *Prolegomena*: xii n.: ". . . should be used with caution." See also Dodds, *Missing Persons: An Autobiography* (Oxford 1977) 28 f., 180 f. On Dodds and Murray, cf. H. Lloyd-Jones, "E. R. Dodds" (1980), in : *Blood for the Ghosts: Classical Influences in the Nineteenth and Twentieth Centuries* (London 1982) 287–94. On Murray and Harrison: *ibid.*, 202 f. [= "Gilbert Murray." Jane Ellen Harrison Memorial Lecture at Newnham College, Cambridge, on 8 February 1980]. The interpretation of tragedy as sacrificial ritual was taken over again especially by Burkert, "Greek Tragedy and Sacrificial Ritual," *GRBS* 7 (1966) 87–121 (cf. 113 n. 61 on Murray and Harrison, though only on the concept of the Eniautos-daimon).

[83] F. M. Cornford (1874–1943), "The Origin of the Olympic Games," in *Themis* (above, note 1) 212–59 (= Chapter VII); cf. Burkert, *Homo Necans* (above, note 38) 109 n. 2, 114 n. 32.

point only to the ancient philosophers' attempts at systematization[84] and, even more, to the Fathers of the Church who built upon them. That the ancient Greek authors from the earliest times on would have presupposed an unbridgeable contradiction between *daimon* and *theos* clearly cannot be proved by quotations from Plato or Plutarch. On the contrary, the synonymous use of the two terms, already in Homer, and above all in tragedy,[85] speaks strongly against Harrison's thesis.

6. *Olympian Contra Chthonian*

Harrison's bias toward philosophically and theologically colored dualism is perhaps most clearly visible in the strict division between chthonians and Olympians which she systematizes in *Prolegomena*.[86] Here too she leans heavily on Plato and Plutarch and does not neglect to quote the notorious passage from Isocrates' *Address to Philip*—where, however, it is not the chthonians, but certain undifferentiated divinities against whom the *poleis* had to perform *apopompai*, who are set in opposition to the Olympians.[87]

[84] Cf. M. Detienne, *De la pensée religieuse à la pensée philosophique. La notion de Daïmôn dans le pythagorisme ancien* [= Bibliothèque de la Faculté de Philosophie et Lettres de l'Université de Liège 165] (Paris 1963).

[85] See G. François, *Le polythéisme et l'emploi au singulier des mots θεός, δαίμων dans la littérature grecque d'Homère à Platon* [= Bibliothèque de la Fac. de Philo. et Lettres de l'Université de Liège 157] (Paris 1957); R. Schlesier, "Daimon und Daimones bei Euripides," *Saeculum* 34 (1983) 267–79.

[86] Cf. especially Harrison, *Prolegomena* (above, note 11) 1–31 (Ch. I: "Olympian and Chthonic Ritual"). Harrison could not, at any period, take the Olympians seriously as gods that commanded respect (perhaps because of the lasting effects of her strict Christian upbringing?). In her first book she jokes, "We are sorry to find that these goodly craftsmen [sc. the Cyclopes] were put to ignoble use by Olympian matrons. . . . Let us hope the Olympian babies had good nerves": *Myths of the Odyssey* (above, note 21) 25 f. In *Mythology & Monuments* (above, note 8) iv, she presupposes a strict division "between popular *local* cults with their endless diversity and the orthodox and ultimately dominant Olympian hierarchy;" cf. 588 f. On Harrison's preference for the chthonians and Murray's equally stubborn adherence to the Olympians (*Five Stages* [above, note 54] 38–75), cf. Stewart, *J. E. Harrison* (above, note 11) 31: "In the characteristic postscript to her very first letter to G. M. [i.e., Gilbert Murray, 24. August 1900; Jane wrote to him: "I hope to send you soon the Diasia with the Fleece of Cursing stolen by the impostor Zeus," *ibid.*, 30; cf. note 103, below], Jane manages to convey her feelings about the Olympian gods. Her lifelong antipathy to these too perfect, magnified humans became a standing joke. The superposing of the official cults on the primitive chthonic nature-cults was the theme of the *Prolegomena*, and her sympathy was always with the superseded underdog."

[87] Isocrates 5 (*Philippos*) 117; cf. Harrison's "Pandora's Box" (above, note 40) 108 f.; *Prolegomena* (above, note 11) 8. See especially A. D. Nock, "The Cult of Heroes. Appendix 3: Deities and Rites of Aversion" (1944) in *Essays on Religion and the Ancient World*, ed. Z. Stewart (Oxford 1972; second edition: 1986) 599–601; Burkert, "Glaube und Verhalten: Zeichengehalt und Wirkungsmacht von Opferritualen," in O. Reverdin and J. Rudhardt (eds.), *Le sacrifice dans l'antiquité* [= Entretiens sur l'antiquité classique 27, Fondation Hardt] (Vandoeuvres-Genève 1981) 116 f.; J. D. Mikalson, *Athenian Popular Religion* (Chapel Hill and London 1983) 63 f. For older views, cf. P. Stengel, *Opferbräuche der Griechen* (Leipzig and Berlin 1910; reprint: Darmstadt 1972) 29;

Unfortunately it remains uncertain in the context who and what Isocrates means. As for Plato's genuinely clear and distinct separation of chthonian and Olympian divinities, this is presumably to be understood less as a document in the history of religion than as an expression of Plato's theory of religious reform.[88] Harrison can with greater justice point to Aeschylus' *Oresteia*. It is nevertheless doubtful whether the actual existence of a rigid separation between Olympians and chthonians in the Athens of the fifth century or earlier, or in other places at a similar time, can be deduced from Aeschylus' tragedies. Even in the case of Aeschylus we probably ought to reckon with attempts at theological reform.[89]

But when these qualifications have been made, it nonetheless remains true that Harrison forcefully and profitably drew the attention of historians of Greek religion to the difference between two utterly divergent categories of cult and sacrifice, which she characterized with the Latin formulae "do ut des" (the "Olympian" ritual of giving) and "do ut abeas" (the "chthonic" ritual of aversion).[90] It is questionable, however, whether this polarity

---

Wilamowitz, *Der Glaube der Hellenen*, vol. 1 (Berlin 1931; reprint: Darmstadt, fourth edition, 1973) 27; L. Gernet and A. Boulanger, *Le génie grec dans la religion* (Paris 1932) 287 f.

[88] Plato, *Leges* 8, 828 c: ἔτι δὲ καὶ τὸ τῶν χθονίων καὶ ὅσους αὖ θεοὺς οὐρανίους ἐπονομαστέον καὶ τὸ τῶν τούτοις ἑπομένων οὐ συμμεικτέον ἀλλὰ χωριστέον κτλ. See also 4, 717 a–b; cf. Harrison, *Prolegomena* (above, note 11) 349 with n. 3.

[89] The chorus names the ὕπατοι along with the χθόνιοι in Aeschylus, *Agamemnon* 89 (on the history of the interpretation of this passage, cf. J. Bollack, *Agamemnon 1. première partie: Prologue. Parados anapestique. Parodos lyrique I* [= Cahiers de Philologie 6] (Lille 1981) 98–101; *Supplices* 24 f. On Aeschylus' reforming intentions, cf. note 78, above; see also K. Reinhardt, *Aischylos als Regisseur und Theologe* [= Sammlung Überlieferung und Auftrag. Reihe Schriften 6] (Bern 1949).

[90] See Harrison, *Prolegomena* (above, note 11) 3, 7; on the problem of the term "aversion:" 10 n. 2; cf. *Themis* (above, note 1) 134, where she distances herself from the "gift-theory" of the formula *do ut des* and understands *do ut abeas* as a "variety" and "modification" of the *do ut des* theory of sacrifice; " she adds, "*do ut abeas* probably precedes *do ut des*." See also *Epilegomena* (above, note 49) 1: "The religious impulse is directed, if I am right, primarily to one end and one only, *the conservation and promotion of life*. This end is served in two ways, one negative, one positive, by the riddance of whatever is conceived to be hostile and by the enhancement of whatever is conceived of as favourable to life. Religious rites are primarily of two kinds and two only, of *expulsion* and *impulsion*. Primitive man has before him, in order that he may live, the old dual task to get rid of evil, to secure good. Evil is to him of course mainly hunger and barrenness. Good is food and fertility. The Hebrew word for 'good' meant originally good to eat." See also, for this and for Mexican parellels, *Themis* 139 and 280. For (implicit) agreement with Harrison, cf. G. van der Leeuw, "Die *do-ut-des*-Formel in der Opfertheorie," *Archiv für Religionswissenschaft* 20 (1920–21) 241–53. On the theory of the reciprocity of giving (in archaic societies and in Roman, Indian, and Germanic law) as "potlatch," *nexum*, "Pfand," etc., see *Essai sur le don* (1923–24), in *Sociologie et anthropologie* (Paris 1950; third edition: 1966) 143–279, by Durkheim's nephew and student Marcel Mauss (1872–1950). A development of Harrison's dualistic separation between "Olympian" food-offerings and "chthonic" offerings destined for destruction is in K. Meuli, "Griechische Opferbräuche," in *Phyllobolia für Peter Von der Mühll zum 60. Geburtstag am 1. August*

corresponds to the contrast between spirits and gods, as Harrison maintains. Zeus Chthonios, for example, is for her only a ghost in snake form, with a new name.[91] But the epithets Chthonios and Chthonia, which refer to the earth and the underworld and are attested for widely different divinities, as well as Olympios and Olympia and many other epithets, seem rather to express the specificity of the Greek gods described by their locally variable and often contradictory cultic functions; the epithet "Olympian," in the epic and (in part) in the literature influenced by it, may well belong to a literary tendency toward stylization and universalization.[92] If this is true, then the contrast between chthonians and Olympians (though Harrison thought it self-evidently true) would scarcely be compatible with a model of cultic and social evolution.[93]

1945 (Basel 1946) 185–288 (with reference to paleolithic hunting) [= *Gesammelte Schriften*, ed. T. Gelzer, vol. 2 (Basel 1975) 907–1021]. Burkert follows Meuli at *Homo Necans* (above, note 38) 20 ff.; see also "Glaube und Verhalten" (above, note 87) 109 ff.; and "Greek Tragedy" (above, note 82) 102 ff., especially 103 f. n. 36.

[91] Zeus Chthonios (cf. *Prolegomena* [above, note 11] 17), in Harrisons's view, does not conflict with her interpretation of the festival of the Diasia (cf. also above, note 86) and her explanation of Zeus Meilichios as originally a snake-daimon, whose cult Zeus had violently appropriated: 8, 12–24. See also "Pandora's Box" (above, note 40) 114: "Meilichios is demonstrably nothing but a snake, the emblem of a hero cult." In *Themis* (above, note 1) 298, Meilichios is included in the class of ultimately undifferentiated "daimons of fertility." But already in *Prolegomena* 642 she writes, "Zeus Ktesios is not the Olympian of the thunderbolt, he is Zeus in nothing but the name. *Ktesios* is clearly an old divinity of fertility, of the same order as Meilichios." See *Themis* 300 on Zeus Ktesios as "*daimon* of fertility" and "house-snake." Harrison's interpretation of Zeus was in conflict with that of her Cambridge colleague Arthur Bernard Cook (1868–1952); from the first volume (1914) of his monumental work *Zeus: A Study in Ancient Religion* ("Zeus God of the Bright Sky"), of which she read the proofs (just as he had done for *Themis*, cf. xxiii f.), she adopted "many suggestions," without accepting Cook's Christian-inspired Olympian and monotheistic basic concept. On Cook, see Hans Schwabl (in this volume).

[92] As far as I am aware, no extensive study of the epithets Chthonios, Chthonia, Chthon, and Olympia, Olympioi, Olympiades is yet available. Even Ge could receive the epithet Olympia in Athens (Pausanias 1. 18. 7), as could Eileithyia in Olympia (Pausanias 6. 20. 2). The epigraphical evidence too presents no unambiguous evidence for a dualistic systematization of the gods; cf., e.g., τοι Δι' Ολυνπιοι, *Sylloge Inscriptionum Graecarum*, ed. W. Dittenberger (third edition: Leipzig 1915–24) 9.6: Elis, sixth century B.C. On Demeter Chthonia and the Chthonia festival in Hermione: Pausanias 2. 35. 5; on Demeter, Dionysos, Hecate, and Zeus-Hades as Chthonioi, see Burkert, *Griechische Religion* (above, note 3) 308; on Dionysos Chthonios cf. also note 122, below.

[93] Fundamental on this point is Rohde, *Psyche* (above, note 60), vol. 1, 204–15; on this work and its influence, cf. H. Cancik, "Erwin Rohde—ein Philologe der Bismarckzeit," in *Semper Apertus. Festschrift Universität Heidelberg 1386–1986*, edited by W. Doerr, vol. 2 (Berlin/Heidelberg/New York/Tokyo 1985) 471–76, 498–501. For agreement with Harrison, cf. S. Wide, "Chthonische und himmlische Götter," *Archiv für Religionswissenschaft* 10 (1907) 257–68. On the problem of this antithesis, see Burkert, *Homo Necans* (above, note 38) 16 f. n. 41; *Griechische Religion* (above, note 3) 306–12.

7. Matriarchy Prior to Patriarchy

The development of human society, in Harrison's view, falls into two historical epochs; these are to be found in all societies but are recoverable with particular clarity in Greece: the original state is matriarchy, which is based on the "natural" preeminence of the mother over the father. Then patriarchy forcibly displaces matriarchy as the physical strength of the man, "naturally" greater than that of the woman, prevails through the institutionalization of marriage. "A man when he married by thus obtaining exclusive rights over one woman violated the old matriarchal usages."[94]

Harrison sees the priority of blood-relationship over the conjugal rights of the man as a never wholly repressible relic of matriarchy, presided over by the Erinyes and other chthonians.[95] She understands the unmarried state of mother or maiden divinities as a survival of "matriarchal conditions,"[96] which continue to be represented by the chthonian goddesses, and also by a few goddesses admitted to Olympus, even after the rise of patriarchy. In her view the female divinities and also figures like Pandora[97] are in essence all-embracing earth-goddesses who have, however, been limited and departmentalized in function by "patriarchal mythology" or even reduced to subordinate, harmful, and morally inferior beings.

[94] Harrison, *Prolegomena* (above, note 11) 131; cf. 285: "Matriarchy gave to women a false because a magical prestige. With patriarchy came inevitably the facing of a real fact, the fact of the greater natural weakness of women." In *Themis* (above, note 1) 494, Harrison distinguishes between "matrilinear" and "matriarchal," which allows her to construct a matrilinearity which is embodied in Themis and which is exalted above power, sex, and weakness and makes woman the "social center." But cf. already *Prolegomena* (where otherwise the term "matriarchal" is interpreted in a thoroughly positive sense) 261, in reference to Themis-Gaia: "These primitive goddesses reflect another condition of things, a relationship traced through the mother, the state of society known by the awkward term matriarchal." On Harrison's rejection of the institution of marriage, cf. *Alpha & Omega* (above, note 12) 11; 254: "Marriage *is* exclusion and jealousy, state-sanctioned." See also *Reminiscences* (above, note 11) 88: "By what miracle I escaped marriage I do not know, for all my life long I fell in love. . . . I do not doubt that I lost much, but I am quite sure I gained more. Marriage, for a woman at least, hampers the two things that made life to me glorious—friendship and learning. In man it was always the friend, not the husband, that I wanted. Family life has never attracted me. At its best it seems to me rather narrow and selfish; at its worst, a private hell."

[95] On the Erinyes, cf. above, note 78.

[96] Harrison, *Prolegomena* (above, note 11) 302, interprets the birth of Athena from the head of Zeus as "a desperate theological expedient to rid an earth-born Kore of her matriarchal conditions;" cf. 273, on the dyad Demeter and Kore: "these early matriarchal, husbandless goddesses."

[97] As early as 1900, in "Pandora's Box" (above, note 40) 103, Harrison interprets Pandora's *pithos* as "grave" and the evils that fly out of it as "ghosts." Hesiod, she maintains, has made of Pandora (who in reality is the Earth-Mother herself) a "curious and fatal woman," an "Eve"—without being conscious of the "original" significance (*ibid.*, 104 f.). On the "substantial identity of Pandora and the Earth-Kore," cf. *Prolegomena* (above, note 11) 281 *passim*. Cf., *contra*, Gruppe, *Bericht* (above, note 24) 586 f.

The dyad of mother and maiden (or daughter), according to Harrison, has typical matriarchal characteristics, which she regards as an original expression of the two periods of female life, with their distinct biological functions and experiences; the relation between the two beings, however, is not primarily genealogical.[98] By contrast with the dyad of mother and maiden, that of mother and son does embody a genealogical relation that emphasizes the physical and social dependence of man on woman, who has borne and nourished him yet must not be understood as his lover.[99]

Harrison reacted with enthusiasm to Schliemann's and Evans's discovery of the Minoan-Mycenaean civilization and hailed it as a revelation. In her view these discoveries provided unambiguous confirmation of the religious and social dominance of the matriarchy in prehistorical times.

> Somewhere about the turn of the century there had come to light in the palace of Cnossos a clay sealing which was a veritable little manual of primitive Cretan faith and ritual. I shall never forget the moment when Mr. Arthur Evans first showed it to me. It seemed too good to be true. It represented the Great Mother standing on her own mountain with her

[98] For Harrison, Demeter and Kore are paradigmatic of this relationship: *Prolegomena* (above, note 11) 271–76. This "twofold form" of a goddess, corresponding to the "two stages of a woman's life," is followed (according to Harrison) by "Women-Trinities" as the next stage of development (*ibid.*, 286), who in patriarchal Olympus "faded away into mere dancing attendant maidens" (291). On the sequence dyad-trinity, cf. already "Delphika" (above, note 40) 218 f.

[99] Cf. Harrison, *Themis* (above, note 1) 41: "The divine figures of Mother and Child reflect the social conditions of a matriarchal group with its rite of adolescent initiation; its factors are the mother, the child and the tribe, the child as babe and later as Kouros. But when, chiefly through the accumulation of property, matriarchy passes and patriarchy takes its place, the relation of mother to child is less prominent; the child is viewed as part of the property of the father. Moreover with the decay of matriarchy, initiation ceremonies lose their pristine significance. It is not hard to see that, given women worshippers and a young male god grown to adolescence, the relation of son to mother might be misconceived as that of lover to bride." For Harrison, the prototype of such a son (whose mothers bear various names) is Dionysos (see note 122, below); cf. *Prolegomena* (above, note 11) 560 f.: "the Son is, as is natural in a matriarchal civilization, at first but the attribute of motherhood;" 561: "The Mother and the Son were together from the beginning;" 562: "But the modern mind, obsessed and limited by a canonical Olympus, an Olympus which is 'all for the Father,' has forgotten the Great Mother, robbed the Son of half his grace, and left him desolate of all kinship save adoption." On the other hand, for Harrison the relationship of the "matriarchal, husbandless goddesses" (cf. above, note 96) to the "male figures" that accompany them is not, in the "modern" sense, "feminine;" "It seems to halt somewhere half-way between Mother and Lover, with a touch of the patron saint. Aloof from achievement themselves, they choose a local hero for their own to inspire and protect. They ask of him, not that he should love or adore, but that he should do great deeds. . . . With the coming of patriarchal conditions this high companionship ends. The women goddesses are sequestered to a servile domesticity, they become abject and amorous:" *Prolegomena* 273. That Harrison here idealizes her own experiences and stylizes them into an objective analysis (as scholars of both sexes so often do) is obvious from her biography; cf. Schlesier, "J. E. Harrison" (above, note 8)

attendant lions, and before her a worshipper in ecstasy. At her side, a shrine with "horns of consecration". And another sealing read the riddle of the horns. The Minotaur is seated on the royal throne, and the Minotaur is none other than the human King-God wearing the mask of a bull. . . . here were the true *Prolegomena*.[100]

The Olympian gods, on the other hand, she relegates to the cold and harsh North and to its patriarchy, to the rough and brutal tribes who came to conquer the southern countries, to thrust aside or subjugate the mild matriarchal goddesses worshipped there, and to usurp their spheres of power.[101]   But Harrison's empathetic aversion is directed less against Dionysos than against the "parvenu" and "woman-hater" Apollo in particular[102] and against Zeus, "the archpatriarchal *bourgeois*."[103]   Even the

---

[100] *Reminiscences* (above, note 11) 72. On Harrison and Evans (1851–1941), cf. also *ibid.*, 83: "Arthur Evans set sail for his new Atlantis and telegraphed news of the Minotaur from his own labyrinth; perforce we saw this was a serious matter, it affected the 'Homeric Question.'" On Harrison and Schliemann, cf. above, note 63. Freud reacted as enthusiastically as Harrison to both excavators and to their intuition, which he also construed as confirmation of his own insights; cf. *Der Mann Moses und die monotheistische Religion. Drei Abhandlungen* (1939), in *Gesammelte Werke*, vol. 16 (third edition: 1968) 174 f. But Freud (unlike Harrison) was surprised at the worship of pre-patriarchal mother-goddesses (cf. *ibid.*, 146 f. n. 1), particularly since it had consequences for his theory of stages of development in the psychology of the individual; see *Über die weibliche Sexualität* (1931), in *Gesammelte Werke*, vol. 14 (fourth edition: 1968) 519: "Die Einsicht in die präödipale Vorzeit des Mädchens wirkt als Überraschung, ähnlich wie auf anderem Gebiet die Aufdeckung der minoisch-mykenischen Kultur hinter der griechischen." Nonetheless, Freud sustained his theory of the *Urvater*. On Freud and Harrison (who integrated into her later works the psychology of religion set forth in *Totem und Tabu* but rejected Freud's sexual theories), cf. above, note 73.

[101] Cf. Harrison, *Themis* (above, note 1) 490–92; cf. also 109, where she calls for sympathy with a "mild, peace-loving Pelasgian," who has the "incoming thunderer Jupiter" thrust upon him. For a text-book outline of this polarity between north and south, cold and warm, father and mother (mixed together from passages in Herodotus and Tacitus), see also Harrison, *The Religion of Ancient Greece* [= Religions: Ancient and Modern 2] (London 1905) 27–34.

[102] Apollo, "parvenu:" Harrison, *Prolegomena* (above, note 11) 92; "woman-hater:" *ibid.*, 394. As serpent-murderer, "usurper" of a Gaia-Themis-oracle, and enemy of the Erinyes, Apollo gets a bad press in Harrison's work—until *Themis* (above, note 1) 439–44, where she neutralizes him by interpreting him as originally a year-daimon, side by side with Dionysos. Cf. 443: "There came then to Delphi, tradition tells us, two Kouroi, the greatest Kouroi the world has ever seen, Apollo and Dionysos. Were they, who seem so disparate, really the same? So far as they are Kouroi and Year-Gods, yes. But they are Kouroi and Year-Gods caught and in part crystallized at different stages of development. Apollo has more in him of the Sun and the day, of order and light and reason, Dionysos more of the Earth and the Moon, of the divinity of Night and Dreams." Thus the Romantic and rationalizing interpretation of myth, an interpretation dominated by the polarity of sun and moon against which Harrison had campaigned in her earlier works, is here restored and is linked with a polarity of the Apollinian and Dionysian, which (unlike Nietzsche's formulation) associates dreams not with Apollo but with Dionysos and makes the latter the patron not of intoxication but of "communion," "life as one with nature." On the antecedents of Nietzsche's dichotomy, cf. M. L. Baeumer, "Nietzsche and the Tradition of

female divinities who have been granted a place in the "man-fashioned Olympus"[104] are only shadows of their former omnipotent selves. Athena, according to Harrison originally a mother and nurse like all other goddesses, is now "all for the father,"[105] and Demeter, the earth-goddess *par excellence*, "in Olympus, is but a lovely metaphor."[106]

But already in *Prolegomena* Harrison is not quite happy with the term "matriarchal," which plays on the double sense—"beginning" and "domination"—of the Greek word *arche*. She characterizes it as "awkward"[107] and finds "the clearest and most scientific statement of the

---

the Dionysian," in J. C. O'Flaherty, T. F. Sellner, and R. M. Helm (eds.), *Studies in Nietzsche and the Classical Tradition* (1976; second edition: Chapel Hill 1979) 165–89; on its influence, cf. A. Henrichs, "Loss of Self, Suffering, Violence: The Modern View of Dionysus from Nietzsche to Girard," *Harvard Studies in Classical Philology* 88 (1984) 205–40. Harrison never forgave Apollo, the "ill-mannered prig," although Murray, friend of the Olympians, finally got her to admit that she was "inclined to make it up with old Zeus," so she wrote to Murray at the end of 1925; see Stewart, *J. E. Harrison* (above, note 11) 194. On Dionysos, cf. note 122, below.

[103] Harrison, *Prolegomena* (above, note 11) 285; cf. 284, where "*bourgeois*" and "pessimistic" appear as virtually synonymous terms. Zeus is already called a "patriarchal bourgeois" in "Pandora's Box" (above, note 40) 108. See also *Prolegomena* 12–31 for Zeus as the prototypical usurper of older cults. For Zeus as "impostor," see above, note 86. In *Themis* (above, note 1) 100, Harrison characterizes Zeus by simply adding to a translation the word "pretender." *Themis* is the work in which she makes her most radical attempt to strip Zeus of his power. The book begins by speaking of him as Zeus the father but then redefines him as *primus inter pares*, the Megistos Kouros of the hymn of the Kouretes, who is ennobled only as the "child Zeus,"son of "Mother Rhea" (39). In the course of the book his divinity (as before in *Prolegomena*) is described merely as a stage in a process of decadence, and finally Harrison refuses to allow him any divine identity at all, ranking him among the "monotonous" class of the periodically dying and rising year-daimons, who together dance and leap about to the greater glory of Themis. On Harrison's identification of Zeus Kouros with Dionysos, cf. above, note 80.

[104] Harrison, *Prolegomena* (above, note 11) 285. The terms masculine, Olympian, anthropomorphic, non-religious (as well as the respective contrasting terms) are increasingly classed together in Harrison's work as associated or even synonymous expressions.

[105] *Ibid.*, 95; cf. also above, note 99. "All for the father" is in Harrison's works a quasi-liturgical, omnipresent anathema, with which, for instance, she pillories Aeschylus because he is a "monotheist;" cf. note 113, below.

[106] Harrison, *Prolegomena* (above, note 11) 314; on Demeter as "Earth," cf. *Themis* (above, note 1) 299.

[107] Harrison, *Prolegomena* (above, note 11) 261; cf. also above, note 94. The debate about "matriarchy" was inaugurated in Great Britain by the works of Maine, McLennan, and Morgan; cf. above, note 46. Independent of them (and without influence on them) was the work of the historian of law and archaeologist Johann Jakob Bachofen (1815–87). Harrison refers with approval to his epoch-making two-volume work *Das Mutterrecht* (1861) in *Prolegomena* 262 n. 1: "Other instances of the survival in Greek mythology of traces of matriarchal conditions are collected by Bachofen in his *Mutterrecht*, a book which, spite [sic] of the wildness of its theories, remains of value as the fullest existing collection of ancient facts." What Harrison means by "wildness" is obscure. That she could not help regarding as abominable his thesis that "Gynäkokratie" was preceded by "Hetärismus," an original stage of promiscuous "Sumpfzeugung," may be accepted as

facts" not in the speculative historian of law Bachofen but in the Quaker E. B. Tylor.[108] Later Harrison preferred to use the term "matrilinear,"[109] which is less objectionable from the point of view of historical theory and is at the same time ethnologically legitimate. This verbal change corresponds to the shift of emphasis in the direction of comparative religion and sociology which occurs in *Themis* and which was based on the work of Frazer and the school of Durkheim.[110] Nevertheless, Harrison's polemical, antipatriarchal

certain; his affectionate treatment of the "chthonian" element and the cult of graves could only be sympathetic to her. In his review of Meuli's edition of *Mutterrecht*, L. Gernet (1951) called attention to the analogy between Harrison's *Themis* and Bachofen's "dessein," in *Les Grecs sans miracle*, ed. R. di Donato (Paris 1983) 119. On Bachofen, cf. *Archäologenbildnisse* (above, note 24) 41 f. On the antecedents of Bachofen's theories, cf. A. Bäumler, *Das mythische Weltalter. Bachofens romantische Deutung des Altertums* [= "Bachofen der Mythologe der Romantik," introduction to the selection of Bachofen's works *Der Mythus von Orient und Occident* (1926)], with an Epilogue "Bachofen und die Religionsgeschichte" (München 1965); H.-J. Heinrichs (ed.), *Materialien zu Bachofens "Das Mutterrecht"* [= suhrkamp taschenbuch wissenschaft 136] (Frankfurt am Main 1975). On the theory of matriarchy in Bachofen, Friedrich Engels, and Freud, cf. H. Zinser, *Der Mythos des Mutterrechts. Verhandlungen von drei aktuellen Theorien des Geschlechterkampfes* (Frankfurt am Main/Berlin/Wien 1981).

[108] Cf. *Prolegomena* (above, note 11) 261 n. 3. On Harrison and Tylor, see also above, notes 21 and 39.

[109] On "matrilinear structure," cf. Harrison, *Themis* (above, note 1) 492–505; this chapter is the programmatic synthesis of the book (492): "If then we would understand the contrast between the Olympians and their predecessors we must get back to the earlier Themis, to the social structure that was before the patriarchal family, to the matrilinear system, to the Mother and the Tribe, the Mother and the Child and the Initiated young men, the Kouretes." In modern ethnology too the term "matrilinear" is preferred to "matriarchal;" in Harrison, however, this occurs for different reasons (cf. 386). By "matrilinear system" she means not simply the legal rules deduced from matrilinear descent but the religious principle itself as a principle of law, portrayed quasi-allegorically in the figure of Themis; *ibid.*, 387: "Themis is a conception so dominant, so integral to religion . . . . In the figure of Themis, if we are right, we have the utterance, the projection, and the personification, of *the* religious principle itself." For a non-universalistic discussion of Themis as goddess and legal concept, cf. R. Hirzel, *Themis, Dike und Verwandtes. Ein Beitrag zur Geschichte der Rechtsidee bei den Griechen* (Leipzig 1907; reprint: Hildesheim 1966).

[110] On Harrison's agreement with Durkheim, see *Themis* (above, note 1) xiii; 29 (against the identification of religion with theology); 63: "Le sacré, c'est le père du dieu;" 139 n. 1 (against Frazer: totemism and exogamy go together); 477 n. 1 (categories as modes of collective thought); 486–88 (definition of religion as social "pratique" and of divinity as "épisode secondaire" in the history of religion); cf. also above, note 62. Also of great importance for Harrison was the work of the students of Durkheim, H. Hubert and M. Mauss (see also above, note 90), especially *Essai sur la nature et la fonction du sacrifice* [= *Année Sociologique* 2 (1899)], in M. Mauss, *Oeuvres. T. 1: Les fonctions sociales du sacré* (Paris 1968) 193–307, cf. Harrison, *Themis* 137 n. 1 and 148 n. 2; and *Equisse d'une théorie générale de la magie* [= *Année Sociologique* 7 (1902–03) 1–146, in *Sociologie et anthropologie*], with whose criticism of Frazer's conception of magic as rudimentary science and pre-religious stage she agrees, cf. *Themis* 85; *Alpha & Omega* (above, note 12) 173 n. 1. Frazer's works were for Harrison a decisive stimulus (cf. above, notes 11, 13, and 22), especially in their conception (which went back to Mannhardt) of the dying and reborn "vegetation spirit," which, however, she universalizes to a greater degree in her

thrust is by no means given up in *Themis*; instead it here reaches its anthropologically and "naturally" based acme.

8. *Monotheism*

Harrison's concept of religion looks back to an *interpretatio christiana*, and not only *ex negativo*. This is perhaps most evident in her concept of monotheism. According to her *Prolegomena*, monotheism is the original form of religious belief; polytheistic multiplicity and the parceling out of the spheres of divine activity is essentially a poetic invention.[111] This would seem to be indicated by the worship of a divine trinity, by the local cults, by the fusion and lack of differentiation between different ghosts and gods (which she assumes to be a primitive characteristic), and by the namelessness of *daimones* and divinities (which she interprets as the original state), later replaced by polyonymy. In the earlier stages of evolution, however, monotheism would exist in a yet unconscious manner. Only the later development of thought into theology or mythology and into philosophy would make possible the development of a conscious monotheism—for instance, through the creation of abstractions like Tyche or through synthetic concepts of divinity like Zeus and the category of the *theion*.[112] For Harrison, the most important champion of the monotheistic

---

concept of the "Eniautos-daimon" (cf. above, note 80), *Themis* xvii: "My own debt to Dr Frazer is immeasurable. But even 'Vegetation Spirit' is inadequate. A word was wanted that should include not only vegetation, but the whole world-process of decay, death, renewal. I prefer 'Eniautos' to 'year' because to us 'year' means something definitely chronological, a precise segment as it were of spatialized time; whereas *Eniautos*, as contrasted with *etos*, means a *period* in the etymological sense, a cycle of waxing and waning." On Harrison's criticism of Frazer, cf. also an unpublished letter to him, 18 March 1911 (Trinity College Archives Add. Ms. b. 36[31]): *"Never, never* have I believed that a sun-god or a moon-god or any god was developed out of an *abstract idea*: that is what I am fighting against; but I do believe that the social form in which a god is *projected* is developed out of a *collective* emotion and I believe that all modern psychology is at my back."

[111] Of course for Harrison the existence of monotheism presupposes a religious prehistory without god and gods; it is nothing "primitive:" cf. *Prolegomena* (above, note 11) 17, 20. Yet she seems to presuppose that an original unity preceded the multiplicity of gods and that theology reverted to this unity (164): "Theology, after articulating the one into the many and diverse, after a course of exclusive and determined discrimination, after differentiating a number of departmental gods and spirits, usually monotheizes, i.e. resumes the many into the one." Thus the "monotheism" of the "Orphics" (cf. 462, 625) is actually, according to Harrison, a reaching back "behind the Olympian divinites" and a mystification of the "earlier figures of the Mother or the Daughter" (*ibid.*, 271).

[112] On the "omnipotence of Zeus" as "monotheism," cf. already Harrison, "Pandora's Box" (above, note 40) 108. On Tyche and the "growing philosophic monotheism" that was inspired by Orphism, cf. *Prolegomena* (above, note 11) 270. On "Orphic" mingling of gods, such as Zeus-Zagreus-Dionysos, as a tendency toward monotheism, see *ibid.*, 479; cf. 500. On Harrison's own equation of Zeus and Dionysos, see above, note 80. Citing Gilbert Murray as her philological authority, Harrison interprets "the meaning of θεῖος as 'magical' and θεός as primarily 'medicine-man,'" *Themis* (above, note 1) 95 n. 3 (on a quotation from Hesiod); cf. *Prolegomena* 137 (on the θεσμοί of the Thesmophoria

idea, besides Aeschylus,[113] is the figure of the "martyr" Orpheus, whom she regarded as historical. It is especially in her description of the "new religion" propagated by "Orpheus" that Harrison unembarrassedly uses terms like "sin," "hell," "evil," "atonement," "church," etc., although she does not avoid such terms elsewhere when describing the "normal" characteristics of ancient Greek religion.[114]

Here too, then, Harrison presupposes a cyclic pattern in religious history: monotheism is at once the origin and the goal. In *Prolegomena* she seems rather to regret than to welcome this supposed fact and is obviously far more fascinated by the multiformity and contradictory relationship of the Greek gods and ghosts than by the figure of a unique god and everything that resembles him. In *Themis*, on the other hand, she explicitly affirms and even magnifies the unifying tendencies in the theory of religion. By now the different names of gods are without significance for Harrison, since they always represent, *mutatis mutandis*, the same thing. Be it Herakles or Ion, Hermes or Zeus, Dionysos or Apollo—whatever the name, it is always the same prehistoric cosmological "Year-Spirit," whose death and rebirth are "mimetically" reproduced in seasonal cultic plays.[115] Thus the

festival): "The root θεσ is more vivid and has the blood of religion, or rather magic, in its veins."

[113] Aeschylus as "monotheist:" *Prolegomena* (above, note 11) 254, 390; see also *Themis* (above, note 1) 386.

[114] In her work Harrison never hesitates to apply Christian terms to ancient Greek religion; she speaks of "orthodoxy" and "church" especially in connection with the poets' portrayal of the Olympians and with the Orphics. See, e.g., a letter to Murray, March 1902: "No wonder Euripides wrote so sadly that 'we (i. e. the Established Church) do not reverence Erôs'" (Stewart, *J. E. Harrison* [above, note 11] 48); "the blood of some real martyr may have been the seed of the new Orphic church" (*Prolegomena* [above, note 11] 468). It cannot therefore be maintained that Arnold Toynbee was the first to use the term "church" of the Orphics—thus Burkert, "Craft Versus Sect: The Problem of Orphics and Pythagoreans," in B. F. Meyer and E. P. Sanders (eds.), *Jewish and Christian Self-Definition*, vol. 3: *Self-Definition in the Graeco-Roman World* (London 1982) 183 n. 4. In *Themis* (above, note 1) xiv, the term "church" is equated with "thiasos;" Herakles or Asklepios is the type of the "half human Saviour" (*ibid.*, xix; 381; 384: "greater than any Olympians"). Prototypical for "resurrection" (Harrison's translation of ἀναβίωσις) is (thus Plutarch) Dionysos: *ibid.*, 157. For the Christian quality (despite her withdrawal from churchy Christianity) of Harrison's interest in the history of religion, see a letter (6 February 1887) to her friend MacColl, who had alienated her from classicistic tastes in art (cf. also above, note 54) in Peacock, *The Mask* (above, note 30) 71: "I had grown into a sort of Salvationist for Greek art— . . . the faith in my gospel was the secret of my strength." At the age of ninety Murray wrote of Harrison, "She is always looking for the new gospel" (Stewart xiii). Therefore, the "anthropological approach" did not result in a real liberation "from the tyranny of Christian inhibitions and preconceptions" (thus G. S. Kirk, *Myth: Its Meaning and Functions in Ancient and Other Cultures* [= Sather Classical Lectures 40 (1970); reprint: Cambridge/Berkeley/ Los Angeles 1971 3) either for Harrison or for her colleagues.

[115] See above, note 80. Harrison's concept of the "Eniautos-daimon" was sternly rejected by Cook (cf. above, note 91); see Ackerman, "Some Letters" (above, note 60) 118. Farnell in Oxford (cf. above, note 60), who certainly did believe that some heroes

"commemorative" or "anticipatory" δρώμενον becomes for Harrison (in contrast to her earlier functionalistic theory) a synonym for ritual *par excellence*.

> A δρώμενον is . . . not simply a thing done, not even a thing excitedly and socially done. What is it then? It is a thing *re*-done or *pre*-done, a thing enacted or represented. It is sometimes *re*-done, commemorative, sometimes *pre*-done, anticipatory, and both elements seem to go to its religiousness . . . The important point to note is that the hunting, fighting, or what not, the thing done, is never religious; the thing re-done with heightened emotion is on the way to become so. The element of action re-done, imitated, the element of μίμησις, is, I think, essential. In all religion, as in all art, there is this element of make-believe. Not the attempt to deceive, but a desire to *re*-live, to *re*-present.[116]

The unanimity of society and its harmony with the regular course of nature were renewed by the *dromena*, which were allied with male puberty-

---

were originally "vegetation-daimones," and Ridgeway, at that time Cambridge's leading archaeologist, also opposed Harrison's universalistic demonology. Harrison heard the lectures of William Ridgeway (1853–1926) on the origin of the gods in "social custom" (cf. Stewart, *J. E. Harrison* [above, note 11] 17; see also *passim* her disagreements with him), and she cites him in the "Introduction" to *Prolegomena* (above, note 11) xiii f. Cf. an unpublished letter to Frazer (above, note 110): "But so far as I have understood you in your lectures the cult of a necessarily mythical hero precedes the individual actual hero, who is feared for a brief time in the interval of incarnation whereas the mythical totemic ancestor is a permanent power for good & evil. It is the blank euhemerism of Prof. Ridgeway I find unsatisfactory." See also Harrison's "Sophokles, *Ichneutae*, Col. IX.1–7, and the δρώμενον of Kyllene and the Satyrs," her contribution to the Festschrift *Essays and Studies presented to William Ridgeway*, edited by E. C. Quiggin (Cambridge 1913) 136–52, where she interprets Hermes as an "Eniautos-daimon." Ridgeway's theory that tragedy originated not from annual rituals of rebirth but from ceremonies relating to the cult of the dead (see especially *The Origin of Tragedy with Special Reference to the Greek Tragedians* [Cambridge 1910] and also his disagreement with the views of "Miss Harrison and her partners" Murray and Cornford: *The Dramas and Dramatic Dances of Non-European Races in Special Reference to the Origin of Greek Tragedy with an Appendix on the Origin of Greek Comedy* [Cambridge 1915; reprint: New York 1965] 51–64) were not accepted by Pickard-Cambridge, *Dithyramb* (first edition, see above, note 75) 174–206, any more than was the theory of Harrison and Murray. But cf. Meuli's (implicit) recourse to the theory of Ridgeway in *Der griechische Agon. Kampf und Kampfspiel im Totenbrauch, Totentanz, Totenklage und Totenlob* (1926; Köln 1968). Harrison's concept of the "Eniautos-daimon" was adopted especially by Carl Robert (cf. above, note 36), who used the concept to interpret the figure of Oedipus in *Oidipus* (Berlin 1915) and by Adolphe Reinach (a member of the school of Durkheim who died at the battle of the Marne in the First World War), "Thémis. Un nouveau livre sur les origines sociales de la religion grecque," in *Revue de l'histoire des religions* 69 (1914) 323–71, especially 352 f.; cf. Harrison, *Themis* (above, note 1) x.

[116] Harrison, *Themis* (above, note 1) 43; cf. her earlier definition of the rituals, of the δρώμενα, as "things done" and of the δρᾶμα as "Thing Acted:" *Prolegomena* (above, note 11) 567. See also above, note 52.

rites;[117] from the *dromena*, according to Harrison, arose the *drama* on a level of evolution specific to Greece.[118] But the worship of the polyonymous "Year-spirit," the "Eniautos-daimon," was not performed for its own sake

[117] Harrison borrows the term "rites of passage" from Arnold van Gennep, *Les rites de passage* (1909; reprint with additions and corrections: Paris 1969 and 1981), but she understands these rituals not primarily as means to facilitate the crossing of social and physical thresholds but as attempts to resolve conflicts by means of the experiences that one gains in the mysteries, with mimesis of death and rebirth at every stage. Van Gennep in his book had opposed the first appearance, in *Prolegomena*, of this universalistic theory, as he opposed the "procédé 'folkloriste' ou 'anthropologique'" in general (*Rites de passage* 127). Instead he tried to determine the specific "séquences" of each rite of passage. Nevertheless he too emphasizes the structural similarities and the drama of the rites of initiation; cf. 258–63. For Harrison's reaction to van Gennep's book, cf. an unpublished letter to Murray (beginning of 1910? Newnham Archives, Box 3, no. 418.2/442.2): "Have you read Van Gennep's *Rites de passage*? You need not read it for the whole gist is in the title. He had a trenchant criticism of me on mysteries in the middle. I wrote to him to say how absolutely to the point I felt it was, I had never seen the importance of the unalterable *sequence* of rites—pre-liminal—liminal—post-liminal—it is really what I was worrying about with rites of sacrifice—entry, sanctification, exit—and all rites de passage have the same *schema*, birth, marriage, initiation, death, they are all *initiations*: and I think it will work out that all true myths as opposed to legends have the *schema*." On van Gennep's importance for Harrison, cf. also *Themis* (above, note 1) 20, 184, 290, 507. On the specificity of masculine initiation societies, Harrison refers (*Themis* 19 n. 1; 26 f.) to H. Schurtz, *Altersklassen und Männerbünde. Eine Darstellung der Grundformen der Gesellschaft* (Berlin 1902), which became one of the basic books of the youth movement in Germany (cf. H. Blüher, *Die Rolle der Erotik in der männlichen Gesellschaft. Eine Theorie der menschlichen Staatsbildung nach Wesen und Wert*, vol. 2: *Familie und Männerbund* [Jena 1919] 91–101, as well as the emphasis *passim* on homosexuality, which Schurtz had hardly touched upon), and later was taken into the Nazi ideology (cf., e.g., A. Bäumler, *Männerbund und Wissenschaft* [Berlin 1934]). The term "initiation" (in van Gennep's sense) is today established in many different disciplines, independently of their method; cf. C. J. Bleeker (ed.), *Initiation* [= Studies in the History of Religions. Supplements to *Numen*, 10] (Leiden 1965). One of the first to build upon Harrison's association between initiation and mystery cult was L. Gernet, "Frairies antiques" (1928), in *Anthropologie de la Grèce antique*, edited by J.-P. Vernant (1968; Paris 1976) 50 f. Harrison's theory about puberty rites (with Usener's interpretation of the Kouroi) served as a "fil conducteur" for H. Jeanmaire, *Couroi et Courètes. Essai sur l'éducation spartiate et sur les rites d'adolescence dans l'antiquité classique* [= Travaux et Mémoires de l'Université de Lille, Nouv. Sér. Droit-Lettres 21] (Lille 1939) 5 f.; cf. A. Brelich, *Guerre, agoni e culti nella Grecia arcaica* [= Antiquitas, Reihe 1: Abhandlungen zur Alten Geschichte 1] (Bonn 1961) 81 f.

[118] Cf. Harrison, *Themis* (above, note 1) 327–40, especially 334: "The dithyramb, which was but the periodic festival of the spring *renouveau*, broke and blossomed so swiftly into the Attic drama because it found such plots to hand; in a word—*the forms of Attic drama are the forms of the life-history of an Eniautos-daimon; the content is the infinite variety of free and individualized heroic saga—in the largest sense of the word 'Homer.'*" Cf. Murray (above, note 82). But see already Harrison, *Prolegomena* (above, note 11) 567–71. Nietzsche had already held that not only "das narkotische Getränk" but also "der Frühling" was responsible for the wakening of "dionysische Regungen" and for the "dionysische Kunst" emerging from them, dithyramb and drama: *Die Geburt der Tragödie aus dem Geiste der Musik* (1872) in *Nietzsches Werke. Kritische Gesamtausgabe*, edited by G. Colli and M. Montinari, section 3, volume 1 (Berlin and New York 1972) 24 f.

but to the greater glory of all-embracing maternal divinities, whose names are likewise arbitrary, since they can all be reduced to a single functionality. "Above as well as below each and every god,"[119] as Harrison puts it, reigns Themis. She presides as the genderless embodiment of the harmony that follows natural laws and preserves life, and as a projection of social solidarity she rules over the initiation into matriarchal mysteries.

9. *Mystery, Ecstasy, and Asceticism*

For Harrison, religion *sui generis* is crystallized in the term "mystery" and in the phenomena of the mystery cults.[120] Here is the focus of the prejudices and preferences to which she adhered from the beginning. The mystery cults, according to Harrison, preserve the memory of earlier stages of religious evolution, are nearest to the origins of religion, realize the fundamental natural and social experiences in a simultaneously spiritual and practical way, represent dramatically the making of gods and ghosts in the image of human beings, and sanction the dominance of the daimon over the god, the chthonian over the Olympian, the matriarchal over the patriarchal.[121]

In Harrison's view, the late and triumphant rise of Dionysos[122] and Orpheus[123] demonstrates most vividly how powerful, how irrepressible,

---

[119] Harrison, *Themis* (above, note 1) 485; cf. also the variations on this theme, *ibid.*, xxi: "Above the gods, supreme, eternally dominant, stands the figure of Themis;" and (lyrically) xxii: "behind Gaia the Mother, and above even Zeus the Father, stands always the figure of Themis."

[120] Cf. Harrison, *Prolegomena* (above, note 11) 29: "it is these rites of purification belonging to the lower stratum, primitive and barbarous, even repulsive as they often are, that furnished ultimately the material out of which 'mysteries' were made—mysteries which, as will be seen, when informed by the new spirit of the religions of Dionysos and Orpheus, lent to Greece its deepest and most enduring religious impulse." Cf. 363 f.: "Just when Apollo, Artemis, Athene, nay even Zeus himself, were losing touch with life and reality, fading and dying of their own luminous perfection, there came into Greece a new religious impulse, an impulse really religious, the mysticism that is embodied for us in the two names Dionysos and Orpheus." In *Themis* (above, note 1) 490, "mystery," mediated by Themis, becomes the embodiment of "social conscience,"the fundamental religious concept *par excellence*: "The instinct of those who, in framing the old definitions of religion, included 'mystery' and 'the infinite,' was right—though their explanations were wrong. The mystery, the thing greater than man, is potent, not only or chiefly because it is unintelligible and calls for explanation, not because it stimulates a baffled understanding, but because it is *felt* as an obligation. The thing greater than man, the 'power not himself that makes for righteousness,' is, in the main, not the mystery of the universe to which as yet he is not awake, but the pressure of that unknown ever incumbent force, herd instinct, the social conscience. The mysterious dominant figure is not Physis, but Themis."

[121] Harrison, *Prolegomena* (above, note 11) 150–62, discusses the "Eleusinian Mysteries" as paradigmatic for the mystery cults in this sense.

[122] Harrison's interests centered increasingly on Dionysos—at least since her reading of Rohde's *Psyche* (for her review, see above, note 40), but at the latest during the writing of *Prolegomena*, as she confesses in a letter to Murray (Stewart, *J. E. Harrison* [above, note

11] 25): "the whole centre of gravity of the book has shifted. It began as a treatise on Keres with a supplementary notice of Dionysus. It is ending as a screed on Dionysus with an introductory talk about Keres." Dionysos is for Harrison in *Prolegomena* (above, note 11) 34, as for Rohde, a chthonic god, "Lord of Souls," and a "late-comer" (364, *passim*), an "immigrant god" from the North, "that home of spiritual impulse." He had been at first a god of mead (μέθυ) and the fermented juice of grains—a conclusion which she derives from the assumption of his "northern" Thracian origins (see above, note 74) and etymological speculation, especially in the case of the word βρόμος, oats (with which she associates "Bromios" and "Braites," two epithets for Dionysos): 415–24. Cf. also above, note 75, on the Satyrs and τράγος = "spelt." In the third edition of *Prolegomena* 453 n. 1, however, she retreats from this position. On Dionysus as originally the god of fermented honey, before becoming the god of wine, cf. K. Kerényi, *Dionysos. Urbild des unzerstörbaren Lebens* (München and Wien 1976) 41–49, 316–18. On the problem of the "chthonian Dionysos" see (*contra* Harrison) G. Zuntz, *Persephone: Three Essays on Religion and Thought in Magna Graecia* (Oxford 1971) 407–11. On Harrison's interpretation of Dionysos with reference to Rohde and his friend Nietzsche, cf. P. McGinty, *Interpretation and Dionysos: Method in the Study of a God* [= Religion and Reason 16] (The Hague/Paris/New York 1978) 71–103, 207–222; Henrichs, "Loss of Self" (above, note 102) 229–32. On Harrison's attitude toward Nietzsche see (in addition to the sources cited in Henrichs, 229 n. 62) an unpublished letter to Murray of December 1909 (Newnham College Archives, Box 3, No. 412): "I have just been re-reading Die Geburt der Tragödie (Nietzsche[)], do you remember that it ends with a rather wonderful forecast of you.—'*Sage auch dies, du wunderliche[r] Fremdling: wie viel musste dies Volk leiden, um so schön werden zu können?*' Have you read the book at all lately, it is real genius, and if you hate the German there is a French translation." On Nietzsche, cf. also above, notes 31, 32, 47, 48, 118. For a divergent view of the polarity between Dionysos and Apollo in Nietzsche and Harrison, cf. above, note 102. A sublime understanding of Dionysos (which, however, is already found in Nietzsche) was given to Harrison by Bergson; *Themis* (above, note 1) xii: "I saw in a word that Dionysos, with every other mystery-god, was an instinctive attempt to express what Professor Bergson calls *durée*, that life which is one, indivisible and yet ceaselessly changing." In *Prolegomena* Harrison discusses Dionysos as the prototype of the son of matriarchal goddesses (cf. above, note 99), who dies and is resurrected (cf. above, note 114) and as the mystic nurseling of divine nurses; cf. the translation [!] of Euripides, *Bacchae* 522: τὸ Διὸς βρέφος, "The Babe of God, the Mystery" (373), or of Sophocles, *Oed. Col.* 678–80: ἵν' ὁ Βαχιώ-/τας ἀεὶ Διόνυσος ἐμβατεύει / θείαις ἀμφιπολῶν τιθήναις: "Where the Reveller Dionysos with his nursing nymphs will go" (396; 401, translated by Harrison's long-time counsellor and travel-companion D. S. MacColl, on whom see above, note 54); cf. Murray, *Jane Harrison* (above, note 24) 7 [= 563, ed. Wilson]. Next she devotes an extensive paralipomenon ("Mystica Vannus Iacchi" [above, note 40]) to the Liknites ("He-of-the-Winnowing-Fan"), which provides the transition to the interpretation (developed in *Themis*) of Dionysos as an Eniautos-daimon *par excellence* (see above, note 80). Cf. also Harrison to Murray, in Stewart, *J. E. Harrison* (above, note 11) 57, on an essay of A. W. Verrall in a book dedicated to Murray, *The Bacchants of Euripides and Other Essays* (Cambridge 1910) 1–160, especially 71–73: "Do you know AWV has discovered that the earthquake and fire in the Bacchae are all hallucinations? (hallucinations were at the time the subject of Mrs. Verrall's psychical investigations). I didn't realise he hated the Bacchos, when I love him so; he sympathises with Pentheus." See also Harrison's last word on Dionysos, *Myths of Greece and Rome* (London 1927) 77: "Dionysos is a human youth, lovely with curled hair, but in a moment he is a wild bull and a burning flame. The beauty and the thrill of it!"

[123] Harrison continued to think of Orpheus in the euhemeristic manner (cf. above, note 59) and so opposed the conception of Orpheus as an "underworld god," as it was developed in E. Maass, *Orpheus. Untersuchungen zur griechischen, römischen, altchristlichen*

how necessary is the essentially religious tendency that finds expression in the mystery cults. The higher stage of religion that had been attained in the worship of the Olympians had shown itself to be ultimately irreligious.[124] The mysteries of Dionysos and Orpheus lead back beyond this stage to primitivism, and thus they are able to restore the genuine religious element to its rights, until this task is taken over by an even more triumphant and consistent monotheistic mystery cult, Christianity.[125]

It is typical of Harrison's ambivalence about all things religious, of her mixture of ethical rationality with emotional wildness, that she is always at once attracted and repelled by ecstasy and asceticism.[126] She applauds the

---

Jenseitsdichtung und Religion (München 1895; reprint: Aalen 1974) 129 ff.; cf. Harrison, *Prolegomena* (above, note 11) 455 n. 2. On Orpheus and Orphism, cf. also above, notes 111 and 120, and notes 126, 127, and 128, below.

[124] See Harrison, *Themis* (above, note 1) xi f.: "My sense of the superficiality of Homer's gods had deepened to a conviction that these Olympians were not only non-primitive, but positively in a sense non-religious. If they were not, for religion, starting-points, they were certainly not satisfactory goals. On the other hand, the cultus of Dionysos and Orpheus seemed to me, whatever its errors and licenses, essentially religious. I was therefore compelled reluctantly to face the question, what meaning did I attach to the word *religion*? My instinct was to condemn the Olympians as *non*-religious, because really the products of art and literature though posing as divinities. Could this instinct stand the test of examination, or was it merely a temperamental prejudice masquerading as a reasoned principle?" Harrison's "instinct," incidentally, was already expressed in her second book, although here the attitude was pro-Olympian; see *Introductory Studies* (above, note 66).

[125] Numerous remarks in Harrison's work imply that she must have viewed the "primitive" initiation rites as well as the Dionysian and Orphic mysteries, which she considered a higher form of these rites, as a preliminary stage of Christianity; cf., e.g.: "the cardinal rite of tribal initiation was a mimetic Death and Resurrection," *Themis* (above, note 1) 511; *Prolegomena* (above, note 11) 120: "the most widely influential of all Greek ceremonials, the Eleusinian mysteries." Or 504: "The early Christians owed some of their noblest impulses to Orphism;" 549, on the proclamation of birth in the Eleusinian Mysteries: "'Unto us a Child is born, unto us a Son is given';" similarly 552: "The mystic child at Eleusis was born of a maiden." See also *Alpha & Omega* (above, note 11) 175: "Mystery-cults and sacraments, the lineal descendents of magic;" 152: "In the Greek Mysteries only we find what we should call a *Confiteor*, and this is not a confession of faith, but an avowal of rites performed." In fact, Harrison could not find the mystic matrilinearity and the ritualism to which she adhered in the Anglican faith of her upbringing; rather, she found them preserved in Catholicism; cf. *Themis* 497: "The Roman Church, with her wider humanity, though she cherishes the monastic ideal, yet feels instinctively that a male Trinity is non-natural, and keeps always the figure of the divine Mother." Even the Greek Orthodox monks of Mt. Athos, who forbade women to approach their sanctuary, she found sympathetic as descendents of the primitive worshippers of the Mountain Mother; cf. the travelling impression described in *Reminiscences* (above, note 12) 69: "It was wonderful to find the Great Mother here in her own Thrace, and worshipped still not by women but by her own celibate priests, the Kouretes."

[126] Orpheus represents for Harrison the "inward ecstasy of the ascetic" (*Prolegomena* [above, note 11] 453) and has nothing to do with madness; cf., e.g., 459: "Orpheus never plays the flute 'that rouses to madness.'" Cf. the interpretation of Orpheus as a "'shamanistic' figure"—which is in agreement with the views of Meuli, "Scythica" (1935), in *Schriften* (above, note 90) 817–79; see also above, note 115; Dodds, *The Greeks and*

"progress"[127] of Orphic mysteries, which spiritualize and ultimately replace the ecstatic religion of Dionysos by the introduction of asceticism. But her approval of asceticism cannot conceal the fact that her emotional sympathies lie not with Orpheus the "reformer"[128] but with the Maenads who tore him to pieces. Her unmistakably anti-Orphic commentary in *Prolegomena* on a certain vase painting reads: "it is impossible not to sympathize a little with the determined-looking Maenad who is coming up behind to put a stop to zall this sun-watching and lyre-playing."[129] Her final word concerning the

---

the Irrational [= Sather Classical Lectures 25] (Berkeley/Los Angeles/London 1951) 147, cf. 71; see also above, note 82—in Burkert, *Lore and Science in Ancient Pythagoreanism* [= *Weisheit und Wissenschaft* 1962] (Cambridge, MA, 1972) 162–65; West, *Orphic Poems* (above, note 80) 4 f. Skeptical toward the theory of shamanism is Detienne, *Les maîtres de vérité dans la Grèce archaïque* (1967; 3ième éd. 1979) 124 n. 80; F. Graf, "Orpheus: A Poet Among Men," in *Interpretations of Greek Mythology* (above, note 76) 83–85, 102 f. On Harrison's idealization of ecstasy, cf. a letter to Murray, 18 May 1909, in Stewart, *J. E. Harrison* (above, note 11) 127: "ectasy [sic] and . . . beauty—same thing;" see also *Prolegemena* 429: "the Maenads, worshipping the god of life, bend in ritual ecstasy to touch the earth, mother of life" (see also above, note 78, and note 129, below). But cf. 206 (on the Sirens): "They stand, it would seem, to the ancient as to the modern, for the impulses in life as yet unmoralized, imperious longings, ecstasies." For her idealization of asceticism, see especially *Epilegomena* (above, note 49) 39: "Asceticism is then not only resistance to the descending wave, it is also, it is chiefly, the rising on the upward wave, buoyant, triumphant." When Harrison sent to Murray this, her last theoretical work, which culminates in praise of asceticism (which Murray often required of her), he wrote to her that this was "the best thing you have ever written about religion. It explains and justifies asceticism, which is almost the most important piece of teaching that the world needs nowadays:" 30 July 1921, in Stewart, *J. E. Harrison* 182. On Harrison's rejection of asceticism (after *Prolegomena*, when she was obliged temporarily to give up the cigarette-smoking and whisky-drinking that she loved), see a letter to Murray, 8 November 1903, in Peacock, *The Mask* (above, note 30) 142: "Also I hate asceticism & am compelled to practice it." On Harrison's use of the term "ambivalence," cf. above, note 73.

[127] On Harrison's appraisal of the Orphic Mysteries as progress, cf. *Prolegomena* (above, note 11) 481: "The Orphics faced the most barbarous elements of their own faith and turned them not only quâ theology into a vague monotheism, but quâ ritual into a high sacrament of spiritual purification." Cf. also 495 (on the story of Dionysos-Zagreus and the Titans): "Perhaps it is not a very satisfactory theory of the origin of evil; but is the sacred legend of the serpent and the apple more illuminating?" On Orphic "Eschatology" and "Cosmology," see 572–658, with Murray's philological "Critical Appendix on the Orphic Tablets," 659–73. On Harrison's "modernization" of Orphism, cf. *Alpha & Omega* (above, note 12) 142: "There was a sect in antiquity, small, despised, persecuted, who made their god in the image of neither a male nor female, but a thing bisexed, immaculate, winged, . . . the Orphics . . . . And if we would worship knowledge, this is the hymn we must chant to-day, together, men and women—to-day and to-morrow." In *Themis*, Orphism is touched upon only briefly, since it belongs not to the origins but to the "reform" of the "religion of Earth;" cf. 462. Harrison emphasizes her renewed interest in Orphism at the end of her life in the Foreword to the second edition of *Themis* (above, note 1) x; cf. also Stewart, *J. E. Harrison* (above, note 11) 195–98.

[128] On Orpheus as reformer, cf. above, note 59. On Harrison's *interpretatio christiana* of Orphism, see also *Themis* (above, note 1) 14, and above, notes 114 and 125.

[129] Harrison, *Prolegomena* (above, note 11) 461; cf. also 567, where Dionysos, "less priest than artist," is contrasted with the mere priest Orpheus (with his "lyre-playing"), for "from the religion of Dionysos sprang the drama." In *Themis*, Harrison grants some status

philosophy of religion[130] in *Epilegomena*, eighteen years later, is paradoxical: it is an ecstatic plea for asceticism.[131]

Freie-Universität, Berlin

even to the sun and to Apollo (cf. above, note 102). She continues to sympathize with the Maenads, interpreting them as "Nurses and Mothers of all that is" (above, note 1) 40, and as a survival of a totemistic cult-federation; see 132 f., her interpretation of a vase-painting of a Maenad tattooed with a deer, with reference to her early paper "Some Fragments of a Vase Presumably by Euphronios," *JHS* 9 (1888) 145 f., where Harrison explains the tattoo as the "special mark of the barbarous Thracian." Dodds, *The Greeks and the Irrational* (above, note 126) 163 n. 44, refers to this without mentioning Harrison's name. Harrison's source for her conceptions of the maenads was the epoch-making paper of A. Rapp, "Die Mänade im griechischen Cultus, in der Kunst und Poesie," *Rheinisches Museum für Philologie* NF 27 (1872) 1–22, 562–611; cf. *Prolegomena* 388 n. 3.

[130] See Harrison, *Epilegomena* (above, note 49) 35–40. Cf. also her final word on the history of religion in the Foreword to the second edition of *Themis* (above, note 1) ix: "I found to my joy that most of my old heresies that had seemed to my contemporaries so 'rash' were accepted . . . : that gods and religious ideas generally reflect the social activities of the worshipper; that the food-supply is of primary importance for religion; that the *daimon* precedes the full-blown god; that the Great Mother is prior to the masculine divinites." A few of these "heresies" are even now "substantiated by a touch-and-handle knowledge and a sort of robust common-sense" (*ibid.*), while others are once again being disputed. What Murray wrote in 1955 is still true today: "Few people would accept the whole of J. E. H.'s conclusions, but nobody can write on Greek religion without being influenced by her work;" Stewart, *J. E. Harrison* (above, note 11) xi. But it must be stated that Harrison's importance in scholarship receives far less recognition than that of her (masculine) colleagues, many of whom had less influence than she or advanced hypotheses as bizarre as hers. Aside from rare (and generally negative) references to her and her work, a *damnatio memoriae* prevails, accompanied by a silent acceptance or rejection of her ideas. A history of the scientific community's response to Harrison's work and personality would be beyond the scope of his paper and is reserved for a future work.

[131] A preliminary version of this paper was presented at the Conference on the Cambridge Ritualists, April 1989, in Urbana, Illinois (organized by W. M. Calder III) and at the van-der-Leeuw Conference, May 1989, in Groningen (directed by Hans Kippenberg). I thank the organizers of these conferences for their invitations to take part; I thank them and the other participants in the discussions for stimulating contributions. My sincere gratitude is owed to Scott Scullion, who helped me to prepare the English version that was read at the Urbana conference, as well as to Michael Armstrong, who produced the final English translation, and Robert Ackerman, Jan Bremmer, Albert Henrichs, Wolfram-A. Maharam, and Sandra Peacock, who gave me important suggestions. My particular thanks go to Churchill College, which welcomed me as Fellow Commoner for the Michaelmas term of 1985, and to Newnham College and Trinity College, which opened their archives to me during this stay in Cambridge and permitted me to study Jane Harrison's unpublished letters.

11

A. B. Cook, *Zeus: A Study in Ancient Religion* (1914 / 1925 / 1940): Nachdenkliches über Plan und Aussage des Werkes

HANS SCHWABL

Es ist mir die Aufgabe zugefallen, im Rahmen dieser Konferenz über A. B. Cooks monumentales Werk *Zeus* zu sprechen, und auf das Werk werde ich mich auch vor allem konzentrieren. Allerdings sind auch einige biographische Angaben als Hintergrund dazu wohl unerläßlich, und so will ich mit diesen zunächst beginnen.[1]

Arthur Bernard Cook (1868–1952) wurde in Hampstead geboren, wo sein Vater eine gutgehende Arztpraxis hatte. Die Mutter entstammte einer Familie, in der kirchliche Berufe Tradition waren.[2] Erzogen wurde Cook in der bekannten St. Paul's School, Kensington,[3] und kam von dort mit einem "Major Scholarship for Classics" 1886 an das Trinity College, Cambridge, wo er ein in jeder Hinsicht glanzvolles und mit einer schönen Reihe von Preisen belohntes Studium absolvierte. Seine Lehrer bescheinigen ihm dabei nicht zuletzt die literarische Befähigung und die besonderen Leistungen

[1] Meine Skizze basiert auf dem Nachruf von Charles Seltman in den *Proceedings of the British Academy* 38 (1952) 295–302 (Plate 19 gibt eine Portraitphotographie) und auf A. B. Cook betreffenden Angaben in den Büchern von P. G. Naiditch (*A. E. Housman at University College, London: The Election of 1892* [Leiden 1988], 158f. [mit ausführlichen biobibliographischen Angaben]) und R. Ackerman (*J. G. Frazer: His Life and Work* [Cambridge 1987], 197–200 [über die zeitweilig enge Zusammenarbeit von Frazer und Cook nach Cooks kritischer Besprechung von *The Golden Bough*, 2nd ed., in *CR* 16 (1902) 365–80 unter dem Titel "The Golden Bough and the Rex Nemorensis"]). Ferner verdanke ich der Großzügigkeit und Freundlichkeit von P. G. Naiditch die Kenntnis des Bewerbungsschreibens und der die Bewerbung unterstützenden "testimonials," die Cook im April 1892 gedruckt eingereicht hat (aufbewahrt in der D.M.S. Watson Library, University College, London, College Collection, Application Classics 1892). Einige Angaben über die Zeit vor der Bewerbung am University College entstammen diesen Dokumenten.

[2] Seltman 295 schreibt darüber: "His mother, Harriet, sister of a bishop of Exeter, was of the Bickersteth family which produced several eminent ecclesiastics and hymn-writers of the evangelical persuasion."

[3] A. B. Cook hat der in Anm. 1 genannten Bewerbung auch "testimonials" von zweien seiner dortigen Lehrer beigefügt (F. W. Walker; J. E. King).

in "Greek and Latin composition." Die beiden abschließenden Prüfungen des "Classical Tripos" ("Pure Classics" bzw. "Pure Classics, Philosophy, and Archaeology") legte Cook in den Jahren 1889 und 1891 ab.[4] Dann wurde er, auf sein eigenes Ansuchen hin, nach einer Reihe von drei Vorlesungen über die Akropolis als Lecturer zugelassen.[5] 1892 bewarb sich Cook um die freie Professur für Griechisch bzw. (im Falle der Nichtberücksichtigung) für Latein am University College, London. Er hatte damit nicht Erfolg,[6] wurde jedoch im Jahre darauf (1893), fünfundzwanzigjährig, zum "Professor of Greek" am Bedford College, London, ernannt. Gleichzeitig erhielt er ein auf sechs Jahre befristetes "Fellowship" am Trinity College, wo er also weiter verblieb und studierte, während er wöchentlich zum Unterricht nach London fuhr.[7] Philosophische Themen beschäftigten Cook damals zunächst (es ist das eine Art von biographischer Parallele zum jungen Frazer), und es ist auch für bestimmte Aspekte in seinem Hauptwerk *Zeus* nicht ohne Interesse, daß er 1895 ein Buch mit dem Titel *The Metaphysical Basis of Plato's Ethics* veröffentlicht hat.[8] Man darf aber—auch ohne genauere Kenntnis diesbezüglicher biographischer Materialien—gewiß davon ausgehen, daß Cooks Freude an

[4] Für das Studien- und Prüfungssystem vgl. Ackerman, *J. G. Frazer*, Kap. 2 ("Trinity undergraduate"). Von den bei der Bewerbung am University College eingereichten "testimonials" (insgesamt 18) kommen die von R. D. Hicks, H. Montagu Butler, H. C. Goodhart, A. W. Verrall, H. Jackson, R. D. Archer-Hind aus dem Trinity College, andere stammen von R. C. Jebb (Regius Professor of Greek), J.E.B. Mayor (Professor of Latin) und J. E. Sandys (St. John's College). Verrall bescheinigt Cook "a singularly complete knowledge of the classical field, both in the more ancient parts and in those more recently acquired." Es fällt auf, daß ansonsten neben den allgemeinen Aussagen, welche die Belesenheit ebenso wie die sprachliche und die literarische Kompetenz hervorheben, nur das Gebiet der griechischen Philosophie ausdrücklich betont wird. Es geschieht das in der besonders warmen Charakteristik Cooks durch R. D. Hicks und in dem an letzter Stelle stehenden Schreiben des Barons F. von Hügel, der als Cooks Schüler bezeugt: "We are now in the midst of a fifteen weeks' course of Pre-Socratic and Platonic philosophy; and the thorough and stimulating manner in which he has piloted me through all the most metaphysical parts of Plato, has earned him my warm gratitude." Ein Nahverhältnis zu griechischen philosophischen Texten mit theologischer Relevanz wird in Cooks *Zeus* vor allem dort kenntlich, wo der Autor sie in seinen Zusammenfassungen (allerdings oft ein wenig kurzschlußhaft) zur Angabe des Zielpunkts der Entwicklung heranzieht.

[5] Zwei "testimonials" von Beauftragten des "Local Examinations and Lectures Syndicate" beziehen sich darauf, wobei das von dem Mathematiker A. Berry stammende auch den Gegenstand nennt: "I attended two out of a course of three Lectures on the Akropolis which he gave to a general audience of about 50. The lectures struck me as clear, forcible and interesting; and the second lecture was a marked improvement on the first."

[6] "Probably because of his youth and lack of experience in teaching." (P. G. Naiditch, *A. E. Housman at University College*, 159, mit Verweis auf diesbezügliche Briefe).

[7] Seltman 299 erwähnt, daß Cooks "manuscript lecture notebooks" in der University Library, Cambridge, aufbewahrt werden. Ebendort auch zu den Materialien für einen Theokritkommentar (vgl. dazu auch Gow, *Theocritus* I p. xii).

[8] Seltmans Urteil darüber (297) mag man anführen: "Had Cook's studies continued along these lines...he would undoubtedly have faded into the academic backcloth as yet another 'forgotten don'."

Anschauung von "Realien" und sein Trieb, das antike Leben an seinen konkreten Äußerungen zu erfassen, auch damals schon sehr lebendig gewesen ist. Es genügt dafür der Verweis auf die genannte erste Vorlesungsreihe über die Akropolis, auf Cooks eigene Angaben über Reisen zu den Stätten der alten Welt bei seiner Bewerbung am University College,[9] und Seltman berichtet über die regelmäßigen Besuche im British Museum sowie über Cooks eigene Tätigkeit als Sammler. Um die Jahrhundertwende wechselte Cook, nach dem Auslaufen seines Fellowships am Trinity College, als Fellow an das Queens' College, womit gleichzeitig ein Auftrag als Classical Lecturer verbunden war. Doch die Richtung seiner späteren Hauptinteressen zeigt sich deutlich in der 1902 erschienenen Besprechung der zweiten Auflage von Frazers *Golden Bough*, und sie erfährt ihre entscheidende Wendung in einer daran anschließenden Zusammenarbeit mit Frazer, welche zu der Artikelreihe "Zeus, Jupiter and the Oak" bzw. "The European Sky-god" geführt hat.[10] Freundliche Kontakte zwischen Cook und Frazer hat es aber gewiß auch schon vor der Periode der engen Zusammenarbeit (1902–05) während der gemeinsamen Zeit als Fellows am Trinity College gegeben, und Ackerman zitiert auch einen Brief an Cook aus Liverpool (1908), in dem Frazer in Erwartung seiner Rückkehr nach Cambridge auf die Wiederaufnahme der gemeinsamen Spaziergänge und Gespräche hofft.[11] Cook hatte in der Zwischenzeit (1907) die Professur am Bedford College in London aufgegeben und stattdessen die Stelle eines "Reader in Classical Archaeology in the University of Cambridge" übernommen, womit auch die Betreuung des archäologischen Museums verbunden war.[12] Die Zeit dieses sichtbaren Wechsels zur Archäologie fällt zusammen auch mit dem Beginn der planvollen Arbeit an seinem großen Werk, wobei Cook im Vorwort zum ersten Band die Atmosphäre von Cambridge als für dessen Durchführung wesentlich bezeichnet hat: "Life in Cambridge," so sagt er, "has indeed afforded me, not merely access to a great Library, but—what is better still—ready access to many personal friends both able and willing to enlighten ignorance" (I p. xv). Und auch hier bekennt sich Cook zu dem Impuls, welcher von "Sir James G. Frazer's Arician hypothesis" auf ihn ausgegangen sei, und wie das die genannten Aufsatzreihen bedingt habe, in denen die Untersuchung auch auf den keltischen, germanischen und lettoslawischen Bereich sich ausdehnte und

---

[9] "I have travelled through Greece and Italy, partly in order to deepen my own knowledge of classical sites, partly with a view to arousing the interest of pupils by the reminiscences of an eye-witness."

[10] "Zeus, Jupiter and the Oak," *CR* 17 (1903) 174–86, 268–78, 403–21; 18 (1904) 75–79, 325–28, 360–75. "The European Sky-god," *Folk-Lore* 15 (1904) 264–315, 364–426; 16 (1905) 260–332.

[11] Ackerman, *J. G. Frazer*, 215.

[12] Von 1931 bis zu seiner Emeritierung (1934) war Cook dann der erste "Laurence Professor of Classical Archaeology in the University of Cambridge," und von 1935–52 fungierte er als "Vice-President of Queens' College."

dem Problem des "European Sky-god" nachgegangen wurde. Cook berichtet jedoch auch, daß ihn schließlich L. R. Farnell durch freundliche Kritik von dem zunächst eingeschlagenen Weg abgebracht habe:[13] "I resolved," so fährt Cook fort, "to start afresh on narrower lines, restricting enquiry to the single case of Zeus," und wenn er zu dieser Aussage noch hinzufügt "even so the subject has proved to be almost too wide" (I p. xii), so wird jeder, der sich einen auch nur einigermaßen passablen Überblick über die Quellen zu verschaffen versucht hat, dem ohne jede Einschränkung beipflichten müssen.[14] Im übrigen hat Cook die auch durch den Titel seines Werkes signalisierte Konzentration auf den griechischen Zeus in Wahrheit nie ganz vollzogen.

Einen direkten Einfluß von J. G. Frazer hat Cook im übrigen auch für sein großes Werk festgehalten: "It was Sir James G. Frazer who first advised me to put together in permanent form the materials that I had collected," heißt es im ersten Band (p. xiv), und noch der dritte und abschließende Band hat eine dem entsprechende Aussage (p. ix):

> Zeus, I am happy to say, has been begun, continued, and ended under the auspices of two old friends, old in years, but young in outlook—Sir James Frazer and Dr. Rendel Harris. It was they who first welcomed the inception of the work, and, though quite aware that I often dissent from their findings, they have wished me well from start to finish.

Aber daneben tritt vor allem im ersten Band auch die Hervorhebung einer besonderen Verpflichtung gegenüber Namen wie O. Gruppe, G. Murray, Miss J. E. Harrison und auch F. M. Cornford, also dem Verfasser der *Griechischen Mythologie und Religionsgeschichte* (München 1906) und dem als "Cambridge Ritualists" zusammengefaßten Kreis von Freunden, der diese unsere Tagung besonders interessiert. Otto Gruppe bezeichnet A. B. Cook dabei als "the greatest mythologist of modern times" (p. xi), und neben dieses enkomiastische Urteil tritt die nicht weniger preisende Aussage, Gruppe habe "in his *Handbuch* and elsewhere...set up a standard of thoroughness that must for many a long day be kept in view by all writers on the subject of classical religion" (p. xiv), und im Vorwort zum zweiten Band bedauert Cook mit sichtlicher Anteilnahme Gruppes Tod als schweren Verlust für die Wissenschaft.[15] Gruppe ist auch der in den ersten beiden Bänden offenbar am häufigsten angeführte Autor, während im dritten Band die Verweise auf ihn deutlich abnehmen. Von Anregungen durch Gruppe, zu

---

[13] "I had meant to go further along the same road. But at this point Dr. Farnell in the friendliest fashion put a spoke in my wheel by convincing me that the unity of an ancient god consisted less in his nature than in his name" (I p. xii).

[14] "I incline to think that a full treatment of any of the greater Greek divinities, such a treatment as must ultimately be accorded to them all, properly demands the co-ordinated efforts of several workers," sagt Cook (I p. xiii).

[15] "Otto Gruppe too is gone—a grave loss to learning—leaving as one of his latest writings a brief but masterly paper on 'Die Anfänge des Zeuskultus' (*Neue Jahrb. f. klass. Altertum* 1918 xli–xlii.289–302" (II p. ix).

denen sich Cook bekennt, mag beispielhaft allein die schöne ikonographische Reihe "Gradual elimination of the thunderbolt" genannt sein, welche sich im zweiten Band (p. 722ff.) findet. Insgesamt hat Gruppe aber natürlich als der Verfasser des "Handbuchs" diese besondere Stellung, und so wird man neben ihm gerechterweise auch die Autoren von Materialsammlungen anführen, auf denen Cook aufbaut, so unter den Archäologen J. Overbeck, E. Gerhard, A. Furtwängler und S. Reinach, unter den Numismatikern B. V. Head, F. Imhoof-Blumer und J. N. Svoronos, und unter den Mythologen und Religionshistorikern nicht zuletzt auch die Verfasser von Artikeln in Roschers *Mythologischem Lexikon* oder in Pauly-Wissowas *Realencyclopädie*, wobei Cook die Abhängigkeit stets gewissenhaft registriert.[16] Vor allem zu nennen sind sodann aber auch unter dem Aspekt der Materialsammlung die Namen von Jane E. Harrison, L. R. Farnell und J. G. Frazer, dessen *Golden Bough* Cook gleichfalls besonders häufig anführt und einmal (II.417) als "that amazing monument of helpful research" in singulärer Weise hervorhebt.

Was die Gruppe der sogenannten "Ritualisten" angeht, so tritt unter ihnen auch bei Cook J. E. Harrison besonders hervor. Cook dankt ihr auch noch im zweiten Band (p. x) für das Mitlesen der Fahnen, aber es ist naturgemäß der erste Band, in dem ihre Anteilnahme am Cookschen Werk am deutlichsten wird, wobei Cooks Danksagung sich auch mit einer Abgrenzung verbindet (die sich mit der gegenüber Frazer und Rendel Harris im dritten Band vergleichen läßt): "Miss J. E. Harrison, to whose wide range and quick synthetic powers I am indebted for several valuable suggestions: I am the more anxious to acknowledge this debt because on matters of the deepest import we do not see eye to eye" (I.xivf.). Im Werke selbst findet sich dann nicht selten der Dank für mündliche und schriftliche Mitteilungen, und man mag davon vielleicht beispielhaft hervorheben, daß Cooks Verweis auf S. Freud, *Totem und Tabu* (1913), für das Problem der Entmannungsmythen[17] ebenso der Rührigkeit von Jane Harrison verdankt wird wie die Erkenntnis, daß die Gleichung der Dioskuren mit den beiden Himmelshemisphären ein neueres Weltbild voraussetzt.[18] Sonst seien hier

---

[16] Z.B. II 1160,7 im Falle von O. Höfer, "that excellent enquirer...to whose article I am much indebted."

[17] II p. 450, 1 "Miss Harrison has further brought to my notice the latest attempt to solve the problem, that of the psychoanalyst" (mit nachfolgendem ausführlichem Zitat aus Freud a.O. 120f). Allerdings ist zu fürchten, daß Cook (und Harrison?)—sosehr der Verweis im Prinzip natürlich relevant ist—die heute jedermann vertraute Terminologie Freuds nicht ganz verstanden, und so den (in "Ödipus-" bzw. "Kastrationskomplex" vorhandenen) Verweis auf Mythologie breiter angesetzt hat als es an der Stelle der Fall ist.

[18] II p. 432,4. Das Bedenkliche an dieser Stelle ist, daß Harrisons Kritik die ganze Cooksche Sequenz über die Dioskuren viel entscheidender in ihrem Ansatz trifft, als dem Autor bei seiner Annahme derselben bewußt gewesen zu sein scheint. Denn Cooks Ausgangspunkt impliziert in II p. 422 ziemlich genau das, was in II p. 434 sich als "Greek speculation from Hellenistic to Byzantine times" darstellt. Und auch hier redet Cook, ähnlich wie bei seinen Aussagen über die Urzeit von "the animate sky." Vgl. hierzu auch

nur Punkte erwähnt, an denen auch ein gewisser Eindruck von einem Freundeskreis entsteht, wie z.B. bei Behandlung der Zagreusmythen, wo Harrison, Cornford und Murray als einheitliche Gruppe erscheinen, deren Deutung Cook im übrigen sich zu modifizieren bemüht (I.649,7), beim Dank an Cornford und Harrison für den Hinweis auf einen angeblich zu dem kretischen Talos passenden Kultbefund auf Sardinien (I.723,3), oder auch bei einer Äußerung zur akustischen Wirkung des Rhombos, wofür Cook sich auf eine praktische Demonstration durch Cornford beruft (I.650,1: "I have heard Mr. Cornford swing [a bullroarer] in the darkness with great effect"). Weitere Einzelheiten dürfen wohl beiseite bleiben, doch mag man in diesem Zusammenhang die allgemeine Feststellung wagen, daß es in Cooks großem Werk streckenweise eine dem Autor selbst unbewußte Verursachung von Themensequenzen gibt, die sich letztlich leichter aus dem besonderen Interessenkreis von J. Frazer und der "Cambridge Ritualists" als aus den Notwendigkeiten des Themas "Zeus" verstehen lassen. Und die Sequenz Omophagie, Ursprung der Tragödie, attische Dionysosfeste, Satyrdrama wird man jedenfalls dazurechnen.[19]

Wir wollen nun eine der zusammenfassenden Äußerungen Cooks über sein Werk uns etwas ausführlicher vergegenwärtigen und wählen dafür Aussagen des dritten und abschließenden Bandes, die auch das Problem der Darstellung zur Sprache bringen und gleichzeitig zeigen können, wie sehr A. B. Cook bereit war, die Leistungen von anderen in fairer Weise zu würdigen. Er tut das in unserem Zusammenhang angesichts des Artikels "Zeus" in Roschers *Mythologischem Lexikon* (der im übrigen viel einem Manuskript von O. Gruppe und auch Cooks *Zeus* I–II verdankt), hebt davon aber auch seine eigene Weise des Verfahrens ab. "The work as a whole," so sagt Cook (III.viif.),

> sets out to survey the range and influence of the Greek Sky-god. It would, I suppose, have been possible to do this in less discursive fashion by means of tabulated statements and statistics—a list of his cult-centres, an index of his appellations, a classified catalogue of his representations in art—in short, to adopt the dictionary-method, admirably carried out by E. Fehrle, K. Ziegler, and O. Waser towards the end of Roscher's great Lexikon (VI.564–759). But my notion of a survey is somewhat different. I find a road-map less helpful than an

---

Ackerman, *J. G. Frazer* 331,10, wo es über Jane Harrisons kritische Bemühungen um Cook schließlich heißt: "Finally she despaired of getting him to understand the importance of clarity in exposition."

[19] Vgl. I p. 651–705 (als Teil eines Abschnitts "The Significance of the Bull in the Cults of Zeus"); Ausgangspunkt ist p. 651 Frazer über vermutete Königsopfer im Adoniskult, doch enthält der in Frage stehende Abschnitt auch die Aufnahme von bzw. Auseinandersetzung mit G. Murrays "ritualistischer" Theorie über den Ursprung der Tragödie und des Satyrspiels (bei Harrison, *Themis* 341–63). Für Cooks Kritik am "Eniautos Daimon" und einen erklärenden Brief Murrays siehe I p. 680f. Es versteht sich, daß das hier angesprochene Problem sich mit dem noch zu besprechenden Problem der Faszination Cooks durch Parallelen zu Christlichem auf das engste berührt.

ordnance-sheet. The former may simplify things and enable you to get more directly to your destination. But the latter invites you to explore the neighbourhood, marks the field-paths, puts in the contour-lines, colours the water-ways, and prints in Gothic lettering the local antiquities. Time is lost, but knowledge is gained, and the traveller returns well-content with his trapesings. So I have deliberately chosen the more devious method, and I can only fall back on Herodotos' plea, that "my subject from the outset demanded digressions". Indeed it was just this need for latitude that lead me to widen the title *Zeus* by adding the subtitle "a Study in Ancient Religion". That is the real justification for long-winded footnotes and a fringe of Appendixes.

Das Resultat ist eine—wie M. P. Nilsson, *Geschichte der griechischen Religion*[2] I.389,1 gesagt hat—"große, grundgelehrte und das entlegenste Material musterhaft vorführende Monographie," eine (so O. Weinreich, *Arch. f. Rel. wiss.* 34 [1937], 137) "wahre Hekatombe von Gelehrsamkeit strengster Art," und man wird diesen Urteilen auch dann ohne allzu gravierende Einschränkung beipflichten, wenn man selber empfindet, daß die Anordnung des riesigen Materials unter den beiden Kapiteln "Zeus God of the Bright Sky" und "Zeus God of the Dark Sky" ihre nicht leichtzunehmenden Probleme hat, ferner auch über Cooks Weise der Aggregation und der Assoziation sich gelegentlich nicht wenig gewundert hat. Fürwahr: "ce livre étrange," eine Charakteristik durch L. Robert,[20] ist nicht danebengegriffen.

Inwieweit A. B. Cook manchmal selbst Zweifel an der Zweckmäßigkeit seiner Anordnung gekommen sind, vermag ich nicht zu sagen, doch darf man wohl vermuten, daß die freudige Registrierung von Otto Weinreichs Zustimmung (a.a.O.138) in der Preface zum dritten Band auch eine Antwort auf diesbezügliche Kritik darstellt, die A. B. Cook nahegegangen ist.[21] Ich möchte auch diesen Passus und den Kontext, in dem er steht, etwas ausführlicher zitieren; wir erhalten damit gleichzeitig auch einen Überblick über das ganze Werk, so wie der Autor selbst es am Ende seiner Mühen gesehen hat bzw. sehen wollte. A. B. Cook sagt (III p. vii):

> This at least I can claim that, year in, year out, I have steadily pursued the plan originally laid down for the scope and contents of the book. Volume I was to deal with Zeus as god of the Bright Sky, Volume II with Zeus as god of the Dark Sky—an arrangement of essentials approved by the authority of Otto Weinreich (Archiv f. Rel. 1937 xxxiv.138). Accordingly, Volume I included not only the Hellenic worship of the Bright Zeus, god of the Upper Sky, but also the Hellenistic attempts to

[20] Leider kann ich das nur aus dem Gedächtnis zitieren.
[21] Weinreichs "Zustimmung" bezieht sich allerdings—genau besehen—weniger auf Cooks Anordnung als auf die Entwicklungsgeschichte des Gottes, zu der er entschieden für P. Kretschmers Ansatz (*Glotta* 13 [1924], 108ff.), der von der Etymologie und den durch Vergleich kenntlichen indogermanischen Voraussetzungen ausgeht, und gegen Wilamowitz, der vom Blitzgott ausgeht, Stellung nimmt.

connect him with Sun, Moon, and Stars, while Volume II was devoted to the Dark Zeus, god of Thunder and Lightning, in all his multifarious aspects. Thunder and Lightning proved to be so wide-spread and far-reaching that much had perforce to be left over for a third, at first uncontemplated, volume. This concerns itself with Zeus in his relations to a further series of cosmic phaenomena—Earthquakes, Clouds, Wind, Dew, Rain, and Meteorites. But I need not here enter into a detailed account of sections and subsections, as I have later endeavoured to trace in sequence the whole evolution of the cult of Zeus (pages 943 to 973), concluding with a statement of what I conceive to be its ultimate significance (pp. 973, 974).

Schlägt man das Ende des Bandes auf, so findet man dort nach der, wie angekündigt, gegebenen Zusammenfassung von etwa 30 Seiten auch die versprochene Aussage über die "ultimate significance" des Zeuskults und seiner Entwicklung, und dieselbige umfaßt, wenn man den Umfang abzählt, gerade 28 Zeilen. Gesprochen wird dabei unter Nennung des Pherekydes von Syros, des Aischylos, des Arat und des Dion Chrysostomos von den Vorahnungen des Gottesreiches und des Gotts der Liebe und Wahrheit durch die griechischen Dichter und Denker. Die Verweise, die diese Aussage sorgfältig begleiten, gehen dabei zunächst auf die Motti der drei Bände des Werkes, die den Zeushymnus im *Agamemnon* des Aischylos (I p. v), das Prooimion der *Phainomena* des Arat (II p. v) sowie das Fragment B 3 des Pherekydes[22] und eine markante Stelle aus der Verteidigungsrede des Phidias im *Olympikos* des Dion bieten (III p. 5). Berücksichtigt wird im Werke selbst davon in erster Linie Dion,[23] und zwar vor allem im Kontext des Abschlusses des dritten Bandes (p. 963), wo der Zeus des Phidias einen Höhepunkt darstellt; berücksichtigt wird ferner auch noch Pherekydes (II p. 316), dieser jedoch in einem Abschnitt über "The *Kabeiroi* or *Megaloi Theoi*," wo zu der Vermutung "that Axiokersa was the Mother [=die Erdgöttin], Axiokersos the Father [=der Himmelsgott], and Axieros the Son conceived as a rebirth of the Father" (p. 314) als vermeintliche Parallelen Hesiods Trias Chaos, Gaia und Eros, aber auch die (angeblich) bei

[22] Es ist wohl nötig darauf hinzuweisen, daß das meiste in diesem "Fragment" offenkundig der Ausdeutung des Proklos gehört. Wenn man die "Verwandlung des Zeus in Eros" akzeptiert, so hat Pherekydes seinem Zas (so der Name bei ihm) an einem bestimmten Punkte die Funktion des kosmogonischen Eros gegeben. Zas, Chronos (Kronos) und Chthonia bilden die uranfängliche Trias des Pherekydes.

[23] Der *Olympikos* des Dion hat auf Cook offenkundig besonderen Eindruck gemacht. Er zitiert ihn bereits I p.xi sq. ("Dion Chrysostomos in a memorable sentence declared Zeus to be 'the giver of all good things, the Father, the Saviour, the Keeper of mankind'.") in einem Kontext, der in nuce Cooks Entwicklungsvorstellungen enthält und Dion eine Art Zielpunkt auf dem Wege "towards our own conceptions of the Deity" sein läßt. Umso markanter ist es, daß Cook, wie wir noch sehen werden, Dions Aussage über die Gotteserfahrung der Urmenschheit offenbar bewußt unter Frazerschen Voraussetzungen umformuliert hat.

Pherekydes gegebene Trias "Zeus, Chthonia and Eros" (mitsamt der Verwandlung des Zeus in Eros, fr. B 3) gestellt werden.[24]

Man wird nicht umhin können zu registrieren, wie oberflächlich diese Parallelen sind, aber das ist eine (bei Cook freilich nicht isolierte) Einzelheit. Für unsere Absicht ist zunächst allein wichtig die Beobachtung, daß das was für A. B. Cook selbst als der Zielpunkt der Entwicklung des Zeuskults galt, in seinem Werk im Grunde nicht mehr zur Darstellung gekommen ist. So ist denn auch die irrtümliche Erwartung eines vierten Bandes, welcher O. Weinreich bei seiner Besprechung der ersten beiden Bände Ausdruck gegeben hat, alles andere als abwegig. Die unmittelbare Quelle für Weinreichs Erwartung war jedoch eine Aussage, die Cook an die ziemlich genaue Ankündigung des Inhalts des 3. Bandes noch angeschlossen hat: "I shall hope," so schrieb Cook, "to conclude at long last with a general survey of the Sky-god and his cult as constituting one factor in the great fabric of Greek civilisation, indeed as in some sense a contribution to Christianity itself" (II p. vii).

Daß dies einen weiteren großen Band in Aussicht stellen sollte, wird man bezweifeln, nicht gut bezweifeln kann man jedoch, daß Cook doch an etwas mehr als 28 Zeilen oder auch einige zusammenfassende Seiten gedacht haben wird, und das heißt wohl auch, daß man Cooks Werk für auch nach seiner eigenen Idee nicht ganz vollendet anzusehen hat. Die Gründe dafür sind wohl nur zum Teil äußerer Art,[25] sondern liegen tiefer. Sie liegen wohl schon im wissenschaftlichen Ansatz Cooks, der bei seiner Erforschung des griechischen Himmelsgotts die Naturphänomene ganz in den Vordergrund gerückt hat und sich dabei auch besonders auf die Daten des Kults und der Bildüberlieferung konzentriert, sie liegen aber wohl auch in einer Art von Widerspruch, der zwischen der Position des gewählten und übernommenen wissenschaftlichen Ansatzes und der Position von Cooks eigener und nirgendwo verhüllter religiösen Überzeugung besteht.[26] Ich werde versuchen, etwas davon deutlich zu machen.

---

[24] Vgl. Anm. 22.

[25] Vgl. z.B. II p. ix: "The episodical character of the book with its sections and subsections is due, at least in part, to the circumstances in which it has been composed. I have throughout been in full work as College Lecturer in Classics and University Reader in Classical Archaeology...Such a life...tends to produce a certain mental attitude, the habit of thinking in compartments" (etc.). Man muß sich jedenfalls vergegenwärtigen, welche Zeit und Konzentration es erfordert hat, um den gegebenen Rahmen auszufüllen.

[26] Vgl. III p 974: "Let us be bold to assert that throughout all ages and in every clime God has been making his mute appeal to men, drawing them, Jew and Gentile alike, with the cords of love nearer and nearer to Himself. Progressive illumination has been given them from above as they were able to bear it." Die Absicht, "sundry points of contact between Hellenism and Christianity" mit zu berücksichtigen, ist schon I p. xii ausgesprochen, wobei "our own conceptions of Deity" als Zielpunkt der Entwicklung erscheinen. Seltman 301f. registriert die Kritik, die Cook bei Erscheinen des ersten Bandes für seinen Standpunkt erhielt, tendiert aber dazu, die Bedeutung desselben für das Cooksche Werk zu unterschätzen. Seine abschließende Feststellung, daß mit dem dritten Band "a delicate change had occurred and earlier missionary evangelicalism had been

Aus der Anordnung des Gesamtwerks, das sich allein an den sichtbaren Erscheinungen des Himmels orientiert, ergibt sich mit Notwendigkeit, daß A. B. Cook nur in über das ganze Werk verstreuten Einzelbemerkungen sowie in der Weise von Anhängen jeweils am Ende der beiden letzten Bände von den Entwicklungslinien sprechen kann, auf denen die Vorstellungen über Zeus sich erweitern und von den zugleich immer vorausgesetzten Naturgrundlagen sich lösen. So endet der zweite Band, der den "God of Thunder and Lightning" zum Gegenstand hat, schließlich beim Gott der Gerechtigkeit und bei der Gotteskonzeption der Philosophen (p. 852), wofür als Illustration eine Behandlung der Dareiosvase (pp. 852–54) und ein Abschnitt mit dem Zeushymnus des Kleanthes (pp. 854–58) folgt. Das wichtigste Element ist dabei für Cook der Blitz und die allmähliche Entwicklung seiner symbolischen Bedeutung. Er sagt dazu (852):

> The populace, taught by the playwrights, was vaguely conscious that above the shifting scenes of human life somewhere and somehow Zeus sat enthroned to mete out justice with impartial balance. If he used his thunderbolt, it would be to punish the proud and to lay their towering ambitions in the dust. The philosophers with clearer insight perceived that Zeus must be all or nought. Most of them, amid much diversity of detail, grasped the same essential fact that there is a Power Supreme, which in every moment is engaged in the godlike task of turning chaos into cosmos. Not a few of them—Pherekydes, Herakleitos, Empedokles, Platon, the Stoics—spoke of It, spoke of Him, as Zeus. And to these the thunderbolt was but a symbol of his omnipotence.[27]

Auch der Abschluß des dritten Bandes führt nach einer Zusammenfassung (p. 943f.) zu einer entsprechenden Aussage, wobei bei ihrer Formulierung diesmal auch Einflüsse von G. Foucart, R. Pettazzoni

---

purified into a calm and considered deist philosophy," deckt sich nicht mit meinem Eindruck. Das interessanteste Problem liegt denn auch nicht in diesem Standpunkt selbst, sondern in seinem Nebeneinander mit rationalistischen Modellen Frazers, die sich damit nicht gut vereinbaren lassen.

[27] Die in erster Linie relevanten Verweise betreffen I pp. 27–33 ("Zeus identified with Aithér...in Philosophy and Poetry"), wobei mehr eine Reihe von Erwähnungen als eine Darstellung der Entwicklung vorliegt. Eigenartig sind Cooks schwankende Bewertungen, wie der Anfang des zitierten Abschnitts zeigen kann. Cook sagt dort mit Bezug auf die (offenbar dem Bedürfnis nach Schönwetter entsprungenen) Epiklesen *Aithrios* und *Aitherios*: "Lying at the back of such usages is the half-forgotten belief that Aithér, the 'Burning Sky,' itself is Zeus. Zoism dies hard; and this belief can be traced here and there throughout the whole range of Greek literature. In particular, it has left its impress on philosophy and poetry." Zur Definition von "Zoism" s. ebd. p. 27,4. Ferner verweise ich auf I p. 13,1, wo Cooks Versuch, sich von dem Frazerschen Modell zu lösen (dem er sonst im Grunde folgt), zu der Aussage führt: "Indeed, it would not be absurd to maintain that this pre-anthropomorphic conception was in some respects higher, because more true, than later anthropomorphism." Die Wertung ist sonst auch bei Cook die umgekehrte, und die Differenz zwischen dem anthropomorphen Gottesbild der Griechen und seiner Aufhebung bei den Philosophen bleibt bei ihm, soweit ich sehe, ziemlich weitgehend verwischt.

und Pater Wilhelm Schmidt[28] eine Rolle spielen dürften. Cook sagt mit Bezug auf "the physical foundations of the cult of Zeus" (an denen sein Werk sich ja ausschließlich orientiert):

I have used them throughout as providing a convenient framework for a somewhat discursive investigation of his worship. But the more nearly we study these aspects of it, the more clearly we perceive that they were after all just the ground-plan or lower storey of a greater and grander whole. Resting upon them and rising all the time, here a little and there a little, was a structure of fresh religious concepts, whose height and breadth—pinnacles of individual aspiration and prospects of interracial understanding—were quite without parallel in the pagan world. The fact is that always and everywhere the cult of a Sky-god has proved to be an elevating and widening force. Inevitably so, for it tends to raise the thoughts of men from earth to heaven. And the quick-witted Greeks were prompt to seize the opportunity of such uplift and expansion.[29]

Die folgenden Beispiele sind keineswegs einheitlich, sie formen aber eine Linie, welche Cooks Grundintention überaus deutlich macht. Die Linie beginnt mit Zeus Hypsistos, für den (keineswegs evidentermaßen) der Übergang von ursprünglichem Bergkult zu der Konzeption eines höchsten Gottes vorausgesetzt wird, welche seit hellenistischer Zeit in der Gleichung des Zeus "with the supreme deity of more than one non-Hellenic people, and not the least of the Jews" sich ergeben hat. Ähnlich wird die Gleichung des Zeus mit der Sonne und mit solaren Göttern von Ägypten, Nordafrika und Syrien bewertet,[30] was schließlich zum "solar monotheism of Aurelian" geführt habe. Auch die jeweils bestehenden Beziehungen der verschiedenen Götter zu Widder und Stier hätten diese Gleichungen gefördert.[31] Und dann betont Cook wiederum den Gott des Blitzes: einmal im Hinblick auf die Vergottung des vom Blitz Getroffenen, dann für die Erscheinung des *Horkios* als Blitzeschleuderer, und schließlich für die Umformung, Umdeutung und Ersetzung der Blitzsymbole. Im Blick sind dabei Entwicklungslinien sowohl zum Monotheismus und zur Vergeistigung des Gottesbilds als auch zu Christlichem, wobei die Herleitung von Symbolen neben die Darlegung von (freilich nur teilweise stimmigen) Analoga tritt:

---

[28] Cook zitiert Pater Wilhelm Schmidt (III p. 944,21) für seine Zusammenfassung von und Kritik an den Positionen von Foucart und Pettazzoni. Zu Pettazzonis Kritik an der Theorie des "Urmonotheismus" s. *Numen* III (1956) 156ff. und V (1958) 116ff., ferner *The All-Knowing God*, London 1956.

[29] III p 944f.; vorausgeht, wie gesagt, eine Zusammenfassung der drei Bände. Die Aussage bleibt offenbar auf der Ebene einer "natural history of religion"; vgl. dagegen die Anm. 26 zitierte Aussage.

[30] Genannt sind "Amen-Râ at Egyptian Thebes, Sarapis at Alexandreia, Ba'al- ḥammân in north Africa, Ba'al-šamin in Syria," ferner Mithras und anderes.

[31] Der Widder verbindet nach Cook Ammon und Sabazios. Für den Stier sind im wesentlichen ursprüngliche Wettergötter genannt.

In general it may be said that from the sixth century onwards the
thunderbolt of Zeus begins to be replaced, surviving mainly as a
symbol of omnipotence or continuous divine activity. Indeed, under
Constantine its old Anatolian form, the *labrys*, was deliberately
reshaped into the *labarum* and adopted as the emblem of the all-
conquering faith.

Allmacht, Allwissenheit und Allgüte, Zeus als Herr des Kosmos, als Garant
des Rechts und als Gott, dessen Erscheinungsformen auch die Züge von
"Clemency, Mercy and Love" zeigen (p. 951), all das wird besonders betont.
Und dann führen die Vorstellungen, welche sich mit Zeus *Hiketes* verbinden,
und die Deutung von Zeus *Alastor* als "Zeus 'the curse'" (p. 952) in der
Zeichnung Cooks direkt auf Christus hin:

> ...a daring and desperate identification of the deity with the sinner.
> These things are strangely suggestive. Simple souls dwelling around
> the Mediterranean were prepared to believe that any day a god might
> appear in their midst in the likeness of a man. Why not as "the man
> Christ Jesus"? Further it would not stagger them to think that such an
> one might somehow condescend to identify himself with the sinner and
> even to "become a curse for us."[32]

Und dann kommt noch die Trinität, indem Cook hier wie auch sonst
besonderen Wert auf Göttertriaden legt, wobei das von ihm rekonstruierte
"thrako-phrygische Modell" die intendierte Grundanschauung wohl am
besten wiedergibt: "a sky-god Dios, an earth-goddess Zemela, and their offspring Dios *Nӯsos*, Dios 'the Younger'. The son was held to be a rebirth of
the father, whose name and nature he duplicated" (952). Von hier aus wird
auch der Attiskult bewertet: "Even the rites and *formulae* of Attis might
pass muster as quasi-Christian" (ebd.). Und selbst Arat und die auf ihn
Bezug nehmende Areopagrede des Apostels Paulus werden, keineswegs ohne
Künstlichkeit,[33] damit verknüpft. Höhepunkt und Schluß ist aber dann eine
Behandlung der Zeusstatue des Phidias in Olympia mit den sie ausdeutenden
Zeugnissen (p. 954ff.), vor allem dem (rein auf der Ebene der Ausdeutung
bleibenden) Zeugnis der Verteidigungsrede des Phidias im *Olympikos* des
Dion (p. 961–64).[34]

---

[32] Die Zitate beziehen sich auf 1 Tim. 2, 5 und Gal. 3, 13. Zeus als Schützer der
Bittflehenden und Schwachen läßt sich legitim mit Christlichem vergleichen. Der Fall von
Zeus Alastor liegt auf einer ganz anderen Ebene.

[33] An Kronos, Rhea und den kretischen Zeus (= Zagreus) wird der (nur bei Byzantinern
gegebene und sehr zweifelhafte) Zeus Asterios geknüpft, dann Arats berühmtes ἐκ σοῦ γὰρ
γένος εἰμέν (*Phaen.* 5) wegen der bei Arat an anderer Stelle auch noch vorkommenden
Behandlung des Zeusmythos (ebd. 30ff.) auf den kretischen Zeus bezogen, und schließlich
das Aratzitat in der Areopagrede mit landsmannschaftlicher Affinität von Paulus und Arat
assoziiert, usw.

[34] Für die Weise der Ausdeutung, aus der sich keine Hinweise auf den Ausdruckswillen des
Phidias ergeben, s. Verf., "Dichtung und bildende Kunst (Zum *Olympikos* des Dion

Damit haben wir zusammenfassende Aussagen des Autors selbst über sein Werk betrachtet. Es empfiehlt sich, daß wir nun den Aufbau und Plan des Ganzen mitsamt den daraus folgenden Konsequenzen uns noch etwas genauer vergegenwärtigen. Der Überblick wird sehr erleichtert durch die peinlich genaue Disposition des Cookschen Werkes mit seiner Einteilung in zwei Kapitel (Kap. 1=Vol. I, Kap. 2=Vol. II–III), die sich weiter in Paragraphen mit Haupt- und Einzelthemen sowie deren Abschnitte und Unterabschnitte gliedern. Dabei unterstützen römische und arabische Ziffern, lateinische Buchstaben, kleine römische Ziffern und griechische Buchstaben die Sichtbarkeit der Gliederung des Texts, den eine Fülle von unter Umständen wieder in sich gegliederten Anmerkungen begleiten. Dazu treten Anhänge, die zum größten Teile als solche wohl von allem Anfang an geplant waren und nach lateinischen Großbuchstaben geordnet sind.[35] Sie können den Umfang von ganzen Büchern annehmen und enthalten immer eine Präsentation des jeweiligen Materials in möglichster Vollständigkeit und in größter Übersichtlichkeit. Nie wird an Raum gespart, Inschriften werden grundsätzlich ausgeschrieben, aber auch literarische Texte sind sehr häufig in vollem Wortlaut gegeben, so daß, wer Cook liest, auch dort wo er mit den Kombinationen des Autors überhaupt nicht einverstanden sein will (und das mag nicht selten der Fall sein), fast immer die Grundlagen in extenso vor Augen hat und so zum eigenen Schluße befähigt wird. Und dazu kommt, keineswegs an zweiter Stelle, sondern oft den Leitfaden abgebend, das archäologische Material, welches in mehr als 170 Tafeln und mehr als 2.500 Abbildungen präsent wird. Auch Volkskundliches fehlt—in der Linie Mannhardts und Frazers—nicht. Und zu guter Letzt ist alles noch durch Indizes von staunenswerter Präzision erschlossen, die es ein leichtes machen, das gesamte Werk als Thesaurus nicht nur für Zeus, sondern auch für fast alle Themen der Religionsgeschichte zu benützen. Der Untertitel des Werkes, sehr bewußt gewählt, lautet ja auch einfach "A Study in Ancient Religion."

Was nun die Gliederung im einzelnen angeht, so hat sich Cook an einer logischen Anordnung orientiert, die man (wir haben gesehen, daß O. Weinreich das getan hat) insofern auch historisch rechtfertigen kann, als die Etymologie des Gottesnamens auf den "hellen Himmel" (oder genauer auf die Bereiche "Tag" und "heller Himmel") führt. Unter diesem Gesichtspunkt kommt der "Gott des hellen Himmels" ohne Zweifel zurecht vor dem "Gott des dunklen Himmels," und es hat so dann auch eine gewisse klassifikatorische Zweckmäßigkeit, wenn man daraus die zwei Hauptkapitel einer Monographie gewinnt, von denen das erste ("Bright Sky") die Abschnitte "Zeus and the Daylight" (§ 1), "Zeus and the Burning Sky" (§

Chrysostomos)" in: Πρακτ. XII διεθν. συνεδρ. κλασ. Αρχ., 'Αθήνα 1983, τόμος β΄(Athen 1988) 259–65 (Kurzfassung) sowie 'Αρχαιογνωσια 4 (1985–86 [Athen 1989]) 59–75.

[35] Cook entschuldigt sich für angekündigte und schließlich nicht verfaßte Appendices in III p. viii. Betroffen sind davon immerhin der Zeus von Olympia und der Zeus von Dodona.

2), "Zeus *Lykaios*" (§ 3), "Zeus and Olympos" (§ 4), "The Mountain-cults of Zeus" (§ 5), "Zeus in relation to the Sun" (§ 6), "Zeus in relation to the Moon" (§ 7) und "Zeus in relation to the Stars" (§ 8) enthält. Das zweite Kapitel gilt dem "Dark Sky" und erhält so dann die großen Einheiten "Thunder and Lightning" (Vol. II) und "Earthquakes, Clouds, Wind, Dew, Rain, Meteorites" (Vol. III). Einzelne Elemente der genaueren Unterteilung sind zum Teil schon oben genannt, und wir werden gewisse thematische Sequenzen daraus unten noch etwas genauer betrachten. Für uns ist jetzt allein wichtig der grundsätzliche Umstand, daß Cook sämtliche Gegebenheiten der Zeusverehrung und der Zeusmythologie in den Rahmen der sichtbaren Erscheinungsformen des Himmels mit allen seinen Meteora (zu denen auch die in den Himmel ragenden Berge sich stellen) eingeordnet hat.   Das bedeutet eine Vorentscheidung, die eine Affinität zu Naturmythologie einschließt und in ihrer Tragweite gerade auch dort spürbar werden muß, wo Cook sich um die Aussage einer Entwicklung bemüht, bei welcher dieser Rahmen transzendiert wird.[36]

Beginnen wir zunächst mit der durch Cook wie selbstverständlich vorausgesetzten ursprünglichen Anschauung des Himmels, die er seinem Bild von der Entwicklung des Gottes zugrundelegt. Paßt sie wirklich zu den wenigen Elementen, die durch die Etymologie und die Analoga im Indischen (Dyaus) und Lateinischen (Iuppiter) sicher scheinen? Der Vergleich führt auf einen Gottesnamen und die appellativische Verwendung desselben für den "Tag" und den "leuchtenden Himmel," und schon das Vorliegen eines Nomen agentis ebenso wie die offenbar bereits auf der indogermanischen Stufe gegebene Charakterisierung des damit bezeichneten Wesens als "Vater" scheinen eine andere als die personhafte Auffassung entschieden auszuschließen.[37]   Man wird demgegenüber also fragen müssen, ob sich diese Grundgegebenheit mit dem religionsgeschichtlichen Entwicklungsmodell verträgt, das A. B. Cook offenbar als selbstverständlich voraussetzt.   Nach ihm gibt es ja zu allererst die Vorstellung von einem "impersonal life" des Himmels, ist Zeus ursprünglich "the animate sky" auf einer Entwicklungsstufe "before Zeus became a personality," bis sich schließlich "the shift from Sky to Sky-god" ereignet, ein Vorgang, dem A. B. Cook die höchste Bedeutung beimißt: "the shift from Sky to Sky-god was a momentous fact, a fact which modified the whole course of Greek religion, and its ultimate consequence was nothing less than the rise of faith

---

[36] Am wichtigsten ist die durch den gleichen Bezugspunkt gegebene Beschränkung, denn ohne Zweifel bringt etwa die Tendenz zu "ritualistischer" Erklärung neue Ansätze. Wie sehr aber z.B. Mond- und Sonnenmythologie nachwirkt, kann man (trotz mancher vorher im einzelnen geübter Kritik an Roscher oder auch Frazer) an dem folgenden Resultate sehen: "it can hardly be doubted that these bull-and-cow myths hang together with the conception of the sun as a bull and the horned moon as a cow" (I p. 740).

[37] Vgl. *RE* Suppl. Bd. XV 999ff. (Schindler) und 1009ff. (Schwabl), = H. Schwabl, *Zeus* (München 1978 [mit derselben Paginierung]).

in a personal God, the Ruler and Father of all."[38] Liegt es nicht nahe, so
wird man dagegen fragen dürfen, die Grundzüge von dem, was hier als
Endpunkt dargestellt wird, schon auf der indogermanischen Vorstufe des
Zeus anzusetzen? Und wenn das zutrifft, dann müßte—etwas pointiert
formuliert—wohl auch gelten, daß von dem ersten Augenblick an, bei dem
es sinnvoll ist, von Griechen zu sprechen, es keinen Zeitpunkt gibt, wo
diese nicht "in a personal God, the ruler and father of all" geglaubt hätten.
Man wird dabei gewiß nicht verkennen, daß es gravierende Entwicklungen
gegeben hat, aber A. B. Cooks Formel ist (sobald man die intendierte
monotheistische Nuance nicht betont) doch so weit dehnbar, daß sie
gleichzeitig sowohl den homerischen Zeus (den Vater, nach dessen
Ratschluß sich alles vollendet) als auch das (als Zeus immerhin benennbare)
Vernunftprinzip Heraklits und den (ohne Einschränkung mit Zeus
gleichbaren) historisch damit zusammenhängenden Gott der Stoa
einschließen kann. Die historische Entwicklung des Gottes führt bei den
Griechen von einer personhaften Grundanschauung als Ausgangspunkt hin
zu einem besonders ausgeprägten Anthropomorphismus, und von diesem
führt die Entwicklung wieder fort zu Konzeptionen wie denen der Stoa.[39]
Cooks Zuneigung—es ist gewiß auch der Trieb des Archäologen, der hier im
Spiele ist—gilt im übrigen offenbar nicht zuletzt dem von den Griechen
entwickelten anthropomorphen Bilde (an das er daran anschließende Tradition
der Darstellung Gottvaters und Christi anzuknüpfen weiß), als Höhepunkt
und Ziel erscheint bei ihm aber dann doch die Aufhebung desselben. Man
wird nicht fehlen, wenn man von einer gewissen Inkonsequenz spricht.[40]

Vielleicht ist hier der Ort, daran zu erinnern, daß nachdenkliche Griechen
selbst die Meinung vertreten haben, die Religion der frühen Menschheit und
so auch ihre eigene Urreligion sei von einer ähnlichen Art gewesen wie die
(am Kosmos und an der ihn dominierenden Gottheit orientierte) Religion der
Philosophen.[41] Etwas von solchen Anschauungen ist auch bei Cook dort
verwendet, wo er (ohne—wie es scheint—die Hintergründe der Quellen
ausreichend zu untersuchen) antike Aussagen über die bei Fremdvölkern
vorliegende Naturreligion heranzieht. So wird Herodots Angabe (1,131)
über die Verehrung des Himmels durch die Perser zum Beleg der primitiven
Anschauung. Und aus ähnlichem Arsenal wird für die Italiker der Übergang
von der ursprünglichen zu der neuen Anschauung belegt, wenn nach Cook (I
p. 10) in einem von Cicero immer wieder zitierten Enniusvers ("aspice hoc
sublime candens, quem invocant omnes Iovem") "the religious thought of
the Italians in its transitional phase" durch den Dichter zum Ausdruck

---

[38] Vgl. I pp. 3, 6, 9.

[39] Für eine allgemeine Skizze dieser Entwicklung vgl. "Vom Wandel des Gottesbildes im
alten Griechenland" in: *Wiener Studien* 98 (1985) 41ff.

[40] Vgl. Anm. 27. Cooks Ideal der Darstellung des Zeus ist wohl weitgehend der Zeus des
Phidias, letztes Endes gesehen mit den Augen des Dion Chrysostomos.

[41] Für Urreligion = Naturreligion, s. Plat. *Kratyl.* 397c. Ein besonders eindrucksvolles
Beispiel für die gemachte Aussage ist der *Olympikos* des Dion (s. Anm. 23).

gebracht sei: "behind him is the divine Sky, in front the Sky-god Iuppiter" (p. 10f.). Eine solche Aussage läßt sich nur durch die Dominanz eines an die Quellen herangetragenen Modells erklären, denn—so sehr Ennius in der Geschichte der lateinischen Literatur seinen frühen Platz hat—es hindert das doch nicht, daß er im Grunde nur als hellenistischer Dichter verstanden werden kann; und ein Vers wie der zitierte hat als Hintergrund die ganze Geschichte des Nachdenkens der Griechen über Ursprung und Rechtfertigung des Götterglaubens, wobei hier im einzelnen euripideische Verse ebenso wie Aussagen von Philosophen vorausgesetzt sind. Was kann ein solcher Vers also für eine von allgemeinen anthropologischen Vorstellungen her gedachte Entwicklungslinie der römischen Religion als Beleg beitragen?!

Wichtiger ist die direkte und indirekte Beziehung auf antike Vorstellung über den Ursprung des Gottesglaubens im Falle eines Autors, der uns schon kurz in der Rolle eines der Lieblingsautoren von Cook begegnet ist. Ich meine Dion Chrysostomos. Und hier ist die Benützung dieses Autors deshalb besonders interessant, weil Cook nicht nur bestimmte Aussagen aus dem *Olympikos* des Dion zur Kennzeichnung des Zielpunkts einer Entwicklung ausführlich herangezogen hat, sondern weil er bei seinem Entwurf eines Bildes über die Erfahrungen der Urmenschheit im Angesicht des Himmels ganz offenkundig das Gegenbild zu einem analogen Bilde gestalten wollte, das gleichfalls im *Olympikos* sich findet. Faktur (Dion) und Gegenfaktur (Cook) bilden den Kontrast der antiken Lehre von der primären Uroffenbarung durch die Gottheit mit einer modernen Konzeption, die das religiöse Phänomen offenbar erst als sekundär sich erklärt. Cook schreibt (I p. 9):

> When those who first used the word *Zeus* went out into the world and looked abroad, they found themselves over-arched by the blue and brilliant sky, a luminous Something fraught with incalculable possibilities of weal or woe. It cheered them with its steady sunshine. It scared them with its flickering fires. It fanned their cheeks with cool breezes, or set all knees a-tremble with reverberating thunder. It mystified them with its birds winging their way in ominous silence or talking secrets in an unknown tongue. It paraded before men's eyes a splendid succession of celestial phenomena, and underwent for all to see the daily miracle of darkness and dawn. Inevitably, perhaps instinctively, they would regard it with awe—that primitive blend of religious feelings—and would go to conciliate it by any means in their power. This is the stage of mental and moral development attributed by Herodotos to the ancient Persians.

Dion, von stoischen Voraussetzungen ausgehend, gibt seinem Bild andere Akzente, aber deutlich sind Zeichnung und Farben an sehr wesentlichen Punkten vergleichbar (sodaß die von uns angenommene Bezugnahme Cooks wohl sicher ist). Dion spricht vom θεῖον, in dem die Menschheit verwurzelt ist und das sie besonders in ihren Anfängen erfuhr:

...illuminated as they were on every side by the divine and magnificent glories of heaven and the stars, of sun and moon, by night and by day encountering varied and dissimilar experiences, seeing wondrous sights and hearing manifold voices of winds and forest and rivers and sea, of animals tame and wild; while they themselves uttered almost pleasing clear sound, and taking delight in the proud and intelligent quality of the human voice, attached symbols to the objects that reached their senses, so as to be able to name and designate everything perceived, thus easily acquiring memories and concepts of innumerable things. How, then, could they have remained ignorant and conceived no inkling of him who had sowed and planted and was now preserving and nourishing them, when on every side they were filled with the divine nature through both sight and hearing, and in fact through every sense? (etc.)[42]

Der allerwesentlichste Unterschied bei Cook gegenüber Dion liegt darin, daß der Himmel als Gegenstand der ursprünglichen religiösen Verehrung möglichst zum Neutrum gemacht wird, dann natürlich auch im stärkeren Einfließen der Komponente der Furcht, und schließlich wird man mit Interesse registrieren, daß zur Erläuterung der im Begriffe "awe" ("Furcht, Scheu, Ehrfurcht") vorauszusetzenden Mischung der Empfindungen Verweise auf Literatur über die Entwicklungsstufe der "Pre-Animistic Religion" gegeben werden.[43] Warum jedoch das Neutrum? Wir haben es schon gesagt: gewiß nicht wegen des Namens "Zeus" (bei dem die Sprachgeschichte allenfalls ein Schwanken zwischen Masculinum und Femininum offenhält), sondern wegen einer modernen (und ebenso auch schon antiken[44]) religionsgeschichtlichen Theorie, die von den—wie man meint—realen sichtbaren Gegebenheiten ausgeht und also fragt: "How came the Greeks in general to think of Zeus, not as the blue sky, but as a sceptred king dwelling in it?" (p. 11) und zur Beantwortung dieser Frage eben einfach von "the blue and brilliant sky, a luminous Something" (p. 9) und den natürlichen Erscheinungsformen des Himmels ausgeht. Und bei dieser Anschauungsweise kommt man dann auch erst dadurch, daß man das Bild des

---

[42] Dio Chrys., *Or.* 12, 28f.: ἄτε δὴ περιλαμπόμενοι θείοις καὶ μεγάλοις φάσμασιν οὐρανοῦ τε καὶ ἄστρων, ἔτι δὲ ἡλίου καὶ σελήνης, νυκτός τε καὶ ἡμέρας ἐντυγχάνοντες ποικίλοις καὶ ἀνομοίοις εἴδεσιν, ὄψεις τε ἀμηχάνους ὁρῶντες καὶ φωνὰς ἀκούοντες παντοδαπὰς ἀνέμων τε καὶ ὕλης καὶ ποταμῶν καὶ θαλάττης, ἔτι δὲ ζῴων ἡμέρων καὶ ἀγρίων, αὐτοί τε φθόγγον ἥδιστον καὶ σαφέστατον ἱέντες καὶ ἀγαπῶντες τῆς ἀνθρωπίνης φωνῆς τὸ γαῦρον καὶ ἐπιστῆμον, ἐπιθέμενοι σύμβολα τοῖς εἰς αἴσθησιν ἀφικνουμένοις, ὡς πᾶν τὸ νοηθὲν ὀνομάζειν καὶ δηλοῦν, εὐμαρῶς ἀπείρων πραγμάτων μνήμας καὶ ἐπινοίας παραλαμβάνοντες. πῶς οὖν ἀγνῶτες εἶναι ἔμελλον καὶ μηδεμίαν ἕξειν ὑπόνοιαν τοῦ σπείραντος καὶ φυτεύσαντος καὶ σῴζοντος καὶ τρέφοντος, πανταχόθεν ἐμπιμπλάμενοι τῆς θείας φύσεως διά τε ὄψεως καὶ ἀκοῆς συμπάσης τε ἀτεχνῶς αἰσθήσεως; (κτλ.). Ich habe, um den Vergleich zu erleichtern, die englische Übersetzung von J. W. Cohoon gegeben (Loeb Cl. L.).

[43] Verwiesen wird (I p. 9,2) auf R. R. Marett, "Pre-Animistic Religion" (*Folk-Lore* 11 [1900] 168) und W. Wundt, *Völkerpsychologie* (Leipzig 1906) II.2.171ff., "Die präanimistische Hypothese."

[44] Es genüge hier der Verweis auf Demokrit fr. B 30 D.–K. und Kritias fr. B 25 D.–K.

irdischen Wetterzauberers und Wetterkönigs auf den Himmel überträgt, zu der personhaften Vorstellung:[45] "...the real prototype of the heavenly weather-king was the earthly weather-king, and...Zeus was represented with thunderbolt and sceptre just because these were customary attributes of the magician and monarch. So Zeus, in a sense, copied Salmoneus" (p. 12). Es folgt ein Räsonnement über die Entwicklungsschritte, die dorthin führten, und schließlich wird als Ergebnis festgehalten: "In short, the transition from Sky to Sky-god was a result, perhaps the first result, of conscious reflexion upon the *modus operandi* of primitive magic" (p. 13). Und als Resultat der ganzen ausgeklügelten Analyse wird schließlich formuliert, sie habe (p. 14)

> ...detected two distinct elements, both of primitive sort—on the one hand the vast mysterious life of the blue sky, on the other the clear-cut form and fashion of the weather-ruling king. To speak with logical precision, though in such a matter logic was at best implicit, the primeval sanctity of the sky gave the content, the equipment of the magician-turned-king gave the form, of the resultant sky-god Zeus.

Ich denke dagegen, man kann ohne Bedenken den "sky-god Zeus" an den Anfang stellen und muß dann auch noch jenes Charakteristikum des Gottes besonders betonen, das mit seinem Namen mehr oder weniger ursprünglich mitüberliefert ist, nämlich seine Bezeichnung als Vater. Man braucht deshalb weder den Wettermacher noch die Komponente der magischen Machtmittel im ursprünglichen Bilde des Gottes bestreiten, doch kommt es hier wohl sehr auf den Grad der Betonungen an. Muß man, wenn man der Aigis primär den rituellen Hintergrund des Wetterzaubers gibt,[46] das deshalb auch beim Blitz und Donner tun, die doch wohl primär dem Gotte (und nicht seinem irdischen Imitator) gehören, und so fort?!

Im übrigen erhebt sich hier die Frage, nicht ob (denn das ist unbestreitbar), sondern an welchem Ort und in welchem Umfang ritualistische Erklärungsmodelle brauchbar sind. A. B. Cook tendiert dazu, in Fällen, wo (mit Recht oder Unrecht) auf den Himmel bezogene rituelle Handlungen ins Spiel gebracht werden, nicht den Himmel, sondern den Akteur der rituellen Handlung als den eigentlichen Zeus zu betrachten. Hier liegt ein Modell vor, für das sich auch im Mythos gewisse Anhaltspunkte finden lassen, und die Übertragung des Namens Zeus auf Menschen ist ja aus dem Herrscherkult genügend bekannt. Man sollte sich aber nicht darüber täuschen, daß die Verwendung des damit gegebenen Modells für die Erklärung von sonst anscheinend Unerklärlichem (wie im Falle der Bildung einer Vorstellung vom Himmel als Person) sehr deutlich eine moderne Variante des Euhemerismus darstellt, die allerdings mit dem Bezug auf Ritus einen generalisierenden Ansatz hat. Bei Cook finden sich auch sonst nicht

---

[45] Cook schließt hier an Ausführungen Frazers im ersten Band des *Golden Bough*[3] an.
[46] R. L. Fowler, *Phoenix* 42 (1988) 111f. zieht dies in Zweifel.

wenige Beispiele für vergleichbare Interpretation: so im Falle des Minotauros, der sich ihm als kretischer Kronprinz in ritueller Funktion und Maske erklärt, auch im Falle der Pasiphae, die als kretische Königin und durch die Rolle, welche dieselbe in einem Hieros Gamos hat, verständlich gemacht wird.[47] Und sosehr hier manches aufgehen mag, so zeigt sich dabei doch überdeutlich die Gefahr der Eliminierung des Wunderbaren und Phantasievollen zugunsten der rationalistischen Erklärung. Auch zeigt sich überall dort die Gefahr des Zirkelschlusses, wo euhemeristische Quellen zur Bestätigung herangezogen werden.[48]

Wir wollen jetzt noch, am Beispiel vor allem des ersten Bandes, uns Probleme vergegenwärtigen, die aus der Anordnung des Cookschen Werks sich ergeben, dessen "masterly structure"[49] auch ihre dunklen Seiten hat. Ich denke, allein durch das bisher Betrachtete mag schon deutlich geworden sein, daß es für einen Autor, der sich vorgenommen hat, in seiner Monographie über Himmel und Himmelsgott zunächst das Thema des "hellen Himmels" zu behandeln, nicht leicht ist, bei dieser Beschränkung zu bleiben. Da stehen wir zunächst vor dem blauen Himmel, aber dann kommt auch schon, um den Gott ins Spiel zu bringen, der Wettermacher mit seinem Donner und Blitz. Es ist denn auch nicht eine irgendwie deutliche Entwicklungslinie oder auch nur eine Reihe von thematisch klar begrenzten Gegebenheiten der "Zeusreligion," was im ersten Band untersucht wird, sondern es ist einfach die mehr oder minder logische Abfolge der Begriffe "Tag" (Heméra), Aithér, Licht, Anhöhe (Olymp und Bergkulte) sowie Sonne, Mond, und Sterne, welche den Untersuchungen eine Art von Gerüst gibt. Gefragt wird jeweils, wieweit es (vor allem) Kult gibt, der von den genannten Phänomenen ausgeht oder auf sie Bezug hat. Und Cook scheut sich nicht, an das Ende einer langen Untersuchung unter Umständen auch das Resultat zu setzen, daß eine solche Beziehung nicht vorliegt. Es hat das aber bei einem Autor, der in jedem Falle bestrebt ist, eine begonnene Sache möglichst in ihrem ganzen Umfang und mit allen Seitenzweigen (samt allem dazu Assoziierbaren) zu behandeln, im Grunde doch sehr eigenartige Konsequenzen. So wird z.B. der Zeus Ἁμάριος, welcher bei genauerer

---

[47] "...the Minotaur. He was the crown-prince of Knossos in ritual attire, and his bull-mask proclaimed his solar character" (I p. 490). "Behind the myth, as is so often the case, we may detect a ritual performance, in which the Cnossian queen actually placed within a wooden cow was symbolically married to a bull representing the sun-god" (I p. 522). Der euhemeristische Interpretationstypus liegt vor auch bei der Erklärung von Ios Verwandlung (I p. 441) sowie bei der der Proitiden (p. 453).

[48] z.B. I p. 496 für die Erklärung des Minotauros Diodor I 61f., wo im übrigen der Minotauros im Zusammenhang mit dem Labyrinth nur gerade erwähnt ist und dann eine euhemeristische (und ritualistische) Erklärung der Verwandlungen des Proteus gegeben wird. Daß Frazer und Cook darauf zur Bestätigung ihrer Annahme als auf eine "important passage" (496,3) verweisen konnten, zeigt den Grad ihrer Abhängigkeit von dem antiken Erklärungsmodell. A. Lang, dessen Widerspruch Cook registriert, kann hier nur recht behalten (*Folk-Lore* 21 [1910] 145).

[49] Seltman (*supra* n. 1) 302.

Überlegung nur die Bedeutung eines "Bundesgotts" haben kann,[50] auf den (freilich bis zuletzt nicht ganz aufgegebenen) Verdacht hin, er könne zu ἦμαρ gehören, eben unter dem Abschnitt "Tag" abgehandelt. Doch dasselbe widerfährt (wegen sporadischer dementsprechender Ausdeutungen oder Verschreibungen) auch dem Zeus Panamaros, bei dem auch Cook selbst offenbar von allem Anfang an kaum Zweifel daran gehabt hat, daß er zu den karischen Zeusfiguren und zu dem für uns unverständlichen Ortsnamen Panamara gehört. Der Abschnitt über Aithér führt sehr rasch zu den mit diesem Begriff verknüpften Gottesvorstellungen der Philosophen und zur Darstellung des "blauen Himmels" durch hellenistische Künstler, zu Themen also, die gewiß hochinteressant sind, aber ihren besten Platz wohl doch nicht am Anfang einer Monographie über Zeus haben. Es folgt der als Lichtgott[51] gedeutete Zeus Lykaios (was sich gewiß gut vertreten läßt), und daran anschließend führen gewisse (für eine Frühzeit gewiß zu schematische) Überlegungen über die Schichtung von ἀήρ und αἰθήρ sowie die dabei angenommene Beziehung der Olymphöhe zu der Sphäre des letzteren zu einer allgemeinen Behandlung der Bergkulte des Zeus; deren Abschluß bildet ein Traktat über "Zeus as a Mountain-god superseded by Saint Elias," in welchem zunächst überhaupt über das Nachleben heidnischer Götter im Gewande christlicher Heiliger gehandelt und dann anhand eines umfangreichen und sehr interessanten Materials dargetan wird, daß der Prophitis Elias in einem weiten Gebiet Europas und Asiens den alten Donnergott ersetzt hat. Und in diesem Zusammenhang fallen (in Anlehnung an Jacob Grimm) auch die Namen des slawischen (Perun) und des germanischen Donnergotts (Thor/Donar), also von Göttern, mit welchen uns die Entsprechung für "Thunder and Lightning" (=Vol. II) gegeben ist. Schließlich ist bei den Gegebenheiten, welche in den weiteren Teilen des ersten Bandes unter den Paragraphen "Sonne" (pp. 186–730), "Mond" (pp. 730–40) und "Sterne" (pp. 740–75) abgehandelt werden, der Anteil von Dingen, welche keinen primären Bezug zu Zeus haben, wohl bei weitem in der Überhand gegenüber solchen, wo es einen derartigen Bezug gibt. Auch hat A. B. Cook selber als Resultat dieser Abschnitte festgehalten, daß das von ihm behandelte Material nur auf eine "post-classical connexion" des Zeus mit Sonne, Mond und Sternen führt (II p. vii). Doch auch unter dieser Einschränkung bleibt noch, wie es scheint, die Frage legitim, ob es denn sinnvoll ist, den synkretistischen Komplex des Ζεὺς Ἥλιος μέγας Σάραπις (also einen Gott, der nach seinem primären Ansatz wirklich nur als chthonisch klassifiziert werden kann[52]) unter "Direct identifications of Zeus with the Sun" und den Zeus Ὠρομάζης (=Ahura Mazda) der

[50] Vgl. *RE* X A 270f.

[51] Cook hat das mit Recht nicht gehindert, auch die Wolfsassoziationen bei Zeus Lykaios zu besprechen, er fügt dann aber auch noch eine Abhandlung über "Zeus-like deities in wolf-skin garb" aus dem römischen Rheinland (und Analogien aus etruskischen Gräbern) an.

[52] Vgl. Artemidoros II 34 und 39 (p. 158,5; 175,8 Pack).

kommagenischen Könige unter einem Abschnitt über Zeus und die Sterne abzuhandeln. Angeführt sei auch, daß im Abschnitt "Sonne" vor allem die Motive "Sonnenrad" (Solar Wheel), "Widder" (Ram) und "Stier" (Bull) hervortreten,[53] wobei Cook offenkundig hofft, insbesondere mit Hilfe von ägyptischen Daten einen Fundus von griechischem (und nicht zuletzt kretischem) Mythos und Kult aufzuhellen. Es scheint, daß hier neben Verbindungslinien, die man immer wieder als möglicherweise wichtig, jedenfalls aber als anregend empfinden kann, auch Verknüpfungen stehen, die den Eindruck der vorschnellen und unkontrollierten Assoziation machen. Man darf, so denke ich, auch diese Seite von Cooks Werk nicht verschweigen, und man darf dann wohl auch auf deren Illustration nicht verzichten. Zwei solcher Beispielen mögen genügen.

Das erste illustriert die Leichtigkeit in der Verwendung von Analoga: I p. 401 wird Libysches, Phrygisches (und Orphisches) an einer zusammenfassenden Stelle auf die folgende Weise verbunden: "It follows that there was no small resemblance between Zeus *Ammon* and Zeus *Sabázios*. In both cases a ram-god developed into a sun-god. In both the deity became a snake. The Libyan god had his sacred oak. The Phrygian Zeus as Bagaîos was an oak-god" (usw.). Selbst wenn die hier vorausgesetzte Bedeutung von Bagaîos (sie ist nicht sehr wahrscheinlich, aber der Urheber der Vermutung ist immerhin P. Kretschmer) richtig sein sollte, eine Assoziationskette solcher Art hebt sich wohl von selbst auf.

Das zweite Beispiel mag die Entschlossenheit zeigen, mit der eine intendierte naturmythologische Erklärung durch Kombinationen erreicht werden kann: bei der Erklärung der Geschichte vom verschwundenen Minossohn Glaukos (I p. 470) kommt A. B. Cook von der dreifarbenen Kuh des Minos und den damit in Verbindung gebrachten Farben der Maulbeere folgendermaßen auf den Mond: "Now a common folk-lore explanation of the moon's spots is that they are a thorn-bush carried by the man-in-the-moon. It might therefore be maintained that the bramble-bush or mulberry-tree was a possible description of the moon. And, if so, then the three-coloured cow, or calf that changed its colour three times a day, was merely another way of describing the moon" (usw.). Es dürfte einleuchten, daß das die Methode ist, mit der sich leicht ein jegliches Ding in jedes gewünschte andere permutiert.

Wichtiger als solche Einzelheiten sind schließlich aber die Konsequenzen, die der charakterisierte physikalische Grundplan des Werks für die Erfassung von solchen Aspekten des Gottes Zeus hat, die nicht den

---

[53] Bei diesem Komplex liegt, trotz aller Umwege, eine historisch verankerte Fragestellung zugrunde, die Cook anläßlich des Themas "Bull" folgendermaßen formuliert (p. 430f.): "As before, we shall begin by noticing certain Egyptian, and therefore non-Indo-European, cults, which were at an early date more or less assimilated by the Greeks. As before, we shall end by showing that the Greeks themselves had inherited from their own Indo-European ancestors ideas so similar that they were readily fused with those of the surrounding foreigners."

Naturphänomenen zugehören. Es gibt im Grunde keinen organischen Platz für sie, es sei denn dort, wo von einer Entwicklung geredet wird, die über die "physical foundations of the cult of Zeus" hinausgeht. Doch gerade hier ist, wie man sich klarmachen sollte, eine Vorentscheidung im Spiele, die nicht primär auf dem Material beruht, das für Zeus und vergleichbare Götter zur Verfügung steht, sondern auf einer modernen Optik, die wir schon kurz zu charakterisieren versuchten. Hier muß es genügen, wenn wir nur für einen wichtigen Aspekt beispielhaft auf die Arbeiten von Raffaele Pettazzoni zum Typus des Himmels- und des Hochgotts verweisen, aus denen wohl mit einiger Evidenz sich ergibt, daß etwa der Charakter der "Allwissenheit" im Bilde eines solchen Gottes schon ursprünglich seinen Platz hat und es also auch prekär ist, dergleichen erst zu derivieren. Natürlich wird man nicht leugnen, daß es auf allen Ebenen, also auch beim Begriff des Wissens, Entwicklung gibt, aber das schließt nicht ein, das alle anderen Ebenen als die der bloßen Naturphänomene erst sekundäre Entwicklung wären und im Grundentwurf des Himmelsgottes fehlten.[54]

In seinem Ansatz ist A. B. Cook von J. G. Frazer beeinflußt und zwar wohl noch mehr als ihm selber bewußt war. Trotzdem besteht die oben zitierte Aussage Cooks über unterschiedliche Auffassungen auch im Blick auf Grundsätzliches zurecht. Denn Frazer war entschieden Aufklärer, und Cook war es an wichtigen Punkten nicht. Und so muß auch Cooks Versuch, die Geschichte des griechischen Himmelsgotts unter Frazerschen Voraussetzungen anzugehen und gleichzeitig in ihr eine Linie zu finden, die zur größeren und endgültigen religiösen Wahrheit führt, einen eigentümlich zwiespältigen Eindruck hinterlassen. Mag sein, daß Cook eine Stelle bei Frazer, auf die R. Ackerman mit Recht besonders hingewiesen hat,[55] für eine ernsthafte Möglichkeit genommen hat. Doch das kann den Eindruck des konglomerathaften Nebeneinander zweier grundsätzlich verschiedener Positionen nicht aufheben. Man wird das auch nicht allzusehr Cook zum Vorwurf machen, sondern eher als Diagnose eines für die Zeit nicht uncharakteristischen Zustands buchen. Stimmig werden kann Cooks Perspektive nur, wenn beim Ausgehen von dem ursprünglichen Blick auf

---

[54] Wichtig ist, sich klarzumachen, daß die ursprüngliche Begriffsbildung gewiß nicht durch die Reduktion auf das reine und konkrete Phänomen gewonnen werden kann. Für die bei der Struktur des Cookschen Werks sich ergebende Weise des punktuellen Anhängens von Daten, die nicht zum Ordnungssystem passen, sei z.B. auf die Behandlung der Geburt des Dionysos aus dem Schenkel des Zeus im Paragraphen "Clouds" verwiesen. Die Anknüpfungsmöglichkeit bietet die allegorische Erklärung derselben bei Euripides (*Bacch.* 286f.), welche die Gleichung Zeus=Luft (αἰθήρ) voraussetzt. Cook sucht dann selbst die Erklärung in einem "very ancient ritual of adoption" (III p. 80f.). Für Pettazzoni, s. Anm. 28.

[55] R. Ackerman, *J. G. Frazer* 169, wo eine von Frazer (*The Golden Bough*[2] III 198) formulierte Alternative referiert ist, bei der der Christ, "faced with the resemblances between the death of Jesus and that of the myriad of other ritual martyrs in the Levant" die letzteren im Sinne von Vorläufern auffassen wird, während der Skeptiker von ihnen als "victims of a barbarous superstition" ausgeht.

den Himmel das religiöse Phänomen auch eine objektive Komponente erhält, wie das bei Dion der Fall ist, und bekanntlich haben auch noch Moderne eine vergleichbare Position eingenommen.[56] Mit J. E. Harrison und F. Cornford verbindet Cook wohl das Interesse an urtümlichen Kulten und die Faszination, die davon ausgeht, es trennt ihn seine christliche Perspektive.[57] Diese selbige aber ist es gewiß auch, die Cook immer wieder auf die entsprechenden Frazerschen Themen zurückführt, auch dort wo man das an sich in einer Geschichte des Zeus sich nicht erwartet.

Cooks *Zeus* wird bleiben als eine Art Thesaurus und als ein staunenswertes Monument geduldiger wissenschaftlicher Einzelarbeit. Es ist ein Werk von eigentümlicher Widersprüchlichkeit, vor der Fragen auftauchen, die nicht nur die bloße Gelehrsamkeit betreffen. Und wo man sich diesen Fragen stellt, berührt es dann auch als das nicht unwichtige Zeugnis einer Person und ihrer Zeit.

Universität Wien

[56] Zu nennen sind etwa F. A. Welcker, Max Müller, auch Andrew Lang in seiner späteren Phase und Pater Wilhelm Schmidt.

[57] Vgl. Anm. 26. Wichtig ist ein Grundgedanke, der schon I p. xiii ausgesprochen ist und auch in den Einzeluntersuchungen immer wieder auftaucht: "Zeus god of the Bright sky is also Zeus god of the Dark sky; and it is in this capacity as lord of the drenching rain-storm, that he fertilises his consort the earth-goddess and becomes the Father of a divine Son, whose worship with its rites of regeneration and its promise of immortality taught that men might in mystic union be identified with their god, and thus in thousands of wistful hearts throughout the Hellenic world awakened longings that could be satisfied only by the coming of the very Christ." Zu vergleichen sind hierzu auch die positiven Aussagen über den Attiskult (II p. 303): "The cult of Attis had points of contact with Christianity itself. A Father manifesting himself anew in the person of his Son, a Son bearing the name of his Father—such beliefs naturally predisposed men to faith in the Son whom the Father sent to be 'the effulgence of his glory, and the very image of his substance'" (Hebr. 1,3). Und: "The rites of Attis, apart from certain crudities, might almost have passed for Christian usage—witness the body of the divine Son affixed to the pine-tree, the lamentation over his prostrate form" (usw.). Besonders wichtig erscheint, daß Cook dort auch auf Vergleichsmaterial bei Firmicus Maternus hinweist und die Methode desselben als Vorstufe zu der von Modernen auffaßt, die ihn selber profund beeinflußt haben: "The same method of comparative study has been followed with conspicuous success by W. Mannhardt *Wald- und Feldkulte*[2] Berlin 1904 I 572f. 1905 II 291ff. and by Frazer *Golden Bough*[3]: The Magic Art II 59ff., ib.[3]: The Dying God p. 251ff."

12

William Robertson Smith

MORTON SMITH

Of all the people who will be discussed in this conference, I suppose Smith was in his day the most famous and, for English society, the most influential, and is now generally the least remembered. Grote's work is a monument of British historiography, he sleeps with Macaulay and Motley; Jane Harrison is now celebrated as the first British woman to achieve professional distinction in classical studies (whether or not she was is of no more concern than what she wrote); Murray's *Five Stages* and Cornford's *Thucydides* stay in print because they are short, readable assignments that provoke discussion; Cook and Frazer are inexhaustible warehouses, constantly looted and occasionally cited; Lang is remembered for his fairy tales; but Smith and *The Religion of the Semites*, when they are remembered, are identified, with some difficulty, as nineteenth-century curiosities.

In Smith's primary field, the Old Testament, the most influential German *Einleitung* of the post-war period, Eissfeldt's,[1] mentions him only twice and then only by entries in a bibliography. The best American introduction, Pfeiffer's, adopts two of his minor suggestions, rejects a major one,[2] and twice includes his work in bibliographies. The currently fashionable introduction of Fohrer likewise includes his name in two places, likewise without further comment.[3] His most important Old Testament work was done on Isaiah 1–39 and on the history of sacrifice. In the recent revision of the leading Protestant commentary on Isaiah, Kaiser's,[4] I have not found a reference to him. The basic texts for the Old Testament's treatment of sacrifices and food rules are Leviticus 1–7, 11, 16, and 17. In Elliger's full commentary on these chapters, I have found no reference to

---

[1] O. Eissfeldt, *Einleitung in das Alten Testament*[3], Tübingen, 1964.

[2] Accepted: that Abiasaph was made a Koraite to make the Asaph singers Levitical (Ex. 6:24); that II Chr. 19:5–11 reflects a Jerusalem court of the editor's time (here Smith followed Wellhausen). Rejected: that Hosea 3 is spurious. R. Pfeiffer, *Introduction to the Old Testament*[2], New York, 1953.

[3] G. Fohrer, *Introduction to the Old Testament*, tr. D. Green, Nashville, 1968, pp. 18 and 27.

[4] O. Kaiser, *Isaiah 1–12*[2], Philadelphia, 1983; there is no index.

Smith's work.[5] The forthcoming commentary by Baruch Levine, however, does mention Smith's theory of totemic sacrifice—but only to refute it: there is no evidence that unclean animals were ever offered as sacrifices in native Israelite cults, nor that any animal suitable for sacrifice was ever prohibited as food.[6]

Against these facts it might be argued that Smith's books on Old Testament criticism—*The Old Testament in the Jewish Church* (Edinburgh, 1881) and *The Prophets of Israel* (Edinburgh, 1882)—were essentially apologetic. In both he was trying to demonstrate that his interpretation of the Old Testament satisfied the requirements of the Westminster Confession, could much increase the Bible's homiletic utility, and would thus benefit its readers. Since his interpretation of the Old Testament was in the main that of Kuenen, Wellhausen, and Ewald (with various modifications), the scholarly content of these books was not mostly new. Smith packed much of his own learning into the appendices, but nobody reads appendices. What he contributed in the main text were the brilliant arguments and powerful homiletic developments of which he was a master, and by which he at first hoped—vainly—to win enough support to keep his Aberdeen chair of Hebrew and Old Testament, in spite of the evangelicals' campaign to depose him. Such virtues do not recommend books for scholarly citation.

We should therefore expect his enduring influence to be exercised by his later books, *Kinship and Marriage in Early Arabia* (Cambridge, 1895) and *Lectures on the Religion of the Semites* (Edinburgh, 1889), reflecting the studies that culminated in his professorship of Arabic at Cambridge from 1889 to his death in 1894. This expectation is confirmed by the history of his works' publications. Of the earlier books, the first had a second edition in 1892 and a German translation in 1894, but nothing thereafter; *The Prophets of Israel* had a new edition in 1919[7]; but *Kinship and Marriage* had a second edition in 1903 and was reissued in the Netherlands in 1966 and in the United States in 1967, while *The Religion of the Semites*, besides a

---

[5] K. Elliger, *Leviticus*, Tübingen, 1966 (*Handb. z. Alt. Test.* I.4); again, no index.

[6] B. Levine, *Leviticus*, Philadelphia, 1989 (*The JPS Torah Commentary*), pp. 222–23 and note 17 on 222. Levine is right in saying that Smith misinterpreted Ezekiel 8:10–11. The prophet represents the worship of creeping things *not* as a holier mystery of the cult of Yahweh, but as an alien abomination. Even if we grant (what Levine does not consider) that ophiolatry was age-old in Palestine and that Ezekiel probably saw a secret perpetuation of popular religion which had been public at least to Hezekiah's time (II Kings 18:4), I cannot recall any evidence that snakes were ever sacrificed or eaten. The sacrifices of abominable things in II Macc. 6:4–5 were probably of pigs to Demeter or Dionysus.

[7] The edition of 1885, reported by J. Muilenberg in his prolegomenon to the third edition of *Lectures on the Religion of the Semites* (ed. S. Cook, New York, 1969, p. 6), is not found in the bibliography of J. S. Black and G. Chrystal, *The Life of William Robertson Smith*, London, 1912, nor in that of T. Beidelman, *W. Robertson Smith and the Sociological Study of Religion*, Chicago, 1974. I think it is one of Muilenberg's many mistakes.

German translation in 1899, had three editions in England, the last of which (in 1927) was reprinted in the United States in 1969 and followed by a paperback here in 1972. (This list[8] omits reprints which did not substantially extend the publication span.) The early second editions of all four are explicable by the quality of Smith's writing, its beautiful clarity and remarkable force, but there were other important factors, as well—the notoriety of his trials, the surge of liberal support aroused by his deposition, his great personal charm, enormous learning, position as editor-in-chief of the *Encyclopædia Britannica*, and consequent connexions all over the academic world—which made him one of the outstanding scholars of England and assured his works of attention until World War I swept away the remains of Victorian society. The 1919 and 1927 editions were due to the piety and influence of his student and distinguished successor in Cambridge, Stanley Cook. The revival in the '60's and '70's reflects both the influence of Durkheim and Freud and the increased importance of the "third world" after World War II, with the consequent growth of interest in anthropology and comparative religion.

Even this change, however, has not sufficed to make even Smith's last two works the sort of classics that every student in the field is expected to read. In the first place, the ideas in them were not original. Both books were enlargements and extended defenses of theses developed and presented more coherently and briefly by Smith's friend, John Ferguson McLennan.

McLennan, I learn from the *DNB*, was nineteen years Smith's elder. He graduated from King's College, Aberdeen, when Smith was three, spent half a dozen years in Cambridge but took no degree, returned to Edinburgh, and practiced law there. Smith met him some time after coming to Edinburgh as a graduate student. McLennan made a hobby of the study of legal survivals—otiose expressions, provisions, and procedures required in various legal actions, but meaningful only in relation to social structures and conditions long gone by. Particularly fruitful was his study of the practice and/or pretense of stealing wives and the legal conditions and consequences of such thefts or purchases. Comparative law led him to comparative religion and sociology and to the invention of the terms *endogamy* and *exogamy*.

He reasoned that endogamy was presumably natural and original. Most large mammals mate with members of their own herds or packs—proximity arouses desire, provides occasion, and saves time. For humans, sister-brother marriages have yet more advantages: the parties know each other well, no property will be alienated from the family, no alien customs will be imported, the children's adherence to the clan is assured, and so on. Consequently, we should expect endogamy to be the normal human practice. Nevertheless he found exogamy attested in most of the oldest peoples historically known, and in many of them, compulsory marriages with close

---

[8] Based on the bibliographies cited in the preceding note.

kin being prohibited by religious law. Why? Since the historical material provided only mythical explanations, he turned, for evidence about prehistoric motivation, to the uncivilized peoples, whom he unhappily called "primitives" and incautiously believed to be living examples of how men behaved in the Stone Age—though he occasionally recognized that "A *really* primitive people...exists nowhere."[9]

For the study of these "primitives" the British were well prepared by philosophical speculation from Hobbes on about the earliest societies, and by overseas exploration, trade, and conquests which had given them experience of such peoples. Reviewing the information accumulated from such sources, McLennan found that for much exogamy there was a common-sense explanation: in poor societies that lived by hard outdoor labor, especially the pastoral peoples, men were more valuable than women, and therefore female infants were commonly killed. It was cheaper to let some other tribe bring them up, and then steal only as many as were needed for procreation and recreation. This much was clear. But besides this, and even in societies where women did as much of the productive labor as men, or more, marriages between offspring of the same mother were often prohibited because it was believed that both parties would have the same fetish, usually an animal or plant. These fetishes were thought to be inherited, like bodily characteristics, from the mothers, and such societies were usually matrilineal and often matriarchal. This combination of fetishism, matrilineal descent, and consequent exogamy McLennan termed "totemism."[10] He set forth these findings and theories in a book, *Primitive Marriage* (1865), which dealt mainly with the evidence for exogamy, and an article, "The Worship of Animals and Plants," in *The Fortnightly Review*, vols. 6 and 7 (1869–70). This article I know only from Smith's acknowledgement and subsequent discussions.

Smith became a close friend of McLennan, publicized his work, took up his ideas, and in *Kinship and Marriage* tried to show that the early Arabian tribes and the original Israelites were matriarchal; the patriarchal systems reflected in the Old Testament and the Koran were secondary developments, as proved by the presence in both texts of many "survivals" of the sorts identified by McLennan. Similarly, in *The Religion of the Semites*, Smith tried to show that the Arabs, including the Israelites, at first practiced totemism. For McLennan, as a lawyer interested in "survivals," the practice was the essential thing. What had to be *done*? The different interpretations that might be given, in different times or societies, to the

---

[9] J. McLennan, *Primitive Marriage*, Edinburgh, 1865, emphasis in the original.

[10] "Totem" is derived from an Ojibwa term indicating relationship, probably known to McLennan from an inaccurate eighteenth-century account: C. Lévi-Strauss, *Totemism*, tr. R. Needham, Boston, 1963, pp. 13, 18, 19. Why people with the same fetish should be forbidden to marry is not explained.

same practices (or legal formulae, or the like) were merely the temporary myths that might be used to explain or excuse the enduring ritual.

In the many forms of totemism reported from all over the world, it was occasionally possible to find instances in which the totemic animal, believed to be the god of all its clan members, and therefore sacred, was itself sacrificed and eaten by those members. Arguing that the purpose of such sacrifices could only be to enable all members to share and be strengthened and united by the life of the god, and that this increase of their strength also revived the god and increased his/her power, Smith tried both to show that such communion was the original purpose of all animal sacrifices, and to explain sacrifices of which the flesh was not eaten (whole burnt offerings, for instance), and sacrifices designated as gifts to the god, as being secondary developments from the primitive, communal type. In this he was more ingenious than persuasive.

Generally, for his sweeping and unlikely claims, the evidence was inadequate, as he had to admit. Though he argued with brilliance (he was extraordinarily acute in seeing, and clever in developing, the implications of details), he suffered from several weaknesses. He would not recognize and fairly evaluate the evidence against his case. He showed little sense of the relative reliability and importance of different points of evidence.[11] He too rarely recognized the ambiguities of the facts to which he appealed, the different ways in which they might be explained. Finally, he sometimes cited as evidence texts which simply did not say what he said they said. This trick he probably learned from ecclesiastical apologists, since many of the worst cases appear in his own apologetics in his earlier books.

To present and explain such passages takes time, but one important instance may be given: in the heresy charge against him[12] the most important point was his denial that Deuteronomy was written by Moses. This was taken to be a denial of the truth of Scripture, since Dt. 31:24 speaks of "Moses...writing the words of this law[13] on a book to their very end." The Westminster Confession, to which Presbyterian ministers were

---

[11] In particular, he took as history the *Narratio* of Pseudo-Nilus of Ancyra (new ed. F. Conca, Leipzig, 1983) and made its account of Bedouin worship (3.3) a pillar passage of his argument, never suspecting (though well he might have) that its sensational and unparalleled gory sacrifice was a bloody fake. Cf. B. Altaner and A. Stuiber, *Patrologie*, Herder, 1980, p. 334.

[12] This was subsequently dropped. He was never convicted of heresy, but merely of expressing himself so carelessly as to cause grave uneasiness to believers. He was warned that this must stop. He promised to amend, did not keep his promise, and was therefore tried again and deposed from his chair, but never excommunicated. He remained a minister of the Free Church and later was a member of its Assembly: Black and Chrystal, *Life* (*supra* n. 7), 353–4, 357–60, 394–97.

[13] Here there is no particular law to which the text's words, "this law," would naturally refer. The most likely reference is to the whole code, but not the whole of the present book. Smith, *The Old Testament in the Jewish Church*, pp. 331–33, used the failure to refer to the whole book as an excuse for denying the probable reference to the whole code.

required to subscribe, asserts "full...assurance of the infallible truth and divine authority" of Scripture. In fact, Smith held the opinion (now common) that although Deuteronomy contained some laws of which the origin was Mosaic, it had been written as a whole by an unknown author in the time of Josiah.[14] When he had to defend this position in his trial he argued that in Israelite history, when "it became necessary to introduce under...prophetic authority some new ordinance to meet the changing conditions of...religious life,...the only way to make the new law an integral part of the old legislation was to throw it into such a form as if it had been spoken by Moses, and so incorporate it with the other laws." And he concluded, "There is one piece of direct historical evidence which seems to show that they did [this], for in Ezra 9:11 a law is quoted from Dt. 7...and yet the origin of this law is ascribed not to Moses, but to the prophets."[15] This is false. The only thing from Dt. 7 that is quoted in Ezra 9:11 are the words "the land to which you are coming to inherit it," Dt. 7:1. Ezra 9:12 partially paraphrases Dt. 7:3, but there is nothing to the effect that the prophets *originated* either the Deuteronomic commandment or the one they (plural) are thought to have reiterated. Further, it is clear from the content of the command in Ezra that it purportedly was given while the Israelites were still in the wilderness; it refers to "the land to which you are coming." The prophets referred to were therefore probably Moses and Aaron, so if the passage referred to were that in Deuteronomy, the reference would say nothing against Mosaic authorship of it. In any case, a command given in the wilderness about rules to be observed in the promised land can hardly have been introduced "to meet the changing conditions of religious life." In sum, Smith's "one point of direct historical evidence" for his position was a sham.

Such particular points are less important than his defense *as a whole* of the critical study of Scripture, the case argued in *The Old Testament in the Jewish Church* and reargued in *The Prophets of Israel* with special reference to Amos, Hosea, and Isaiah. Briefly stated, his argument is that the documents in the Old Testament, when critically studied, approve themselves a God-given revelation of the work of God to bring into being the people of Israel, separate it from paganism, and make it an environment suitable for the incarnation of His Son to reveal a purely spiritual religion,

---

[14] *The Old Testament in the Jewish Church*, pp. 246, 331–38, 352–69.

[15] Black and Chrystal, *Life* (*supra*, n. 7), 250–51. For his fuller defense, with explicit references to Dt. 31, see *The Old Testament in the Jewish Church* 331–33, where he argues (1) that because 31:24 speaks of Moses in the third person it cannot have been written by him; (2) that "the words of this law" *might* not refer to the whole code, since the same expression has a different reference (probably) in Dt. 27:8 (but he suggests no other likely reference in 31:24). Neglecting this lack he concludes (3) that "it cannot be thought *certain* that the author of Dt. 31 means to convey as an historical fact that...the very code of Dt. 12–26...was written...by Moses" (my italics). He is careful not to ask whether or not it *can* be thought *probable*. The ellipses in the last sentence stand for words intended to obscure the issue and to necessitate an answer in his favor.

free alike of priestly hierarchy, sacrificial ritual, superstitious observances, and ethnic limitations—in one word, Calvinism.

This magnificent conception Smith set forth with great homiletic power in his first two books, but the effectiveness of his presentation depends on his careful neglect of the biblical facts. For example, let me summarize one theme from the account of the conquest of Jericho, adding the references to divine guidance which Smith's theory would require us to understand. When the Book of Joshua opens, the Israelites are in Transjordan, across the river from Jericho. Moses has died. They had previously tried to invade Palestine and had been driven off with losses (Num. 13–14). Now some of the tribes are determined to stay in Transjordan (Num. 32). Should Joshua, the new leader, attempt another invasion? The Lord said to Joshua, "Send spies to discover the attitude of the Canaanites." So Joshua sent two spies to Jericho (Josh. 2). When the spies came into the city, the Lord said unto them, "Go to a whorehouse." They went. Then the Lord said to the King of Jericho, "Two Israelite spies have entered the city, send men to capture them." Then the Lord said to the madam, "The king's men are coming. Hide the spies and lie to the men; tell them the spies have left the city. When they have gone in pursuit, make the spies swear that if you get them out of the city they will, when it is captured, save you and your family. Tell them, too, that everybody here is afraid of the Israelites and expects the capture. Then let them down by a rope outside the wall." The madam (Rahab) did as directed, and the Lord told the spies to give her the promise demanded and follow her directions. She got them out. With more divine guidance, they got back to Jericho, the invasion was undertaken, the city fell, Rahab and her family were spared, and she was rewarded for her treason to her city by marriage into the tribe of Judah and a place in the Messianic line (Mt. 1:5). Meanwhile, the Israelites, on the Lord's direction, continued the revelation of divine love in Palestine by slaughtering all the other men, women, and children of the city, in accordance with the law of the Lord, which destined all Canaanites for genocide. (Much to the Lord's regret, this law was not obeyed, but He tried. Cf. Josh. 2; 6:16–25; Dt. 7:1–3; Judg. 1:19–2:4.)

Clearly the defense of biblical history as a revelation of the ways and nature of God cannot well be used except on the many who are ignorant of the Bible and the few who know what it says but have been so thoroughly brainwashed that they read and revere it without thinking of what it means. Smith may have thought that most of his fellow divines in the Free Church Assembly were of this latter class. He may also have belonged to it himself. Whether or not he did is not our concern. What men think and intend, so long as it remains mere thoughts and intentions, is practically unimportant and certainly uncertain;[16] the certain and important things are what they do.

In this case Smith's arguments probably found many adherents among homiletic exegetes and clergy, whose sermons and commentaries the mercy of God has saved me from reading. In the works of biblical scholarship that I have read, the use of Smith's message has at best (or, at worst?) been marginal. Similarly, his theories about the matriarchal and totemistic background of the Bible have won little acceptance. His reputation, however, is still respected. Krauss, in his history of Old Testament exegesis,[17] described Smith's first book (in its German edition, of course) as a "großartige Krönung" of the series of Old Testament introductions of the customary (i.e., Wellhausenian) sort; he also put the German translation of *The Religion of the Semites* at the beginning of the series of works on the history of religion, which from then on began to replace studies of "biblical theology." These two judgments lead me to believe that he had not read either book. At all events, he says nothing more about them. The two outstanding works of this century on Israelite society and religion have been, to my mind, those of Pedersen and de Vaux.[18] Pedersen argues against the notion of an early matriarchate: the few details that support it are mostly due to special circumstances, and the decisive evidence against it is that the children are always reckoned to the father's family (pp. 75–76; Smith is mentioned only in a note on one detail, p. 508). As to sacrifices, however, he accepts and extends the communion theory, allying it with the renewal of the covenant (pp. 322–23), and he later praises Smith's remarks on sacrifices burnt outside the camp: they cannot be interpreted as gifts "in the modern sense" (pp. 344–46). However, he objects to Smith's "dubious interpretations" of details, and to the absolute primacy of the totemic theory as "too narrow"—other sorts were also aboriginal. De Vaux is less favorable. As to matriarchy, many have followed Smith, but much of the evidence is dubious and all of it together would not suffice to demonstrate that the system was ever prevalent. It is mainly associated with small-scale cultivation; pastoral societies are usually patriarchal and the Israelites, throughout the history known to us, were emphatically so (I, 19f.). On sacrifice, he does not mention Smith, but often argues against his positions (esp. II, 433–56), and often from theological presuppositions which need

---

[16] The uncertainty extends even to private lives, where conscious, verbalized thoughts and desires are, as it were, our private myths, by which we screen from ourselves not only our sub-conscious motives, but our non-ritualistic actions.

[17] H.-J. Krauss, *Geschichte der historisch-kritischen Erforschung des Alten Testaments*, Neukirchen, 1956, pp. 339, 344.

[18] J. Pedersen, *Israel, Its Life and Culture*, 2 vols., Oxford, 1926, 1940 (Danish, 1920, 1934). R. de Vaux, *Les institutions de l'Ancien Testament*, Paris, 2 vols., 1958, 1960, considerably revised as *Ancient Israel*, 2 vols., New York, 1961. My citations are from *Ancient Israel*.

neither specification nor refutation. All in all, as was said above, Smith's position in Old Testament criticism is that of a nineteenth-century eccentric.

I know little of the history of Arabic religion. The few recent works I have seen (J. Teixidor's *The Pagan God*, Princeton, 1977, the best of the lot; *Le antiche divinità semitiche*, ed. S. Moscati, Rome, 1958; J. Hoftijzer's *Religio aramaica*, Leiden, 1968) have not, I believe, mentioned Smith, but have had no occasion to do so, since all deal with the epigraphically-attested religions of particular areas, not with Smith's general concerns.[19]

It was these general concerns which recommended him to the Cambridge Ritualists, to incipient anthropologist-sociologists, and to Freud. To these, therefore, he owes his present place in this conference. My impression is that these scholars have rather used him than discussed him. Of the few discussions I have seen, I am most impressed by Prof. Jones' careful demonstration of how Frazer differed from him.[20] This I think an account of an important judgment, since Frazer had been led by Smith into this field, had worked closely with him while writing the *Britannica*[9] articles "Taboo" and "Totem," and came to acquire a much more extensive and detailed factual knowledge of primitive religions than anybody else in his generation. Conversely, I should attach least weight to the judgments of Durkheim and Freud. I find that the more general the problems attacked by a sociologist, the less he is apt to know in particular of what he is talking about. As for Freud—to use a Napoleonic metaphor—*Moses and Monotheism* was his Egyptian campaign; surviving that disaster was one of the greatest proofs of his genius. Cook seems to have followed Frazer; he cites Smith here and there for particular details. On "totemism" the starting point for historical discussion should be McLennan, not Smith. Lévi-Strauss, in his booklet analyzing the concept (*supra*, n. 10), did not find it necessary to mention Smith's work. Whatever the fate of the concept, the role of the practice in pre-Islamic Arabia and pre-Mosaic Israel

---

[19] So far as I know, the best general book on "Arabia and the Bible" is still the work of J. Montgomery with that title, first published in 1934, and reprinted in New York, 1969, with a prolegomenon by G. van Beek. In one footnote (no. 27, p. 158), Montgomery declared that "Robertson Smith, Wellhausen, Nöldeke have abundantly registered the similarities between the religion of Israel and that of North Arabia as illustrated in the Muslim tradition of the times of the Pagin Ignorance. To this literature may be added Nielsen, *Die altarabische Mondreligion* (1904) containing some rather venturesome conclusions. I may here simply call attention to the large number of correspondences in religious terminology..." (etc.). In Montgomery's vocabulary, "venturesome" was one of the strongest terms of condemnation. Van Beek's prolegomenon has much to say of topography, tribes, trade routes, and archaeological evidence; the little evidence that is of religious and intellectual significance gets little attention; of course there is no mention of Smith.

[20] R. A. Jones, "Robertson Smith and James Frazer on Religion," in *Functionalism Historicized*, ed. G. Stocking Jr., Madison, 1984 (*History of Anthropology*, 2), pp. 31–58. Beidelman, on Smith and sociology, is most valuable for its bibliography (*supra*, n. 7).

seems hopelessly uncertain for lack of evidence, and its role in Islam and Israelite religion seems limited to uncomprehended survivals.

Since Smith's theories were mainly mistaken and his influence, I should guess, has just about blown itself out, why did I begin by describing him as perhaps, "for English society, the most influential" of the figures we are now studying? Because of his importance as a publicist. Publicity is a form of education, and Smith used it deliberately for important ends. After his pietistic, bibliolatrous upbringing, his conversion to the Kuenen-Graf-Wellhausen critical position in biblical scholarship must have come with almost the force of a revelation and religious conversion. The passionate clarity of the explanations, in his first book on the Old Testament, voice an almost Platonic joy in seeing, understanding, and grasping the truth.

This is the explanation of his determination to be tried. He could have taken the kindly warnings that were given him, kept his mouth shut, and kept his position. When the trials began to go badly, he could have accepted the position at Harvard which Eliot had offered him, and withdrawn from the fray, or he could have taken a position in physics—in which field he had taught with success and published with distinction—but he chose to continue to fight the cases, get the largest possible hearing for his position, and subjected his opponents to the public disgrace of penalizing him for arguments they could not answer.

By his three trials, first for heresy and twice for deposition from his chair, he broke the hold of Calvinistic orthodoxy in Scotland. The trials got full newspaper coverage. The twelve lectures which became *The Old Testament in the Jewish Church* "were delivered in Edinburgh and Glasgow during…three months…and the average attendance on the course in the two cities was not less than eighteen hundred."[21] These were paying customers, and in a world far poorer and less populous than the present. The lectures for *The Prophets of Israel* were also delivered in both cities to large audiences. Those for *The Religion of the Semites* were the first of three series delivered for the Burnett fund in Aberdeen. And these were only the most famous of many other appearances. By his ecclesiastical position (he was never defrocked), his academic connexions, his learning, his brilliance, he made it common knowledge that the opinions of critical scholarship about the Bible were not alien eccentricities to be dismissed out of hand, but raised serious questions about which various positions other than the orthodox might respectably be held. In particular, his exoneration from the charge of heresy enabled many teachers and clergymen to express similar opinions, and so broke open what had hitherto been an intellectual prison. It is therefore no wonder that Black and Chrystal's *Life* (*supra*, n. 7) has the tone of a martyrology and, I fear, the reliability of one.

A second aspect of his publicity campaign were his many articles, and especially his razor-edged reviews. Yet more important was his editorship

---

[21] *The Old Testament in the Jewish Church*, p. v.

of the *Encyclopædia Britannica*, of which he brought the ninth edition to completion, and for which he wrote over two hundred articles. He thus placed the opinions, arguments, and evidence of critical biblical scholarship in an accepted work of reference from which the general public would take them as facts. And these were not only his own opinions, nor was his work limited to biblical criticism. He got the best scholars available in Europe and America to write articles on their specialties, and so made the *Britannica*[9] one of the leading reference works of its time. The hagiographic legend says that he read all the articles. Greater love than this, no man hath.

Other arms in the campaign were his teaching, his huge scholarly correspondence, the time he gave to advise young scholars who wrote him from all parts of Britain, and his work as University Librarian in Cambridge, where he added a building to the library, revised the filing system, and organized the work of securing important publications from all over the world. If epithets were now added to names, as they were in the Middle Ages, we should remember him as "William the Illuminator."

Columbia University

13

Seventy Years Before *The Golden Bough*: George Grote's Unpublished Essay on "Magick"

JOHN VAIO

The practical, as opposed to the intellectual, prehistory of Grote's essay begins in 1814. In that year MacVey Napier assumed the editorship of the supplementary volumes to the fifth edition of the *Encyclopædia Britannica* and invited James Mill to contribute articles on topics in the fields of politics, economics, law, and education. The impact of these articles on contemporary politics and political science was immense, and one of them, the *Essay on Education*, will be of special importance to our study. The working relationship between editor and author was a cordial one, and this phase of it lasted ten years.[1]

On January 3, 1821, Mill wrote a letter to Napier which contained the following paragraph:

> By the by, there is a friend of mine who has written a very learned and, what is more, a truly philosophical discourse on the subject of Magic, which he would be very happy to have printed in your work. From the specimen I have seen, it will prove, I think, not only instructive, but amusing. I am not at liberty to mention the name of the author. He is a young City banker, and the son of a man who is an eminent banker, and is a very extraordinary person, in his circumstances, both for knowledge and clear vigorous thinking.

Bain, who cites this letter, adds, "The city banker was Grote. The article did not appear, and was probably destroyed or transferred by its author; I am not aware of any trace of it in his subsequent works."[2]

But the essay had not been lost. It was found and identified as Brit. Mus. [now Brit. Lib.] Add. MS 29531 by M. L. Clarke in his biography of Grote:

---

[1] See A. Bain, *James Mill: A Biography* (London 1882, repr. New York 1967) 128f, 153ff, 160f, 193, 201ff, 215–59 [henceforth: Bain, *James Mill*]; W. H. Burston, *James Mill on Philosophy and Education* (London 1973) 47–49.

[2] Bain, *James Mill* 193f.

The paper was not published, but it survives in manuscript. It is concerned not with magic as the term is generally understood today so much as with all belief in the agency of invisible beings, and is in effect a reasoned attack on the idea of supernatural intervention.[3]

The MS consists of 89 folios written in a clear and legible hand.[4] On f. 66 someone (Mrs. Grote?) has written "G. Potther his book / a Xmas box 1820." On the same folio Mrs. Grote adds a note dated to 1873: "'Potther' was a nickname given to G. G. [George Grote] by his wife, and he used to be amused to call himself by it in joking with her."

Folios 1–65 contain the essay in question. On ff. 67–89 a condensed version of the first part of the essay is found. These twenty-three folios correspond to ff. 1–22 of the longer version; both ff. 22 and 89 end at exactly the same point. I assume the longer version (dated to late 1820) is the essay referred to by James Mill in January 1821, though it appears to lack the conclusion indicated in its first paragraph. The shorter version may be an attempt to meet the requirements of Napier. Whether it was ever completed or left unfinished in its present state cannot be determined, at least on the evidence of this MS. In the following remarks I refer only to the longer version published below.

Before turning to the essay itself we should consider briefly its biographical context. In November 1820, Grote turned twenty-six; for the previous ten years he had worked in his father's bank. To all appearances he was an active man of business who had not had a university education. But in fact since 1819 he had been part of one of the most important intellectual movements of his time: he had become a "disciple" of the leading Utilitarians, Ricardo, Bentham, and above all James Mill.[5] These great men were Grote's teachers in "Modern Greats," that is, philosophy, politics, and economics in the slang of Oxford. It is Mill's philosophy as well as what Bentham termed the analysis of natural religion that will be of particular importance for our discussion.

Grote begins his essay with a definition of "Magick." This falls into two parts: (1) "supposing the existence and agency of certain excessive and undefinable powers" and (2) "extending the range of those powers with which we are acquainted beyond the limits which experience authorises." Later (p. 278)[6] we find reference to "that excessive and unwarranted range of agency, which falls...under the denomination of Magick." But by pp. 280f the object of enquiry has taken an important and revealing turn: the reader has been led to consider how men "imagine the existence and agency of

---

[3] M. L. Clarke, *George Grote: A Biography* (London 1962) 29 with n.3 [henceforth: Clarke, *Grote*].

[4] The following account is based on a positive microfilm copy of the MS.

[5] See Clarke, *Grote* 19ff (esp. 20 with n.1); H. Grote, *The Personal Life of George Grote* (2nd ed. London 1873) 20ff [henceforth: *Personal Life*].

[6] Page references to Grote's essay are to the text as printed in this volume.

certain designing beings, enfranchised from all the limits and restrictions of visible material bodies." The true object of Grote's philosophical analysis has emerged: religion.

The tendency of this analysis becomes clearer as we read on. For example, on p. 283 "an invisible being" is compared to "an earthly potentate" who wreaks his "utmost vengeance on the wretch who dares to...distrust...his power." Further (p. 284) "a class of persons" emerges who "assume the character of favourites and deputies of these invisible beings...The analogy of earthly potentates...disposes us also to embrace the idea, that unseen beings would be likely to employ a visible *ministry* upon earth" [my italics]. These "ministers" gain "wealth and reputation" as well as "a weightier command over the minds of others, and a greater influence in proscribing and discrediting whatever notions they deem unfavorable to their sway" (pp. 284f.). What began as an analysis of belief in magic has become a full-scale assault on organized religion.

Such views have a distinguished British pedigree going back to Hume and Hobbes, but of more immediate interest to us is their place at the center of the Utilitarian attack on religion, in particular the religious views of Bentham and the philosophy of the elder Mill. The latter's *Analysis of the Phenomena of the Human Mind* was begun in 1822 and published in 1829, but its principal ideas had been sketched in the *Essay on Education*, written according to Bain in 1818.[7] As for Bentham, in December 1821 he turned over his copious notes on religion to Grote himself, who with great labor and zeal produced the volume entitled *An Analysis of the Influence of Natural Religion on the Temporal Happiness of Mankind*, published in 1822 under the pseudonym "Philip Beauchamp." The great man's instructions to his editor are worth citing:

> ...the best way would be to stop in the first instance at the subject of the natural Jug [="Juggernaut," Benthamite slang for "religion"]; showing its inefficiency to useful purposes, and then its efficiency to mischievous purposes: bringing in the question of verity, considered in respect of its inefficiency to useful purposes for want of *sufficient apparent verity*.[8]

Compare here the *cri de coeur* that follows Grote's analysis of belief in superhuman agents (p. 281):

> It is easy to comprehend how readily and infallibly all our erroneous associations will connect themselves with this supposition. The course of nature rejects them, and they of course claim alliance with that which is above nature. Under its ample and impenetrable shield all

[7] Bain, *James Mill* 247; cf. Burston (*supra* n. 1) 48 n.23.

[8] The letter, dated December 9, 1821, is cited from Clarke, *Grote* 30; see also the discussion in the same work at 29ff. Bentham's polemic against religion goes back at least to 1817: see C. M. Atkinson, *Jeremy Bentham: His Life and Work* (London 1905; repr. Westport, Conn. 1970) 210f.

conceivable errors find a ready shelter, which not only renders them unassailable by all the weapons of reason, but also invests them with a portion of that terrific and mysterious character which so much unhinges and disarms the mind in dwelling upon superhuman agents. They not only become true, but even privileged and consecrated above all other truth.

The close relation between master and disciple becomes even clearer if we bear in mind the remarks on the "earthly potentate" quoted above and consider the following from M. "Beauchamp":

> From men's...dogmas it would seem that [the invisible Being] is a capricious tyrant...If, then, we regard [him] as a capricious despot, and moreover, as a despot who knows every word we utter, we shall never speak of him without the highest eulogy, just because we attribute to him the most arbitrary tyranny. Hence, the invisible despot will specially favour the priests whose lives are devoted to supporting his authority...

Moreover, "religion, besides each separate mischief, 'subsidises a standing army for the perpetuation of all the rest.' The priest gains power as a 'wonder-worker,' who knows how to propitiate the invisible Being..."[9]
Grote's association with Bentham was especially close in this period (1819ff). As Mrs. Grote puts it, her husband "caught the [Benthamite] infection with readiness, and not only became a reader of Bentham's works...but he also frequented the society of the recluse author: not without sensible advantage to his inquiring and impressionable mind."[10] One may safely assume that Bentham entrusted his ideas on "natural religion" to Grote before he entrusted his copious notes. That his influence pervades the essay of 1820 should be no surprise.
"Beauchamp's" reference to priests as "wonder-workers" brings out another interesting point of contact. On p. 284, Grote writes:

> The reputed possession of magical powers constitutes a source from whence many persons derive uncommon affluence and dignity, and the interest of this class will of course direct the employment of all their efforts in cherishing the errors by which they profit so abundantly. And as superiority of talent is one of the most frequent among those causes which lead the ignorant to ascribe magical powers to any individual, it thus happens that the most eminent intellects acquire an interest in prompting error and deception among their fellows. Nor does this corrupt interest cease to operate, when the production of magical effects is attributed not to men, but to unseen agents. For the

---

[9] Taken for convenience from the paraphrase in L. Stephen, *The English Utilitarians* (London 1900) 2.342, 346; cf. "Beauchamp," *Analysis*, pt. 1, chap. 3; pt. 2, chap 2.6. The work was first published in 1822 and reprinted with altered pagination in 1866 and 1875. On Bentham's other writings against religion, see Stephen *op. cit.* 1.315f, 323f.
[10] *Personal Life* 24.

same class of persons, to whom the possession of such powers was previously attributed, now assume the character of favourites and deputies of these invisible beings. They affect an acquaintance with the character and attributes of the latter, and are supposed to possess the secret of calling forth or arresting at pleasure the irresistible arm of their superhuman patrons. The same preeminence of talents, which before procured for its possessor the reputation of a magician in his own right, will still continue to obtain for him the most exalted post; and, where invisible agents are supposed to exist, no higher situation can be awarded to any individual than that which is only subordinate to them, and which carries with it the dispensation of their favours and injuries. The analogy of earthly potentates, and our observation of their constant partiality for favourites, disposes us also to embrace the idea, that unseen beings would be likely to employ a visible ministry upon earth.

Grote here considers two phases of development: (1) a period in which "the production of magical effects is attributed…to men," and (2) a period in which such production is attributed to "unseen agents." During the first a powerful class of magicians arises. These are men of superior talents, each of whom has "the reputation of a magician in his own right." Later, when "invisible agents are supposed to exist" and to possess these magical powers, the ex-magicians become their deputies.

As Professor Morton Smith points out to me (*per litt.*), "No major occidental society of which Grote could have known anything (except perhaps the Celtic, and I doubt that he knew much of that) ever possessed any such ruling class of magicians. These are the Christian clergy, and their 'magic' is eighteenth-century 'priestcraft.'" Grote's "magicians" are essentially a philosophical abstraction; their connection with any historical or ethnographic reality is virtually zero. But like the "Primitive Man" of later anthropologists, their "mission" was "Theologians all to expose."[11]

Grote on magicians also offers some striking points of contact with *The Golden Bough*. Sir James' magicians like Grote's develop into a *class* that includes "some of the ablest and most ambitious men"; these men possess "acuter minds," and their career "holds out to them a prospect of honour, wealth, and power." They combine "the keenest intelligence and the most unscrupulous character" and are men of "superior ability." Their purpose is often "to dupe their weaker brother and play on his superstition for their own advantage"; they depend on the reputation for "wonderful powers which the credulity of [their] fellows ascribes to [them]." In Sir James an "Age of Magic" is distinct from an "Age of Religion," which it precedes; but at a transitional stage "the functions of priest and sorcerer were often combined or, to speak more correctly, were not yet differentiated from each other." Finally, as we noted above, Grote distinguishes two phases of

---

[11] See G. W. Stocking, *Victorian Anthropology* (London & New York 1987) 190f with n.8 and index *s. v.* "Religion, weakening of."

"Magick"; the second, being characterized by belief in unseen agents, is, in effect, religion; for Frazer belief in unseen, superhuman beings ushers in the "Age of Religion."[12]

There could hardly be a greater contrast than that between *The Golden Bough* and Grote's exercise in abstract philosophical speculation, lacking as it does any citation of historical or ethnographic examples. But the basic developmental scheme of both, at least in this area, is surprisingly similar. Grote's essay, which stands squarely in the tradition of Enlightenment and Rationalist thought on magic and religion, looks ahead some seventy years to the standard account of these matters given by one of the leading Victorian anthropologists.[13]

We turn now to the first part of Grote's essay (pp. 275–85), in which the mental processes leading to the two phases of "Magick" noted above are analyzed. In Phase I the "principal aids" employed by the "unguided savage" in interpreting the phenomena of nature are "the senses and the associating principle." There are two *laws* of *association*: one, "the law of succession," the other, the law of *resemblance* or similarity (p. 276). After examining "the melancholy certainty of error" to which "this mode of acquiring knowledge" is prone (p. 276ff), Grote concludes by noting that this is how "belief in magical powers" arises: "Unimportant phenomena are connected in our imaginations with a particular result, merely because they happen to precede it in the order of time, and thus become invested with that excessive and unwarranted range of agency, which if not detected and rectified by subsequent observation, falls afterwards under the denomination of Magick" (p. 278).

Here the principles of association psychology are used to explain the mental processes resulting in a belief in magic. Several points merit consideration: (1) the importance and influence of James Mill, (2) the anticipation in part of Frazer on magic, and (3) the anti-religious tendency of Mill's philosophy.

> With the domain of mental science [James Mill] had an almost unlimited acquaintance, having read every author of eminence, and sounded the depths of metaphysical inquiry in all its ramifications. At the time I am writing about [1818–20], he was composing a treatise on psychology, which he not long afterwards published under the title of

---

[12] The quotations from *The Golden Bough* are taken from the third edition (London 1911, repr. New York 1966) Part I, vol. 1, pp. 215f, 220, 237 (=abridged ed. 52f, 60, 65). Of special interest is pp. 224f n.2: "When I wrote this book originally I failed to realize the extent of opposition between magic and religion, because I had not formed a clear general conception of the nature of religion, and was disposed to class magic loosely under it" (cf. *GB* [1st ed., London 1890] 1.7ff). The view found in the third edition was first presented in the second (London 1900) 1.9ff, 61ff.

[13] We may now add the evidence of the essay to the discussion of Frazer's debt to Enlightenment thought at R. Ackerman, *J. G. Frazer: His Life and Work* (Cambridge 1987) 40ff.

"Analysis of the Human Mind," in two volumes. It was on this subject...that the young disciple...sought instruction at the hands of James Mill, and in his new acquaintance he found a master...

Thus Mrs. Grote on her husband's "tutorials" with the elder Mill.[14]

In fact, James Mill was the chief purveyor of association psychology to the 19th century, and by way of his son and Herbert Spencer, exercised a considerable influence on later anthropology.[15] In 1866 Grote himself praised his master's work as follows:

...the "Analysis of the Phenomena of the Human Mind," is a model of perspicuous exposition of complex states of consciousness, carried farther than by any other author before him; and illustrating the fulness which such exposition may be made to attain, by one who has faith in the comprehensive principle of association, and has learnt the secret of tracing out its innumerable windings.[16]

The writing of the *Analysis* did not begin until 1822, but Mill's serious work in this field dates back at least to 1816, when he was working on the *Essay on Education* (written probably in 1818), which gives a brief account of the theory and its origins.[17] Here it is worth noting that Mill cites Hobbes as the founder of associationism, since it is Hobbes who links one of its principles with the origin of religion (and magic), preceding Grote by some 170 years.[18] Seventy years after Grote it is Frazer who analyzes "magician's logic" in terms of associationism: in particular, "Homeopathic [or imitative] magic is founded on the association of ideas by similarity."[19] *Leviathan* meets *Golden Bough* by way of Grote's "lost" essay.

Finally, in connection with the anti-religious tendency discussed above, we may quote Sir Leslie Stephen's comments on Mill's philosophical theories:

The application of Mill's Analysis to the views of orthodox theologians required, one might have supposed, as little interpretation as a slap in the face. But a respectable philosopher may lay down what premises he pleases if he does not avowedly draw his conclusions...You may openly maintain doctrines inconsistent with all theology, but you must not point out the inconsistency. The

[14] *Personal Life* 22.

[15] See Stocking (*supra* n. 10) index *s.v.* "Associationism"; H. C. Warren, *A History of the Association Psychology* (New York 1921, repr. Ann Arbor 1966) 81ff.

[16] *The Minor Works of George Grote*, ed. A. Bain (London 1873) 283. Note also that Grote contributed "notes illustrative and critical" to J. S. Mill's edition of his father's book (2nd ed. London 1878); cf. vol. 1, p. xx.

[17] See *James Mill on Education*, ed. W. H. Burston (Cambridge 1969) 45–61; cf. Burston (*supra* n. 1) 47f, 51f, 124-97.

[18] Cf. *Leviathan*, chap. 12 ("Of Religion").

[19] *GB* (3rd edition) Part I, vol. 1, p. 53 (=abr. ed. p. 13). On Frazer and associationism, see Ackerman, *loc. cit.*, (*supra* n. 12).

Utilitarians contented themselves with sapping the fort instead of risking an open assault.[20]

Mrs. Grote later accused Bentham of having destroyed James Mill's religious faith and the latter in turn of doing the same for her husband, who "suffered much in giving up old beliefs."[21] The *Essay* shows that by 1820 the suffering had largely passed.

As noted above, Grote distinguishes two periods of "Magick," one preceding, the other based on, belief in "invisible beings." The next section of the essay (pp. 278–84) deals with the foundations of such belief. Another of "the laws of succession between natural effects" comes into play, namely, "the connection between design and volition in itself, and the effects which follow it." It is "the inference of design" that leads by various stages to belief in "the existence of willing and designing agents" (or *beings*), who are at the same time "invisible" and "omnipotent" (pp. 280f). This belief is aided by certain factors: distance, darkness, fear, and other emotions such as confidence and its opposite (pp. 282–84). Finally, our old friends, the magicians, help to foster this belief (pp. 284f).

On p. 285, Grote summarizes the first part of his essay: "We have thus endeavoured to sketch a concise review of the belief in magick, to trace the various shapes which it assumes in the human mind, and to notice some of the principal circumstances which appear to suggest and support it." After a few preliminary remarks he then turns to the next subject of enquiry, namely, the question "whether there is any ground for supposing, that there exist unseen and unlimited beings who produce effects around us; and what portion of those effects should be ascribed to their agency" (pp. 285–86).

Grote begins by considering the criterion of *rarity*: "...when we observe in an event the character of rarity,...are we authorized to attribute the production of this event to design?" The answer is negative for the following reasons. (1) The criterion is insufficiently exact, since it is "always relative to the observer." (2) It would be applicable only if we had knowledge of "the whole course of nature" both in the present and the future. (3) It is impossible to get a clear notion of the necessary "degree of rarity" needed to establish the validity of the criterion. (4) Given "the infinite variety of possible combinations which the particles of matter may assume,...there is no substance in nature which is not rare and even singular" (p. 286).

In the following section (pp. 286f), Grote enlivens his abstract discussion by considering a concrete example. A king cures the scrofula with his touch. Are we then entitled to "infer the aid of an invisible being" merely because we can find no difference between the king and other men sufficient to explain his unusual ability? Such an answer, declares Grote, would be presumptuous in view of (1) our limited powers of observation

---

[20] *The English Utilitarians* (*supra* n. 8) 2.338.
[21] *The Amberley Papers*, ed. B. and P. Russell (London 1937) 1.421.

and (2) our incomplete knowledge of nature. Moreover, we cannot first classify the king as a *man* and then base our argument upon that classification. Nor can we determine beforehand that certain qualities to which we assign the term *man* "shall never be found in connection with the property of healing scrofula," any more than we can "decide that they shall be found in connection with it." "Lord Bacon," the "Father of Experimental Philosophy," would hardly allow such a procedure.

Next (pp. 287ff), Grote argues that we cannot "introduce a supposition in order to account for certain facts, which are affirmed to be inexplicable without it, while we refuse to apply it to certain other facts which are equally inexplicable." If we "introduce invisible agency in order to explain" our scrofula-curing king, then we must also apply it in the case of a pig "whose scent was so remarkably fine and keen that it was employed in hunting game." The principle *Magna di curant, parva neglegunt* will not do. The supposition of invisible agency must be applied consistently or not at all; it must either be trivialized or dropped altogether.

In the section that follows (pp. 289f), Grote's aim is to show that the hypothesis of invisible agency "is exposed to the very same difficulties, as the facts which it is brought to explain, and that if admitted as a fact, it does not render the body of our knowledge more coherent or intelligible than it was before" (p. 295). The hypothesis is worthless from a philosophical and scientific point of view, as those who employ it implicitly concede when forced to admit "that the nature of those invisible agents, whose existence they maintained, was unknown and incomprehensible" (p. 289).

The fifth section (pp. 289–94), which concludes the essay, is for us by far the most important, in that it affords an early look at the principles that underlie Grote's treatment of Greek myth and legend in *A History of Ancient Greece*, a fundamental book in the classical studies of the nineteenth century, written by a scholar "who would not only transform British thinking about Greek myths but also redirect the course of the fledgling British study of Greek religion, history and philosophy for over fifty years." The quotation is from Frank Turner's major study, *The Greek Heritage in Victorian Britain* (p. 85), and it is to Professor Turner that we owe a full discussion of Grote's importance as mythologist and religious historian (*ib.* pp. 83–104). Again, it is Turner who emphasizes "the continuity of thought" that links Grote with the Cambridge Ritualists in this area (*ib.* pp. 116–19).

Grote began work on the first draft of the *History* two years after writing his essay. On October 14, 1822, he writes, in a letter to G. W. Norman:

I am deeply engaged with the reading necessary for my history. I am now going through Strabo, and shall devote myself almost entirely to Greek now for God knows how long. About the early periods I find such prodigious want of certainty and authority, that I am amazed how men can have gone on asserting as unquestionable truths what the witnesses reporting could not by possibility have ascertained.[22]

Three months later (January 14, 1823), Grote writes again to the same correspondent:

> I am at present deeply engaged in the fabulous ages of Greece, which I find will require to be illustrated by bringing together a large mass of analogical matter from other early histories, in order to show the entire uncertainty and worthlessness of tales to which early associations have so long familiarized all classical minds. I am quite amazed to discover the extraordinary greediness and facility with which men assert, believe, and re-assert, and are believed. The weakness appears to be next to universal...[23]

In the last part of his essay, Grote is principally concerned with "the notion of a prodigy" as it relates to "the laws of proof." A *prodigy* is "an event produced by superhuman interposition," that is, by an "invisible agency overruling the course of nature." *Proof*, on the other hand, "is the result of testimony," which in turn is defined as "the communication...of the belief of one man to another"; and this belief is validated or invalidated only by an "appeal to the laws of nature." Grote's aim is to show that "the supposition of a prodigy is inconsistent with the fundamental assumption on which the process of inference rests," and so "must be deemed inadmissible" (pp. 292, 290f, 294f).

The considerable debt owed here to Hume's "Of Miracles" was pointed out to me by Dr. Paul Keyser, and it is odd that Grote nowhere cites either it or its author. His acknowledged philosophical heroes, at least to judge from his citations, are Bacon and Locke. Why then is the name of their greatest successor absent? Certainly one would hesitate to accuse Grote of intellectual dishonesty.

True, in 1817 he writes, "Hume's essays, some of which I have likewise read lately, do not improve, in my view, on further knowledge."[24] But there he is apparently contrasting Hume's moral philosophy with that of Aristotle, which he much admires. Moreover, association with James Mill, who had a deep respect for Hume, must have affected Grote's assessment.

Why then no mention in the *Essay*? The answer, I think, lies in the following. In his recent edition of Hume's essay, Anthony Flew notes that:

---

[22] G. Grote, *Posthumous Papers*, ed. H. Grote (privately printed, London 1874) 20.

[23] Cited at *Personal Life* 41. On the inception of the *History* see Clarke, *Grote* 33f; A. D. Momigliano, "George Grote and the Study of Greek History," *Studies in Historiography* (London and New York 1966) 60 with n.2 (=*Contributo alla storia degli studi classici* [Rome 1955] 218); and J. Vaio, "George Grote," in *Classical Scholarship: A Biographical Encyclopedia*, edd. W. W. Briggs and W. M. Calder III (New York/London 1990) 120.

[24] From a letter to G. W. Norman (dated April, 1817), cited at *Personal Life* 20.

...during the nineteenth century, in the edition of Hume's *Essays*...in Sir John Lubbock's best-selling Hundred Books series, both this Section X ["Of Miracles"] and the subsequent Section XI are excised, to appear only in a reluctant Appendix. This has a remarkable initial note beginning: "These essays are generally omitted in popular editions..."

Flew also refers to a later editor who dismisses "Of Miracles" "as an irrelevant and offensive addition, to be explained only by reference to 'Hume's ambition to disturb "the zealots" at all costs.'"[25]

To avoid the threat of prosecution in 1822, Grote and Bentham used a pseudonym and a printer already in jail to publish the attack on religion discussed above. In his essay, Grote is at pains to cloak his attack on religion and priestcraft under the terms "Magick" and "magicians." It may well have been the obvious tendency of the essay in spite of these precautions that prevented its publication. The proper acknowledgement of Hume was impossible in these circumstances, as it would have given the game away all too clearly. Indeed, the term *miracle* is used only once, in citing an English divine who in fact believed in such phenomena.

The divine in question is one Dr. Berriman, who "in vindicating the authority of the legends relating to the 5th and 6th centuries remarks, 'I see no reason why we should dispute the facts on account of the natural incredibility of them, unless it can be proved, as it certainly cannot, that miracles were ceased in that age'" (p. 292).[26] Now for Grote, the philosopher of religion, it could never be adequately *proved* that any miracles had ever occurred; and for the future historian the authority of the myths and legends relating to Greece before the 8th century B.C. was to be removed entirely from the arena of history. The essay of 1820 reveals an early stage in the development of the scepticism that was to inform the first part of the *History* published in 1846.

Hume's influence on that scepticism has been noted above. Here we may add that "Of Miracles" had much to teach regarding historical as well as philosophical method. Its importance for the philosophy of history is well brought out by Flew, who directs our attention to Hume's concern with "the criteria by which we must assess historical testimony, and the general presumptions which alone allow us to interpret the detritus of the past as

[25] D. Hume, *Of Miracles*, ed. A. Flew (LaSalle, Illinois 1985) 3 [henceforth: Flew, *ed.*); cf. Flew, "The Impossibility of the Miraculous," in *Hume's Philosophy of Religion* (Winston-Salem 1986) 9 with nn.2–3 [henceforth: Flew, *art.*]. The editor in question is L. A. Selby-Bigge, whose edition of Hume's *Enquiries* for the Clarendon Press "has been and is the most widely used edition...in our century" (Flew, *ed.* 3). ("Of Miracles" is Section X of Hume's *Enquiry Concerning Human Understanding*.)

[26] See W. Berriman, *An Historical Account of the Controversies...concerning the Doctrine of the...Trinity* (London 1725) 356 note q. Grote cites Berriman from the "Introductory Discourse" to C. Middleton's *A Free Inquiry into the Miraculous Powers*, etc. = *id., Miscellaneous Works* (2nd edition, London 1755) 1. lxix. Grote paraphrases Middleton, who in turn paraphrases Berriman. It should be noted that the Garland reprint of *Free Inquiry* (New York and London 1976) omits the "Introductory Discourse."

historical evidence."[27] In the words of C. S. Pierce, "the whole of modern 'higher criticism' of ancient history in general...is based upon the same logic that is used by Hume."[28]

Nor should we overlook the valuable lessons in historical method that could be learned from Conyers Middleton, whose *Free Inquiry*[29] is cited by Grote in his discussion of prodigies. By critically re-examining the evidence for the post-apostolic miracles of the first four centuries A.D., Middleton sought to expose those miracles as fraudulent. The success of this enterprise earned the lavish praise of Bentham,[30] from whom Grote learned of the importance, if not the existence, of Middleton's treatise.

Thus the final pages of Grote's essay on "Magick" shed new light on the formation of the critical method responsible for the historian's mature achievement. To the list of illustrious and influential predecessors compiled by earlier scholars—James Mill, Vico, Comte, K. O. Müller, and above all Niebuhr[31]—we may now add Hume and Middleton, noting that their contribution to the study of religion had a significant impact in the next century on the thought of the major British ancient historian of the Victorian age.[32]

University of Illinois at Chicago

[27] Flew, *ed.* 13; in general, see *ib.* 12ff. The discussion is reprised with few changes at Flew, *art.* 21ff.

[28] *Values in a Universe of Chance*, ed. P. P. Wiener (Stanford 1958) 292f; cited by Flew, *art.* 21 with n.32 (cf. Flew, *ed.* 12).

[29] See above, n. 25.

[30] Cf. Gamaliel Smith (=Bentham), *Not Paul, but Jesus* (London 1823) iii–iv. The MS of this book was edited in 1817: see G. Wallas, *The Life of Francis Place* (2nd edition, London 1918; repr. 1925) 84 n.4.

[31] On the crucial influence of German scholarship and especially Niebuhr on Grote, see U. Muhlack, "Die deutschen Einwirkungen auf die englische Altertumswissenschaft am Beispiel George Grotes," *Philologie und Hermeneutik im 19. Jahrhundert II*, edd. M. Bollack and H. Wismann (Göttingen 1983) 376ff. I owe this reference to Dr. Renate Schlesier.

[32] I wish to thank the Manuscripts Librarian of the British Library for permission to quote extracts from Brit. Lib. Add. MS 29531. Thanks are also due to Professors Robert Ackerman, W. M. Calder III, Howard Jacobson, and Morton Smith for reading Grote's essay over and supplying me with much valuable comment. An earlier version of the present paper was generously and beneficially read by Professor Evelyn K. Moore. Much of value was also learned in the discussion following the presentation of this paper at the colloquium on the Cambridge Ritualists held at the University of Illinois at Urbana-Champaign April 27–30, 1989. Above all, I wish to thank Professor Calder for his encouragement and support.

14

An Unpublished Essay on Magick by George Grote (1820)[1]

edited by JOHN VAIO

Though it is not easy to comprehend in a few words all the circumstances which the term Magick is usually understood to embrace, yet the belief in it may generally be described as supposing the existence and agency of certain excessive and undefinable powers, or extending the range of those powers with which we are acquainted to an height beyond the limits which experience authorises. We shall attempt to trace this belief to its source in the human mind, and to sketch a short account of its origin and progress; We shall then examine the truth or falsehood of those arguments which have usually been urged in vindication of it; And we shall conclude with a brief review of those phenomena to which it has most commonly been applied, together with the particular circumstances most universally found to accompany it in the different countries where it has prevailed.

The root from which this belief springs lies deeply seated in the human mind, and in order to discover it completely, we must carry back our view to the condition in which rude and early observers of nature must have been placed, before any portion of our present experimental knowledge had been treasured up. That knowledge consists of a series of propositions asserting various resemblances and differences among the phenomena of nature, and assigning also the rules according to which they succeed each other. But the steps by which nature has thus been interpreted are tardy and laborious, and

[1] [Editor's note] For a description of the MS on which this edition is based, see the editor's paper in this vol. (Vaio, "Seventy Years") 264. The present edition is a *Lesetext* based on a positive microfilm copy of the longer version of Grote's essay (ff. 1-65 of the MS); that is, the variants (mainly Grote's) are not recorded, nor are the divergences of the second, partial version (ff. 67-89). The editor's purpose is to give the text of the longer version as corrected by Grote, whose conventions of spelling and punctuation are maintained. Notes 2-9 (by Grote) have been numbered in the modern manner, but are otherwise unchanged. Grote's citations (except for punctuation) are left in their original form. I wish to thank the Manuscripts Librarian of the British Library for permission to publish the text of Grote's essay, and Ms. Annette Dewberry for making the initial transcript of the text from photocopies of the microfilm. See also Vaio, "Seventy Years " n. 31.

the path of truth is originally so little distinguishable from that of error, that the unguided savage can only be informed of his mistakes by a painful experience of their consequences. His principal aids, in commencing this task of interpretation, are the senses and the associating principle. Impressions are made upon the senses in a particular order and this immediate succession seems to constitute the primary link which unites them together in the mind. But association does not only connect together those objects which have been observed to succeed each other; By another law of its operation, one phenomenon will awaken the recollection of any thing similar which we may have previously witnessed. And the subsequent part of the process consists in applying the law of succession observed in the latter as a corrective of that remembered in the former. The similar circumstances in each will have been presented to us twice; The points of difference but once; Consequently the former, by their more frequent recurrence, outweigh and obliterate the latter, and those circumstances in which the first phenomenon resembled the second, and in which the first law of succession resembled the second, will be left exclusively connected together in our minds. Repeated processes of this kind, and a comparison of many distinct occurrences, each contributing to fix in our associations its points of resemblance with the preceding, enable us at last to set apart that circumstance among them all which is subject invariably to the same law of succession.

The slightest inspection of this mode of acquiring knowledge must suffice to exhibit its extreme tediousness and difficulty, as well as the melancholy certainty of error which it ensures. The associating principle acts according to its own laws, and connects together in the mind certain events which may have occurred in two following moments of time. But this succession may possibly be quite accidental. Nor is there any discernible character in the antecedent which can guide a mind perfectly inexperienced, in deciding whether it is the constant and natural precursor of that event which is associated with it as its consequent, or whether its prior occurrence may have been casual and confined to this single instance. Indeed as the correct supposition can be but one, and the number of possible errors, in a compound train of circumstances, is very considerable, it is infinitely more probable that the result will at first be false, and consequently a wrong law of succession treasured up in our minds. And amidst this multitude of probable errors, there is not one which can be exposed in its true and genuine colours, until subsequent facts shall have occurred to detect it.

But if the attainment of truth is thus difficult, when we have two visible trains of circumstances to compare together, how much must the liability to error be enhanced, where one train of circumstances alone has been presented to the senses and another similar series is to be supposed or inferred? When our minds have coupled together two phenomena as antecedent and consequent, we are irresistibly impelled to imagine, when an event recurs similar to the latter, that it has been preceded by something similar to the former. This principle we uniformly apply whenever the second consequent happens not to be preceded by any phenomena which excite our attention, and when therefore our minds demand that it should be assimilated to some other course of succession which has already been presented to us. Now when we remark, between two consequents, a partial similarity, it is impossible, prior to experience, to decide whether the antecedents have been similar or otherwise. No human foresight can determine, whether the connection hinges upon those circumstances in which the two events resemble, or upon those in which they differ. Neither of these suppositions can be rejected, until the other has occurred and has been shown by experience to be real.

The following passage from Mr. Stewart's *Philos. of the H.M.* (Vol. 1. Cap. 5. Part 2. Sect. 1.) presents some just remarks upon this topic; "As the connections among physical events are discovered to us by experience alone it is evident that when we see a phenomenon preceded by a number of different circumstances, it is impossible for us to determine by any reasoning a priori, which of these circumstances are to be regarded as the constant, and which as the accidental antecedents of the effect. If in the course of our experiences the same combination of circumstances is always exhibited to us without any alteration, and is invariably followed by the same result, we must for ever remain ignorant whether this result be connected with the whole combination, or with one or more of the circumstances combined, and therefore if we are anxious, upon any occasion, to produce a similar effect, the only rule that we can follow, with perfect security, is to imitate in every particular the combination which we have seen. It is only where we have an opportunity of separating such circumstances from each other, of combining them variously together, and of observing the effects which result from these different experiments, that we can ascertain with precision the general laws of nature, and strip physical causes of their accidental and unessential concomitants."

We may remark however that the error of a rude mind by no means necessarily consists in associating all the preceding circumstances, important as well as unimportant, with the result. The defect which is inseparable from the human constitution, lies in the incapacity of distinguishing casual accompaniments from invariable sequences; Nothing but time and experience can correct this original disability. But the associations of an early observer usually fasten upon some circumstances to the exclusion of the rest and comprehend but a limited portion of the properties of an object. Vague and slight resemblances attract his notice and occasion him to overlook the points of difference. The most trifling similarity in the object will induce him to infer similarity in the laws of succession which belong to it. Some circumstances likewise will excite his hopes or fears more powerfully than others, and these emotions will lead him to ascribe a distinct and peculiar importance to that which occasions them. Though therefore our early associations will almost always fasten upon some particular department of a compound train of circumstances, to the exclusion of the rest, yet this preference is not to be attributed to any original and inherent symbol of truth which we can detect in the former, but simply to certain accidental properties about it which urge themselves more forcibly upon our attention.

In this rude stage of the human mind, the belief in magical powers takes its rise. Unimportant phenomena are connected in our imaginations with a particular result, merely because they happen to precede it in the order of time, and thus become invested with that excessive and unwarranted range of agency, which if not detected and rectified by subsequent observation, falls afterwards under the denomination of Magick. Of the innumerable errors which the early incompetency of the human faculties in this manner obtrudes upon us, the greater proportion do indeed find their corrective from the hand of time, and are insensibly obliterated by the more frequent recurrence of the genuine connections of nature. But there are some among them which accident has stamped very deeply upon our associations, and which have become indelible from the absence either of capacity or opportunity to expose them. In phenomena which occur but rarely, or in a confused and complex manner, there may have been no possibility of detecting the error of our primary belief; in other cases, terror or some other emotion may have so bewildered the judgment as to render it incapable of a calm and accurate comparison of past and present. Under either of these circumstances, those primary associations, which ascribe the production of inexplicable effects to some erroneous and unimportant cause, are likely to be of unusual durability. When, in other respects a correct view has been attained of the genuine connections of nature, these remnants of our early ideas appear to stand out at variance and inconsistent with the other branches of our knowledge. They do not seem to recognize those limits which experience has taught us to apply to the properties of other subjects. And the gradual collation of many other effects, together with the increasing quantity and value of analogical evidence, would unquestionably proscribe and extinguish them, were they not kept alive by a particular sort of confusion in which the early dawning of our faculties infallibly involves us, and which we shall now proceed to explain.

Of all the laws of succession between natural effects, that which first becomes known to a child is, the connection between design and volition in itself, and the effects which follow it. This is a connection which it is impossible for him either to mistake or to disregard. He becomes even in the earliest period intimately and familiarly acquainted with it, and as it is the only rule of sequence which he possesses, it may be said to represent to his mind all the laws of nature. Whenever therefore changes occur in the phenomena around him, he will have no other method of explaining and rendering the succession in which they occur intelligible, than by assimilating it to that single law which he has treasured up. The resemblance between the effects of his own design, and the change to which he annexes a similar interpretation, may be really slight, but to his vague and inaccurate survey, it will be perfectly sufficient to authorise the transition. We should recollect that the distinction between a slight and a close resemblance is the fruit of a later period, when various degrees of resemblance have been frequently submitted to our inspection.

But besides prior acquaintance, there is another remarkable property in this law of succession. Design in other bodies is never subjected to our perceptive powers, nor does experience ever instruct us of its existence or agency except in ourselves. Hence it follows, that when a child has once accounted for any changes presented to him by supposing volition and design, no subsequent fact which ever occurs can positively negative the hypothesis. In the case of any other phenomenon which he may have mistaken for an invariable antecedent, the recurrence of the consequent without it will instantly reveal to him his error. And it is only by a comparison of these scattered and various combinations of phenomena, as we have before explained, that casual conjunctions can be separated from the genuine connections of nature. But the inference of design is from its very essence, destitute of this wholesome and important corrective.

Though a child however infallibly commences his interpretation of nature by applying the notion of design, and though no positive fact occurs to contradict this hypothesis, yet there are circumstances which gradually restrict the number of occasions on which he will employ it. In proportion as he extends his remarks, the laws of succession in many of the phenomena before him, will appear perfectly similar and unvarying. Instances of similar sequence will be progressively coupled together and familiarised to his associations. As soon as those have been frequently submitted to his notice, the close resemblance and regularity which they exhibit among themselves will insensibly displace in his mind the fainter resemblance which they bear to the phenomena consequent upon volition in himself. He will then learn the existence of something which is not designing, or the distinction between animated and inanimate bodies. The latter class will at first comprehend only such substances as stones, for example, or other bodies the changes in which are few in number and uniform. Trees or flowers will remain still personified, until the greater variety of the phenomena which they present is in some degree arranged and familiarised to the mind. But the changes which occur in men and animals are so irregular and multifarious, that the supposition of will and design will remain constantly annexed to them, from the impossibility of discovering any resemblance among themselves sufficiently close or uniform to exclude it. A child will unquestionably become sensible in time of the similarity between their corporeal formation and his own. This however is a discovery which may tend to confirm his previous conclusion, but does not form the primary foundation of it.

These two properties therefore belonging to the notion of design; first, our familiarity with it when we know no other connection in nature, which compels us to apply it to whatever phenomenon we may then wish to account for; secondly, its unsusceptibility of positive contradiction from experience; inevitably give birth to a laxity in reasoning about it, far greater than that to which any other inference is exposed. Before we imagine the operation of any other antecedent, we always observe with more or less precision, the rules of experimental interpretation; We demand some special resemblance between the result which previous observation has connected with it, and the phenomenon to be explained. But the original law of our faculties impels us to annex the supposition of design to all phenomena, whatever be their nature, when they do not present a visible and positive conformity to some other known law of succession. And the only argument which we acknowledge, as proving that this supposition is incorrectly applied to any fact, is the discovery of some other established natural connexion, to which the fact may be shewn to belong.

The foregoing remarks explain to us why this belief of excessive and unauthorised power so frequently attaches itself to design; and why the words, looks, and all signs of volition in our fellow creatures have been so universally invested with that undue and undefinable range of operation which we term magical. In time also, most of those early errors which have guided our association of other phenomena, fasten themselves more or less remotely upon the supposition of design, and justify themselves by the reference of that which appears supernatural in their mode of agency to the will of a thinking being. And anything, as we have observed, becomes sufficiently understood when it can be traced up to volition.

It is obvious that we cannot pretend to apply this hypothesis as a satisfactory solution of all occurrences, indiscriminately, without investing design with an unbounded range of agency, and imagining it to be omnipotent. But that design, which we annex to the visible material bodies around us, can never be thus exalted, and though we may ascribe to the volition of our fellow creatures a number of effects with which it has no real connection, we still can never endue it with unlimited power. The narrowest experience cannot fail to notice the melancholy proofs of weakness which all men exhibit. The pain and sickness to which all are exposed, their frequent inability to satisfy the most urgent desires, and the restrictions which the laws of the material universe constantly impose upon their modes of gratification—all these are exhibitions but too striking of the confined sphere which human powers embrace. Though also the changes in human bodies still continue so various and irregular, that we are compelled to suppose them designing, yet time invariably discovers to us certain rules or bounds which they do not and cannot exceed. Hence, while there is not that particular reason for withdrawing the supposition of design from human bodies which had previously withdrawn it from other material systems, yet design, in this shape, becomes incompetent to those explanatory functions which our original constitution uniformly leads us to ascribe to it. There is but one mode of reconciling this discrepancy. We overleap the boundary which our senses present to us, and we imagine the existence and agency of certain designing beings, enfranchised from all the limits and restrictions of visible material bodies.

By this supposition, we retain the liberty of employing the notion of design with the same latitude as before, while we seem at the same time to maintain the uniformity of those laws which regulate the material world. The hypothesis of invisible design, therefore, supposes that some conception has been attained of a limited system of properties throughout nature. It involves an admission that the omnipotence originally attributed to design is wholly disclaimed and contradicted by experience, and that if we will still allow so indiscriminate a range of action it can be supposed to exist only where no observation can reach to detect it. Yet though it includes in this respect an important truth, it still irrevocably confirms to design all that unlimited power connected with it in the early mind, by detaching it finally from those material concomitants which experience might penetrate and circumscribe. At the same time that we frame a notion of a regular and systematic course of nature, we nevertheless suppose the existence of a class of willing and designing agents, who possess an unbounded privilege of altering and over ruling it at pleasure.

It is easy to comprehend how readily and infallibly all our erroneous associations will connect themselves with this supposition. The course of nature rejects them, and they of course claim alliance with that which is above nature. Under its ample and impenetrable shield all conceivable errors find a ready shelter, which not only renders them unassailable by all the weapons of reason, but also invests them with a portion of that terrific and mysterious character which so much unhinges and disarms the mind in dwelling upon superhuman agents. They not only become true, but even privileged and consecrated above all other truth. In a progressive state of society, for instance, it is quickly deemed absurd to suppose any connexion between the state of an animal's entrails, and the subsequent loss of an engagement. But when this event can be represented as the signal of impending wrath and vengeance on the part of an invisible being, the absurdity is veiled from our eyes and appears to vanish. We shall not now anticipate, what will come presently under our consideration, the question of the reality of this hypothesis, on its own grounds. Thus much however we shall not hesitate to affirm, that the human intellect never harboured any principle which has been so prolific and efficacious in originating, and perpetuating, credence in false facts, as this which is now under our review. Nor shall we apprehend any contradiction on this head, when it is recollected; That while every nation in the world has numberless tales of invisible interference in which it reposes implicit faith, there is no one individual nation which does not reject and deride all other tales except its own. The firmest believer therefore in the reality of the supposition cannot deny, that for one truth which is affirmed concerning it, there are a thousand falsehoods to which it gives currency. And this forcibly reminds us of the remark of Fontenelle; "Je ne suis pas si convaincu de notre ignorance par les choses qui arrivent, dont la raison nous est inconnue, que par ceux qui ne sont pas, et dont cependant nous trouvons la raison. Cela prouve que non seulement nous n'avons pas les principes qui menent en vrai, mais que nous en avons qui s'accommodent très facilement avec le faux."

Though it may appear to be a violent transition from the idea of will and energy in a material substance which we see before us, to the supposition that there exists a thinking and active being, when we have no evidence whatever for the existence of any thing—yet there are circumstances which lead the mind from one to the other by an easier route than might be imagined. There are many phenomena which take place at a great distance from us, so that even though there were designing beings in those spots, to whose agency the events might be referred, yet these beings would still be beyond the reach of our perceptive powers. Residents in the sky, or beneath the earth, would be so situated that human vision could afford no testimony of their existence. There are also many hours during every revolution of the sun when darkness renders our eyes wholly useless. It is during those hours that the impression of surrounding beings, whom we cannot see, and who are yet acting around us, is fastened upon our minds in the strongest manner. It is distance and darkness therefore which inform us, that beings may exist and produce effects, although not within the range of our vision, and which consequently prepare the mind for the notion of invisible agency in general. Besides this, an invisible being is not considered as immaterial, but as merely possessed of a degree of power which enables him to fascinate and elude our gaze. We ascribe to him superior attributes, by virtue of which he becomes invisible at pleasure. And the alarm and uneasiness which we feel at the sight of an unintelligible occurrence, always disposes us to represent as unlimited and irresistible the power by which we imagine it to be produced. Our passions, as Father Malebranche remarks, all justify themselves, or suggest to us opinions which justify them, and when we are once afraid of anything, we readily believe every circumstance which can render it still more the object of our apprehension.

The same fear which urges thus powerfully upon the understanding the notion of invisible agency, acts with equal efficacy in maintaining and keeping alive such ideas when once admitted, and in excluding all such considerations as may offer themselves on the other side of the question. We naturally couple with the notion of design certain modes of feeling in the possessor by which we imagine the direction of that design to be determined. The dispositions which we ascribe to invisible agents are copied from those which we observe to influence the great and mighty of earth. Extreme jealousy and irritability of temper, the liveliest sense of everything which tends to exalt his might, and the most unbounded hatred and resentment against everything which would question or diminish it, are the usual accompaniments of power in a fellow creature. An earthly potentate views any distrust of the magnitude of his power as a mark of defiance, and as a signal for the extension of his arm to wreak its utmost vengeance on the wretch who dares to entertain such a sentiment. But in an invisible being, the power is essentially and inseparably linked with existence, and the certainty of each is testified and manifested by the very same phenomenon. To disbelieve therefore or even to doubt his existence is precisely the same as to disbelieve or doubt his power, and is viewed as equally offensive and criminal in his eyes.[2] Hence we observe, that the very conception of an invisible agent infallibly introduces along with it an apprehension of impending punishment, if he should really exist, and if at the same time we should be even involuntarily, so far misled as to call his existence in question.   And since the imagination represents this punishment as incurred by the simple act of doubt or disbelief, there arises a bias in the mind which imprints most forcibly every thing which can be urged in favour of the supposition, while it terrifies and scares away the attention even from a review of the arguments on the opposite side. The operation of fear in thus suspending the impartiality of the judgment and in deterring it from embracing those sentiments whence future evil may possibly ensue, is striking and undeniable, and acts with peculiar influence on the present case. For if the question were, whether any other supposition should be adopted or rejected, no person would apprehend any punishment as likely to result from an involuntary misconception of the subject. But the dispositions which we annex to the idea of an invisible agent, present to us inevitably the mere act of disbelief, if that disbelief should be erroneous, as attended with the highest peril—while, on the opposite side, belief, even if it should be unfounded, is at any rate perfectly secure and harmless.

Nor is fear the only emotion which contributes to perpetuate and strengthen these notions in the human mind. In all those cases where man is either actively or passively concerned, it is well known how much the result will depend upon the tone of thought which may happen to govern the individual engaged. Cheerfulness and confident anticipations of success will inspire him with a vigour and energy which would be incompatible with a depressed and sinking spirit. Strong expectations in his mind, whether favourable or unfavourable, act very powerfully in realising themselves. But should he be impressed with the full persuasion, that there exist invisible beings of great power, which they are ready to employ in order to assist in the accomplishment of his wishes, his expectations of success will of course be infinitely enhanced. Should he view them as inimical, his hopes of a prosperous issue will be proportionally destroyed. In either case the difference of result, which is in reality owing to the

---

[2] By the same rule, it is considered as likely to draw forth his indignation, though in a less degree, if we endeavour to resolve effects, generally ascribed to his interposition, into the laws of nature. Such a contraction of the extent of this sway and efficiency is supposed to insult him.

increase or diminution of his own energies, will be ascribed to the invisible agents who are the objects of his belief. And thus the supposition of their existence and efficiency will appear to be visibly manifested, and will be practically illustrated and confirmed by the result which they are imagined to have brought about.

The considerations which we have just urged seem to be peculiarly and almost exclusively applicable to the present subject. But there are likewise other circumstances, which assist in maintaining and perpetuating among mankind errors of every sort, and the influence of these circumstances on the present case is very distinct and striking. The reputed possession of magical powers constitutes a source from whence many persons derive uncommon affluence and dignity, and the interests of this class will of course direct the employment of all their efforts in cherishing the errors by which they profit so abundantly.

And as superiority of talent is one of the most frequent among those causes which lead the ignorant to ascribe magical power to any individual, it thus happens that the most eminent intellects acquire an interest in promoting error and deception among their fellows. Nor does this corrupt interest cease to operate, when the production of magical effects is attributed not to men, but to unseen agents. For the same class of persons, to whom the possession of such powers was previously attributed, now assume the character of favourites and deputies of these invisible beings. They affect an acquaintance with the character and attributes of the latter, and are supposed to possess the secret of calling forth or arresting at pleasure the irresistible arm of their superhuman patrons. The same preeminence of talents, which before procured for its possessor the reputation of a magician in his own right, will still continue to obtain for him the most exalted post; and, where invisible agents are supposed to exist, no higher situation can be awarded to any individual than that which is only subordinate to them, and which carries with it the dispensation of their favours and injuries. The analogy of earthly potentates, and our observation of their constant partiality for favourites, disposes us also to embrace the idea, that unseen beings would be likely to employ a visible ministry upon earth. Nor should it be forgotten that the conception of an invisible power, though highly convenient in reconciling our original tendency to explain all phenomena by design, with the laws of the material world, is yet of a nature so very shadowy and incomprehensible, that the mind eagerly catches at any sensible object to associate with it. Certain animals, certain spots of ground, certain occupations or amusements, are always selected as the objects of their peculiar preference. We need not be surprised therefore, that whether magical powers are supposed to reside either in human or in superhuman agents, there infallibly arises in either case a class of persons, whose affluence and dignity is built upon this belief, and who consequently employ all their energies in cherishing and perpetuating it. And the very wealth and reputation which they acquire by the prevalence of this doctrine, imparts to them a weightier command over the minds of others, and a greater influence in proscribing and discrediting whatever notions they deem unfavorable to their sway.

We have thus endeavoured to sketch a concise review of the belief in magick, to trace the various shapes which it assumes in the human mind, and to notice some of the principal circumstances which appear to suggest and support it. Let us now examine the reality of the principle, and the grounds on which the belief in it may be vindicated. Now when any powers whatever are supposed to reside in a substance which we see before us, we are possessed of a simple and infallible test, by which the validity of the belief can at once be ascertained. We can, almost always, cite the substance in question before the tribunal of experiment, and unless the verdict received sanctions and verifies our supposition, we do not hesitate to pronounce it inadmissible. There are doubtless many phenomena, to which, from the particular mode of their occurrence, the application of this test can be neither easy nor frequent; yet still it remains, as the indisputable arbiter of truth or falsehood, whenever we find an opportunity of appealing to it. But design is never subjected to our experience and therefore when we suppose it to exist, unconnected with that visible material system which is its usual concomitant, our former criterion fails us. Our perceptive powers never inform us of the action of design in anyone besides ourselves. The only test therefore which we can employ, is a comparison of those changes in ourselves which we observe to have followed the action of design, with other phenomena, in order to ascertain whether there is sufficient similarity to warrant us in ascribing the latter to the same cause as the former. Yet even this, though by no means so exact as that experimental test which we apply to visible material substances, is not resorted to in the case of design. Our original tendency, as has been before remarked, is, to explain every thing by the supposition of design, without demanding any special resemblance whatever, and the only mode by which we can exclude the idea of design from any event, is by discovering a positive conformity which it presents to some other known law of nature. There is a degree of indistinctness in the mode of applying this supposition, which is above all things favorable to the continuance of error,[3] and we shall therefore attempt to explain and examine it at considerable length. In order however to obviate misconception it should be premised, that this is wholly unconnected with the question whether there exists a Supreme Cause, to whom the original production of all things is to be referred. Our enquiry is destined to ascertain, simply, whether there is any ground for supposing, that there exist unseen and unlimited beings who produce effects around us; and what portion of those effects should be ascribed to their agency. As this supposition is merely the introduction of design, in its most convenient and unfettered shape, the question is, when we observe in an event the character

[3] "Citius emergit veritas ex errore, quam ex confusione. " Bacon, *N.O.* 2.20.

of rarity, or want of conformity to certain connections which our minds have treasured up as laws of nature, are we authorised to attribute the production of this event to design? Or when we remark no difference between two antecedents, while the consequents are yet dissimilar, are we justified in affirming that there has been a particular interference of design to bring about that dissimilarity?

1. Rarity, or frequency, are always relative to the observer. A phenomenon which to one man appears strange and inexplicable, will to another of more extended research, seem perfectly ordinary and familiar. To every one, in early youth, all phenomena are necessarily rare. Nor can we determine whether a phenomenon is really rare or not, until we become acquainted with the future, which is as much a part of the course of nature as the past, and to which we may look for an explanation of the phenomenon in question. "In interpretatione naturae," says Lord Bacon, "animus omnino taliter est praeparandus et formandus, ut et sustineat se in gradibus debitis certitudinis, et tamen cogitet (praesertim sub initiis) ea quae adsunt multum pendere ex iis quae supersunt." Before we assert that any phenomenon is not conformable to the course of nature, we must be acquainted with the whole course of nature, nor should we presume to ground our negative upon the mere inspection of a part of it. We must suppose in that case, that we are omniscient, and that the future has nothing to reveal to us. Besides, the most limited portion of past experience must convince us, that all phenomena do not occur equally often. What degree of rarity shall we therefore decide to be necessary, in order to justify us in attributing any occurrence to an invisible agent? Increasing experience has convinced us, with regard to many phenomena, that it is their nature to recur but seldom. Now if this be admitted, ought it to appear unaccountable, that others should happen but once during an infinite space of time? The latter fact differs from the former, merely in extending somewhat further the period of recurrence.

Again, if we consider the infinite variety of possible combinations which the particles of matter may assume, we may venture to affirm, that there are no two substances throughout nature in which these particles are thrown together after a manner completely similar. At least the chances against this occurrence are as infinite to one. Consequently there is no substance in nature which is not rare and even singular. If this needed confirmation, we might adduce the notorious circumstance, that every individual, whose contemplations have been habitually directed towards any particular class of objects, never fails to detect differences where the eye of a common observer would perceive nothing but undeviating uniformity.

2. If this be correct, we must ascribe the absence of any sensible difference between two substances merely to our incomplete inspection and comparison of them. When therefore we affirm, that of two things between which there is no apparent difference, the one possesses properties which the other is without, the proposition merely means, that amongst all the points

of difference discernible between them, there is none which can be assigned as a satisfactory account of the different properties which they exhibit. If, for example, we should witness a king who cured the scrofula with his touch, we should infer the aid of an invisible being, not because there was absolutely no difference between him and other men, but because there was no difference which appeared to us to afford an explanation of this exclusive property. But this is surely a presumptuous anticipation of nature, to assume, that none of these distinct appearances which we discover are connected with this peculiar property, merely because we happen to be unacquainted with such a connection. To suppose that amidst the circumstances which we observe to precede an event, none of them is really connected with the event, is at least an act of mind as unphilosophical as it is to mistake an accidental concomitancy for an established connexion. It would indeed be subversive of all advance and accumulation in our knowledge of nature, since we can only enlarge our acquaintance with her laws by generalising upon the exceptions to them which are constantly occurring; "Neque desistendum ab inquisitione (is the exhortation of Bacon) donec proprietates et qualitates, quae inveniuntur in hujusmodi rebus quae possunt censeri pro miraculis naturae, reducantur et comprehendantur sub aliqua forma sive lege certa; ut irregularitas et singularitas omnis reperiatur pendere ab aliqua forma communi; miraculum vero illud sit tandem solummodo in differentiis accuratis, et gradu, et concursu raro, et non in ipsa specie; ubi nunc contemplationes hominum non procedant ultra, quam ut ponant hujusmodi res pro secretis et magnalibus naturae, tanquam incausabilibus, et pro exceptionibus regularum generalium."

If it be urged that this single subject would thus possess a property which none of his species enjoy, and that this is incredible, the answer is, that this is not a question of fact, but merely of classification and application of a common name. A resemblance is remarked between certain individuals, and the properties which they possess in common are designated by the term *man*, which is applied to each of these individuals. If these properties are discoverable in the king whom we before cited, then the term *man* is applicable to him. But if, among these qualities, we choose to include the incapability of healing the scrofula, then the term *man* will no longer be applicable to him. If therefore the king possesses certain properties which are not to be found in any of his species, it is merely ascribable to that arbitrary classification, by which we ourselves place him in that species. For, with regard to any of the qualities themselves, we can no more pretend to determine beforehand, that two leggedness and self motion shall never be found in connection with the property of healing scrofula, than to decide that they shall be found in connection with it. Would not the Father of Experimental Philosophy pronounce us guilty in either case of a flagrant anticipation of nature, wholly inconsistent with the character of her servants and interpreters?

3. But will it really be contended, wherever two substances exhibit different properties, while we are unable to point out the visible marks with which this difference is connected, that we are to introduce invisible agency in order to explain it? If this principle were allowed and adopted, the appeals to this mode of elucidation must indeed be numerous and frequent. A particular taste or smell is agreeable to one man and odious to another. But who can detect the organic conformation upon which the production of these distinct effects depends? All the various shades of mental capacity are merely inferences from the different tenor of action which we observe in individuals, nor can we assign any discernible mark on which the performance of a particular class of actions depends, or which can be considered as the characteristic of lofty or defective intellect. There are some few in whose hands a hazel rod will twist and bend when suspended over a landspring, while it remains stedfast and immoveable under the grasp of every one else; And Daniel in his Rural Sports informs us, that Sir H. Mildmay's gamekeeper in the New Forest lately possessed a pig whose scent was so remarkably fine and keen that it was employed in hunting game. Here are examples of individuals differing from the remainder of their species by the possession of a peculiar property, with the exercise of which not the smallest visible distinction can be shown as exclusively connected. Should we therefore pursue the principle on which the appeal to invisible agency is vindicated, we cannot with any consistency refuse to call in its explanatory aid on these occasions.[4]

But we are told that we are not to expect the interposition of unseen beings on slight occasions, but only when interests of importance are involved. "Nec vero ita refellendum est, ut si segetibus aut vinetis cujuspiam tempestas nocuerit, aut si quid e vitae commodis casus abstulerit, eum cui quid horum acciderit aut invisum deo aut neglectum a deo judicemus. Magna Dii curant, parva negligunt [sic]."[5] (Cicero, de Nat. Deorum 2.66) Yet surely nothing can be more gratuitous or unauthorised than this distinction. We introduce a supposition in order to account for certain facts, which are affirmed to be inexplicable without it, while we refuse to apply it to certain other facts which are equally inexplicable. We leave the latter to account for themselves and do not attempt to suggest any other explanatory medium. Nothing more need be said to shew the futility of this distinction. But it is of importance to remark, that many nations, in

[4] Indeed all those circumstances, which we commonly ascribe to *chance*, possess an equal claim to be considered as instances of particular interposition. By the word *chance*, we simply express our ignorance of the cause why any phenomenon happens as it does. That is, we can point out no visible mark peculiarly belonging to that law of succession under which it occurs.

[5] What is meant by the term *importance*? It is perfectly relative. The ruin of the vintage or harvest may be of the utmost importance to the proprietor, while it will not excite the attention of any other man. The former therefore would be authorised in admitting a particular interference, the latter in rejecting it, on the very same occasion.

pursuance of this very principle, have imagined, that they could specify the occasions on which invisible beings would be induced to interfere, and have endeavoured to apply the supposition to fact. They believed that nothing could be more worthy of invisible beings, even of the highest order, than to shield and extricate the innocent from unmerited suffering, and hence when their own minds were not sufficiently versed in the laws of proof to detect truth if artfully blended with falsehood, they had recourse to the trial by ordeal. Yet we now universally deride this establishment, as the summit of human folly, while we admit principles from which it follows as a just, obvious, and useful conclusion!

4. But farther, if we examine this supposition more closely, we shall find it exposed to the very same difficulties, and involving at least as many inexplicable points, as the facts which it professes to account for. A person who touches for the scrofula is doubtless a rare phenomenon, and exercises a property which none of his species possesses, without any visible distinction which we know to be connected with this peculiarity. But surely we suppose, in an invisible agent, something equally rare and without parallel. We imagine him to perform an action, which we have never before witnessed in any designing being. Yet can we point out any difference between him and the rest of this class, which we know to be connected with the singular and exclusive property thus supposed to be inherent in him? We are compelled therefore, if we refer this cure to him, to affirm, that there is some unknown distinction between him and other designing beings, by virtue of which he produces an effect to which they are incompetent. But is it not equally simple and easy, and much more philosophical, to assert this of the visible agent whose touch we observe to precede the cure? "What safety, what advantage to any one is it for the avoiding the seeming absurdities, and to him, insurmountable rubs which he meets with in one opinion, to take refuge in another, which is built on something altogether as inexplicable, and as far remote from his comprehension?" (Locke, *H.U.* 2.3.6)

Indeed, in the reasoning employed by the advocates of this supposition, we may detect an unqualified admission that it does not explain the facts. Consult Glanvill's vindication of the belief in witchcraft, or the reasonings of Quintus Cicero in support of divination; You will find each of these disputants eluding all objections by an open avowal of ignorance, and allowing fully that the nature of those invisible agents, whose existence they maintained, was unknown and incomprehensible.[6] This is a confession, that nature, or the facts which we see around us, even taken

---

[6] It is remarkable however, that the very same persons who at one time acknowledge their complete ignorance of the nature of invisible agents, will at another resort to the distinction which has just been noticed, and will gratuitously determine what events ought or ought not to be ascribed to them. Though the alliance between dogmatism and ignorance is extremely close, yet it will not be easy to point out any other case in which they alternate in a manner so glaring and unwarrantable.

together with invisible agency, is still incomprehensible. But nature cannot be more than this, without such a supposition. And an hypothesis, which when admitted to the rank of a fact, is still allowed to be irreconcileable with other facts, must be instantly rejected as destitute of all pretensions to our belief. What would have been the treatment bestowed on the hypothesis of LeSage, when that philosopher attempted to account for gravitation by means of infinitely small particles of matter, if, on listening to objections which he was unable to remove, he had ventured to retain the theory, coupled with the admission that these particles of matter were not only invisible, but incomprehensible?

5. But the supposition of invisible agency overruling the course of nature is exposed to an objection still more direct and conclusive. It is inconsistent with the laws of proof, and all employment of this process in support of it must necessarily involve a sophism. A concise dissection of the process will exhibit this in a clear and undeniable manner.

Proof is the result of testimony, and testimony is the communication (either attempted or effected) of the belief of one man to another. By the utterance of certain sounds the latter is made sensible that the former believes in the reality of a particular fact. Why is it that on some occasions, this belief in the mind of the speaker is uniformly followed by belief in that of the hearer, on others not? It is solely from the indirect support afforded by the laws of nature, with which the hearer is previously acquainted. He knows the general principles according to which valid and trustworthy belief is commonly excited in the mind, and he inquires whether the belief of the witness can be authenticated by a conformity with these laws. Has the latter seen what he relates? Has he derived it from a spectator? If these questions receive a satisfactory reply, we deem the fact well attested; if not, the naked belief of the witness is discarded as of no value. We see therefore, that in order to procure the reception of a fact which we have not ourselves witnessed, it is necessary that the particular testimony of an individual should be produced, and that his belief should have been framed according to those laws of nature, which, by a comparison of previous cases, are known to justify the formation of such a sentiment.

Nor is this sufficient. In the greater number of instances, it is not merely intended to communicate the isolated fact which has been submitted to the senses of the witness, but also some ulterior circumstances, indeed sometimes a long chain of other events. In order to ascertain whether the testimony offered to us is sufficient to establish these ulterior events, we must recur not only to the usual marks of sound or unsound evidence, but also to other laws of nature. We must take into our calculation the properties of the object to which the fact relates. Two men are accused of murder; Of the one, it is deposed, that he stabbed the deceased with a dagger in the left breast; Of the other, it is merely proved that he touched the deceased with his finger. Before we can decide which of these men is guilty or innocent, we must be obviously acquainted with those principles which regulate the extinction of the vital functions. Wherever therefore any thing is to be established beyond that which is actually submitted to the senses of the observer, the most unimpeachable testimony is useless, if we cannot produce a certificate from nature, sanctioning the connection between the fact perceived and the fact conjectured to depend upon it. Again, when we refute any assertion, our only method is to offer positive proof of something which is inconsistent with that assertion. Since therefore this counterproof is indispensably necessary to a complete refutation, all that appeal to the laws of nature, which proof has been remarked to involve, must likewise be included in the process of disproof. But whence comes it that the reality of one fact is assigned as demonstrating the untruth of another? Simply from the accompanying testimony of experience which pronounces the reality of both to be incompatible. Unless therefore this appeal to the voice of nature be allowed, all attempts at refutation must be defective and ineffectual.

The preceding analysis of proof and refutation discovers to us, that both these processes involve an appeal to the laws of nature, or an assumption, that two things which we have formerly observed to happen together, will continue connected together in the present case. We necessarily, in other words, anticipate the stability of the course of nature, and therefore gratuitously exclude the agency of any over ruling power. But when we employ, in behalf of supernatural interference, a proof, in which we have already taken for granted that no such interference is to be expected, our reasoning is perfectly fallacious and sophistical. No prodigy therefore could ever be established, if real; nor disproved, if unfounded.

Mr. Locke in his Chapter on Faith and Reason, has an argument which is strictly applicable to the present question. "Before we can receive any thing as a Revelation, our reason must be convinced that it comes from God. Consequently if any fact be affirmed on the authority of Revelation, which our reason pronounces to be manifestly untrue, the evidence against it being equal to the evidence in its favour, no ground remains for believing it." As we cannot assign the authority of Reason for disbelieving the dictates of Reason, so we are not entitled to plead the stability of the laws of nature, as a ground for believing their violability. In the one case, it is the mental faculty which determines as much against us as in our favour; in the other case, it is the evidentiary matter or ground on which the decisions of the judgment rest.

But if no proof can be introduced in behalf of a prodigy, supposing it to be true, it is even more manifest, that no mode of refutation can be brought to discredit it, if false. The whole weight and efficacy of disproof consists in the certificate which we produce from nature, declaring the incompatibility of the fact contained in the counterproof, with that which is alleged on the other side. But how can we decide what is consistent or inconsistent with an event, in the production of which all the connexions of experience are confessedly disregarded and annulled? In disproving the grossest fiction imaginable, we can do no more than demonstrate, that it is inconsistent with the laws of nature. But this is part of the definition of a prodigy.[7] The essence therefore and character of a prodigy exactly resembles that of a fiction. They both agree in possessing that attribute which is the sole discernible mark of falsehood, inconsistency with the laws of nature; and the sole difference between them is, that a prodigy is a species of fiction against which we will not allow the weapons of disproof to be employed. We cannot refute it, because it is already in the state of a refuted proposition; we cannot slay it, not because it is invulnerable, but because it is already slain.

Since both proof and refutation are equally inapplicable to the case of prodigies, there cannot possibly be any distinction of these events into true and false. Yet it is strange, that every nation in the earth implicitly believes some of them, while it treats those received by the rest of mankind as the most ridiculous and contemptible fictions. This difference in their credibility is in reality perfectly groundless and imaginary. For with what arguments can the believer in a well-attested prodigy assail an adversary who reposes implicit faith in all events whatever of this class? He can shew that his adversary's belief has not been framed according to those circumstances which the laws of nature usually connect with valid belief, and consequently that these laws do not confer any credit upon the prodigy in question. But this mode of reasoning can neither be employed with any consistency by himself, nor will it make any impression upon his adversary. To demonstrate to the latter that his belief in this unattested prodigy is not sanctioned by the laws of nature, is perfectly fruitless and irrelevant. Had the adversary recognised an appeal of this kind, he would never have attempted to maintain, that which is by its very definition an infringement of those laws. And he may with justice retort, that his assailant discovers amazing inconsistency, when he adopts one event, in spite of its incompatibility with the course of nature, while he disbelieves another to which no farther ground of rejection can be shewn to belong.

Dr. Berriman, in vindicating the authority of the Legends relating to the 5th and 6th Centuries remarks; "I see no reason why we should dispute the facts on account of the natural incredibility of them, unless it can be proved, as it certainly cannot, that miracles were ceased in that age".[8] This proposition involves a most important truth, when generalised to the extent of which it is susceptible. We learn from it, that any one who admits even in a single instance the reality of supernatural interference, is precluded by this concession from ever rejecting any other assertion on the ground of incompatibility with the laws of nature, unless he can assign some special reason for excluding, in this latter case, the agency of any overruling power.

---

[7] In common conversation we may remark that a prodigy and a fiction are considered as synonymous terms.

[8] See Dr. Middleton's *Free Enq.* [p. no. cannot be read: see, Vaio, "Seventy Years " n. 25].

The above remarks, it should be recollected, apply exclusively to the notion of a prodigy, or an event produced by superhuman interposition. For as to the naked fact which the prodigy contains, stript of all reference to supernatural agency, the preceding arguments do not in the least impeach its credibility. They simply demonstrate, that the fact, if received, must be deemed reconcileable with the course of nature, by supposing our acquaintance with her laws to be incomplete, and by expecting from the future such farther insight into them, as will evince their perfect compatibility with the event in question. And we have attempted to show, that the very laws of proof preclude us from admitting the fact, and then annexing to it the supposition of invisible agency; Because in justifying our belief of this or of any other fact, we necessarily introduce the laws of nature as an indispensable element in the evidence; By which appeal we avowedly subscribe to her authority, and pledge ourselves not to disallow her testimony, when it can be pleaded against us. And because, in vindicating our disbelief of any fiction whatever, the most triumphant refutation can extend no farther, than to shew its inconsistency with the laws of nature. Whence it follows, that unless human reason is inconsistent with itself, we cannot admit that to be true, to which the sole and essential attribute of fiction is allowed to belong. For by such a proceeding we obliterate and annul the test of falsehood, and consequently that of truth also, which we can never hope to attain where there is no mode of detecting the presence of error.[9]

It may perhaps be asserted that we have been combating a mere verbal distinction, inasmuch as invisible beings, if any such exist, are a part of nature, as much as those which are visible. To this we reply, that it is their supposed possession of powers either without limit in themselves, or without any limit discoverable by the human faculties, which necessarily places invisible agents beyond the sphere of nature. That which renders knowledge attainable is, the limited properties of every thing around us. Before we can establish a single proposition, it is requisite for us to discover these limitations, or, in other words, the laws of nature, and to incorporate them with the body of our proof. When a man has been seen to plunge a dagger into the bosom of his enemy, who instantly falls down dead, we infer that the former is the murderer. If he has been observed merely to touch the deceased with his finger, we pronounce him innocent. In the former of these inferences, we negative the agency of all the other substances in nature; In the latter, we exclude the action of the immediate subject mentioned in the

---

[9] "Quicquid oritur, qualecumque est, causam habeat a natura necesse est; ut etiam si praeter consuetudinem exstiterit, praeter naturam tamen non possit existere. Causam igitur investigato in re nova atque admirabili, si poteris. Nihil enim fieri sine causa potest; nec quicquam fit, quod fieri non potest; nec si id factum est quod potuit fieri, portentum debet videri. Nulla igitur portenta sunt... Illa igitur ratio concluditur, nec id, quod non potuerit fieri, factum unquam [sic] esse; nec quod potuerit, id portentum esse; ita omnino nullum esse portentum. " Cicero, de Divin. 2.28.[60].

proposition. Every act of inference, whether positive or negative, therefore, necessarily involves the imposition of a limit, and as both proof and disproof require the aid of inference, we could not pretend to apply either of these processes to the substances of nature, if unsusceptible of limits. But even on the supposition, that most of the substances around us were limited in their properties, while some few alone were unlimited, the result would be precisely the same as if they were all of the latter character. We could never apply the processes of proof or inference to the former, and therefore never acquire any knowledge of them, because we could never presume to exclude the agency of the latter. If therefore nature were composed of substances partly limited and partly unlimited, our only practicable mode of acquiring knowledge would be, to detach and disregard the latter class as substances whose agency was not cognizable by the human faculties.

These considerations appear to suggest a reply to the arguments of the late Dr. Brown who in his Essay on Cause and Effect, vindicates the credibility of prodigies. "According to him, there is, in addition to all those circumstances which we observe to precede an effect, an immediate exertion of the Divine Will, by means of which the perceived effect is brought to pass. This volition is to be numbered among the natural antecedents of the effect, and if when all the visible antecedents were the same, a different effect should take place, we ought to ascribe it to an altered determination in the preceding will of the Deity. Hence he deems it incorrect to describe a prodigy as a violation of the laws of nature. For as the will of the Deity, one of the requisite natural antecedents, is altered, a change in the effect is really warranted by the laws of nature, and is in perfect conformity to them. Whenever therefore satisfactory evidence of a prodigy is offered, we are merely required to believe, that an event has taken place which the Deity has chosen to produce in a manner different from his habitual agency."

This train of reasoning however, though we should concede all the principles on which it is founded, does not seem to extricate the supposition in question from the difficulties and inconsistency which have been pointed out. If all effects around us result from the constant and immediate impressions of the Deity, then what we term the laws of nature must be certain general principles, gathered by observing that he uniformly exerts the same act of volition on the same occasions. Hence when we remark the recurrence of any particular visible antecedent we are led to infer its consequent or to expect that the Divine Will is to reproduce the latter immediately after the former. Every act of inference therefore involves this assumption, that as the visible signs remain the same, the thing signified will infallibly succeed; In other words, it includes the negation of any possible change in the will of the Deity, so long as the indications of that will which are discernible by man continue to be the same. But the supposition of a prodigy is allowed to imply the very reverse of this—an altered volition on the part of the Deity, while all the visible signs remain perfectly unchanged. Consequently the supposition of a prodigy is inconsistent with the fundamental assumption on which the process of inference rests. The latter therefore can never be employed to prove the former; And as the human faculties furnish no other means of proof, the notion must be deemed inadmissible, as well under this definition, as under the preceding.

To recapitulate the substance of the foregoing arguments; In the first and second, we have offered reasons to prove, that neither rarity, nor a dissimilarity in the laws of succession among phenomena while there is no visible difference which we know to be connected with it, can ever authorise us to suppose the agency of invisible beings; In the third we have attempted to shew, that if these circumstances were admitted as a sufficient ground for resorting to such interference, the occasions in which we must introduce it would be innumerable, and far more frequent than its warmest advocates would venture to acknowledge; In the fourth we have urged, that the supposition itself is exposed to the very same difficulties, as the facts which it is brought to explain, and that if admitted as a fact, it does not render the body of our knowledge more coherent or intelligible than it was before; The fifth is destined to prove, that such a supposition is inconsistent with the laws of proof, and therefore that every attempt to give evidence of its reality must infallibly involve a sophism.

Any one of these five objections, supposing it to be well founded would suffice to annihilate any hypothesis whatsoever.